GERMAN EXPLORATION
OF THE POLAR WORLD

GERMAN EXPLORATION
of the POLAR WORLD

A HISTORY, 1870–1940

David Thomas Murphy

UNIVERSITY OF NEBRASKA PRESS
LINCOLN AND LONDON

Library of Congress

Cataloging-in-Publication Data

Murphy, David Thomas, 1960–

German Exploration of the Polar World:

a history, 1870–1940 / David Thomas Murphy.

p. cm.

Includes bibliographical references and index (p.).

ISBN 0-8032-3205-5 (cloth : alk. paper)

1. Polar regions—Discovery and exploration—German—History.

2. Explorers—Germany—History.   I. Title.

G587 .M86 2002

919.8—dc21

2001048090

"N"

Illustrations 1–7 are reprinted from Verein für die deutsche Nordpolarfahrt zu Bremen, ed., *Die zweite deutsche Nordpolar-fahrt in den Jahren 1869 und 1870 unter Führung des Kapitän Karl Koldewey* (Leipzig: F. Brockhaus, 1873); illustrations 8–11 and 13 are reprinted from Erich von Drygalski, *Zum Kontinent des eisigen Südens* (Berlin: Georg Reimer Verlag, 1904); illustrations 12, 14, and 15 are reprinted from Wilhelm Filchner, *Zum sechsten Erdteil* (Berlin: Verlag Ullstein, 1922); illustrations 18–25 are reprinted from Else Wegener, *Alfred Wegeners letzte Grönlandfahrt* (Leipzig: Brockhaus, 1932); illustrations 26 and 27 are reprinted from Karl Koldewey, *Die erste deutsche Nordpolar-Expedition im Jahre 1868* (Gotha: Justus Perthes Verlag, 1871); illustrations 28–31 are reprinted from Alfred Ritscher, *Deutsche antarktische Expedition 1938–39* (Leipzig: Koehler und Amelang, 1942).

CONTENTS

ILLUSTRATIONS

PREFACE

The boldest voyagers, today and earlier, wagered active lives to solve this question; but science still looks toward those regions of our globe, without being able to lift the veil that hangs over them.

BREMISCHEN COMITE,
Die zweite deutsche Nordpolar-Expedition, 1870

This study explores exploration itself. It tells a little-known story, that of German exploration in the polar world at a time when popular interest in the Poles was at its peak. As part of that story, this work considers what such exploration reveals about German society during these years. It is not, and does not intend to be, a detailed account of every one of the many German forays into polar regions in the years between 1870 and the Second World War. Instead, I have selected the most significant polar episodes representative of each of the four German political systems in the turbulent decades under consideration: the competitive, multistate Germany of the pre-Unification era, the aggressive and powerful Wilhelmine Reich, the pluralistic and internationalist "Weimar" democracy of the interwar period, and the Third Reich of Hitler and the Nazis. The pages that follow tell the story of these episodes, consider their political and scientific significance for German society, and place the polar world in the German popular imagination of the era.

German polar enthusiasts tried during these years to establish their country as a leading exploring nation. They failed, despite scientific successes and a number of fascinating and heroic adventures. Nonetheless, the story of the German polar endeavor is both engaging in its own right and historically valuable. The Poles were the last imperial frontier for Germans and other Westerners, and the drama of their opening shaped ideas about the environment, the public uses of science, and the character of non-European cultures. And while the German public thrilled to tales of the valor and self-sacrifice of individual adventurers, in retrospect the story of German exploration reveals a subtler but more historically significant dynamic: the steadily expanding link between science and the state and the gradual absorption of scientific exploration in the political aims of the state.

No work of history is written alone, and this study is indebted to many scholars and institutions. These include the Deutscher Akademischer AustauschDienst (DAAD), the Falls Faculty Development Fund of Anderson University, and colleagues Guillaume de Syon, Susan Solomon, John Mc-

Cannon, Alan Steinweis, Lynn Nyhart, and Peter Fritzsche. I am grateful as well to Harry Liebersohn, to Clark Whitehorn, and to D. Blake Janutolo and J. Douglas Nelson of Anderson University. Madeline F. Murphy provided valuable research assistance. The staffs of many libraries and archives were also generous with their expertise, including those of the Bundesarchiv Potsdam, the Bundesarchiv Koblenz, the Geheimes Staatsarchiv preussischer Kulturbesitz in Berlin-Dahlem, the Berlin Document Center, the Politisches Archiv des auswärtigen Amts in Bonn, the Staatsbibliothek preussischer Kulturbesitz, the Wisconsin State Historical Society Archive in Madison, and the Nicholson Library of Anderson University, particularly that institution's patient and resourceful interloan librarian, Jill Branscum. Translations, except where otherwise indicated in the notes, are mine. Above all, I am grateful for the inspiration and critical insight provided by Marcia Martin Murphy. This book is dedicated to her.

WEIGHTS AND MEASURES CONVERSION CHART

METRIC UNIT	APPROXIMATE U.S. EQUIVALENT
LENGTH	
centimeter	0.39 inch
meter	3.28 feet
kilometer	0.62 miles
AREA	
square kilometer	0.39 square miles
VOLUME	
cubic kilometer	0.24 cubic miles
CAPACITY	
liter	0.26 gallons
MASS AND WEIGHT	
kilogram	2.20 pounds
metric ton	1.20 short tons

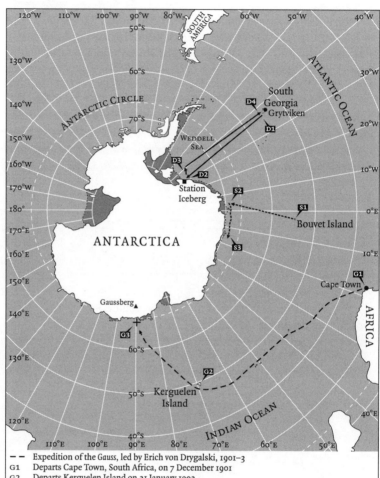

— — Expedition of the *Gauss*, led by Erich von Drygalski, 1901–3
G1   Departs Cape Town, South Africa, on 7 December 1901
G2   Departs Kerguelen Island on 31 January 1902
G3   Frozen in ice, 22 February 1902 – 2 February 1903

——   Expedition of the *Deutschland*, led by Wilhelm Filchner, 1911–12
D1   Departs Grytviken, South Georgia, on 10 December 1911
D2   Filchner erects house and equipment at "Station Iceberg", 9–18 February 1912
     (position 77°45′ south latitude, 34°34′ west longitude)
D3   Frozen in Weddell Sea ice pack, 15 March–26 November 1912 (initial position
     73°7′ south, drifting northwest at around 8.5 nautical miles per day)
D4   Arrives back in Grytviken, South Georgia, on 19 December 1912

······ Expedition of the *Schwabenland*, 1938–39
S1   Arrives in sight of Bouvet Island on 15 January 1939
S2   Arrives at Antarctic coast on 20 January 1939 (69°10′ south latitude, 4°15′ west longitude)
S3   Cruises the Antarctic coast eastward, finishing on 6 February 1939 (near 15° east longitude)

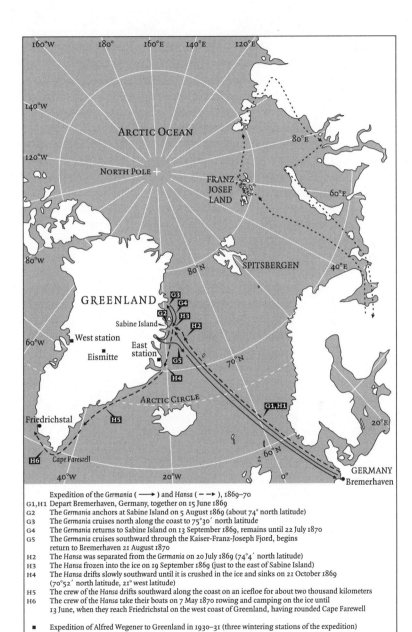

Expedition of the *Germania* (⟶) and *Hansa* (– ⟶), 1869–70

G1,H1 Depart Bremerhaven, Germany, together on 15 June 1869
G2   The *Germania* anchors at Sabine Island on 5 August 1869 (about 74° north latitude)
G3   The *Germania* cruises north along the coast to 75°30′ north latitude
G4   The *Germania* returns to Sabine Island on 13 September 1869, remains until 22 July 1870
G5   The *Germania* cruises southward through the Kaiser-Franz-Joseph Fjord, begins
       return to Bremerhaven 21 August 1870
H2   The *Hansa* was separated from the *Germania* on 20 July 1869 (74°4′ north latitude)
H3   The *Hansa* frozen into the ice on 19 September 1869 (just to the east of Sabine Island)
H4   The *Hansa* drifts slowly southward until it is crushed in the ice and sinks on 21 October 1869
       (70°52′ north latitude, 21° west latitude)
H5   The crew of the *Hansa* drifts southward along the coast on an icefloe for about two thousand kilometers
H6   The crew of the *Hansa* take their boats on 7 May 1870 rowing and camping on the ice until
       13 June, when they reach Friedrichstal on the west coast of Greenland, having rounded Cape Farewell

■   Expedition of Alfred Wegener to Greenland in 1930–31 (three wintering stations of the expedition)

◄- - - Flight of the Graf Zeppelin into the Soviet Arctic

INTRODUCTION
The Lure of the Great Deed

A great task must be greatly conceived! For such tasks, one must be a great man, a great character . . . If you have doubts or scruples, back out now. I hardly believe that this great work will be brought to its conclusion without the loss of ships and human lives. And why should thousands of noble lives be slaughtered only in inhumane wars? Is not such a great affair also worth a few lives?

AUGUST PETERMANN, 1869

The great men of German polar exploration are largely forgotten. Despite heroic and sometimes mortal struggle at the ends of the earth by Germans, it is the agents of Germany's rivals such as Britons Robert F. Scott and Ernest Shackleton, Americans Robert Peary and Richard Byrd, and Norwegians Fridtjof Nansen and Roald Amundsen who endure in popular memory. Even in Germany, the renown of the nation's polar explorers survives in large part thanks to a handful of historians at scientific institutions.[1] And, in a sense, the historical gloom enshrouding the names of Wilhelm Filchner, Erich von Drygalski, Karl Koldewey, and others is appropriate. Their descent into obscurity is a fitting metaphor for their nation's encounter with the Poles. The expeditions they led to the Arctic and Antarctic ended most often in recriminations, broken dreams, and spiritual exhaustion. Despite scientific successes, they attained none of the polar "firsts" the public craved. Their fates mirrored the experience of their nation, for which the drive to polar exploration, born of scholarly idealism, political ambition, and public enthusiasm, withered over the decades into perceived futility and widespread indifference.

At the time, however, German explorers played key roles in the dramatic drive to chart the Poles, and no one could have foreseen their subsequent obscurity. During the "golden age" of polar exploration, from the mid–nineteenth century to World War II, Germans threw themselves into the race for polar glory with an ardor that matched that of their better-known English, American, and Scandinavian counterparts. Though the men of other nations claimed the great prizes (to be first at the Poles by land, sea, or air), German expeditions made important, if less spectacular, discoveries, particularly in Greenland and the Antarctic. In the seven decades from 1868 to 1938, Germany sent out dozens of Arctic and Antarctic voyages.[2] Three elements shaped the German expeditions: urgent nationalist motives, the setting of the polar environment, and the expeditions' participants, tools, and patrons.

The Challenge of the Poles

Why did Germans care about the Poles? Much of the earth's geography was still a mystery, and from the Western perspective, simply that the Poles were unknown sufficed to make the quest to find them a self-evident necessity. Equipped today with technology that instantly calibrates vast amounts of data from remote distances, we easily forget how recent is our mastery of the earth's most inaccessible areas. When the midpoint of the nineteenth century had come and gone, many blank spaces remained on Western maps. The origin of the Mississippi had not been established for more than a generation, and the riddle of the Nile's source was at last solved by John Speke only in 1862. Great reaches of Africa and Asia were uncharted, and fanciful mountain ranges such as the "Mountains of Kong" still decorated European maps. Much of the globe continued to defy the Western scientist and explorer.

This was especially true of the Poles. The higher latitudes for the most part were completely unknown when the first German expeditions set out at the end of the 1860s. The Greenland ice cap had not been charted. No one knew, in fact, whether Greenland was an island or an arm of either the Eurasian or American land masses, joined with one of these under the ice. It was impossible to be sure what the North Pole was like. Opinions varied as to whether it was covered with land, ice, or open water. Such uncertainty naturally bred the most fanciful speculation. Well-known scientists, including August Petermann, the hotheaded father of German Arctic exploration, believed that swirling warm water from the Gulf Stream preserved a navigable, ice-free sea at the top of the world.

Knowledge about the southern regions was, if anything, even murkier. Though Antarctica had been circumnavigated by James Cook in the 1770s, its outlines were a mystery, concealed by the great flange of ice girding much of the continent. Bodies of land like Bouvet Island, incorrectly charted during the 1730s, were lost and not rediscovered until the close of the nineteenth century. No human being had yet set foot on the main portion of the Antarctic continent.[3] The polar world seemed a land, as Shackleton wrote, of "secrets preserved inviolate through all the ages."[4]

The uncertainty surrounding such basic geographical matters provoked scientific inquiry. The West believed in science. The clash of science and faith that had scandalized earlier generations was fading late in the nineteenth century, and society had not yet learned the nuclear age's fear of uncontrolled science. Scientific knowledge seemed to be remodeling the world for the better, and the practitioners and supporters of science believed that their achievements represented the triumphal progress of truth. No nation upheld this idea more wholeheartedly than Germany. Living standards had improved, and science received much of the credit. All the rising indices of material well-being seemed to vindicate Goethe's optimism, written as the nineteenth century dawned, that science would "awaken to ever-elevated life new proficiencies that avert the harmful and introduce the useful."[5] Many Germans naturally believed they had a duty to replace the mystery of the Poles with the certainties of science.

The pretensions of Western science, however, were only a small part of the obsession with polar discovery. The polar race of the 1890s and early 1900s, when as many as six nations at a time dispatched expeditions to polar waters, was driven by many forces. When Petermann and other Western scientists appealed to their nations' sense of duty to discover the Poles, they were joined by a chorus of businessmen, soldiers, politicians, and reporters. Changes in technology, politics, and culture persuaded growing numbers of Germans and other Westerners that ignorance of the exact nature of the polar worlds was a luxury they could no longer afford.

Simple practicability was partly responsible for the century's surge of interest in the Poles. By the 1860s, chances that an expedition might reach a remote destination in the high latitudes and return without loss of life were very good. This had to do in part with improved marine technology. Ships driven by mechanical means could overcome the challenge of ice fields and hostile weather more efficiently than wind-powered vessels. Though feeble and fickle by later standards, the steam engines assisted sails, an improvement over exclusive reliance upon the wind. The first German attempt at a voyage to Arctic zones, in the rented British ship *Queen of the Isles*, ended, to the mortification of its sponsors, in mechanical breakdown on the day it set out in August 1865. The *Germania*, the specially constructed main ship of the German expedition of 1869, was somewhat more successful but still, by later standards, absurdly underpowered with a steam engine of a mere thirty horsepower.[6] Despite such limitations, however, mechanically powered ships drastically simplified the matter of maneuvering in polar seas.

Steam was only the earliest of the innovations that would facilitate Western incursions into the polar environment. Rapid technological change, often taking unexpected forms, characterized the next six decades of polar exploration. For example, the harpoon gun and steam launch, both introduced by Svend Foyn, revolutionized the whaling industry, leading to huge annual kills and a resulting contraction in the ranges of marine mammals toward the Poles. The need to maintain goods and profits derived from whaling therefore became one of the most effective motivations for polar exploration.[7] In addition, though tools and insulating fabrics made of synthetic materials would come later, advances in food preservation, medicine, and communication (the first use of radio transmitters in the Arctic predated World War I) gradually lessened the danger of polar adventurism. Aviation was especially important. The rapid aerial evolution from balloon to rigid airship to monoplane opened in decades lands that had resisted human intrusion for centuries.

Scientists were not alone in noting the opportunities that technology was creating for exploring the polar world. Chauvinists in every technologically advanced nation viewed the exploration of the Poles as a competitive test of national character. When, during the Franco-Prussian War, the crew of the German ship *Hansa* were saved after nine months of shipwreck, their survival on ice floes off the coast of Greenland was hailed as a triumph of Germanic virtue: "Just as on the bloody field of honor in France," wrote one commentator later, "so Germany gained a magnificent victory on the peaceful field of science in the North."[8] Enthusiastic nationalists, many of them scientists, exhorted their compatriots not to be left out of the race for polar glory. Soldiers heartily agreed, and every branch of the modern German military eventually lent funds, equipment, or personnel to polar expeditions.

Imperialist politicians also eyed the Poles. After parceling out Asia and Africa among half a dozen developed nations, the largely uninhabited, unclaimed circumpolar world beckoned to Westerners as the last great region of territorial acquisition. Entrepreneurs believed it concealed valuable ores from whose wealth no industrialized state could risk exclusion. Few imagined that international cooperation, not conflict, would largely characterize the future of polar territories. These regions seemed instead to be new sites of imperial competition, leading the great polar incursion between 1870 and World War II to become part of the final stage in the effort to create an all-encompassing world order centered on the Western imperial system.

In short, new technological and political developments gave Germans many reasons to be interested in the Poles. However, a history that simply examines that interest or that merely traces the routes and recounts the hardships of successive expeditions will miss much of the significance of the West's engagement with the Poles. Polar history includes not only what was done at the Poles but also the ways the Poles were perceived. The Poles then had a glamor that is difficult to re-create today. To understand this glamor and its impact, one has to ask why ordinary working men and women on the streets of Berlin or Frankfurt or Munich who understood little science and had no direct material stake in exploration were nonetheless enthusiastic about it. What did polar exploration as a popular cultural spectacle mean?

In part, of course, it meant money. The new media of mass communication, newspapers especially, quickly learned that images of exotic Eskimo, spectacular scenery, and heroic death could turn a profit.[9] But this answer begs a more basic question: why did Germans want these images? There is no simple answer. Germans derived many meanings, for example, from their confrontation with polar nature. A deeper appreciation for that nature itself seems to have been one of these. Stories of the freakish beauty of the pristine world at the Poles, of its auroras, solitude, danger, sublime majesty, and surprisingly rich and diverse fauna all fostered an environmentalist sensibility that went beyond the sentimental naturalism embraced by the romantics.

Perhaps surprisingly, Germans also derived from their images of the polar world a more complex appreciation for non-European peoples. At a time when racist ideologies were gaining appeal in Germany, the popular image of the native inhabitants of the northern polar lands grew increasingly positive. Though misunderstood, sentimentalized, and sometimes patronized in German polar literature, the Eskimo, so called, acquired greater stature as Western explorers adopted "native" ways of coping with the extremes of the polar environment.

An intriguing paradox also heightened the popular appeal of polar exploration. Elaborate technological, social, and political structures made possible the presence of Germans in the polar regions. The individual explorer who was the beneficiary of this complex system of support, however, was seen as the embodiment of independent human resourcefulness and self-reliance. The glamor of the Poles derived in large part from this entirely mythical conception—that the polar explorer, or his small team, represented man battling alone against a hostile environment. Nothing could have been further from the truth. Only the strictly marshaled

5

resources of the world's most materially sophisticated civilization, that of the West, enabled human beings to reach the Poles. But at the very time that the application of new technological devices helped open the Poles, the images of polar explorers that were most popular expressed a more primitive and antitechnological ideal. It is easy to understand why. In a society where men and women may have felt unable to exercise meaningful autonomy, the heroes of polar exploration demonstrated that man was more than the money or science or political ideology behind him. In the polar lands, a man—and the polar hero was always male—still seemed master of his own fate. Personal character, courage, and determination could still shape destiny.[10]

A strain of Germanic polar mysticism also contributed to interest in the Poles. Ignorance breeds superstition, it is said, and the scientific darkness around the Poles gave rise to fantastic notions. Ancient legends of ultima Thule stimulated wild occultist speculations, some blending with the racial myths of Aryanism, which also attracted believers in turn-of-the-century Germany. Old visions of the mystical significance of the top and bottom of the globe, of reaching the very axis upon which the earth spun, fed these fantasies. For the credulous adherents of such legends, the Poles as places in the physical world were of no consequence. They were important only as sites for the construction of dreams. Exploration, in fact, ultimately corroded the dreams of polar mystics. Once the secrecy of the Poles was finally and thoroughly violated, when they had been mapped and charted and drawn into the mundane world of everyday science, the eccentric speculative literature that had grown up around them died. Polar fantasy faded as science ascended.

The Nature and Politics of the Polar World

No one seems certain where to draw the boundaries of the "polar world." Geographers and explorers have argued for decades over what criteria best define the "Arctic" and "Antarctic." The most straightforward response— those regions that fall within the Arctic and Antarctic Circles—is unsatisfactory on a number of counts. The polar circles, at 66°33' above and below the equator, are astronomical concepts. They denote the points beyond which one encounters uninterrupted sunlight for one or more days a year—"midnight sun." However, many regions characterized by Arctic flora, fauna, and climatic conditions, such as the heavily glaciated regions of southern Greenland, fall outside this astronomical abstraction.

Similarly, parts of the Antarctic continent, which displays an emphatically polar character, are outside the Antarctic Circle. In the same way, northern Norway and other regions that enjoy a clearly temperate climate fall within the circle's limits. Hence, the circles themselves do little to define the polar world.

Objections can be raised to other all-embracing definitions of the Arctic and Antarctic. The range of floating ice fields is occasionally used to trace the bounds of the Arctic, but this definition has no use in continental polar regions of Canada and Siberia and omits even clearly polar maritime regions such as western Greenland. The limit of the tree line is more reasonable, perhaps, than many other definitions of "polar," but it suffers from the fact that the tree line in the North is not clear-cut. The border separating dense forest from barren tundra is gradual and in some areas very broad. The line of the permanently frozen layer of subsoil, or permafrost, as well as various climatic boundaries also have their partisans as the preferred means of separating polar from nonpolar regions. And, obviously, neither the tree line nor the permafrost border has any relevance in the frozen, treeless Antarctic. There is, in short, no clear, universally accepted definition.[11]

To the explorer, however, defining the polar world was simple: it comprised those unexplored and unmapped regions beyond latitude 65° north and south of the equator. Expeditions to such lands were considered to be "North Polar" and "South Polar" expeditions, even though the German expeditions were rarely intended to reach the actual Poles. This use of "polar," referring to the regions of terra incognita surrounding the ends of the earth's axis, simplified and broadened the idea of what polar exploration meant.

The goals of the earliest German ventures, for example, were framed in the most imprecise terms and seem maddeningly vague in contrast with contemporary notions of scientific propriety. The main ship of the German expedition of 1869 and 1870 was instructed merely to land on the coast of Greenland, whence the venture's leaders were to proceed as far inland as possible. This vessel's consort was sent forth "to attempt to attain the highest possible latitude at some point between Greenland and Novaya Zemlya."[12] By later standards, this is intolerably murky, but at the time, with scientific mapping of the polar zones still in its infancy, these directions seemed perfectly clear.

In part, therefore, the definition of "polar world" was operational. Polar lands were those regions at both ends of the globe where detailed geographical and topographical knowledge ceased and basic exploratory work remained to be done. Polar regions were also defined for German (and European) explorers by their general environmental qualities. They were constantly cold. Their landscape seemed barren of all but the simplest vegetation. They were inhabited by humans only very sparsely, if at all. They were the regions where nature seemed to shed its indifference toward humanity and assume a posture of active hostility to human intrusion. As one German chronicler put it, the polar lands were "those fabled regions that have most occupied the fantasy of man, where the year counts only a day of six months and an equally prolonged night; man awaits from there unimagined insights into the nature of our globe, and nowhere in the world were greater dangers and deprivations connected with discovery. Were? It is the same today, and the proverb of the ancient Greek, Sophocles—'Nothing is more powerful than man'—is foiled there, where nature gathers together all her forces."[13]

Given this forbidding aspect of nature at the Poles, the common tendency to ascribe hostile intent to the polar environment seems justified. Conditions in the Antarctic are particularly savage. Deprived of the moderating influence of an underlying body of water, which renders the Arctic just habitable, the climate of the southern continent displays a surreal brutality toward most forms of life. It is incomparably cold. Covered by three thousand meters of ice, the South Pole has an average annual temperature of -49°C. The coldest reading ever, -88°C, was recorded in Antarctica. Winds roar at 249 kilometers per hour at Ross Island off the Antarctic coast, and the continent itself is the windiest on the planet.

The ceaseless scouring of the Antarctic wind creates the blizzard conditions that dominate continental weather patterns. Antarctica is actually a desert (it receives less annual atmospheric moisture than the Mojave), but the wind-driven snow accumulates without melting from year to year atop the continent's blanket of ice. The cold withers most forms of life. Inland from the teeming marine life of its coastal waters, Antarctica sustains only the most basic forms of existence: lichens, mosses, mites, wingless flies, and similarly wretched flora and fauna.

The land's location and features conspire with the climate to frustrate human intrusion. Three oceans, Atlantic, Pacific, and Indian, swirl round the continent uninterrupted by land (the so-called Great Convergence), generating winds, storms, and currents of unmatched ferocity. Ice shelves fringe much of the coast, further complicating access. The greatest, though not by much, is the Ross Ice Barrier, a floating sheet of ancient ice 210 meters thick and as large as California. The shelves are so closely anchored to the mainland that only seismic techniques permit the explorer to distinguish the shelf from the continent proper. The mainland itself, as large as the continental United States and Mexico combined, is no friendlier when reached. It is the highest land mass on earth, with an average elevation above 2,100 meters, and the surface is a jumble of glaciers, sheet ice, snow, and patches of bare rock. Early explorers described it as another world entirely, hardly part of this planet.

The Arctic is mild by comparison. Geographically, the earth's northern end reverses the pattern of the south. Instead of a great land mass hemmed in by oceans, the top of the globe is an icebound ocean of greatly varying depth, nearly surrounded by Eurasia, North America, and Greenland. Though both dry and cold, it never reaches the extremes of the Antarctic and shows greater seasonal variation. Temperatures reach a balmy near-freezing in July. Most of the region receives twenty-five centimeters or so of precipitation in a normal year, creating a dry environment but one slightly better suited to sustaining life than the Far South. The relative moderation of the Arctic climate, due in part to the warm waters of the Gulf Stream, is reflected in the rich diversity of its flora and fauna. Unlike Antarctica's sterile heart, the Arctic teems with the extraordinary variety of marine life found wherever warm and cold ocean currents collide. It also shelters a wide range of nonaquatic birds and native mammals, including polar bears, musk oxen, caribou, foxes, ermine, and many more.

Milder conditions have not made the Arctic less hazardous for its explorers, however. Efforts to navigate the Arctic Ocean were hampered throughout the era of exploration by powerful currents and constantly shifting patterns of ice cover. Ice fields follow wind and water, moving generally from east to west above Siberia, while eddying in a clockwise pattern north of the Canadian archipelago. Great vistas of apparently open and navigable water tantalize polar sailors, only to close overnight into endless fields of jagged ice boulders or to freeze over entirely. While channels of open water between the ice, called leads, appear in the polar ice pack every summer, their existence is transient. They are never in the same place twice. By autumn they always close up.[14] The result of such conditions for exploring vessels was predictable. Ships venturing into the ice fields routinely found themselves imprisoned in pack ice, subject for months to the whims of Arctic wind, tide, and current.

Travel conditions ashore are not much better. Rock, ice, and snow cover most Arctic land regions, save for the tundra. There the underlying layer of permafrost prevents thawed snowmelt from draining and reduces the ground to an enormous sodden bog throughout the summer. The Greenland ice cap, nearly three kilometers deep in places, is one of the Arctic's most remarkable features. This towering mass of prehistoric ice, pierced here and there by the naked rock peaks called nunataks, makes the island second only to the Tibetan plateau as the highest land mass in the Northern Hemisphere. The ice cap's fogs, cliffs, and crevasses render the interior nearly impassable. It was not finally crossed until 1888, by a small expedition under the Norwegian Fridtjof Nansen, and it claimed the lives of explorers well into the twentieth century.

Legal rights in these forbidding wildernesses were as vague as their boundaries. At the dawn of the age of discovery, European explorers simply claimed vast territories on sight. England, for example, assumed sovereignty over great stretches of the Northern Hemisphere by virtue of John Cabot having viewed them before any other European. Spain in 1539 claimed everything south of its Latin American holdings all the way to the Pole. By the time the polar regions began to be explored in an ongoing fashion, however, this style of land grab was an anachronism. The emerging body of international law to which Western states nominally subscribed increasingly recognized territorial claims based not on exploration but on "use," "occupation," or "administration." The precise meanings of these terms, of course, were eminently debatable.[15] In practice this meant that when German-sponsored expeditions first reached polar regions, much of the Arctic and Antarctic was legally *terra nullius*, or no-man's-land.

The two polar regions nonetheless differed politically in important respects. The Antarctic had neither native inhabitants nor contiguous states that might try to extend their domain into neighboring, uninhabited territories. Though the Arctic was indeed home to scattered human communities, the question of investing sovereignty in stateless, nomadic peoples like the Eskimo or the Lapps never occurred to the European and North American states that dominated exploration. When German exploration began, however, Westerners had not made any explicit claims to Arctic territories. Possession of the Canadian archipelago was unclear, though generally presumed to be a sphere of British influence, thanks to the activity of the Royal Navy.[16] Alaskan coastal regions after 1867 were presumed American, just as Russians claimed the northern coast of Asia.[17]

After the turn of the century, as potential and actual resources began to be contested, quarrels developed between Norway and Denmark over rights in northern Greenland. A proposal for a new solution emerged in 1907 with the Canadian advancement of the "sector principle," which asserted that states extending into the polar circle had a natural claim to the longitudinal sectors of the globe above their land regions.[18] The idea had no precedent, but it caught on. In 1908 England extended formal claims from its Falklands holdings over a great swath of territory to the south that came to be called the Falkland Islands Dependency, legitimating its title by reference both to exploration and administration of the region. The English were soon followed by Australia, Norway, Chile, and Argentina, the last named both considering themselves Spain's legatees. All these claims were of dubious validity in international law, and it was significant that neither the United States nor South Africa, both potential claimants, followed suit.[19]

Disputes over Arctic sovereignty even extended to questions about the polar ice pack, which, though not a land mass, was treated as such in international law due to its permanence.[20] Norway and Russia quarreled over ownership of Franz Josef Land, and Britain and Russia disputed ownership of Wrangel, or Vrangelya, Island and a number of other sites. In practice, however, such disagreement was rarely acrimonious. Despite competing claims, the environmental hostility of the Arctic imposed a kind of fellow-feeling upon the West. Territorial jealousy nearly ignited war in other regions—between Russia and Britain on the Northwest Frontier of India or between Britain and France at Fashoda in the Sudan—but not in the Arctic, where international cooperation was more typical than strife. In any event, thanks to a late start in exploration and a lack of territory contiguous to the Arctic Circle, there was never a prospect of any serious German claim to sovereignty in the Arctic.[21] German interests were best served by internationalism, which preserved scientific access to the region and whatever unknown resources it might conceal.

The Antarctic presented a slightly different case from the German perspective. Since systematic exploration of the southern continent began so much later than Arctic research, Germany did not lag especially far behind other Western states. In contrast to the Arctic, the Antarctic had no contiguous neighbors able to claim "natural" extension of their territorial rights. There existed no native population. And, as shall be seen, German expeditions to the Antarctic, particularly those led by Erich von Drygalski and Wilhelm Filchner at the beginning of the twentieth century, ranked among the West's larger and more elaborate efforts. German explorers and politicians noted all these factors, and they helped inspire Nazi Germany's attempted Antarctic land grab on the eve of World War II.

Thanks to the rigors of the polar environment, therefore, each end of the globe constituted a political vacuum at about the time that Western territorial expansion reached its apogee. Nature, in Spinoza's famous maxim, abhors a vacuum. Science and the modern state feel the same. It is not surprising that Western political and scientific aspirations should have been attracted to this vacuum in the late nineteenth century. Those aspirations, the aims of the West's polar adventure, called forth as the tool by which they might be achieved the form of organized cultural activity known as the "polar expedition."

The German Polar Expedition in the Heroic Age

The century after the Napoleonic Wars is so often described as the "heroic" age of polar exploration that the term threatens to become an empty historical cliché. The idea of the polar heroic age remains a convenient shorthand description, however, of an era in which polar exploration was typified by certain traits in a way that was not true either before this period or after World War II. One of these traits was the public attention devoted to such exploration. The exploring endeavor was taken more seriously by governments and followed more ardently by the Western public than at any other time. Expeditions were tracked daily by the media, and they were usually identified with some famous leader.

National prestige was as important as scientific progress. All the technologically advanced nations sought to display their flag in the vicinity of the Poles, even if many of their expeditions were not actually intended to go all the way to 90°. The "expedition" itself was an expression of scientific culture characteristic of the time, a coordinated thrust into the high latitudes meant to last from a season to two years, never more, in contrast with the business-like, permanently inhabited research stations that have characterized polar research since the World Wars. The expedition became a cultural life form with a structure determined by three elements: the men, money, and tools with which it pursued its goals.

The ship itself was the most important implement of German polar research. Since oceans made up both the route to the fields of polar endeavor and, in the case of the Arctic, the actual object of exploration itself, the German expedition was typically conceived as a nautical exercise.

The acquisition and outfitting of a suitable vessel were typically far and away the most expensive elements in the preparation of the expedition. During several German voyages, the ship that transported men, beasts, and equipment to polar regions found itself frozen into the polar ice, sometimes intentionally, occasionally not, and had to serve as the crew's home, sledding base, and laboratory for months at a time. Given the centrality of the ship in the German expedition, it is surprising to find German exploration often characterized by a quality of marine antiquarianism.

Both vessels of Germany's early-twentieth-century expeditions, the Gauss and the Deutschland, for example, were deliberately constructed of wood at a time when metal frames and hulls were already standard. This was by no means a matter of economies. The variety and quantity of exotic woods consumed in specialty ship construction were costly. The Gauss, a compact ship of 590 metric tons, was built in Kiel in 1901 at a cost of roughly five hundred thousand marks. By comparison, one of the largest sailing ships ever built, the Preussen, a gargantuan, five-masted steel vessel several times the size of the Gauss and able to carry 7,250 metric tons of cargo, was built the next year for just nine hundred thousand marks.[22] But the prevailing belief in Germany and England, championed by Colin Archer, the most renowned polar naval architect of the day, was that the elasticity of tough wooden hulls would better sustain the pressure of pack ice than would more rigid metal hulls. And, although mechanically powered vessels had nearly driven sail from the Atlantic trade, both German ships were outfitted with complete sailing rig. Though supplied with small steam engines for ice navigation, they were intended to reach the Antarctic primarily by relying upon the wind.

Aviation gained a readier reception among German expeditionaries. Though they attained no polar flight "firsts," Germans utilized balloons just after the turn of the century and airships and seaplanes in the 1930s. Even here, however, there was a curious strain of technological minimalism, apparent in the refusal of the German Greenland expedition of 1930 to use any air support. There seems at times to have been an unspoken sentiment that polar expeditioning, after all, ought to be hazardous and difficult.

In contrast to their nautical traditionalism, German polar explorers were innovators in the use of scientific tools and instruments. The German zeppelin expedition of 1931 and the German Antarctic expedition of 1938–39 both pioneered complicated new aerial photography techniques and equipment. German expeditions are also notable for their creative use of unmanned aviation tools, such as pilot balloons and kites. German explorers devised special techniques for the remote detection and transmission of polar weather conditions, and they were the first to develop reliable methods for the measurement of ice depth. In the design of polar garb, Germans were also inventive. It was Alfred Wegener, in the course of outfitting the members of his 1930 Greenland expedition, who commissioned the preparation of special jackets modeled on those of Greenlandic natives, thus sparking the popularity of the anorak, or parka, in Europe.

Explorers in all the Western nations adopted some of the methods of the natives of the Arctic, and the Germans were no exception. This was especially true in matters of protecting the human body from the cold. Eskimo patterns became the prevailing models for clothing and sleeping bags. Like the Eskimo, German explorers through most of this period relied for transport on sleds pulled by teams of seven to nine half-wild dogs, normally obtained in Greenland or Siberia. Ponies too were used by German explorers, and they also experimented with mechanical means of overland transportation, such as propeller-driven sleds. The latter illustrated that there were limits to the adoption of native tools and methods, however. The German expedition in general remained dependent for its success upon the importation of European devices into the polar environment—firearms, prefabricated station housing, chronometers, theodolites, kerosene ovens, specially conserved provisions, and so on.

Material resources probably did less to determine success or failure than did the quality of human resources. Here too certain patterns predominated from the 1860s to the 1940s. One of the most consistent characteristics of the German polar expedition was its masculinity. The Poles were a male domain. All of the participants in every one of the expeditions under consideration were male. The polar world was discovered and initially interpreted for Germans, and Westerners in general, through the eyes of men. Polar exploration combined elements of warfare, sport, and science, and it was presumed that it required the same exclusively masculine qualities demanded by these related pursuits.

The leaders of German expeditions were also typically certain kinds of men. They came from backgrounds in the educated middle class—the social stratum of cultured, comfortably well off families known as the Bildungsbürgertum. Most were strongly nationalistic and patriotic without being narrowly chauvinistic. They were generally conservative, displaying no noticeable tendency toward political activism, and tended to identify with and get along with legally constituted authority. Wilhelm Filchner, to take one example, was capable of the most appalling misjudgment of authority figures, admiring the ridiculous and malevolent Kaiser Wilhelm II as a "good and great" man and able to get along with Hitler and the National Socialist government. Hugo Eckener, the great zeppelin entrepreneur, quarreled with the Nazis, but Eckener was, in many ways, an atypical member of the club of German polar explorers.

Typically, the German polar explorer was a civilian scientist in early middle age. Only two, Wegener and Eckener, were past the age of forty when they led their expeditions. The strain killed Wegener, but Eckener, though in his sixties, had only to ride through the air in the gondola of his zeppelin. Germany also typically looked to the sciences, rather than the military, for leadership in polar adventuring. In a nation considered at the time to be notable for its militaristic values and with considerable evidence of military interest in polar affairs, this may seem surprising. Career military officers— Peary and Scott, Bartlett, Byrd, Payer, Koch—figure prominently in the explorations of other Western states at the time. Only one major German expedition was led by a military careerist. Wilhelm Filchner, leader of the Antarctic expedition of 1911, was an army officer, but he later left the military. He was also a scientist with very advanced training in mathematics and geodetics. Though they sometimes made use of military resources, the only German expedition dominated by a military presence was the Nazi Antarctic expedition of 1938, an atypical German mission in nearly every respect.

With scholars and scientists in the lead, German engagement with the polar world displayed a sober, industrious character. Germans derided the Scandinavian and Anglo-American "race for the Poles" as mere exhibitionism, a matter of sport rather than of serious science. There was no doubt a touch of sour grapes in their criticism, since Germans were never serious competitors in that race. And there was obviously an element of appealing romantic adventurism in the German expeditions, however much German scientists may have tried to downplay it at the time. Nonetheless, German expeditions by the turn of the century, even the publicity stunt of the Eckener zeppelin flight in 1931, set forth with ambitious and innovative scientific agendas that went far beyond the basic mapping or the attainment of polar "firsts" that characterized the expeditions of their rivals.

Financially, the German polar expedition was a hybrid. While the German state (or states, in the era before unification) usually provided some funds, successive German governments were often reluctant to assume the full financial burden of polar research. Expeditionary planners therefore turned to a combination of patrons for their wherewithal. One of these was the German public, whose members repeatedly showed great generosity toward polar endeavors, supporting them in fund drives and lotteries. Some expeditions made money by selling publication rights to newspapers and book publishers, an increasingly important source of revenue that was tapped by explorers in all the Western states by the turn of the century. The state also contributed indirect support through its research agencies, including the German Marine Observatory (Deutsche Seewarte), the Institute for Oceanography (Institut für Meereskunde), and other scientific entities. Equipment was commonly tendered free of charge by institutions like the Royal Prussian Aeronautical Observatory (Königlich Preussisches Aeronautisches Observatorium) and the German Geodetic Commission (Deutsche Geodätische Kommission). Before World War I, the German titled nobility was also very active in financial support of expeditions, making personal donations and sometimes serving, like Prince Regent Luitpold of Bavaria, as honorary patrons in charge of fund-raising.

Erich von Drygalski, a leader and active supporter of German polar exploration for more than three decades, once noted that "the very essence of the expedition lies in the cooperation of various forces—science, navigation, technology, and practical life."[23] So, in its most vital aspect, that of its financial underpinnings, did the German expedition always rely upon the cooperation of various forces. In its classical era, the German presence in the high latitudes was never a simple expression of the fiat of the state. It was usually initiated by individuals or organizations not directly affiliated with the state, and it relied for its funding on popular as well as official enthusiasm. Only as the heroic era died, on the very eve of World War II, did German polar exploration become the sole property of the German state. At that point, with expeditioning carried out solely in the service of National Socialist politics, Germany's "heroic" polar era ended.

Until then the mission of opening the Poles was an exhilarating undertaking, charged with risk and reward alike. The threat of disaster and death hung over every expedition. This was counterbalanced by scientific idealism, patriotic duty, and, most alluring of all, the chance at immortal renown. These were high stakes. It is not surprising that they drove generations of enterprising Germans into the polar circles in order, as one of them put it, "to unite the strengths of German scholars and German mariners, to attempt a great deed."[24]

1. GERMANY DISCOVERS THE POLES

*After thirty-two years of having always to enter foreign names on the maps
and surveys of new discoveries that have gone through my hands ("Victoria,"
"Wellington," "Smith," "Jones," and so on), it affords me great satisfaction to
be able to inscribe on the map a few names of that nation that stands behind
no other in today's geographic endeavors.*

AUGUST PETERMANN, 1871

Germans were exploring the Poles long before the nineteenth century.
Adam of Bremen, a medieval historian and Church canon, records that German
sailors set out in 1040 to determine whether the great northern sea was
endless, as legend had it. They may have gotten as far as the Faroes. Later,
during the early days of modern exploration, German scholars and sailors
often accompanied the expeditions of other nations as technical specialists.
Scientists of many backgrounds, including Alexander von Humboldt, one
of the most renowned natural historians of the nineteenth century, made
important contributions to Russian exploration in Siberia. Germans were
also prominent among the first modern European explorers of Greenland.[1]
None of these could really be considered "German" expeditions, however;
no Germany yet existed. Not until the 1860s, when the imperial wars of
Prussia united the many German territories into a single German state,
was the hour ripe for a truly German polar expedition. And just as German
nationalism found in Otto von Bismarck the man who could give expression
to its political dreams, so the German scientific community found in August
Petermann the man who could give life to German polar aspirations.

Petermann still puzzles historians. His character combined outstanding
virtues with disastrous faults. He was undoubtedly a visionary, energetic
and determined, gifted in his field, and possessed of public relations skills
that transformed German exploration. At the same time, he was obstinate,
quarrelsome, vituperative, and wildly misguided in his conception of Arctic
geography. Assessments of Petermann's contributions are as conflicting as
the elements of his personality. Sometimes praised as the man who single-
handedly revived European progress toward opening the Poles, he has also
been denounced as a "hare-brained" eccentric whose fanciful misconstruc-
tion of Arctic geography led a succession of polar explorers to disaster.[2]

Petermann was born in 1822 in the village of Bleicherode. His parents
hoped he would study theology. Instead, in 1839 he entered the geographic
school of Heinrich Berghaus in Potsdam, near Berlin. He won early fame for

the precision and aesthetic quality of the maps he produced to accompany the account of Humboldt's journey through central Asia. Resettling to the British Isles in 1845, he gained further acclaim for his outstanding charts that traced the route of the 1849 British central African expedition. But his English years turned Petermann's attention toward the Arctic as well. Sir John Franklin, one of England's greatest explorers, vanished in the Canadian polar archipelago in 1845. His mysterious disappearance was England's scientific cause célèbre of the day, and Petermann was an enthusiastic advocate of efforts to solve the riddle of Franklin's fate.[3]

Returning to Germany in 1854, Petermann founded *Petermanns geographische Mittheilungen* (Petermann's geographic news), which soon became Germany's leading geographical journal. With a circulation in the thousands, much of which included foreign subscribers, *Petermanns* acquired a transatlantic reputation as Europe's clearinghouse for geographic articles, reviews, maps, expedition accounts, and general scientific gossip. The magazine made Petermann an influential force in European geography. He was named an honorary member of Britain's Royal Geographical Society in 1864, and his translated accounts of foreign expeditions were so popular that publicity-conscious explorers like John Speke insisted on using Petermann as their vehicle for reaching continental audiences.[4]

When it came to the Far North, however, Petermann's geographic instincts betrayed him. He was convinced that the top of the globe was covered by an ice-free, navigable ocean, the mythical "open polar sea." If the circumpolar girdle of ice could be pierced, he was confident that the Arctic Ocean proper would afford clear sailing and a convenient maritime shortcut across the top of the world. "The ice pack as a whole forms a mobile belt on whose polar side the sea is more or less ice free," he wrote. "Ships that break through this ice belt will find a navigable sea in the highest latitudes and to the Pole itself."[5] This was not the limit of Petermann's geographical fantasy. He embraced the so-called Transpolarland hypothesis, which held that a great arm of Greenland, hidden beneath its ice cap, must stretch across the entire top of the world. The elongated land mass he thus imagined to exist had two southern capes, with its Asian terminus at Wrangel Island off the northern coast of Siberia. In 1865 he published a map arguing his case that showed this Greenland extension crossing the Arctic Sea very near the Pole and reaching almost to the northern coast of Alaska. At the other end of the globe, Petermann imagined the Antarctic as largely composed of water with perhaps an island but certainly no continent.

Such notions strike the modern reader as so unlikely, so spectacularly counterintuitive, and in retrospect so wrong that they seem to border upon the deranged. Why would the ice, as one followed a route northward, suddenly cease? Why would anyone suppose Greenland to have such an unusual configuration? In justice to Petermann, however, both ideas, though controversial, were also plausible during the 1860s in a way that they have not been since. Many explorers had noted patches of open water in the Far North, and the great dream of the Northwest Passage, an ice-free route over Canada, tantalized explorers from Hudson's day to that of Franklin and beyond. Nor was Petermann alone in supposing that the Gulf Stream, as it eddied atop the globe, must spend its dying warmth in some ice-free, far northern space. British scientists had advanced this idea in the mid–eighteenth century, and the American explorer Isaac Israel Hayes tried to find such an open Arctic waterway in 1853 and again in 1860. Unsuccessful though he was, he advanced his ideas in a book called The Open Polar Sea. Because of Petermann's interests and his fluency in English, Hayes's work was probably already well known to him when it appeared in German in 1868.[6] Petermann and others also believed that seawater, due to its salinity, would never freeze to an extent sufficient to cover the entire polar zone. The pack ice encountered north of Canada and Russia was attributed to the local influence of fresh water discharged by huge northern rivers like the Mackenzie and the Lena.

In its historical setting, therefore, Petermann's belief in a navigable polar ocean was not so unreasonable. The same may be said for his idea of Greenland's geography. In his day, the island had been neither circumnavigated nor crossed overland. It was by no means certain that Greenland might not be joined to Canada beneath its ice shield. Given the circumstances, reasonable speculation was justified, even though the particular theory of Greenland's shape advanced by Petermann would have given the island a very unusual geography. Although misguided, Petermann's theories in their day were defensible, and they had one valuable consequence that elevates them above the level of mere historical curiosities. Petermann's passionate determination to prove their accuracy inspired in 1865 a public call for the first German-sponsored Arctic expedition.

To the Open Polar Sea: Founding the German Arctic Tradition
Petermann chose his moment well. German nationalism, apparently dormant since the revolutions of 1848, was pulsing with renewed vigor in 1865. A year earlier, Bismarck, acting as minister president of Prussia, had

engineered a successful war with Denmark in which Austria, Prussia, and other German states fought in the name of the Germans of Schleswig and Holstein. The spectacle of united German armies battling foreigners roused ancient dreams of German nationhood, and Petermann exploited the popular feeling that the Germans, as one of the great cultural peoples of Europe, had both a right and an obligation to take part in the general European work of exploration. Patriotic duty, he argued, demanded German exploration: "What a triumph for Germany and the German navy, if the seas and lands beyond 80° north latitude received a *German* nomenclature, if a *German* mariner first advanced there, if a *German* keel first furrowed the floods of the North Pole!"[7]

Petermann had been considering an attempt on the Poles by the eastern coast of Greenland for some years. He would appeal to national chauvinism, if necessary, but he was also moved by solid scientific considerations. He noted that there were obvious benefits to be realized from such a journey in the field of geography, "which may very properly be characterized as a German science." But a host of other sciences (geology, meteorology, zoology, botany, and ethnography), Petermann argued, "culminate in their most interesting problems precisely in the polar region."[8] It was already clear to European meteorologists that polar air masses had an enormous impact upon their weather patterns, and their colleagues in the natural sciences were interested in acquiring greater information on the little-known plant, animal, and human life of the region.

Petermann also believed that the prestige of German science was at stake in the polar project. His connections with the British geographical establishment were close, and he knew that the Royal Geographical Society was contemplating an Arctic expedition. He dreaded seeing German scientists once more compelled to take a backseat to their Anglo-Saxon rivals. While Petermann had been quietly urging a German expedition since 1863 and being largely ignored for his pains, the British began in 1864 to discuss the plans of Sherard Osborn, one of the last of the Franklin searchers, for a renewed attempt at the Pole by a route west of Greenland.

Petermann was fascinated, and it speaks to the integrity of his scientific ideals that he was willing to support a British, rather than German, expedition if it would explore along his own suggested route. In early 1865 he wrote two letters to the president of the Royal Geographical Society, Sir Roderick Murchison, urging the advantages of an expedition along the unexplored eastern coast of Greenland. With an undeviating affinity for the wrong guess, he argued that a route to the west of Greenland, such as the British were discussing, would run into a dead end in the Smith Sound, which he felt to be a mere gulf of Greenland rather than a strait linking two bodies of water.[9] Though the society debated Petermann's proposal, plans for a British expedition were not put into effect along the Smith Sound route for another ten years.

Undaunted and afire with the conviction of his own arguments, Petermann appealed to his countrymen.[10] Though sometimes criticized in light of later experience, he was undoubtedly right to urge the eastern route. The eastern coast of Greenland had been sighted by Henry Hudson in 1607, but by the middle of the 1860s it had not been visited for nearly forty years. Beyond 75° north latitude it was unknown and unmapped. This, clearly, was a site where a great deal of pioneering geographical work remained to be done. It was not a route by which the Pole would be attained, as Petermann hoped. As events over the next five years would show, however, the most significant advances to be achieved by German exploration were attained along the eastern Greenland coast.

For the moment, in the midsummer of 1865, German geographic and naval circles were unimpressed. In July Petermann suggested to the Versammlung deutscher Geographen und Hydrographen (Assembly of German geographers and hydrographers) a "reconnaissance voyage" of six weeks. This he hoped to carry out in the waning summer as preparation for a more elaborate expedition the following year. Skeptics objected that no suitable ship was available in Germany. Money was an even greater obstacle. The general opinion of the assembly was that the cost of Petermann's preliminary expedition would be very high and that a voyage toward the Pole during the current year was in any case out of the question. The assembly voted to wait until at least the next year.[11]

Doubters reckoned without Petermann's persistence. Unfazed by the absence of money, a ship, or scholarly encouragement, he took matters into his own hands. Banking on his personal resources, on 30 July 1865 he offered a prize of one to two thousand Taler to the first German who would undertake a sailing expedition in the remaining summer weeks, with the goal of researching currents and temperatures between Spitsbergen and Novaya Zemlya. The offer was instantly taken up by Reinhold Werner, commander of the Gefion, the Royal Prussian Navy's gunnery training vessel. Captain Werner solved the problem of a ship in short order, renting in London the Queen of the Isles, an iron, steam-powered vessel. Werner further undertook to finance additional costs from his own pocket. However, since Captain Werner was unable to obtain leave from his military duties on such short notice, the actual command of the vessel was turned over to a civilian, Captain Hagemann of Bremen.

It was very late in the Arctic voyaging season. Northern expeditions customarily set out much earlier—mid-May was typical—to maximize their exploitation of warm weather and the seasonal retreat of the ice. Petermann shrugged off the threat of early winter weather in the northern latitudes. Late though it may be, he had every confidence that Hagemann's vessel would reach distant northern waters with little trouble. His nonchalance was typical. Never having traveled beyond the Arctic Circle, and closely familiar with the lethal rigors of African exploration, Petermann scorned the risks of Arctic traveling. From his cozy study in Gotha, he characterized polar sailing as a lark that consisted merely of exploiting the advantages that new technology afforded polar explorers: "For decades, our explorers, one after the other, have let themselves be slaughtered in the interiors of the most dangerous continents, especially Africa, perhaps by fanatical inhabitants, perhaps by the deadly climate, while such dangers and sacrifice occur with Arctic expeditions, at the most, only as rare exceptions."[12]

Any dangers lurking in the North, he felt, would be neutralized by the power of steam. Though steam had been employed in Arctic research since 1829, when John and James Clark Ross used a steam engine to help power the *Victory*, marine engines were growing increasingly reliable and powerful, even if still weak by later standards. By 1845 Isambard Kingdom Brunel's *Great Britain* had substituted iron for wooden hulls and screw propellers for inefficient paddle wheels.[13] Convinced of the navigability of the polar seas, Petermann felt that reaching the Pole required little more than the resolve to fire up the boilers, steam across the ice belt, and cruise at leisure through placid Arctic waters. Reaching the Pole, he argued, would be a "very easy, trivial thing. A suitable steamship, at the right time of year, could carry out a trip to the North Pole and back in two to three months."[14]

Incredible as his opinions seem in light of later experience, Petermann was not alone in his estimate of the ease that steam would bring to polar voyaging. The Russian admiral F. P. Litke, a grizzled polar hand whose expedition failed forty years earlier along the very route now touted by Petermann, still backed Petermann's plan. Litke wrote Petermann, endorsing his scheme and pointing out the advantages the modern explorer enjoyed over the brave sailors of an earlier generation. His own failure along the Petermann route four decades before, Litke insisted, "proves nothing, because my ship was in no way fitted out for a decisive advance into the ice masses, and that was in any case not the goal of the expedition. Above all, however, because one now has what was never at the disposal of us old mariners—steam power applied to ships."[15]

With the determination of Petermann and the practical experience of Werner and Hagemann, preparations during August 1865 pressed forward. Werner used his naval connections to secure a team of German specialists to accompany the ship's English crew, recruiting helmsmen and two scientists trained in geology, botany, and zoology. The Queen of the Isles arrived in Hamburg on 30 August, Werner and the Germans went on board, and, with unusual alacrity, the expedition set out the next morning. Even the formidable resolve of a Petermann, however, was not proof against an unforeseen enemy—mechanical failure. In midafternoon, while the Queen was still churning its way down the Elbe River, the engine gave a series of knocks, sputtered, and died. As the ship anchored, the machinist reported a bent piston rod, requiring at least eight days for repair. Even Petermann conceded that early September was too late to begin a voyage to Arctic waters, and the first attempt at a German polar expedition came to an ignominious end.[16]

Ignominious and, for Petermann, infuriating. The return of the Queen of the Isles to Hamburg in the wake of a tugboat on the very day of its departure was about as humiliating an end as a proud German scientist could imagine. The real cause of the engine's breakdown was never determined, but Petermann and the German crew were convinced, without tangible evidence, that sabotage was at play. "The suspicion of intent occurred to all of us," Captain Hagemann recalled, "strongly increased by the curious nature of the problem" and hinting that it must have been caused by the ship's English mechanics and crew. North German newspapers, too, suggested that the ship, "whose charter had to be paid in advance," had been subverted by the English, arguing that the Queen had to be stopped before attaining the high seas so that no lives, including those of the English on board, would be lost. Petermann's anger only redoubled his commitment to the project. Even though the first German effort never got farther than 53° north latitude ("note that, you Times and Quarterly Review writers, if you want to mock the undertaking in clever articles"), Germany was not out of the business of polar exploration.[17]

"The Most Modest Scale": The First German North Polar Expedition

The breakdown of the *Queen of the Isles* "brought the entire venture into temporary discredit," as Petermann put it.[18] The misfortune only strengthened his resolve, however, and he pursued an exploratory voyage with redoubled vigor in the fall and winter of 1865–66. Deeper pockets were clearly needed, and Petermann now sought to transform the German Arctic venture from a private into a public undertaking. The two leading German states, Prussia and Austria, were obviously the best hope of a wealthy sponsor, and in the fall of 1865 Petermann confidently petitioned both for funds.

Political realities now overtook Petermann's scientific dreams, however. The Austro-Prussian War for preeminence in German Europe was already looming, and Petermann could make no headway. Austrian naval circles were sympathetic, especially young, ambitious officers such as Julius Payer and Karl Weyprecht, both of whom would take part in later polar expeditions. Ultimately, however, the imperial naval inspector, Archduke Leopold, could not stomach the prospect of shared leadership with the Prussian upstarts, and chances of a joint expedition by the major German states faded.[19]

The Prussian government, on the other hand, initially seemed intrigued by Petermann's proposals. The grand conception of German Arctic exploration outlined by Petermann at this time was to begin with a small-scale expedition by a single ship, like that planned for the ill-fated *Queen of the Isles*, as a means for German mariners to acquire experience in polar waters. This would be followed by a large-scale expedition with two ships. One vessel would carry coal and provisions in support of a smaller ship, which would try to push through to the presumed open water at the Pole.[20] In November 1865 Petermann conferred with Bismarck and Albrecht von Roon, the Prussian war and naval minister. Both statesmen received Petermann, in his own words, in "the most obliging and sympathetic fashion," promised the direct support of the royal government, and with the enthusiastic approval of King Wilhelm established a naval commission in December to consider direct governmental involvement.[21]

To Petermann's surprise and dismay, however, and despite Bismarck's apparent interest in the project, the naval commission rejected the idea. This seems to have been Petermann's own fault in presenting unclear and overly ambitious plans. Rear Adm. Eduard Jachmann, later commander in chief of the Royal Prussian Navy, directed the commission, which included six other naval officers (among them Captain Werner) and Petermann as a geographical consultant. Roon asked the commission to answer the most pressing practical questions concerning a German polar thrust—estimated cost, availability of suitable vessels, and, particularly, the specific destinations and goals of such a voyage. Naval involvement in the scheme could occur only "at the expense of the most immediate and pressing official tasks," the commission declared. "A polar voyage is neither a responsibility nor a matter of honor of the royal fleet," was the nearly unanimous judgment. The navy possessed no suitable vessel, nor did it have at its disposal mariners with experience in Arctic navigation. Jachmann was also annoyed by Petermann's inability to estimate clearly the extent of the pack ice barrier. The navy would not sail to the Arctic.[22]

Naval opposition failed to thwart the project, however. Petermann's agitation was bearing fruit, generating unanticipated support for a German expedition. In January the Prussian House of Deputies (Abgeordnetenhaus) urged the king to back the mission. Wilhelm himself, warming to the prospect, ordered "appropriate ministries" to begin planning a voyage with the support of state funds in March.[23] Petermann recognized a favorable wind blowing in his direction. In April he published "Die deutsche Nordfahrt: Aufruf an die deutsche Nation" (The German northern voyage: appeal to the German nation), which, with a title that deliberately evoked one of the founding documents of German nationalism, Fichte's "Reden an die deutsche Nation" (Addresses to the German nation) of 1806 and 1807, linked the completion of an Arctic voyage to the honor of the German people.[24]

The Austro-Prussian War in the summer of 1866 naturally diverted Germans from the question of what the nation might owe to polar exploration. For Prussia, the conflict was a triumphant demonstration of national virtue, a lightning war settled in a few weeks by Austria's crushing defeat at Sadowa. The shockingly rapid victory of Wilhelm's armies inflamed nationalist feeling throughout northern Germany. Widely seen as a victory of Prussian industry and science over a less modern state, the victory also spurred a more militant sense of German economic might. German liberals, with good cause, were unsure whether Bismarck could quite be trusted, but economic nationalists were exuberant.

Petermann rode the wave. In the year after the war, he repeatedly hammered in his journal not only at the theme of German national pride but at the need to expand and protect German economic interests, especially fisheries, in the North.[25] "Only a very small part of the ice sea between

Jan Mayen Island and Spitsbergen has been fished by the whaling fleet,"
as he put it, "and it is with good grounds generally anticipated that an
exploratory expedition will locate new and richer fishing grounds."[26] His
instinct for error remained flawless. Northern whaling grounds were in
fact nearing depletion in the 1860s. But Petermann's rhetoric had its effect.
If the Prussian navy was reluctant to be drawn into a polar expedition of
uncertain utility, private whaling, shipbuilding, and scientific interests were
enthused by Petermann's dream. In the fall of 1867 Petermann met with a
high-powered polar project committee that included Wilhelm Freeden of
the North German Marine Observatory, Arthur Breusing, director of the
Bremen Steuermannschule (Bremerhaven navigation school), and, most
importantly, Albert Rosenthal, a wealthy and influential shipyard owner.

Thus united, German science and German industry convened at Gotha
in October and resolved to undertake a trip to northeastern Greenland,
including an overwintering, an ambitious plan estimated to cost sixty
thousand Taler. Rosenthal offered the use of his new whaling steamer,
the *Albert*, "the first steamship built specifically for the purpose" of cruising
northern seas, according to Petermann.[27] The committee then sought funds
from the German National Union (Deutscher National-Verein), a patriotic
citizens' league, which turned them down—"yet another hope was thus
carried to its grave." One of its members incidentally offered Petermann a
donation of five hundred Taler, however, and this inspired him to turn to
the public at large.[28]

In May 1868 Petermann published a combined expedition plan and
appeal for money. A chord was struck—the response was electric. For
the first time, the German public awoke to the romance of the Poles.
The Petermann expedition became a fashionable charitable cause, and
donations flooded in from German communities throughout the Western
Hemisphere. Queen Augusta of Prussia, the shipbuilder Rosenthal, and the
grand duke of Mecklenburg-Schwerin all chipped in. King Wilhelm provided the largest single donation, five thousand Taler. Geographic societies,
scientific unions, and publishing houses also contributed. Ultimately, over
2,700 groups and individuals gave to the polar cause, with collections taken
up by German youth groups, cultural associations in Paris, and immigrant
clubs on the far coast of the Atlantic in New York.[29] Petermann set the
nationalist tone: "In such undertakings other, less cultivated nations have
already hurried on far ahead of us," he warned. "We see that even in France
the idea of a northern journey has been taken up, and a great national
collection has been created."[30]

With money pouring in, Petermann wasted no time. Still bitter about the lack of state support, he reluctantly downsized his plans to fit financial realities. "Under the circumstances there remained no alternative other than what has in the rule been the lot of scientific efforts and undertakings in Germany: restriction to the most modest scale." A commander was at hand: Capt. Karl Koldewey, thirty-one years old, a civilian navigator trained in Bremen. Koldewey was a young man in a hurry. He had served as helmsman on West Indiamen and, in 1868, was working his way through a series of university courses on physics and mathematics. Leading the much talked of expedition was a magnificent opportunity, and the ambitious Koldewey, who would become Germany's greatest polar explorer of the nineteenth century, leapt at Petermann's offer. He was, in any case, burning with patriotic fervor and willing "to sacrifice all his hopes to take part in the North Pole expedition, even if it costs his life, since one knows one dies for the renown of the German name."[31]

Both Koldewey and Petermann were eager to see the expedition at sea as soon as possible, and they quickly secured vessel and crew. Another Bremen student, Richard Hildebrandt, took the post of first officer. Hildebrandt was only twenty-five years old, but according to his sponsor, he was well adapted by character to expeditions: "Since the commander must be able to demand slavish obedience from every participant in such an expedition, I am particularly happy that Hildebrandt is going along," wrote the director of the Bremen Steuermannschule. "His is such an energetic character that, should anyone contradict Koldewey's orders, he would shoot him down out of hand without batting a lash." Eleven other seamen, Germans all save for two Norwegians, joined the two officers.

No ship suitable for the task could be found in Germany. Though Petermann had been urging a northern expedition for nearly five years, German activity in the seas north of Europe was still so insignificant that the Arctic planners had to look abroad for a vessel fitted to the rigors of northern seas. Since Norwegian firms dominated Arctic whaling, Petermann sent Koldewey to find a ship in Bergen. His luck was good. On the day of his arrival, Koldewey purchased the *Grönland*, a rugged, twenty-meter, single-masted vessel (without steam power) of a type used by the Norwegians for hunting seal and walrus. By purchasing rather than renting, Koldewey gained the right to fly the North German flag and to have the ship specially adapted for the threat of ice by adding iron plating around the bows and reinforcement to the internal structural members.

27

No scientists joined the ship's complement. This curious aspect of a scientific expedition had two sources. One was Koldewey's conception of the venture: "With this preparatory voyage it was intended only to determine in what direction and how far toward the north Greenland extends," he wrote, "because local currents and climatic and ice conditions around the North Pole depend chiefly upon this."[32] The presence of trained scientists was superfluous to goals of such an elementary nature. At the same time, the Grönland was quite a compact ship, crowded with crew and equipment. Under such conditions, the presence of scientists was felt to be a dispensable luxury.

By late May Koldewey had ship, provisions, and personnel ready for a twelve-month stay in the Arctic, in case circumstances should compel a voyage beyond the anticipated autumn return. Skeptics were vocal. Armchair critics in Bremen doubted the Grönland's ability to fend off floating ice, and a Captain Geerken, "one of the oldest experienced Bremen sea captains," predicted mutiny and shipwreck: "If you require sacrifice, exertion, or dangerous measures of a Norwegian crew, they would refuse their obedience. What would you do then? Such an undertaking requires personnel from the navy, who are used to slavish obedience. With a sailing ship it is always extremely dangerous to go into the ice. One never knows if one can get out again." Financial circles in Bremen and Hamburg kept their distance. The fresh scar of Werner's failure fed their doubt, dissuading those who had helped foot the bill and others, like Hermann Heinrich Meier, founder of the North German Lloyd shipping line, who urged a year's wait to fund a larger and better prepared expedition.[33]

Petermann ignored his critics, publishing his "Instruktion für den Oberbefehlshaber der Expedition" (Instruction for the commander of the expedition), a bizarre artifact of the first German polar voyage. After calling God's blessings upon the expedition, the "Instruktion" listed thirty-eight goals for Koldewey to pursue. The chief aim, succinctly stated and perfectly reasonable, was "the attainment of the highest possible latitude," beginning from 74.5° on the eastern coast of Greenland and proceeding northward. Petermann anticipated open water near the coast and felt that if "the coast of Greenland extends as far north as I presume," the ship will be able to attain "the vicinity of the Pole." Failing this, Petermann instructed Koldewey to proceed to Spitsbergen, there to try to reach the central Arctic basin above 80° latitude.

In its other provisions, however, the "Instruktion" reflects an aggressive yet addled aspect of Petermann's character as a patron of science. He clearly suspected that Koldewey and his crew would lack what he called "pluck" and so took great pains to explain repeatedly that, however matters may appear, an Arctic voyage presented almost no dangers to its members. Should the vessel become stranded in the ice, Petermann reminded the crew that "only in the most extremely rare cases are ship and crew endangered," that it is only "extraordinarily rarely" that lives are lost, that it is always possible, should the ship sink in the ice, to take the ship's boats back to "European settlements," and that "no ship of the very numerous exploratory expeditions to Spitzbergen or in the Antarctic seas has ever been caught fast in the ice or at any time been forced to overwinter." Petermann's implicit doubt of Koldewey's nerve found further expression in his note that the ship had been outfitted with a year's provisions "chiefly to inspire the crew with full confidence" and that the expedition was to take pains "to stretch its researches and work as far into the autumn as possible."[34]

Petermann admonished Koldewey to keep a sharp eye out for "Gillis Land," an island sighted east of Spitsbergen in 1707 by the Dutch sailor Cornelis Giles and not rediscovered until 1898. Should the expedition happen upon the island (known today as White Island), they "have the fullest right, upon attainment or sighting of this land, to give it whatever name they choose." Other provisions for naming newly discovered geographic features were discussed, with the reminder that friends and supporters of the expedition were to be recognized but that the most important discovery must be called for King Wilhelm. Nor did Petermann trust solely to patriotic sentiment to ensure the zeal of his sailors. Cupidity was also called into play with the offer of a prize of five hundred Taler for each degree of latitude attained above 83°, and a sum of five thousand Taler would be divided among the crew should the Pole itself be attained.[35]

The strangest aspect of the "Instruktion" pertains to the Eskimo. After reminding the expedition's leaders to gather plants, skins, artifacts, and so forth, Petermann advised the collection of human specimens as well. "Above all, if at all possible, two Eskimo, man and woman, should be brought back to give an opportunity to study more closely this curious human tribe, living entirely isolated in those high latitudes, and through whom the Eskimo language experts in Germany can learn their history." Petermann included no guidance on how such an Eskimo couple was to be induced to accompany the expedition upon its return to Europe (nor how, on a vessel deemed too crowded for scientists, they were to be accommodated), but he warned that "the Eskimo must be handled with all caution, so that they don't become shy and fearful and run away, for example, from the firing of rifles."[36] Petermann's view of indigenous peoples as simply one more natural phenomenon to be studied in Europe was typical of the ethnographic sensibilities of the day. In 1868 there would not have been shock anywhere in the West at what amounted to the abduction of human beings as scientific curiosities. In the United States at the time, for example, an Eskimo couple were being displayed as part of a touring "Lecture on Life among the Esquimaux"—essentially a circus "freak show" tricked out with academic jargon—by Charles Francis Hall, the most erratic of America's Arctic heroes.[37]

Charged with this grocer's list of duties, the Grönland left Bergen on 24 May 1868. The expedition lasted 140 days and began in a promising fashion. The tiny Grönland, more yacht than ship at just under fifty metric tons, pitched so violently that Koldewey could savor the spectacle of his veteran sailors, accustomed to larger and more stable vessels, prostrate with seasickness. Her sailing qualities, on the other hand, were excellent. Koldewey recorded that "she flew over the ocean like a gull" and was able to make a very respectable speed of up to seven knots.[38] The voyagers crossed the line of the polar circle only four days out of Bergen on a northwest course for the envisioned northeastern Greenland starting point. A week later, however, on 4 June, the expedition encountered its first setback, drift ice that, as the vessel neared the coast, grew so dense that "any penetration was completely impossible."[39]

Thus began a series of frustrations that for the remainder of the journey bedeviled the best efforts of Koldewey and his crew. For several days the ship zigzagged south, then north, and back again in a vain effort to find a way through the increasingly thick fields of ice floes. The work, carried out in waters whose temperatures remained constantly near freezing, was extremely difficult in the wind-powered vessel. Early in the second week of June, snowstorms and high winds set in, and on 9 June the Grönland found itself immobilized and frozen in. Koldewey struggled to keep the crew occupied, and during the next two weeks the ship was canted onto its side so that ice damage to the bow and stern might be repaired.

The ice released the vessel on 22 June, and Koldewey resumed feeling his way northward along the edge of the coastal ice fields. But the constant frustration was corroding the morale of his crew. In addition to the cold, Koldewey's sailors were depressed by one of the most frequently remarked phenomena in the polar literature of the time—the seemingly eternal fog that enshrouded the ship. Combined with the inability to break through to the coast, this produced "a melancholy and cheerless mood among officers and men. The daily watch was ordered silently and seriously, and the days dragged slowly and idly by."[40] Under these circumstances, Koldewey resolved to take Petermann's advice and proceed to the waters north of the Spitsbergen island group. Here too the ice blocked a landing, and on 12 July Koldewey put into the harbor of Bellsund.

The stay at Bellsund represented roughly the halfway point of the planned voyage, and to this time none of the primary goals set forth by Petermann had been attained. Remaining at the tiny port only three days, Koldewey set out westward again on 15 July, hoping to find a way through the ice to the Greenland coast. Once more, he was thwarted. Striking the border of thick pack ice on 18 July, he spent more than three weeks in a vain search for a route between ice floes packed so tightly that a "sewing needle couldn't have fallen to the water between them."

Resolved to wring some modicum of scientific good out of the expedition, Koldewey turned his back on Greenland on 11 August, steering for the northern coast of Spitsbergen again. After weathering severe storms, the ship reached the Hinlopen Strait between West Spitsbergen and North East Land. Koldewey remained near the southeastern outlet of the strait from 21 August to 10 September. From here he and his crew mapped parts of the coast and investigated the island's glaciers. The utter desolation of the site greatly affected Koldewey: "A sadder and more barren region cannot easily be imagined; everywhere, naked, dark stones, thrown wildly over one another, without a trace of soil or vegetation. All was dead and barren."[41] Navigation, as Koldewey noted, was extremely difficult. At times, it was impossible to determine whether the ship was in the strait or in open ocean surrounded by ice. On 10 September, with the Arctic winter nearing, the Grönland sailed for home, reaching the harbor of Bergen on 28 September. Koldewey telegraphed news of the ship's return to Petermann, and, after paying out the Norwegian crewmen, he reached German waters at Bremerhaven on Saturday, 10 October 1868.

Koldewey, his crew, and Petermann were all treated as heroes in the wake of the Grönland's homecoming. Bremerhaven's maritime notables steamed out en masse aboard Rosenthal's tug to meet the Grönland in the estuary of the Elbe and celebrate Koldewey's return. Banquets, speeches, and newspaper accounts hailed the voyagers "in such a magnificent fashion as we had truly never permitted ourselves to dream." Nor were Germans, thirsting for national heroes, alone in celebrating the work of the *Grönland*. The Royal Geographical Society awarded Petermann its gold medal for his role as catalyst for the German expedition, and in England he visited Queen Victoria herself, at Balmoral, to discuss the affair.[42]

Judged in terms of its scientific goals, however, the first German expedition was a failure. It had not attained the coast of Greenland and had not found any suggestion of an ice-free route toward the Pole. The expedition's achievements also suffered by comparison with the simultaneous Greenland journey of the Swedes, under Nils Adolf Erik Nordenskjöld, who not only made a successful landfall but journeyed 51.5 kilometers inland. The *Grönland* had, it is true, reached the highest latitude yet attained by a ship, at a little beyond 81° north, but this was not a considerable advance beyond latitudes already achieved.

In less spectacular ways, such as the creation of the first scientific maps for parts of Spitsbergen, the taking of a thorough set of temperature and current measurements, and so on, Koldewey led his ship to modest success. This was not much compensation for the failure in regard to the primary aims of the expedition, however, particularly the inability to find a route through the pack ice. In part, this was a matter of sheer bad luck. Later analysis suggested that the border of the pack ice around Greenland and east to Spitsbergen was unusually broad in the summer of 1868, due to a meteorological anomaly that no amount of careful planning or skillful navigation could have anticipated or averted.[43] A German whaler hailed by Koldewey reported that "there has never been so much ice everywhere as in this year."[44] Koldewey noted that the first German polar expedition had to be considered in this respect "an unfortunate, utterly miscarried" attempt.[45]

On the other hand, the voyage was a smashing public relations success. Petermann and Koldewey won international acclaim for German science, as both noted with pride. Germany had shown it belonged "in the ranks of the great seafaring nations," Koldewey rejoiced, "and if for this time we also returned without success, yet it is success enough to have held upright in every respect the honor of our young North German flag."[46] The two greatest purposes of Arctic voyages, the expansion of geographic knowledge and the cultivation of naval expertise among the nation's sailors, had been well served. Petermann felt the same way, noting that donations in support of German polar exploration continued to accumulate. Furthermore, both the captain and the geographer believed that the voyage did nothing to disprove their conception of a navigable sea at the North Pole.

Quite the reverse. Koldewey noted that the effort made thus far had been supported with insufficient means and argued that ships, not sleds, still had the greatest probability of achieving the Pole. Petermann was even more emphatic—contrary to the charges of its critics, the voyage of the Grönland had proven that "the seas north of Europe, among all the ice seas of the earth, are the most navigable."[47] Most of all, as one observer commented, the first German polar voyage had whetted German public appetites for Arctic adventure, and served, in that regard, "to get the ball rolling" toward a much more elaborate attempt.[48]

2. PERSISTENT DANGERS, UNUSUAL LUCK

From the high valley of the Alps to the foaming Belt,
blossoms now the German, the domestic world;
she reposes there, blessed, a garden of the Lord,
no more beautiful shines forth upon our star.

And yet, you men, so bold and so strong,
and yet impatience drives you forth,
you depart the blooming native strand,
with gazes turned to the icy North.

ANONYMOUS, 1869

Koldewey's voyage was a huge popular success. Public donations flooded in, surpassing Petermann's expectations and generating a surplus for the construction of a new steamer designed to lead a more elaborate follow-up voyage. Whatever its ultimate outcome, both Koldewey and Petermann saw the Grönland voyage as no more than a first effort. In the fall of 1868, accordingly, even before the ship had returned, planning went forward for a second and much more systematic effort at reaching the Greenland coast and finally breaching the ice girdle that they thought encircled the open polar ocean.

Establishing the route and aims of this second German expedition, however, caused controversy and, ultimately, an unbridgeable rift between the geographer and the sailor. The plan formulated by Petermann at the end of October 1868 bears the unmistakable stamp of the armchair explorer. He intended to use two steamers. One would drive for the central Arctic basin between Greenland and Spitsbergen along the lines planned for the first voyage. The second ship would deposit a landing party on the eastern coast of Greenland whose members would be retrieved by the first vessel on its return. The entire project, in Petermann's view, ought to take about five months, from June to October.[1] This plan was grossly overoptimistic in its assessment of what might reasonably be carried out in a summer of Arctic navigation, and it was bound to strike a now-seasoned Arctic hand like Koldewey as the amateurish fancy of a dilettante.

It is a tribute to the youthful Koldewey's great personal tact that he was able to restrain Petermann's ambitions without provoking an immediate quarrel. In March 1869 the two men met to discuss the plan and agreed upon a more realistic program. The voyage through the Arctic basin toward

34

the Pole was abandoned. Efforts now concentrated solely on the task of reaching and exploring the eastern coast of Greenland. A new steamer, the *Germania*, would be built to order as an exploratory vessel. The *Grönland* would serve as a supply ship, and an overwintering in Greenland would be part of the expedition. In contrast to the initial voyage, this expedition would undertake an ambitious scientific agenda, to be carried out by a team of accompanying specialists. After their meeting, which ended on cordial terms, Koldewey departed for a lecture and fund-raising tour through Leipzig, Prague, Vienna, Munich, and half a dozen more central European towns.[2]

The Sinews of Science: Funding and Outfitting the Expedition

With Koldewey working the lecture circuit, Germans rallied to the idea of another polar voyage. Fund-raising committees led by the local well-to-do sprang up in a dozen German cities. Civic leaders in the old Hansa towns, especially Bremen and Hamburg, were particularly effective, as was the dynamic middle-class community at Berlin. In Bremen the polar committee assembled a cross-section of the local bourgeoisie, bringing together Meier of the North German Lloyd shipping line, merchants like Georg Albrecht, industrialists and shipbuilders such as Franz and Johann Tecklenborg, sailors like Koldewey, the publicist Moritz Lindeman, and others. By the end of 1869, this Verein für die deutsche Nordpolarfahrt zu Bremen (Bremen Committee for the German North Polar Journey) had raised over eleven thousand Taler, a fifth of the total gathered in support of the expedition and just about the cost of a vessel like the *Germania*.

Academia's intimacy with commerce was typical of German intellectual life. In Berlin the committee was led by Adolf Bastian, an anthropologist and geographer who is often seen as the founder of modern ethnology, but it included industrialists and businessmen like August Borsig, Werner Siemens, and Albrecht, a generous patron of the sciences who would play a key role in founding the Geographical Society of Bremen (Geographische Gesellschaft Bremen) a few years later, in 1876.[3] In all the appeals, the fund-raisers linked exploration with national pride. The Berlin appeal, distributed by the thousands, was typical.

> Fellow citizens! The question whether the sea around the North
> Pole of our globe bristles with eternal ice, or if there too creative
> nature has spread life on unknown shores, is still unsolved. . . .
> German explorers have already brought high honor to the German

35

name in all the zones of our globe, but in the solving of this question Germany has recently played little part. Thanks to the national rebirth of our fatherland, it is appropriate that it here takes its place among the other seafaring nations. The affair is a truly German matter, since the first exploratory voyages in those icy districts of the North Pole proceeded from Germany more than eight hundred years ago, and the German *Hansa* tested in the northern seas her then still young powers.[4]

Koldewey's triumphant lecture tour also drew funds from the nobility of the many German states. Crown Prince Friedrich, heir to the Prussian throne, heard Koldewey in Berlin, and his father, the Prussian king, donated 2,000 Taler, an example emulated in slightly less open handed fashion by his brother monarchs, the king of Bavaria (400 Taler) and the king of Württemberg (280 Taler), as well as some two score other members of the lesser German nobility. Franz-Josef of Austria, Napoleon III of France, and the Royal Italian Navy gave money, as did German expatriates in London, New York, Bombay, Lima, St. Louis, and a dozen other sites around the globe. From the financial point of view, at least, Petermann's second effort was a pan-German project.[5]

Some supporters of the expedition still felt that Petermann's goals were too ambitious. In response to such doubts, and prompted by worry that the plan allowed too little flexibility to respond to unforeseen problems, Koldewey in mid-March of 1869 published a modified alternative program. This altered Petermann's plan in only one respect: should the coast of Greenland once more prove unattainable, Koldewey suggested that the planned overwintering site might be shifted to the north of Spitsbergen. Though less scientific benefit would be derived from such a change, since Spitsbergen was fairly well known, Koldewey's proposal had the advantage of permitting some constructive response to unanticipated difficulty.

It is not clear whether Koldewey believed he had Petermann's support for his proposal. Petermann, however, was furious, denouncing Koldewey's suggestion as a personal attack against himself and a subversion of the entire German polar endeavor. "Whether your opposition was necessary, whether I deserved it, whether it was just and well considered, I do not wish to consider further," Petermann wrote in his nagging and resentful style. "I can see your plan only as open hostility toward me and the affair, since you promise in it nothing with certainty beyond Spitzbergen, and for our purposes that is not simply nothing but less than nothing."[6] In private, he attacked Koldewey's seamanship, blaming him for the failures of the *Grönland* and suggesting that only Petermann's own forbearance (!) had kept him from openly criticizing his captain.[7] This was an egregious injustice. Koldewey had captained the *Grönland* over three thousand nautical miles through some of the most turbulent reaches of the North Atlantic. Though the ship had not been able to make a landing, as both men had hoped, the voyage was a creditable achievement. Petermann's vindictive anger, however, initiated an enduring estrangement between the two.

Despite the conflict of wills, preparations gathered momentum as the summer of 1869 approached. In sharp contrast with the ad hoc character of the first expedition, the outfitting of the second German North Polar effort was characterized by painstaking attention to detail. The expedition's selection of vessels, personnel, clothing, and provisions typified the way that technologically advanced cultures girded themselves to meet dangerous and little-known environments as the age of exploration closed.

The main vessel of the expedition was built at the Tecklenborg yards in Geestemünde, on Germany's North Sea coast. Tecklenborg already enjoyed a continental reputation for quality and would win new laurels in coming decades with some of the greatest sailing ships ever constructed.[8] The polar ship, begun on 10 March, was launched just four weeks after the laying of the keel and christened, at Petermann's behest, the *Germania*. This was the first ship to be constructed in Germany expressly for research purposes, and its design incorporated a host of ingenious adaptations. The vessel was small, at 143 tons displacement, about the size of the West Indian trading schooners of a slightly earlier day. It was also exceedingly solid in structure—"somewhat fortresslike," as a contemporary account put it. In order to withstand collision with floating ice, the wooden planking of the hull was shielded with a double layer of plate iron, further reinforced at the bow with a network of iron bars. The beams between the decks and the so-called knees of the vessel, joining the frame and deck beams, were made of both iron and wood and were suitable to a vessel several times the tonnage of the *Germania*.

The ship's steam engine and screw propeller were meant for use only within the ice fields. Specially strengthened masts and conventional sailing rig were provided for locomotion to and from the Greenland coast. The *Germania*'s hull, thirty meters long and seven meters wide, was narrow and designed to ride up the ice in which it would eventually be frozen, slipping out of its crushing grip like a squeezed seed. A shallow draft of just three meters would enable it to navigate near shore without difficulty. Appropriate class distinctions would be maintained while aboard—officers, scholars, and common seamen were each housed in separate cabins.

The *Grönland*, originally intended as the consort of the *Germania*, was by the spring of 1869 dismissed as too small. Instead, the *Germania* would be accompanied by the schooner *Hansa*. It was also new, built in 1864 as the Prussian ship *Fulton*. Ironically, the vessel named for the pioneer of motorized navigation had no engine. Purchased for eight thousand Taler by members of the Bremen polar committee, the *Hansa* was reworked into a polar supply vessel, given a skin of iron sheeting over its oak-plank hull, an iron-reinforced prow, and special internal supports to resist the pressure generated by pack ice. The *Hansa* was also specially insulated against the Arctic cold. The walls of its quarters were lined with felt, and a fifteen centimeter gap between the hull and inner walls was filled with sawdust to hinder the penetration of cold and moisture. Special hatches and doubled glass skylights were likewise meant to reduce indrafts of cold air and lessen the chance of condensation gathering within the vessel.

A staggering amount of material was crammed into these two small vessels. The provisioning of the ships was governed by the presumption that the thirty-one members of the expedition (seventeen on the *Germania*, fourteen on the *Hansa*) must be ready to spend two years in the Arctic wilds. Since nothing but fresh meat could be derived from the local environment, and that only at sporadic intervals, the ships had to be supplied with every conceivable necessity for the next twenty-four months—food and drink, clothing, fuel, scientific instruments, spare wood and iron plating, spare screw propellers for the *Germania*, sleds, rope, tools, medical supplies, books "of every genre, from scholarly disquisitions to children's stories," playing cards, ink, pens, paper, ship's tackle, rifles and bullets, knives, nuts and bolts—the list seems endless. In both craft, cargo space was largely consumed by coal, 70 metric tons in the *Germania* and 110 metric tons in the *Hansa*, to fuel the *Germania*'s engine, the ships' ovens, and stoves in the overwintering huts. Much of this coal was carried in the form of compressed briquettes, a circumstance that would prove fortuitous for the *Hansa*'s crewmen.

Merely cataloging the variety of goods necessary to the voyage may fail to convey an accurate sense of the complex material foundations of European scientific expeditions in the nineteenth century. A detailed consideration of the actual contents of three primary categories of items—victuals, clothing, and scientific instruments—shows the dependence of incursions into remote regions upon the financial, material, and technical resources of Western societies. Bread and meat were considered to be the two most important sources of nutrients for the expedition. A quantity of smoked and salted meats was included on both ships, but since a diet too reliant upon salt meat was by this time felt to run the risk of scurvy, canned meat was preferred. One thousand kilograms of canned meats, felt to be equivalent in nutritive value to twice that amount of fresh meat, were taken on board the *Germania*. Hundreds of kilos of pemmican were also stored. Flour rather than bread was shipped to save space and to ease preservation. Canned or jarred vegetables of every kind were added, including spinach, kidney beans, peas, carrots, asparagus, pickles, French cut green beans, potatoes, Brussels sprouts, onions (green and white), sorrel, parsley, thyme, egg yolks, and, to gratify the North German palate of the day, cabbage in three varieties—Savoy, brown, and red. Preserved fruits included cranberries, plums, and others.

Since, as one account of the voyage noted, "good drink is indispensable on Arctic journeys," the *Germania* carried a mind-boggling selection of alcoholic beverages. In addition to what are described as "numerous gifts of wine, and especially French red wine," the ship's cellar boasted the following:

75 liters of rye whiskey
29 dozen bottles of sherry
2 dozen bottles of Jamaican rum
2 dozen bottles of port
4 dozen bottles of berry liqueur
190 liters of Médoc wine
225 liters of Oporto wine
40 crates, 6 carboys, and 75 liters of "diverse wines"
16 barrels, 1 carboy, and 6 dozen bottles of beer
16 crates of diverse "spirits"

It is not possible to determine the precise volume of the containers listed here as "bottles" nor that of the carboys of wine, crates of spirits, or barrels of beer. Clearly, however, the per capita allotment of alcohol taken aboard the *Germania* ran to many liters for each of the seventeen crew members. Preserved milk was also carried, presumably to soothe corroded stomach linings, along with raspberry vinegar and thirty-two carboys of lemon juice as an antiscorbutic.

Great care was taken in tailoring special garments for the explorers. Later generations would turn to the Eskimo for their models. In the 1870s, however, Germans consulted the accounts of English, Russian, and American expeditions as to the most effective means of protecting the human body against cold and exposure. Wool, leather, and furs were the preferred materials, derived from the hides of seal, American buffalo, Russian sheep, and Polish dogs. Seams were sewn exclusively with thread of Angora wool, since both cotton and silk had been seen to lose their tenacity under conditions of extreme cold. Buttons were of so-called vegetable ivory, taken from the hard shell of the corozo nut; the more typical bone buttons sewed on with silk thread were considered too fragile. Fur-lined hoods to shelter face, neck, and shoulders were issued, and gigantic gauntlets, forty-three centimeters long and twenty centimeters wide, were made to fit over hands already covered with leather and woolen gloves. Pelisses of sheep and buffalo hide, as well as buffalo-skin sleeping bags to be used on sledging excursions, were also provided. Hats and gloves were sewn of Polish dog pelts. The Germania was as liberally provisioned with clothing as with alcohol, shipping, among other items, the following:

- 4 dozen pairs of white woolen long stockings
- 6 dozen pairs of brown woolen long stockings
- 3 dozen pairs of white woolen leggings
- 5 dozen pairs of brown woolen leggings
- 3 dozen blue woolen leggings
- 3 dozen Irish jackets
- 8 dozen woolen waistcoats
- 10 dozen pairs of woolen gloves, in white, gray, and colors
- 3 dozen woolen shawls, in brown and white
- 3 dozen hunting caps
- 3 dozen sets of fur hats and gloves
- 24 complete sheepskin outer suits
- 3 dozen pairs of insulated leather boots

All this represented only a part of the ship's complement of clothing. Bolts of woolen fabric, skins, yarn, and sewing implements were included, as were materials for preparing the pelts of animals taken by the expedition.

The scientific outfitting of the Germania was accomplished through donations from many sources, including the Royal Prussian Observatory in

Göttingen, the Royal Physical Department, clock and scientific instrument companies in Germany, England, and France, and the property of individual scientists. Included were a theodolite and a wide range of surveying instruments; two telescopes of 30X magnification and their stands; four microscopes; six compasses; four sextants; four box chronometers and two pocket chronometers; a spectroscope, a magnetometer, and other instruments for measuring geomagnetic intensity; a score of thermometers of various types and graduated according to various scales; and photographic equipment, including a camera and hundreds of plates supplied gratis by "the photographer Herr Harnecker in Wriezen."

This recounting, needless to say, does not approach a complete inventory of the goods and implements thought necessary to the expedition, but it does help illustrate the elaborate preparation behind Western exploratory adventures. When packing up the implements of their civilization, members of the expedition did not forget about the cultures they might encounter. A variety of dime-store baubles and factory trinkets was brought along for barter and gift giving with the native peoples. These included mirrors, dyed cloth, small metal goods such as files, knives, and saws, and glass beads, a staple of exchange between Europeans and indigenous peoples since the earliest days of the African slave trade.[9]

Anticipation built steadily through April and May as the ships were completed and provisioned. Crews were assembled with care, this time including several scientific specialists. All the scholars, as all the crew members, were young. None had passed thirty-three years of age. Half had military experience. On board the *Germania* were two German scientists: Adolf Pansch, the ship's doctor and expert in zoology and anthropology, and Karl Börgen, an astronomer. The ship carried as well an English astronomer, Ralph Copeland, and the Austrian infantry officer Julius Payer, an experienced alpinist, amateur geographer, and decorated veteran of his nation's war in Italy. The *Hansa* carried Reinhold Buchholz, a physician, zoologist, and anthropologist who had served in a field hospital during Prussia's war with Austria, and Gustav Laube, an Austrian geologist. The ships' captains were Koldewey and, on the *Hansa*, Friedrich Hegemann, an experienced whaling captain, like Koldewey thirty-two years old. This was a very young complement, but one not without experience in the persons of Koldewey and Hegemann.

At the end of May, King Wilhelm granted Koldewey an audience at the royal estate in Babelsberg, just outside Berlin. Koldewey traced the planned route of the expedition for his monarch, and Wilhelm promised to attend the ship's departure from Bremen. That ancient seafaring community celebrated departure day, 15 June 1869, as a public festival. This was an important moment in the life of the town. Its citizens had invested considerable sums and great effort toward the realization of the occasion, and the presence of the Prussian king, accompanied by Bismarck, underscored the import of the event. An anonymous admirer smuggled flowers and a poem to Koldewey, reminding "you heroes" of the crew that "German woman has always courage revered / and held magnificent recompense to the gallant due."[10] The crew, costumed in Arctic furs, stood to attention as the king reviewed the *Germania*, and Alexander Mosle, president of the Bremen committee, reminded them of their duty: "The success of the mission depends upon you participants in the expedition, representatives of German science and German maritime affairs. You have committed yourselves to your entire nation, to wager everything to reach the goal. Through you, knowledge of the North Polar sea shall be made accessible to all peoples, to the honor of the fatherland, to the honor of the young German flag, to the honor of German science and German navigation."[11] Then, with the crew saluting their king, their sponsors, and the flag-waving crowds along the quays of Bremen, both ships slipped their moorings and set out for the mouth of the Weser and the North Sea.

Karl Koldewey and the Germania in Greenland

The shared voyage of the *Hansa* and the *Germania* lasted barely a month. Contrary and fickle winds slowed the early stages of the journey, so that the ships required sixteen days to reach the latitude of the Shetlands, a distance normally traversed in ten. Now, at the start of July, the ships sailed beneath the midnight sun, and on clear days the men could read on deck around the clock. On 5 July the vessels crossed the Arctic Circle. They would remain north of the line for nearly a year. Lingering, dense fogs blanketed these waters, and the ships often stayed in contact only by firing signal guns. The first ice appeared on 15 July, a month out of Bremerhaven, and five days later, misreading a flagged signal from the *Germania*, the *Hansa* sailed into a smothering fogbank. The ships would never reunite.

While the men of the *Hansa* would experience the most gripping drama of the expedition over the next several months, the *Germania*, under the leadership of Koldewey and the energetic Payer, won notable scientific success. Resolving after a day's search that contact with the *Hansa* had been lost for good, Koldewey steered northwestward for the eastern Greenland coast. Through the rest of July, the *Germania* cruised the regions between 73° and 74.5°, seeking in vain for a way through the ice. This was not to be a repeat of the futile wanderings of the *Grönland*, however. On 5 August, seven weeks out of Bremerhaven, the *Germania* anchored off the southern end of Sabine Island, a part of Greenland's eastern coastal archipelago. "Amidst general cries of 'Hurrah!' our black-white-red flag was unfurled for the first time in eastern Greenland," Koldewey later recalled. "It was a sobering moment, and we congratulated ourselves joyfully over the first difficult portion of our great task."[12]

Reconnaissance from a nearby hill revealed only ice-choked water to the north. This was a disappointment. Both Petermann and Koldewey had hoped to find open coastal channels at this season. Undaunted, Koldewey steamed northward once more on 10 August. Gingerly picking out a path among the increasingly dense floes of ice, the crew found their way finally blocked at 75°31' north latitude. This was as close to the Pole as the expedition would get by water, and it wasn't very close. Confronted by unbroken pack ice, the *Germania* turned back southward, anchoring in its original small harbor on the south side of Sabine Island on 13 September. Ship and crew would call this site home for the next ten months.

Two tasks now faced the men of the *Germania*. First, the ship had to be prepared for overwintering. Koldewey noted that nights were longer and much colder, unmistakable signs that the brief summer was already passing back into Arctic winter. The crew quickly converted their oceangoing vessel into a snug winter home. The rigging was largely taken down, and the entire deck from bow to stern was roofed with planks and then insulated with moss and snow. Outside, windbreaks constructed of snow and ice were thrown up surrounding the vessel. The result was a cozy and thermally efficient abode. The ship's specially designed ovens were now able to maintain customary room temperature while consuming very little coal.

The other challenge confronting Koldewey and his crew, particularly the scholars, was to begin the execution of their scientific tasks. To this end, two small observatories were constructed ashore, one for astronomical and the other for geomagnetic observations. A kind of meteorological observatory was also erected, consisting of wooden cases open to the movement of air and hung with barometers, devices for measuring wind speed and precipitation, and a variety of thermometers graduated according to several scales. For the next nine months, these instruments were read around the clock on an hourly schedule, providing a wealth of data. Systematic collection of other scientific information also began after the *Germania* had been winterized, including such daily chores as the measurement of ice thickness on land, gathering of soil and rock samples, and collection and organization of specimens of mosses, lichens, crabs, and later the local mammalian fauna.[13]

The *Germania*'s scientific success reflected the enterprise of Koldewey and Payer. Within a day of anchoring, Payer broke out sleds for a short journey, and the icebound months were punctuated by several extended and hazardous trips inland. Neither dogs nor draft animals of any type had been included in the ship's cargo, so the consequent "horse work," as Koldewey termed it, of moving the sleds depended upon the muscle of the men.[14] Both leaders noted that the Germans were initially hindered by their inexperience. The men inclined to pack, as Koldewey put it, "for a European lifestyle and had not yet acquired enough Eskimo simplicity."[15] Payer agreed: "Even though we knew from the Arctic literature in a theoretical sense in what fashion and manner such journeys were to be carried out, none of us had any kind of practical experience with them, so that our entire preparation, as would later become clear, remained faulty."[16] Wisdom came painfully. On one such journey, the ship's first officer, Heinrich Sengstacke, froze his feet so badly that amputation of the toes was considered, and he was confined to his bed for weeks.[17]

The crew quickly grew savvy to the ways of Arctic survival, however. Ultimately, five extended sled journeys were undertaken by parties of four to eight men each, and these accounted for some of the most noteworthy achievements of the expedition. Extreme hardship marked these sledding forays. Fractured terrain, often concealing dangerous ice crevasses, tested the endurance of the crew, as did the cold, which Koldewey reported at times reaching -27° Reaumur, roughly -34°C. The trips reaped a substantial scientific reward, however. Payer and his accomplices made one of the journey's striking finds when they encountered a small herd of musk oxen. To this time, Europeans had noted these animals only along the Arctic coast of Canada.

The prolonged violent storms of the eastern Greenland coast further complicated sledding. "These storms were our greatest hindrance," Koldewey recalled. "They often compelled us to remain dormant in our tents for three days at a stretch, which is by far more difficult, stressful, and harmful to the health than the most exhausting marching days. Snow in the form of fine dust squeezes through all the seams of the tent roof and deposits itself in a two-and-a-half-centimeter-thick layer over the blankets and clothes; body warmth melts some of the snow, you grow moist and damp, shivering sets in, and illness is the inevitable result. Miserable and downcast, we recover after such a storm to begin our horse work anew."[18] On one such trip, lasting over a month in the spring of 1870, Koldewey and Payer reached a latitude of 77°1' north, the farthest ever advanced along Greenland's coast and a record not surpassed until 1907. This trip, lasting thirty-four days and covering 210 kilometers of some of the Northern Hemisphere's most difficult terrain, was a convincing demonstration of the extent to which the Germans mastered the technique of Arctic overland travel.

Nor was it necessary, in this almost entirely unexplored region, to go far from the ship itself to make valuable finds. The remains of an Eskimo village, recorded forty-seven years earlier by an English expedition as the only such settlement on the eastern Greenland coast, were discovered nearby. Though the artifacts of the village were carefully cataloged and closely examined by Pansch, it was not possible to determine why the settlement had been abandoned.[19] Coal was also found nearby. Koldewey viewed this as a discovery of the utmost importance: "Of all the living requirements that one must bring along, it is fuel that first sets limits to the length of journeys inland and to the stay itself. . . . Provisions may be replenished as soon as one disposes of sufficient cartridges. Clothing is not subject to any discernible daily consumption. Fuel, on the other hand, is not only indispensable, but it cannot be replenished."[20]

Koldewey's lack of concern over provisions was well justified. Game was so abundant and taken with such ease that it seemed the *Germania*'s crew might have landed on the coast with no more in the way of provisions than rifles and cartridges and still have gained weight. Foxes, bears, marine mammals, and birds of all sorts were consumed by the expedition, but roasts of musk ox and reindeer comprised the mainstay of their diet throughout the winter. Fresh meat was so plentiful that the conserves were hardly used, and the salt meat went untouched. Polar bear fat provided fuel for the melting of snow.

Not all the game was timid, however, and the hunters on several occasions found themselves the hunted. Angry walrus bulls, for example, repeatedly chased crew members across the ice. A graver threat by far were the polar bears. They were numerous, deadly, and dangerously aggressive, and the men soon learned not to venture far from their compatriots without a rifle at hand. Börgen, the ship's astronomer, was nearly killed by an attacking bear. Returning from his observatory, at some distance from his fellows, he was set upon by a stalking bear at such short notice that he lost his weapon. A strangled cry of alarm alerted Börgen's comrades, but before they could reach him the scientist was dragged several yards by the hood, nearly asphyxiated, and bitten about the head so severely that the skin was torn back from the cranium at several places.[21]

Savage beasts were only one of many hardships the *Germania*'s crew had to surmount. The extensive mapping, sounding, collecting of samples, and recording of data that the little expedition managed to carry on are impressive both for the fact that none of the crew had experience with the hazards of the Arctic terrain and for the extremity of the environmental obstacles encountered. Although the buffalo-hide sleeping sacks proved effective, the cold still penetrated the men's clothing, froze the tents "as hard as iron," and threatened at the least carelessness to cause frostbite and amputation. Elementary tasks, like the collection of shellfish specimens, became tests of emotional and physical stamina. "It was no pleasant work, by the light of lanterns in the cold and dark, to fish the creatures out and secure them, particularly because one had always to keep eyes and ears open for approaching bears and loaded rifles ready at hand."[22] Powerful windstorms, during which movement outside the shelter of the ship or tents was nearly impossible, exacerbated the effects of the temperature. Worst of all was the constant darkness from the fall through early February.

Confinement, tension, isolation, darkness, and the exhausting routine of physical labor gradually eroded group morale. The psychological health of the men had not been neglected when planning the expedition, and efforts were made to supply healthy diversions. A newspaper was attempted (as would be the case later with subsequent German expeditions to Greenland), but it "died of neglect" after five issues. The men passed their spare time reading, writing letters and notes, and practicing such crafts as carpentry, tailoring, and shoemaking. A school of navigation was set up to teach the crewmen the theoretical basis of the mariner's craft. Christmas was observed with special foods and a "tree" of sticks draped with moss.

Still, a sense of slowly building tension and depression can be felt in the participants' accounts of their overwintering. Koldewey noted by late January a marked "slowness and sleepiness" besetting his men and said that, although the mood remained good, "smaller, unavoidable frictions" were common.[23] The captain may have underestimated the impact of the darkness. Others recorded the experience of endless night in more disturbing tones. "Nature is wrapped in a rigid shroud or funeral pall, over which the profound Night broods immovable . . . No wonder, that with such surroundings, we almost succumb to a feeling of utter desolation or that our spirits are prostrated by the darkness that weighs so heavily on Nature animate and inanimate."[24]

The return of the sun, at noon on 3 February 1870, prompted an outburst of high spirits and solemn gratitude. Payer and Koldewey spent the next several weeks preparing for the most ambitious of their sled journeys, one that eventually took them, under the most torturous conditions (whose pains were deadened with opium) to the expedition's northernmost point. Returning at the end of April, the explorers began preparing for the expected summer breakup of the ice around the *Germania*. This began on 11 July, and on the 22nd, over thirteen months after leaving Bremerhaven, the ship left its winter harbor and tried once more to cruise northward.

After a week of fruitless searching for a navigable cleft in the ice, Koldewey resolved to explore southward along the coast, an option not provided for in the plans for the expedition. His decision proved fortuitous. On 5 August the expedition discovered the mouth of the Franz Josef Fjord, a magnificent arm of the sea reaching scores of kilometers inland. Koldewey, Payer, and the scientists understood the significance of their find. "The scenery was stunning, like the Alps. An unknown land, the actual interior of Greenland, opened itself ever more beautifully and imposingly before our astonished eyes. Glaciers, cascades, waterfalls came down from the ever-ascending mountains."[25] Their natural eagerness to explore this dramatic landscape was cut short, however, by increasing concern at the mechanical malfunctioning of the steam engine. To be caught in the windless fjord, should the engine break down, might at this late date condemn ship and crew to a second consecutive overwintering, for which they were both materially and psychologically unprepared. On 22 August, accordingly, Koldewey and the *Germania* began the long journey back to Bremerhaven.

Hansa Agonistes

The fate of the *Germania*'s consort, meanwhile, was far different. When the two ships separated, Hegemann, in command of the *Hansa*, spent a day searching and then plotted a course westward in hopes of finding Koldewey off the Greenland coast. On 13 August the island's dark cliffs were seen in the distance, but the ship's advance was now blocked by the same dense

47

fields of ice that had frustrated the *Germania*'s first attempts to land. Lacking steam power, the *Hansa* spent a month chasing leads and shifting winds through the ice floes, often advancing only by the laborious method of "warping," rowing the ship's anchor ahead in a boat and then propelling the entire vessel forward by hauling at the anchor. The work was difficult and very slow. The ship made little progress, cold weather closed in, and on 19 September the *Hansa* found itself immobilized in the coastal ice pack. As the cold deepened, the grim situation became clear: the ship was trapped in the ice until spring. Thus began the ordeal of the *Hansa*.[26]

Tales of stranded, shipwrecked, and lost expeditions comprise the epics of polar history. Though the drama of the *Hansa* and her crew is a gripping specimen of this genre, it has not won a place with Franklin, Scott, Shackleton, Andrée, and other heroes and martyrs of polar abandonment and salvation. Perhaps the omission of the *Hansa* from polar memory is due to the fact that the crew actually survived and that only a sacrificial and pointless death on the altar of polar adventure, à la Robert Falcon Scott, really guarantees fame. That answer, though, ignores the case of Shackleton and the *Endurance*, arguably the most famous of polar disaster stories, despite the inconvenient survival, from the dramatic point of view, of all the participants. A likelier answer for the obscurity of the *Hansa* adventure is that popular memory has focused upon the Anglo-American and Nordic experiences and missed even significant contributions made by the Japanese, Italians, Germans, and others on the periphery of polar exploration.

Despite the fabled terrors of Greenland's weather, the crew of the *Hansa* faced the looming winter with composure. "We were confident that our ship, which was very sturdily built and internally reinforced with strong beams, would survive," wrote Buchholz. "It had already defied hard shocks and even compression between ice fields without suffering the least damage."[27] The crew set to work immediately, preparing a snug refuge against the elements. As on the *Germania*, the topmasts were struck down, the deck was roofed, and the vessel was secured in place with ropes and ice anchors.[28] Two of the three ship's boats (*Bismarck* and *Hope*) were cleared from the deck, stocked with two months' provisions, and covered with sailcloth to provide escape in an emergency.

The ultimate key to the crew's survival, however, was the captain's decision to construct a shelter on the ice at several hundred paces from the ship. It was laid out, by Hegemann's design, in rectilinear form, six by four meters, with gables two meters high. Using ice axes and shovels, the crewmen cleared the snow from an ice foundation. Walls and a floor of the twenty-three-centimeter-wide coal bricks were then laid masonry-fashion. Snow and water provided mortar. "We had only to strew fine, dry snow in the gaps and seams, pour on water, and in ten minutes all had frozen to a firm, compact mass, from which an individual stone could be taken only with great difficulty." This structure was roofed with sailcloth nailed over spars and planks and then stocked with provisions—150 kilograms of bread, two dozen tins of conserved meat, a side of bacon, coffee and alcohol, barrels of cabbage, and wood for fuel.[29]

The elements smiled upon the crew during the week required to build this "Hansa-House," with temperatures normally between about —17.8° and —9.4°C. The structure, "which in the great, wide fields looked more like a coffin than a human habitation," was initially intended as a store-house.[30] No one yet felt the least cause for panic. Ship, stores, boats, and crew were all sound and still together, drifting slowly southward with the ice fields caught in the Greenland Current.

The maritime routine was quickly resumed. Meteorological and hydro-graphical data were collected at hourly intervals. Crewmen sewed, reshod their boots, repaired weathered ship's tackle, and occupied themselves with other odd jobs. They exercised by hunting game, which, with the exception of the ready supply of Arctic foxes, they found considerably less abundant here than did the Germania, nearer the coast. The scientists filled the spare hours organizing their records. The only aspects of their condition that seemed at all ominous thus far were the growing frequency, length, and power of the storms and the haunting sounds generated by the ice, "which resembled now the pounding of an ironworks, then the brakes of a locomotive, then the cry of many human voices."[31]

The eerie din of grinding ice floes proved to be the prelude to disaster. In the third week of October, a northwesterly storm set in for several days. On 19 October, a day of extreme cold, blowing fine snow, and very little visibility, the entire ice field began to shake and vibrate, as if it were at some point colliding with the land or scraping over a shallow point on the seabed. The screeching of the tortured ice increased in pitch, and the men realized that the ice fields encasing the Hansa were subjecting the ship's hull to overpowering compressive force.

All around the crew, the ship began to come to pieces. Deck seams burst, and the thick planking, yielding to unbearable pressure, began to bulge upward.[32] The men rushed out of their cabins and over the sides to witness a terrifying sight.

> It was a fantastic spectacle, as the massive burden of the ship was slowly lifted three meters upward by the ice masses sliding under it, while all about us the splintered ice blocks threw up a high wall. Now came a second blow that set the ship quivering in all its members and, slanting on its side, thrust the ship a few meters sideways onto the ice wall. During this time the ice under our feet trembled as in an earthquake, deep chasms gaped open all around us, and we expected every moment that the ground beneath us would disintegrate.[33]

This was the end of the *Hansa*. When the icequake finally ceased, the massive ship had been lifted entirely clear of the water, borne upon a cradle of ice with the bow elevated a few meters above the stern. Officers and men clambered back on board to examine the damage and frantically started clearing off all the implements and supplies within reach, in case the ship should actually be about to sink. This was in fact the situation. Early in the afternoon the movements of the ice field calmed, while a gap slowly yawned open behind and beneath the *Hansa*. The ship slid backward, and, as it reentered the water stern first, the mortal nature of its wounds became clear. Ominously, rats began to flee the ship. Water rose quickly in the hold, and though the crew broke their backs turning the ship's pumps the rest of the day and into the night, the water level rose steadily. Distinctions of rank temporarily disappeared in the face of disaster. All worked side by side, "even the captain and the scholars taking a turn," but their exertions were futile. The *Hansa*, apparently supported on a submerged projection of the ice floe, continued to take on water and was clearly beyond repair. The soaked and exhausted crew, after working for hours up to their knees in water barely above freezing, in air so frigid that the oil in the lamps froze, were now commanded to cease pumping and begin removing everything not bolted to the deck. All knew what this meant, and the mood became somber. "The entire crew behaved quietly through all the work, and only the sliding and thrusting of the bales and the commands of the captain broke the stillness. Each may well have been pondering his ordained fate."[34]

Their predicament might have made anyone a trifle thoughtful. Though they were able to spend the next day looting the ship of everything useful not trapped in flooded compartments below, including masts for firewood and tools of every type, the crew faced an Arctic winter with only the most primitive shelter from the elements. Their means of return to Europe was a ruin, they had no hope of resupply of any necessities beyond meat and water, and the long polar night was approaching. They were cut off from communication with the outside world. One of the members of the crew was disabled with fever, another had frozen his toes so badly in the effort to save the ship that he could not walk. To top off the brimming cup of woe, the Hansa, with a hiss and rush, slid beneath the ice during the night of 21 and 22 October, to settle forever on the ocean floor. Though the men salvaged a third lifeboat, the King Wilhelm, from the flotsam, even the least reflective of the small party seemed to sense that death hovered near.

Under these conditions, men and officers set out to make a life as secure and comfortable as possible, and the diaries and subsequently published accounts of the next several months reveal a generally resilient and resourceful spirit among the Hansa community. The Hansa-House was initially cold and wet inside, with temperatures around -7°C. Warming the air within at first increased the suffering of the men, causing thawed ice and snow to drip onto their clothes and sleeping sacks, there to refreeze.

Work and time gradually transformed this primitive shelter into a comfortable home. The crew dug a deep trench around three sides of the hut, then covered it with planks and sailcloth extending from the roof to the snow on the moat's far side. Provisions and supplies were stored here. Raised plank beds were built along each long wall of the shelter, and an oven for cooking and heating was placed opposite the entrance. The coal walls were covered with cloth from on board the Hansa. Crewmen installed a latticed walkway between the rows of beds, mounted bookshelves on the walls, and modified crates to serve as tables and stools. The gold-framed mirror from the ship's cabin graced one wall, the ship's clock another, and clothing and tools hung in nets from the roof.

As the snow deepened around the house—and the storms in December 1869 blew for days at a stretch—it provided insulation, which made the shelter warmer and drier. By the end of the month, the hut was nearly covered in snow and could be entered only by descending a small flight of stairs. As the domestic environs grew cozier, the gemütlich atmosphere waxed. "In our house it is getting more and more comfortable and, most importantly, dry," the captain wrote. "Thanks to that, we are all able to enjoy the best health."[35] Wilhelm Bade, the ship's second officer, imagined the astonishment that a newcomer might have experienced to find "with misery, the greatest luxury . . . as in a bandit's hideout, poverty and wealth

51

all mixed up." The interior decor of the *Hansa*-House was enlivened by a hodgepodge of salvaged items; a travel blanket showing a tiger crouched in the jungle, navigational and medical instruments, scientific journals and popular books, chronometers, cigar cases, four music boxes, knives, daggers, and rifles, as well as "the photograph of a charming feminine form, smiling cordially forth at one."[36]

Nights were passed playing whist, speculating about chances of rescue, and keeping watch against surprise by Eskimo or polar bears. During the day, the men hunted game, which, as winter deepened and the floe drifted southward, became more plentiful. Foxes, bears, seals, and walrus were all taken in such profusion that the sailors acquired the discrimination of Arctic epicures: "In general, we found the roasts of fox an extremely savory dish, next to walrus tongue the best wild game that came to our table," one recalled, "since polar bear hams, though by no means to be disdained, always retained a trace of an oily flavor."[37]

The men made pets of the Arctic wildlife. They tamed a white fox so that it would take food from their hands, although for some reason, ironically enough, it always shunned Buchholz, the ship's zoologist. Hildebrandt then captured the cub of a polar bear whose mother the men had killed while hunting. Chained to an ice anchor outside their house, the cub remained defiant. Unlike the fox, the young bear "behaved most wildly and bit and would not lay its wildness aside, though well fed and also thoroughly chastised many times with a rope, but tore so wildly at its chain that it finally succeeded in breaking this and fleeing. Presumably, it sank in the water because of the heavy chain."[38] Christmas was observed with wax tapers, an imitation tree, and grog.

The floe upon which the men were stranded was at this time enormous, measuring about eleven kilometers in circumference. It was drifting southward on the coastal current, covering about six nautical miles (eleven kilometers) per day. As the winter days passed, however, the weather worsened. Storms confined the men to their tiny dwelling for days at a time, and the nights grew in length to sixteen hours or more. Daytime was always dim. Though the crew and officers seem to have borne the emotional stress of their plight with courage, the two scholars on board began to show signs of mental and emotional breakdown. Within two weeks of the loss of the *Hansa*, Bade noted signs of collapse in both Buchholz and Laube, the geologist.

In passing, I note here that sailors have stronger nerves than

people who have always been on land. While we have long since
recovered our accustomed calm and mental vigor, the two scholars
are still not able to properly regain their balance. Instead of
moving about in the fresh air as we do to divert ourselves, they
sit in the house almost all the time, despite admonitions, pursue
their melancholy thoughts, and corrupt our good humor by their
complaints. Dr. Buchholz is chiefly stricken. Even though Dr.
Laube concedes him almost nothing, he unburdens himself by
picturing our terrible predicament, wishing for his mother, and
cursing the entire expedition.[39]

The condition of the scholars, and the chances of the entire expedition,
worsened radically in January. During the first two weeks of the month,
a series of storms and collisions began to chip away at the edges of the
crew's floating island home. On the night of 2 January, after eight unbroken
days and nights of blizzard, the men were startled from their rest by a
"strong, lasting shuddering of our base." The continuing storm prevented
any further investigation until it abated at midmorning the next day.

When the crew emerged, they found that their enormous raft of ice was
no more. It had shattered into fragments during the night. Theirs was the
largest, but it was now, by Hildebrandt's estimate, only an eighth the size
it had been a day earlier. The men, seeing that they were drifting within
half a German mile, or about three kilometers, of the shore, presumed that
the floe had fractured as it rasped over coastal shallows. Reduced in size,
their ice island now rocked steadily in the storm-whipped waters. This in
turn generated pressure that continually eroded new fragments from the
perimeter. Two days later, the floe broke again, carrying away the store of
firewood and leaving the Hansa-House perched upon the very brink of the
ice.

The men realized they were in extreme peril, and they prepared to take to
the boats at a moment's notice. Watch was kept all night so that they might
not be surprised by a further collapse of the floe. The ship's unflappable
cook, Johann Wupkes, made hot coffee, which the men drank with cognac
and a supper of cold meats. Their series of calamities was not yet ended. On
12 January another violent storm caused an even more devastating fracture
of the ice, bisecting the Hansa-House itself, carrying away one of the boats
(later retrieved), and rendering their shelter an uninhabitable ruin.

Now the Hansa's men faced their greatest trial. They were cast away on
a shard of ice, between one and two hundred paces broad. Their hut was

53

destroyed, much of their fuel was gone, and some provisions were lost. From the remains of the coal hut, the men fashioned a smaller structure with space for four of the fourteen men. Planks and bits of wood were used to make a small cooking closet over the stove. Most of their time, sleeping and eating alike, was now spent "packed like herring" in the boats, wrapped in their skin sacks and covered with sailcloth against the blowing and drifting snow.[40] Their block of ice, grown skittish as its size diminished, now bobbed about like a cork on the waves.

As the spring progressed and the ice raft drifted southward, towering icebergs threatened to crush the crew's sanctuary. They lived in constant terror of further splintering of their floe, leaping from their boats to prepare an evacuation whenever the ice began once more to grind and wail. Their one realistic chance of survival lay in eventually drifting into open water, where they could take to the boats and try to reach an Eskimo or whaling settlement. Prospects were dim, and at least one of the crew—Second Officer Bade—resolved privately to end his own life in the event of any kind of serious injury.[41]

A few of the men succumbed to momentary despair. Fritz Kewell, a sailor, tore open his clothes and begged Hildebrandt to put a bullet through his chest. Both scholars collapsed entirely. Laube "holds that all is lost, and since he believes he will never return to society, he tries in no way to conceal his cowardice. This naturally makes a repulsive impression on us." He feigned illness, hid from work, and was regarded by his fellow castaways as "an old woman." Buchholz seemed to be dissolving into raving insanity. At the end of January, Bade reported that he "has lost all love of life, lying continually in his sleeping bag in the great boat, and does not come out at all. We have to feed him there, so that he does not starve."

This was just the start of Buchholz's descent into lunacy. By March his madness had progressed to such a point that the entire crew was frightened. Bade recorded that "a case has occurred that crowns the most horrible of our experiences," explaining that "madness has broken out among us."

> What the grounds for it may be, I cannot say. Is it the horror and danger of our situation, which can probably shatter a spirit, even more, as is the case with us, when it is bound up with the almighty length of the time that in the end must weaken even the strongest? Is it the climate of the Arctic winter, the cold terrible night of the High North? Is it an inner kernel of this evil that has thereby escaped? Were earlier reasons already at hand to which the

outbreak may be attributed? Over all this we have racked our brains in vain.

Whatever the cause, on the morning of 8 March, Buchholz began to scream, strike about, and bite at his fellows so that he had to be forcibly restrained. Though calming down thereafter, he was clearly a danger and a demoralization to the entire crew. "At times the doctor is extremely droll to see, then again horrible, cutting frightful grimaces, talking crazy nonsense, then again melancholy and sad; it is very depressing. Lately he wants to get away. He secretly vanishes, twice even has left the floe. He possesses now an agility that astonishes all of us." The men had, ultimately, to confine him to a kind of straitjacket and exercise him only at the end of a leash.[42]

Buchholz's mental collapse might easily have provoked resentment or even brutality. He had, after all, become a liability to his comrades' chances of survival. Still consuming a portion of their dwindling supply of provisions, he could in no way contribute to the crew's exertions on their own behalf. On the contrary, he required constant supervision and special care, further taxing the already strained mental and physical energies of the stranded community. What is remarkable and inspiring about the case of Buchholz under these circumstances is the compassion that breathes through the two most thorough diaries of the expedition, those of Hildebrandt and Bade. Despite their own extreme suffering from hunger, cold, exhaustion, and despair, the officers and crew showed not brutality but sympathy and a rough sensitivity for their afflicted comrade. They refer frequently to the plight of the "poor fellow" and the need to treat him with forbearance. Given the extremity of the crew's circumstances and the fact that even the stalwart Bade had determined to take his own life in the case of injury, one might have expected to see the emergence of a ruthless Social Darwinism, an attitude of every man for himself, and "the devil take the hindmost." Nothing of the sort seems to have occurred, and there is no suggestion that the kind of scorn that the crew directed at a coward and deliberate malingerer like Laube was ever attached to one who was genuinely overcome by mental disability, as was clearly the case with Buchholz.[43]

These instances aside, the accounts of the *Hansa* stranding suggest the ship's crew behaved with admirable courage and composure. Both Hegemann and Hildebrandt continued to collect scientific readings, a laudable devotion to duty under the most distracting conditions. The behavior of the ship's cook and carpenter were particularly inspiring examples of grace under utmost pressure. The demented Buchholz himself later recalled that Wupkes, the cook, "even in the greatest extremity never lost his humor."[44] When the splintering of the ice floe destroyed the Hansa-House, it was Wupkes who first helped overcome the shock that beset the crew, climbing over the roof and into the flooded remnant of the hut to make a pot of hot coffee for his stunned shipmates. When, one day at the end of January, Bade inquired after the cook's feelings, he would only remark stoically that, "so long as he had tobacco, it all amounted to nothing." "Such scenes," Bade wrote, "refresh the soul."[45] Wilhelm Böwe, the ship's carpenter and an experienced Greenland sealing hand, was also much valued by his peers as the "court jester" of the ship. With practical jokes and a magnanimous willingness to serve as the butt of teasing, Böwe made a crucial contribution to the maintenance of the crew's fragile morale after the disasters of early January.[46]

The diaries also suggest that the men and officers of the Hansa made an instinctive effort to preserve the structures of their normal routine and the shipboard social hierarchy with which they left Bremerhaven months earlier. It is striking to note, for example, that even in their private writings, the diarists always refer to one another as "Herr" Hildebrandt and "Herr" Bade, never "Richard" and "Wilhelm." Living at the closest and most intimate quarters, sharing hardships and the constant threat of death for months at a time, the men still clung tenaciously to the necessary formalities of social intercourse, which, by their use, impart a sense of dignity and mutual respect to all participants. The two specialists on the ship, the cook and the carpenter, are likewise always referred to by title—"Koch" and "Zimmermann"—rather than by name. The scientists are nearly always, despite their public shame, denoted as "Dr." Buchholz and "Dr." Laube. The sailors, as befitting those at the bottom of the hierarchy, are referred to by surname.

The cycle of holidays was also scrupulously maintained in the midst of disaster. Easter fell on 17 April in 1870, and though by this time the men were subsisting mostly on ship's biscuit, the steadfast Wupkes scrounged together an appropriate feast of remnants—a bit of ham and baloney, a couple of bottles of sherry (one for the officers and one "for the people," as Bade put it), canned soup with carrots, a dumpling of flour and water ("which, with our most healthy appetite, tasted excellently"), and a mug of lime juice.[47] Thus unselfishness and good humor, the preservation of social convention, and the maintenance of cultural routines combined to preserve the Hansa community's threatened social harmony.

By Easter the Arctic spring had returned. The northern lights were again visible. As the days grew longer, however, provisions grew shorter. Some of the men sickened with the warmer weather. The crisis seemed to be intensifying, and Hegemann and the Hansa's officers resolved to try their chances in the boats at the first sign of extended open water. Accordingly, on 7 May the men gave three cheers and took to the water in the Hansa's boats, with Hegemann commanding the Hope, Hildebrandt the Bismarck, and Bade the King Wilhelm. In a perilous month-long journey, sailing by day, bivouacking by night on ice floes, the little flotilla picked its way south and westward. On 13 June the crewmen glimpsed the roofs of the Danish settlement of Friedrichsthal. To their astonishment, they were greeted in their own tongue. "We came closer to the place and saw many people standing on the land, of whom a few were distinguished from the others by their European dress. As we finally drew within range of voices, we heard the words 'That's our North German flag, it is our friends!' It was the (Moravian) missionaries, who now welcomed us in the most friendly way and entertained us with the very best."[48]

The community's Eskimo and even the local Danes, from whom the men had feared a cool reception because of the recent war, gave the castaways a warm welcome. In their two-hundred-day odyssey aboard the ice floe, the Hansa's crew had covered a distance of nearly two thousand kilometers. Amazingly, all had survived, and in fairly sound health. Buchholz, later recovered from his derangement and reflecting on the "amazing way in which we were rescued from persistent dangers," candidly credited the safe return of the entire crew to Germany as evidence of "unusual luck."[49]

The Legacy of the Second German North Polar Expedition

The Arctic argonauts, as a contemporary account described them, returned to a transformed Germany. Carried back to Europe in a Danish vessel, the men of the Hansa were astonished to learn from the Copenhagen harbor pilot that "there is war between France and Germany, and it will go badly for the Germans."[50] This was on 1 September 1870, and the pilot, of course, proved a very poor clairvoyant. The Hansa crew reached German soil by rail two days later at the very time Prussian troops were shattering Napoleon III at Sedan. A little over a week later, on 11 September, the Germania returned to Bremerhaven, slipping undetected through the French blockade by night. Koldewey was at first puzzled by the lack of response to his signal rockets

57

and then grew alarmed at the approach of warships. "A shot across our bow forced us to heave to; officers of our navy came aboard, and now we learned, amazed and exultant, of the magnificent events of the last months."[51]

The expedition was in many respects a resounding scientific success. It had not, it is true, found a way to the Pole along the Greenland coast, as its planners had hoped. This in itself, however, represented a significant contribution to the solution of what Koldewey, Petermann, and others at the time routinely called the "Polar Question": there was no navigable route, in coastal waters at least, to the vicinity of the Pole. Other scientific achievements were of a more positive nature. The exploration of the eastern Greenland coast between 73° and 77° north latitude during the ambitious sledding journeys of Koldewey and Payer, as well as the careful daily collection of data of every sort by the expedition's scientists, provided a wealth of information on a region previously almost unknown. The naturalists on board the *Germania* collected an astonishing variety of specimens, many of them nondescript or never examined in a scientifically systematic fashion. Pansch and Börgen, the *Germania*'s botanists, brought back 247 varieties of mosses, lichens, mushrooms, and algae. The zoological data were equally copious. Specimens of more than two hundred species were brought back to Germany, including fifty-six, gathered from the seabed in soundings, that were previously unknown.[52] Nor were the contributions of the *Hansa* negligible. Though it had been impossible to save any of the ship's specimen collections, the meteorological and hydrographical observations were secure, and these acquired particular value, as Koldewey noted, "through comparison with those of our winter station."[53]

The public at large did not particularly care about the valuable data collected by the expedition. The wreck and survival of the *Hansa*'s crew were what mattered most to Germans. The king in his field headquarters listened to accounts of the *Hansa* with enthusiasm, the queen publicly praised the gallant crew, and the story of the castaways "was in every mouth."[54] Koldewey's discoveries also excited Germans of all nations. In agreement with Payer, Petermann named the most striking geographical find of the voyage the "Kaiser Franz-Josef Fjord." This decision, in the nationalistic atmosphere evoked by the Franco-Prussian War, drew a good deal of criticism in German newspapers.[55] The highest peak sighted on the voyage, at just over 3,650 meters, was named for Petermann. The nomenclature of other landmarks was parceled out among deserving participants and supporters of the expedition: Bismarck Cape, Koldewey Island, King Wilhelm Land, Payer Cape, and so on.

The sensational story of the Hansa, however, won popular acclaim not only in Germany but abroad as well, with French and English versions of the affair brought out almost as quickly as the German editions appeared.[56] There was a considerable public appetite for stories of Arctic exploration in Germany in the late nineteenth century (accounts of English exploration appeared in German translation almost as soon as the originals were printed), and many popular works over the next several decades treated the Hansa's experience.[57]

The earliest accounts, published by Buchholz, Hildebrandt, or, in the next decade, J. Löwenberg, dwelt mostly upon the horrors faced by the crew. "Imagine oneself in the position of a man who for four long weeks under the open sky in the Arctic region, exposed to wind and weather, must carry out the most exhausting tasks every day, without having rest at night, without being able to satisfy a hungry stomach, occasionally rendered snowblind, and, on top of all this, with never a dry thread on his body."[58] These accounts are objective and thoughtful in tone. As already noted, Buchholz attributed survival to luck as much as any other factor, which is perhaps not quite fair to the crewmen who fed him while he cowered in his sleeping bag on the drifting ice floe. The story of the Hansa, Löwenberg wrote fifteen years later, "is one of the most horrible that polar travelers have experienced."

Over the next few decades, however, the tale of the Hansa took on a considerably more triumphalist coloring. Neither the cowardice of Laube nor the breakdown of Buchholz seems to have made it into accounts published at the time. Though both scientists composed memoirs, they and other members of the crew maintained their discretion about the shameful collapse of the academics. Laube did no more than refer to "dark times" and hint at depression. Instead, the crew's fortitude was seen as proof of particularly Germanic virtues. Laube, incredibly, crowed publicly that "the prospect was serious, but why shouldn't it be possible to overcome the risk? God never forsakes a good German!"[59] Ludwig Herz also credited the triumph to German fortitude when concluding his account of the episode in 1896 in *Tropisches und Arktisches. Reise-Erinnerungen* (Tropic and Arctic: travel memoirs):

> That is, in brief, the story of that singular journey: nine months adrift on an ice floe, easily said, but what unmentionable suffering the words contain! Eternal night, storm, blowing snow, hunger,

cold, constant mortal danger, a horrible selection of all the sufferings that man can endure; and it is easily understood when Captain Bade, that otherwise so grave man who can be brought out of his North German phlegm only by stories of his whale hunts, gets tears in his eyes when telling of the suffering withstood. Only German tenacity, German discipline could have borne these dangers— would have continued the duties with the journals, measurements, and so on as on board ship. And if today we celebrate the twenty-fifth anniversary of the victory over Welschland, so should we also recall those who, though indeed unable to participate in the great struggle for unity, for their part yet struggled with an overwhelming enemy, the Arctic winter, and overcame it with the same virtues that permitted the humiliation of the Franzmann, energy, and farsightedness on the side of the leaders, discipline and obedience on the side of the subordinates.[60]

Herz's rhetoric was neither unusual nor extreme for his day. The "popular edition" of the journey's official account, which appeared in 1875, admonished young Germans to remember the work "begun by German men in the greatest spirit of sacrifice and under the most difficult conditions" so that they too "might bring honor to the German name."[61] Books for youngsters—*Heroen der Nordpolarforschung* (Heroes of North Pole exploration), for example—also noted the exemplary Germanness of the survivors: "Despite the frightful situation, discipline never wavered for a moment, the *Hansa* men proved themselves true Germans who knew how to obey." The *Hansa*'s story was "without example in Arctic history," and its successful conclusion was due to the captain, "who knew how to maintain discipline among his people in situations where need and desperation threatened to break all the bonds of order."[62]

Germans undoubtedly had good reason to be proud of the *Hansa*'s crew. Polar history could show many examples of expeditions that had suffered the most disgraceful breakdown of group cohesion under circumstances that the *Hansa*'s men had, for the most part, endured with grace. The American expedition led by Adolphus Greely from 1881 to 1884, for example, provided an abject contrast to the discipline of the *Hansa*, decaying, once stranded, into a catalog of human corruption and degradation: insensate drunkenness, mutiny, theft, suicide, executions, and the death by starvation of most of its members.[63] The men of the *Hansa*, by comparison, had displayed inspiring stoicism. Nor can those outsiders who extolled the Teutonic heroism of Hegemann and his men be fairly chastised for concealing the failure of the two scholars, since this was not commonly known. The diaries of the Hansa's commanders appeared over a century later, and the participants engaged in a tacit conspiracy of silence that avoided revelations that might have exposed either scientist to public embarrassment.

There is, however, an element of very selective memory in later suggestions that something uniquely German ensured the crew's survival. Amazingly, just two years after the safe return of the second German North Polar expedition, the experience of the Hansa was repeated under conditions that were, if possible, even more desperate. Nineteen members of the Polaris expedition, led initially by the American Charles Francis Hall, were cast adrift on a floe of ice off the western coast of Greenland in October 1872. The party included women and even nursing infants. For more than five months they drifted more than 2,400 kilometers southward, kept alive by the hunting skills of two Eskimo members of the party. All survived until their rescue in April 1873.[64]

If chauvinistic chroniclers thus sometimes exaggerated their virtue, the crews of the Hansa and the Germania had nonetheless acquitted themselves with great merit. All the sailors received a bonus of three months' pay above what they had earned on the voyage, while the two scientists aboard the Hansa received a special five-hundred-taler honorarium.[65] Most of the expedition's young officers and scientists went on to distinguished careers. Hegemann and Koldewey took posts at the German Marine Observatory, a remarkable institution whose unsurpassed sailing directions for the Atlantic and Pacific earned a global reputation among bluewater sailors.[66] Koldewey eventually directed the observatory's section for nautical instruments, while Hegemann wrote on navigation and meteorology. Bade dined and lectured for years on his experiences and remained involved in the fishing industry, while Hildebrandt became a naval officer, ending up in the Imperial Naval Office (Reichsmarineamt) in Berlin. Laube enjoyed an active career as a geologist at academic posts in the Habsburg Empire, publishing occasionally until his death in 1923.[67] Buchholz traveled to West Africa in 1872 and died, shortly after his return to Germany, in 1876.

For August Petermann, however, the successful return of the voyagers from Greenland was no triumph. The tragic irony of the second German North Polar expedition is that it led not to acclaim for Petermann, without whom the venture would never have occurred, but to his marginalization.

61

This has largely to do with his stubborn and belligerent personality, which led him to quarrel with nearly all the important figures of German Arctic exploration in the year after the expedition returned. He published a bizarre attack on Koldewey's entirely sound decision not to continue to search for a way northward in the late summer of 1869, and, unlike Koldewey, who felt the notion of the open polar sea had been "thoroughly destroyed" by the expedition, Petermann continued in the face of all evidence to insist that it was still waiting to be discovered.[68] He also quarreled with the Bremen committee, which in 1870 reconstituted itself as the Polarverein (League for German North Polar travel). Though repeatedly invited to join the group, Petermann refused, insisting on changes in the league's structure so that he could exercise control. Nor did he take part in the editing of the official account of the expedition's voyages and scientific discoveries.

There is, indeed, a kind of mania in the stubborn defiance of evidence through which Petermann clung to his belief that a boat could steam to the Pole through open waters. Expedition after expedition ventured forth to the presumed open polar sea to find instead failure, disaster, and death. Between 1858 and 1868 no fewer than four Swedish expeditions searched north of Spitsbergen in vain for navigable water. Petermann concluded they probably got there at the wrong time. Koldewey failed twice in the same undertaking. From 1871 to 1874 the Austrians Payer and Weyprecht tested the same idea, and though they found Franz Josef Land, they lost their ship, the *Tegetthoff*, and barely escaped with their lives. Petermann's refusal to face facts, even an admiring contemporary had to concede, was "a very clear demonstration of how even the great polar theorist gets into a muddle."[69] Even after his death, Petermann's ideas lived on, causing continued mischief. The American expedition of the *Jeannette*, from 1879 to 1881, also sailed north to find the open polar sea. Only thirteen of its thirty-two members returned.

Petermann's insistence on the open polar sea notion had never been without its critics, and his refusal to entertain the possibility that he was wrong was sometimes attributed to academic vanity. "I think it utterly mistaken to try to penetrate with ships to the North Pole between Spitzbergen and Nova Zemlya," Sherard Osborn told Britain's Royal Geographical Society, "and I would be part of an expedition sent out to this goal only if Herr Dr. Petermann personally came along for the journey."[70] In general, however, Petermann enjoyed considerable prestige in Germany through the early 1870s, viewed as the "Polarpapa," a kind of "international president of the geographical world" who knew how to enthuse entire nations for geographical projects.[71] The royal houses of Austria, Italy, Spain, and several less august courts presented him with honorary decorations. A growing depression nonetheless took hold of Petermann after 1875. A connection with the failure of his polar theories is doubtful. This was a common condition among his male ancestors, who had occasionally taken their own lives. In September 1878 Petermann also ended his life in suicide.[72]

Though memorialized in the names of a dozen geographic features spanning the globe, Petermann was quickly forgotten, recalled within a generation as the "half-forgotten" geographer.[73] Even before his death, the momentum sustaining the German drive for the Poles had begun to wane. The Bremen Polarverein began planning for a third and much more elaborate polar expedition as soon as Koldewey returned, confident that now "the German Reich has sprung up anew in the fullness of strength, its helping, sponsoring hand will surely not fail us."[74] But fail the Reich's hand did. The recommendation of a special commission set up by the Reich chancellery to consider using state funds for an expedition was rejected by the federal Senate in 1876.

The German scientific community continued to press loudly for exploration of the polar world, and at the urging of the new director of the German Marine Observatory, Georg Neumayer, Germany participated in the meteorological observations conducted during the First International Polar Year from August 1882 to September 1883.[75] Increasingly, however, there was public questioning of what one of Petermann's biographers called "the positively inexplicable competition among the most various nations to achieve success in the desolate, ice-encrusted, useless polar world."[76] Without the services of Petermann to rouse a successful public fund-raising campaign and little support forthcoming from the imperial government, the German expeditionary drive fell into abeyance. After Koldewey, three decades passed before Germans again sent a large-scale exploratory expedition into the high latitudes.

It might seem that the first German polar endeavors produced no more than a nationalistic legend and a handful of place-names in obscure corners of the globe. In fact, the struggles of Petermann, Koldewey, and the crew of the *Hansa* left a more significant legacy. Scientifically, these voyages produced a valuable body of meteorological, geomagnetic, and hydrographic data, as well as advancing knowledge of the geological and biological characteristics of eastern Greenland. They also mapped an extensive portion of the same area for the first time, bringing to the attention of Western geographers such natural features as the Franz Josef Fjord and some of the mountains of eastern Greenland. In cultural terms, the impact of the voyages was even more significant. While Petermann sank into oblivion, the German scientific community took his polar projects as a starting point. Though often ignored, German natural scientists continued to speak through the century's end of the unfinished scientific business awaiting Germans at the top and bottom of the globe. Eventually, Germans listened. When they did, however, they looked not to the Arctic but to the Far South.

The journey is a gamble; it always brings gain and loss, most often from an unexpected venue; one gets more or less than one hopes.

GOETHE TO SCHILLER, 1797

Germany as a nation had little to do with the opening of Antarctica before the twentieth century, but an individual German scientist had already spurred the region's exploration without leaving the university town of Göttingen. This was Carl Friedrich Gauss, who rose from humble working-class origins to become one of the great mathematicians of the nineteenth century. Gauss was intrigued by geomagnetism and spent decades mapping the contours of the earth's magnetic field. He invented devices for measuring magnetic intensity as well as methods for interpreting geomagnetic data.

Though the earth's magnetic field was already notorious for its inconstancy, and the means of its generation was a complete mystery, Gauss pinpointed the site of the magnetic South Pole in 1838, declaring that it would be found at 66° south latitude and 146° east longitude.[1] It was in part to determine the accuracy of Gauss's provokingly exact calculation that the British expedition of James Clark Ross set out for the Antarctic in 1839, breaching the continent's ice pack for the first time and showing the way for later journeys. Germans interested in the southern polar world could thus claim a distinguished heritage when, generations after Gauss's death in 1855, they began once more to reflect upon the exploration of the Antarctic.

The View to the South

Even while the eyes of their nation followed the *Germania* and *Hansa* northward, a number of Germans advocated exploration of the Far South instead. The most famous and effective German Antarctic enthusiast was Georg Neumayer, a kind of August Petermann for the South Pole. Educated as an astronomer, Neumayer's career linked the world of Humboldt and Gauss with fin-de-siècle German scientists, particularly those concerned with sciences of the earth. A disciple of the legendary Humboldt himself, he was drawn to Gauss's work on geomagnetism and after his studies took passage to Australia as a common seaman to pursue research on the topic. With Humboldt's help, Neumayer during the 1850s persuaded Maximilian

II of Bavaria to fund a geomagnetic observatory in Melbourne.[2]

Returning to Germany in 1864, Neumayer became a tireless promoter of exploration in the Antarctic. He knew much about the region and surmised a good deal more. Neumayer was convinced that the Antarctic held the key to understanding fluctuations in global geomagnetic fields, and he believed that the region of Kerguelen Island was an ideal base to explore what he claimed would prove to be a great embayment on the Indian Ocean coast of Antarctica. In scores of articles and speeches before scientific gatherings throughout Europe, Neumayer urged a southern polar orientation as the most likely to yield significant advances. While Petermann lobbied for German Arctic research at the geographic congress in Frankfurt in 1865, Neumayer pleaded his case for the Antarctic. Though less successful than Petermann at the time, Neumayer's appeal initiated thirty years of Antarctic agitation.[3]

Neumayer was an eloquent speaker who cultivated a deliberately striking figure. In an age of short-haired men, his flowing locks affected to the end of his life the tonsorial fashion of the romantic, polymathic scientists of earlier generations. The Cato of German science, Neumayer closed his speeches not with the Roman's "Delenda est Carthago" (Carthage must be destroyed) but with the cry "Auf zum Südpol!" While extolling the scientific utility of Antarctic exploration, he also appealed to the idealism of his listeners. His concern with the practical benefits of such research, Neumayer assured German scientists,

> was not occasioned by the conviction that in our fatherland a material impulse is needed to promote scientific undertakings. On the contrary, I am convinced that no people on earth understands as well as the German how to nurture research exclusively for the sake of research, intellectual endeavor exclusively for the sake of knowledge. The history of our culture, the development of our nation to its present world rank among the cultured peoples of the earth, fills me with the certain confidence that the German nation will appear at its observation posts in this essential scientific matter, and that the scholars called to the promotion of the undertaking will take second place to the scholars of no other nation in their efficiency, self-sacrifice, and devotion to the cause of systematic polar research.[4]

Neumayer won some successes. During the southern summer of 1873–74, for example, the German sailor Eduard Dallmann made the first use of a steam-powered vessel in the Far South when he took the *Grönland* on an exploratory cruise through Antarctic waters. In general, however, Neumayer argued that scarce research funds were better employed in the establishment of permanent research stations rather than in such ad hoc, short-term expeditions. The International Polar Year was one example of his impact.

As director of the German Marine Observatory from 1876 until 1903, Neumayer was a significant figure in German academic life, and his drive for Antarctic research garnered a wide range of backers. Friedrich Ratzel, an influential dilettante who dabbled in ethnology, journalism, and political geography, joined Neumayer in urging Germany to "turn its view to the South Polar region."[5] A steady stream of popular books kept polar exploration before the public eye, and politicians liked the idea, too.[6] Rudolf Virchow, Germany's most distinguished physician and a founder of the science of anthropology, was also a Reichstag deputy who enthused about polar exploration and polar peoples such as the Lapps. In 1881 he led the Reichstag in urging Bismarck to "take suitable measures to ensure German participation in the research of the polar regions."[7]

Bismarck was not interested. The ardor he once expressed for German exploration had cooled with age. He remained aloof from the pleadings of Neumayer, much as he remained personally detached from the rantings of Germany's colonial fanatics. He was, it is true, willing to grant a hearing to polar enthusiasts, as he had done with Petermann. But the Iron Chancellor refused government support for polar projects and apparently declined even to contribute a token amount to Petermann's fund drive, despite the popularity of the cause with thousands of other Germans.[8] He concurred with the Reich commission's rejection of the plan for a third Arctic expedition in the 1870s, he ignored the International Polar Year, and, when the German-American millionaire Henry Villard offered to put up half the cost of a German Antarctic expedition in 1888, Bismarck declined without comment.[9]

One can only speculate upon his reasoning, but it is not hard to imagine Bismarck's distaste for the possible diplomatic complications arising from something as unpredictable and beyond his control as a band of idealistic German expeditionaries set loose at the Poles. In the increasingly volatile climate of European politics, Bismarck may have regarded polar claims as one more headache he didn't need, as he clearly felt about the African entanglements upon which he reluctantly entered.[10] It is also likely that the calculating and cynical eye of the chancellor saw neither point nor profit in the alleged scientific value of polar ventures.

Whatever the reasons for Bismarck's polar apathy, in combination with Petermann's death it certainly contributed to a lag in German polar work. To his own surprise, however, Bismarck was not politically untouchable. In 1890 he was dismissed, and the new political landscape altered the prospects of German polar advocates. The new kaiser, Wilhelm II, was a passionate young man, and his enthusiasms were many. Most failed to engage his attention in any lasting fashion, but his commitment to German naval power endured. Though the decision to build a German "battle fleet" was a diplomatic disaster for his nation (the "risk" in Admiral Tirpitz's "Risk Theory" turned out to be for Germany, not its rivals), it was a boon to the advocates of German Antarctic exploration, since the kaiser initially saw polar exploration as part of the establishment of German naval parity with Great Britain.[11]

On this point, Wilhelm's judgment was uncharacteristically sound. The geopolitical climate at the bottom of the earth was warming up as the nineteenth century ended, and German sailors, scientists, and politicians agreed that the Antarctic must not be left to the disposal of their rivals. While the 1880s saw no major expeditions aimed at actual exploration of the continent, the 1890s saw Britain, France, Norway, and Belgium send ships to the coasts of Antarctica.[12] The German scientific establishment was sensitive to the growing competition and for the first time in decades found that a supportive government shared its concerns. The view gained ground that "South Polar research is now a more pressing requirement than North Polar for the scientific development of geography and for the natural sciences as a whole."[13] Accordingly, in April 1895 the German geographic congress convened a commission for South Polar research to plan an Antarctic journey.

"Beneath Our Cherished Hopes": The First German Antarctic Expedition, 1901–1903

The commission linked the old guard of German polar exploration with a new generation. Neumayer, the director, was joined by key figures from Petermann's days, including Moritz Lindeman, Karl Koldewey (now the elder statesman of German polar journeying), and Koldewey's old Austrian sledging comrade, Julius Payer. Ferdinand Freiherr von Richthofen, founder of the Berlin Institute for Oceanography in 1899 and the most distinguished German geographer of the time, was also a member. Meeting six times between 1895 and 1898, the commission determined the course, outfitting, and personnel of the proposed expedition and worked to mount the kind of successful publicity/fund-raising drive at which Petermann had proven himself so adept.

The German public, however, was inexplicably cool to polar adventure. While the Arctic voyagers of Petermann's day generated a groundswell of popular support to sweep along a foot-dragging government, Neumayer's dream of a German Antarctic thrust in the 1890s was realized thanks to a reversal of the earlier pattern: this time, enthusiastic government support was met by tepid popular feeling. Neumayer and his colleagues were no match for Petermann when it came to persuading Germans to part with their money. Though again employing Petermann's proven method of forming local committees of notables to beat the polar drum, they failed to inspire the massive, voluntary giving that had propelled earlier expeditions into the Arctic. The fund drive in Munich collected less than 3,000 marks, a miserable pittance that hardly justified the time involved in its raising.[14] Nationally, the commission collected just 35,000 marks—roughly a third of it from the single source of the Leipzig Geographical League (Geographischer Verein Leipzig). This was less than half the cost of the expedition's scientific instruments alone and was a mere drop in the bucket toward the expense of a research vessel.[15]

German popular indifference to the Antarctic cause at the end of the 1890s is puzzling. A few Germans argued that polar lands had little value, and certainly the public was preoccupied with controversies and agitation of many other kinds.[16] Perhaps the remote Antarctic interested Germans less than the Arctic world just beyond their doorstep. It may be, too, that the Antarctic seemed less likely to yield gain for Germany than did the development of German colonies. Whatever the cause, the polar consciousness of the German public contrasted sharply with that of the English, who contributed the equivalent of nearly 2 million marks to a simultaneous Antarctic fund drive. The lapse in German popular support lasted only a few years, however; within the decade, massive public lottery sales would fund German Antarctic research.

Meanwhile, official enthusiasm soothed the pain of popular indifference. In one crucial respect, Neumayer succeeded where Petermann had failed: he gained direct state support. The eagerness that the kaiser and his government brought to Germany's first effort at Antarctic exploration, breaking with the distance cultivated by the Bismarckian establishment, was in part a natural byproduct of the great naval building program overseen by Adm. Alfred Tirpitz. Appointed naval secretary in June 1897, Tirpitz moved rapidly to create a fleet of German battleships. He convinced an initially hostile Reichstag to pass the First Navy Law (Erstes Flottengesetz) in 1897–98 and then called into being a modern, high-powered publicity apparatus—the Naval League (Deutscher Flottenverein)—to manipulate German public opinion. Tirpitz's navy was intended to be a powerful element in the European military balance and to symbolize Germany's new place among the world's most advanced states. The German maritime profile was expanding rapidly in any case (North German Lloyd's liner, *Kaiser Wilhelm der Grosse*, took the British Cunard line's transatlantic speed record in 1897, holding it for a decade), and the navy's interest in exploratory voyages dovetailed precisely with the generally increasing official attention to things nautical.[17]

In February 1898 the chief of Nautical Section of the Imperial Naval Office (Nautische Abteilung des Reichsmarineamts), Count von Baudissin, offered Neumayer his support. Baudissin was already involved with the so-called Valdivia Deep-Sea Expedition (Valdivia Tiefsee-Expedition), an oceanographic research journey that sailed in August 1898 under the biologist Carl Chun. This was the first scientific expedition of the decade to be funded entirely through public means, an unequivocal sign of the new attitude.[18] Baudissin believed that "with the powerful boom of the navy, its active participation in scientific undertakings for the research of the seas was also appropriate. Great sea powers have based their rise on such undertakings and have thus schooled and tested their naval personnel; one must know the seas to be able to rule them."[19] In recognition of the link between marine research and naval might, the Imperial Naval Office (Reichsmarineamt) had supported the establishment of the Institute for Oceanography, and similar considerations now drove the navy to back the Antarctic endeavor.

It is not surprising that Baudissin, a career naval officer who later commanded the kaiser's yacht, appreciated the value of exploratory navigation. Less predictable, however, was the extent to which politicians in the Reichstag and bureaucrats in many other branches of the German government shared a profound conviction that polar exploration was simply de rigueur for a great nation like the newly united Germany. The kaiser's officials and professors were committed to active German cultural propaganda both at home and abroad, and in this spirit German elites rallied to the polar cause.[20] Friedrich Schmidt-Ott, for example, a counselor in the Royal Prussian Ministry of Culture (Kultusministerium) was an avid booster of the Antarctic project and would later be a pivotal figure in the revival of German exploration after World War I.[21] Arthur, count von Posadowsky-Wehner, the powerful head of the Imperial Ministry of the Interior (Reichsministerium des Innern), devoted himself to securing funds for the mission. In the Reichstag, too, deputies from the far right to the moderate Catholic Center party were keen and vocal supporters of an Antarctic voyage. "I stress that the question of dispatching a South Polar expedition has now become a matter of national honor," thundered Deputy Gröber of the Center party.

> Once upon a time Germany could not seriously have considered sending such an expedition. That was in the days when Germany consisted of a fragmented collection of individual states, days when our navy was underdeveloped and our overseas interests were less than those of other peoples. Those days are gone, thank God! Then, our German scholars were obliged to turn to others to test their theories and to conduct practical experiments. Today we can expect the aspirations of German scholars to be realized by German expeditions. Germany has very nearly the second most powerful navy in the world. Here is a matter on which all can be united![22]

Two beliefs propelled the drive for a German Antarctic expedition. Polar exploration, many felt, proved that united Germany was a far greater nation than the politically splintered Germany of the Koldewey era. And, conscious of swelling German naval power, polar enthusiasts believed that Germans had both a right and a responsibility to take up the polar question. The "white man's burden" in the colonies had its parallel in the "white lands burden" of opening the Poles, a note sounded again and again in public and private by military officers, bureaucrats, and politicians.[23]

Genuine scientific and commercial considerations were also influential. Insight into magnetic fields promised to aid navigation, information on iceberg patterns would make shipping safer, and fertile new marine mammal hunting grounds would profit German business.[24] In the literature of the time, however, the passion is saved for appeals to national unity and naval might, and these carried the day. German colonial enthusiasts saw a natural affinity between their own aims and those of Antarctic exploration, reasoning that "colonial policy is only one branch of our entire overseas policy," while exploration was another.[25] In May 1899 the mission received the royal assent of the kaiser. The Commission for South Polar Research (Deutsche Kommission für die Südpolarforschung), its task accomplished, dissolved itself, and the Reichstag voted 1.2 million marks in support of the project.

Meanwhile, the commission had agreed upon a leader, a ship, and a plan of action. The leader, by unanimous consent, was Erich von Drygalski, a thirty-four-year-old professor of geophysics who had already taken two expeditions to western Greenland on behalf of the Geographical Society of Berlin (Gesellschaft für Erdkunde zu Berlin). Though for a time suspect as a mere adventurer rather than a true scholar, Drygalski won scientific legitimacy with the publication of the expedition's results in 1897.[26] He boasted a formidable reputation as a man of "complete engagement, untiring diligence and high organizational skill, to whom success was never denied."[27] He also enjoyed a high standing in the global community of polar explorers. At the International Geographical Congress in Berlin in 1899, Norway's famed Fridtjof Nansen mounted a table to toast the German expedition, privately telling Schmidt-Ott to rest easy: "You have the man, that is the main thing."[28]

On the question of the ship, too, there was general unity. Designed by the navy, the Gauss, as the vessel was eventually christened, was considered to be a model of polar marine technology. The construction of such a craft, Drygalski later observed, was a matter of arriving at a series of judicious compromises. The ship must have space to house sailors, scientists, equipment, fuel, and provisions through a polar winter while remaining sufficiently compact to negotiate narrow leads of open water along the coast. The engine required power to propel the vessel through ice-choked seas but must not be so large that its fuel supply ate up cargo space or limited the vessel's range from coaling stations. The hull must be rounded to resist the compressive force of ice fields while remaining sufficiently narrow to guarantee stability in the high seas sure to be encountered en route to the Antarctic.

This careful cross-breeding of nautical traits produced a three-masted vessel of the type known as a "topsail schooner." As with the Germania, the 325-horsepower steam engine of the Gauss was not intended as the vessel's main source of locomotion but as an aid to navigation in the ice. The ship was larger than Koldewey's Germania but had steel sheathing only at the bow and stern. Every effort was made, in fact, to restrict the use of metal so as not to interfere with magnetic readings. Like Shackleton's *Endurance* and Nansen's *Fram*, the *Gauss* was built of timber. "A huge amount of wood," Drygalski recounted, "gradually vanished into the ship during its construction." German oak from the royal wharves at Danzig was used for the hull; Oregon pine was used for the masts; teak, Scotch pine, and American pitch pine provided the knees, supports, decks, and inner planking of the hull. The "ice skin," or outer sheath of the hull, was of fifteen-centimeter-thick slabs of greenheart, an extremely tough South American wood that could be worked only with specially hardened tools. It caused a number of injuries among the dock workers unused to its ways. Walls were insulated with cork, while a mixture of tar and cork was added between the layers of floorboards.[29]

The commission crafted a plan to coordinate the work of the *Gauss* with British and Swedish expeditions in a joint "concentric attack" upon the continent to be launched in 1901. The Germans were to explore Antarctica's Indo-Atlantic sector, working south from an astronomical observation post they would establish on Kerguelen Island toward the unmapped regions west of the point known as Termination Land.[30] Neumayer was delighted. Just as Petermann believed one could penetrate to the North Pole by water, so Neumayer thought the proper ship in this sector might carry explorers very near the South Pole. Neumayer believed that a great current of warm water must flow south from Kerguelen as a counterstream to cold northward flows from other Antarctic regions. Such a current might create a seasonal opening in the ice-covered bay that he thought indented the Antarctic coast in this sector, thus providing an opportunity to steam to a very high latitude.[31] He also considered Kerguelen a good site for astronomical observation and noted that the German sector was the least known region of the Antarctic. Neumayer and Koldewey pushed for a two-ship expedition, a notion rejected on fiscal grounds.[32] Drygalski also planned to use dogsleds, a proposal that so alienated Koldewey, a traditionalist grown testy with age, that he withdrew entirely from the preparations. Finally, though he regarded it as a distraction, Drygalski agreed to carry along personnel and equipment for a small observatory on Kerguelen.

The German plan seemed simple. The *Gauss* would proceed in the late summer of 1901 (in the late Antarctic winter, therefore) to Kerguelen Island by way of Cape Town. Drygalski would rendezvous with the members of the Kerguelen station, who were to precede the main expedition, take on coal and sled dogs, and in the first days of 1902, during the high Antarctic summer, proceed as far south as possible, exploiting the anticipated open waters to reach the mainland. The expedition team would spend the winter iced in on the coast, gathering meteorological and geomagnetic data, and return during the Antarctic summer of 1903. Drygalski planned to go by land as far as possible toward both the geographic and the magnetic Poles. With an anticipated return date of 1 June 1903, the expedition would last almost two years. If no word of Drygalski was received by the northern summer of 1904, a rescue expedition would be dispatched.[33]

This was, in fact, an audacious scheme. Only one ship had ever over-wintered in the Antarctic ice—the Belgica, a Belgian research vessel sent out in 1898—and that was by accident. No nation's explorers had as yet set out deliberately to freeze in their ship as a scientific base. "The plan that governs this German expedition is bolder and more comprehensive," Richthofen declared at the christening of the Gauss in April 1901. "The ship shall advance into the ice and serve for more than a year as the fixed point from which to make attacks into the ice world. In the midst of a fearfully desolate nature, it shall be the home and domicile of the Antarctic travelers. He who imagined the task is himself leader of the undertaking."[34]

While details of the expedition's plan were worked out in the winter and spring of 1901, the final outfitting of the Gauss went forward. Equipping the expedition became a test of national prestige, proof that Germany had attained parity with its longer established polar rival, and the mission's promoters made it a point of honor to meet the needs of the journey without recourse to foreign sources. The chemical and zoological laboratories, nearly all the scientific instruments, and the complete photographic needs of the Gauss were met by German suppliers, including the Royal Prussian Airship Department (Königlich Preussische Luftschifferabteilung) in Berlin, which furnished a balloon—"an aid to navigation in the ice, not yet used by earlier polar expeditions"—and 450 steel cylinders of hydrogen, sufficient for six ascents. A German trading agent in Vladivostok shipped sixty-seven sled dogs, complete with three Siberian attendants, to Kerguelen via Hong Kong and Sydney.[35]

The furnishings of the ship were plush, at least for the elite of officers and scientists. Each occupied a private cabin, with individual heating stoves, bookstands, desks, and other amenities. The officer's mess was an opulent and spacious chamber, paneled in American walnut and furnished with a great mirror, gleaming buffet, specially designed piano, and several paintings, including a portrait of Wilhelm II presented by the kaiser himself.[36] A sofa lined each wall, and the bored or tired polar explorer could divert himself with a "plentiful library of works of scientific and entertainment literature," the gift of German publishing houses. "The crew's mess," Drygalski noted tersely, "contained benches and tables in simpler appointment and was likewise adorned with an image of His Majesty the Kaiser."[37]

The expedition's personnel were young. When the Gauss left Germany, the average age on board was twenty-six years. Of the scientists, only one was over forty, Ernst Vanhöffen, a zoologist and botanist. The others—Hans Gazert, a medical doctor; Emil Philippi, a geologist and chemist; and Friedrich Bidlingmaier, meteorologist and "magnetist"—ranged from twenty-six to thirty-one years of age. All were products of the German university system, employed as untenured lecturers or assistants, and all were unmarried.[38] Three scientists were intended for the Kerguelen station: meteorologist Josef Enzensperger and "magnetist" (actually physicist) Karl Luyken, who traveled with the equipment by way of Sydney. Emil Werth, a zoologist, would sail with the Gauss. None of the naval officers were yet forty, including the thirty-eight-year-old captain, Hans Ruser.

In addition to being young, the crew was inexperienced. Only Drygalski and Vanhöffen, who had joined Drygalski in Greenland and sailed with the Valdivia Deep-Sea Expedition, had journeyed into the high latitudes. Captain Ruser, though enjoying a reputation as a skilled navigator, spent most of his career ferrying emigrants across the North Atlantic on vessels powered not by wind, like the Gauss, but by steam and constructed of metal rather than timber. Though he had been first officer on the Valdivia's short trip and made a brief Arctic excursion in the summer of 1900 to familiarize himself with navigation in the ice, Ruser was not an experienced polar sailor.[39] Nor were most of the crew, twenty young Germans and Scandinavians recruited from Hamburg and other North German ports. The lack of polar experience may have prompted the decision of Germany's chancellor, Bernhard von Bülow, to place the entire expedition under the direct control not of its naval personnel but of the civilian Drygalski, the man aboard with the most polar expertise.[40]

The Gauss sailed on 15 August 1901. Those inclined to find ill omens did not have far to look. The Empress Frederick died on the eve of departure, casting a pall of mourning over all the setting-forth ceremony. A crewman died of a fall, on a clear summer's day, as the Gauss was carrying out a short "shake-down" passage through the Kiel Canal. And the ship proved disappointing on the trip to Cape Town. Despite Drygalski's assurance that "it was the best polar ship that has yet existed," the *Gauss* drew critical comment even before the journey's start.[41] Stepan Makarov, who built and then captained the Russian steel icebreaker *Ermak* on a journey north of Spitsbergen, dismissed the *Gauss* as fifty years behind the times, underpowered and handicapped by its wooden construction.[42]

He may have been right. The vessel never attained its alleged 7-knot speed, and the captain complained that his ship was unstable in high seas. The main boom could not be moved without lowering the funnel (Drygalski notes that a telescoping funnel would have been sensible), and the engine room was a scalding Roman bath. The skylighting of the cabins was insufficient, necessitating the constant use of lamps to dispel the gloom. And, while crossing the Tropics, the pitch insulation melted, dripping through the planks, plugging ventilators, and creating a general mess. Later, a leak in the stern that took months to locate consumed half a ton of coal per day in driving the ship's pumps.[43] Drygalski claimed the sailors felt that work on the *Gauss* was easier than on other vessels, but six men, nearly a third of the crew, had already had enough and left the ship at Cape Town. Eight new members were taken on.

Despite the loss of the crewmen, the sojourn of the *Gauss* in Cape Town from 23 November to 7 December 1901 was a happy one, demonstrating the extent to which polar exploration transcended nationalistic rivalry. The turn of the century is conventionally seen as an era of mounting tension between Germany and the Western states, but both the British and French foreign offices declared themselves ready to extend every aid to the Drygalski expedition.[44] The *Gauss* arrived at Cape Town in the midst of the bitterest phase of the Boer War, when the brutality of full-scale guerrilla combat had been going on for over a year. Although the Germans were resented for sympathizing with the Boers (many in England believed German officers must be serving with them), the British community of the town celebrated Drygalski's men as heroes. Scott had preceded the Germans at Cape Town by a month and according to Drygalski had exerted himself to prepare the city for the reception of the Germans.[45] Had their stomachs been able to endure it, a local German reported, the crew of the *Gauss* could have eaten at honorary dinners three times a day. The mayor of Cape Town, the South African Philosophical Society, the German consuls (there were three at the time), and more feted the voyagers. Most moving of all was the celebration of their departure. Drygalski invited all the local supporters of the *Gauss* on board ship.

> Then we drank—naturally with German *Sekt* [champagne]—to reunion here or in the beloved fatherland. About noon a steamer appeared with the harbormaster, who invited those remaining behind to board his ship and accompany the *Gauss* a bit of the way. The station commander had sent a military choir shortly before who performed on the pier in honor of the guests. As the polar ship finally steamed from the harbor, all the ships in the area signaled, and from the English troops all around rose the cry "Hurrah!"[46]

German ship choirs in the harbor serenaded the departing explorers with "Deutschland, Deutschland über Alles."

Ruser and Drygalski set a southeast course for Kerguelen (earlier known as Desolation Island).[47] Arriving in late December, they found the observatory nearly finished. Luyken, Enzensperger, and a sailor named Georg Weinke had been at work for two months. They had taken passage from Sydney aboard the steamer *Tanglin* with the expedition's dogs. The ship's Chinese crew was ill with beriberi and unable to help with the unloading or construction of the station and its equipment. The *Gauss* shipped coal, wood, and the dogs, leaving Werth and another sailor behind to join the Kerguelen staff before setting forth on the last day of January 1902.

Three days later, the *Gauss* anchored at Heard Island, a site frequented by American sealers, and officers and scientists spent a day hunting, climbing glaciers, and collecting specimens. They then continued southeastward, exploiting the prevailing westerly winds, for their first encounter with terra incognita. Drygalski hoped to determine the status of the land supposedly sighted by the American Charles Wilkes in 1840—Termination Land. Here the expedition made one of its first significant scientific discoveries, albeit a negative one. On 15 February, at the site where Wilkes had logged an island or the tip of a peninsula, soundings taken on the *Gauss* revealed an ocean depth of about three thousand meters. Termination Land, probably an optical illusion, could be stricken from the maps.

The signs of southern winter were by now increasingly obvious. On 14 February Drygalski counted thirty icebergs, glittering blue-green colossi in the shape of tabletops and truncated pyramids, stretching out to the horizon in every direction. The day before, air temperatures below freezing were recorded for the first time. The drift ice, in chunks a meter or two across, was thickening. From 15 to 18 February Ruser and Drygalski zigzagged south and west, navigating through the dense floating ice only with great difficulty. The wind, blowing from the east and southeast, seemed to Drygalski to have the qualities of continental wind.

The twenty-first was a memorable day and the last on which the ship would proceed southward. Crossing the Antarctic Circle, Drygalski spotted the thirty-five-meter cliffs of the continental ice cap glimmering in the distance. This was uncharted territory, now christened Kaiser Wilhelm II Land. Drygalski, though unaware of the fact, was as far south as he would get. Steering westward along the coast at dusk, Ruser and Drygalski pursued a narrow lead northward between two masses of looming ice. As darkness fell, the ice closed in, and at 4:00 A.M. on 22 February, the *Gauss* found itself frozen in the Antarctic pack.

While this was precisely the task for which the vessel had been constructed, the venue was disappointing in the extreme. The *Gauss*, just past 66° south latitude, was not even within the Antarctic Circle. After three days of violent snowstorm, open water beckoned just a tantalizing kilometer away. Drygalski tried dynamiting a path to the sea. When this failed, opening only a small patch of water immediately fore and aft of the ship, Drygalski had to resign himself to wintering on the spot. The stations of the vessel therefore had to be set up not on land, as had been planned, but over three thousand meters of water, complicating the work of the geologist, Philippi. The only consolation was that the ice field in which the *Gauss* found itself was fast rather than drifting and would remain so until the end of the following January, providing a fixed and stable station for scientific observation.

Making the best of the circumstances, the men of the *Gauss* created a considerable scientific station on the Antarctic ice. An astronomical observatory, two magnetic observatories, and a meteorological station, built of ice blocks and wood, were all tended several times daily. Some of the most demanding work was overseen by Bidlingmaier, who supervised magnetic readings taken four times a day through the entire year the ship spent immobilized. As part of the international research agenda of the British, Swedish, and German expeditions, specific days, such as 1 March 1902, had been set aside for detailed comparative readings. On these dates, magnetic data were collected every twenty seconds from noon to 1:00 P.M., Greenwich mean time. Geological samples and oceanographic readings were taken from openings maintained at the bow and stern of the *Gauss*.

Drygalski was clearly right to include the dogs, which were essential to exploiting the ship's location. Seven extended sledding journeys were undertaken in the year the *Gauss* spent in the ice, varying in duration from four to twenty-four days. Drygalski himself spent nearly two months away on such trips. On the first of these journeys, during the third week of March, Philippi and Richard Vahsel, the ship's second officer, reached the Antarctic mainland, ninety kilometers away, where they discovered the Gaussberg, an extinct volcano towering 335 meters over the surrounding sheet ice. The barren dome of rock provided the first evidence of earlier volcanic activity on the Antarctic continent. Later expeditions involved as many as eight members using four sleds, each drawn by teams of seven to nine dogs. Up to 250 kilograms of equipment, including scientific instruments, tents, provisions, and sleeping bags, were transported on each sled. Slowly, the crewmen learned basic skills, such as securing the dogs when stepping off the sled to prevent the repeated tendency of the animals to dash back to the *Gauss*. Without the dogs, the expedition might have reached the mainland, but crews could not have remained there and would have achieved "only a fraction" of their aims.[48]

The balloon seems to have worked out, too, though it was used only once, at the end of March 1902. The hydrogen cylinders consumed a good deal of cargo space, but they permitted Drygalski to ascend to a height of 457 meters, where he remained for two hours. On a day of crystalline atmospheric clarity, the view was magnificent, revealing the distant Gaussberg when Drygalski was no more than 45 meters high. His naval eye noted that the best chance for the *Gauss* to navigate farther, when the ice should break, lay toward the west, where, far off, he thought he could discern broken ice. Though the air warmed noticeably as he rose (he had to remove some of his winter clothing), Drygalski repeatedly dropped the thermometers, so that his meteorological readings remained incomplete. After the twelve-man balloon crew hauled him down, Ruser and Philippi followed Drygalski aloft, the latter taking a series of photographs.[49]

As the weather turned savage, the sledding journeys diminished in both frequency and duration. Temperatures sank to -34°C, accompanied by winds in excess of 110 kilometers per hour. On one sledding journey, Drygalski and his men were confined to their tent for forty hours without a break. Even the simplest foray could have mortal consequences. Guide cables laid from the ship to various stations did not always help. A sailor named Stjernblad nearly paid with his life for venturing out to the toilet during a blizzard in April. Though only ten meters from the boat, he became disoriented on the way back. Fortunately noting Stjernblad's failure to return, the entire ship's complement, roped together for safety, went out in search of him. He was discovered huddled at the foot of the meteorological hut, forty meters from the *Gauss*.

Despite its many defects, the *Gauss* had the great virtue of remaining warm and dry through the coldest months. Comfort, rather than deprivation, characterized the expedition. The crew remained physically sound—many gained weight on the trip.[50] But despite the fact that the vessel was north of the zone of constant winter darkness, Gazert, the ship's doctor, reported many of the signs of confinement-induced depression—loss of appetite, sleeplessness, nervous irritability. The greatest medical concern aboard the *Gauss* was psychic, rather than physical, health, and this was maintained in tried German fashion with clubs, music, cards, drinking, and tobacco. Bidlingmaier found shipboard society comforting:

> Sunday was beer night, Wednesday lecture night, but Saturday evenings were the finest. There we sat with a glass of grog and gathered ourselves for play or entertainment. Clubs sprouted up like mushrooms out of the earth. The skat club Harmony competed with the skat club Blank-Ten in its game, the Knösel-Club (devoted to pipes) held a general assembly in the cabin next door, while the fine gentlemen of the Gentlemen's Smoking Club smoked only cigars as a matter of principle, at least those they hadn't gambled away in the skat club. The cigars were our money on board—eighty points in skat equaled a cigar. The sounds of a quartet singing of beautiful Schwabenland carried forward from the crew's cabin at the stern, a bit antarctically raw, but still gladdening to the heart.[51]

In addition to the music (and there were songwriting competitions, regular violin and piano performances, and a second choir on board), lectures were offered by Gazert on first aid, by the captain on mathematics and navigation, and by various members on Antarctic exploration. A good deal of drinking went on, too. Drygalski later felt called upon to explicitly defend the practice, declaring that if some drank a bit much, the use of alcohol "was decidedly good, because it contributed to well-being and in many down-hearted hours enlivened the mood beneficially."[52]

In general, the crew of the *Gauss* seem to have taken their long imprisonment very well. Active and resourceful, they found ingenious solutions

1. The *Germania*

2. The *Hansa*

Matrofen im   Winterkoſtüm.

Dr. Ad. Panſch.   Oberlieutenant Payer.   Dr. Börgen.
Kapt. Koldewey.   Dr. A. Petermann.   Kapt. F. Hegemann.
       Dr. Laube.   Dr. Copeland.   Dr. Buchholz.

3. Leaders of the second German expedition

4. The *Germania* off Shannon Island

5. Slain musk oxen

6. The *Hansa*-House

7. Pet polar bear

8. Georg Balthasar von Neumayer

9. The *Gauss* upon completion

10. Emperor penguins awaiting their fate

11. Josef Enzensperger

12. Wilhelm Filchner

13. Richard Vahsel

14. The station house under construction

15. The station house after its catastrophe

16. Eckener and an early zeppelin lifting off. Courtesy of Bundesarchiv Koblenz.

17. The return of the zeppelin. Courtesy of Bundesarchiv Koblenz.

18. Alfred Wegener

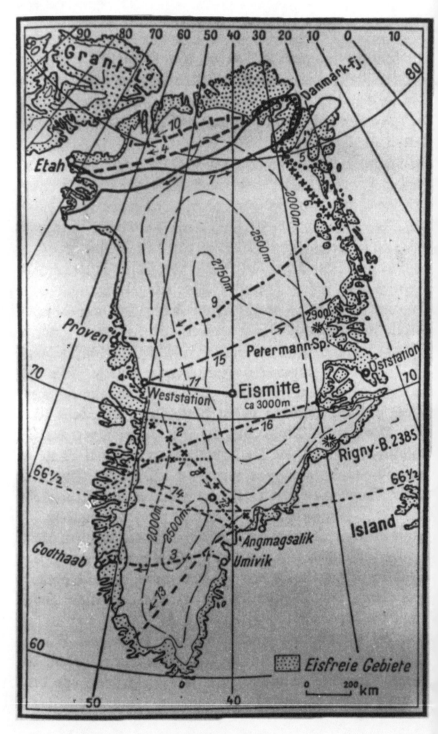

19. Map of Greenland

20. The propeller sleds going up the glacier

21. The propeller sleds at Ice Central

22. Dogsled on the way to Ice Central

23. Georgi and Loewe in their ice hole

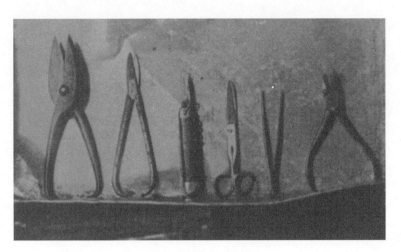

24. "Surgical" tools

25. Alfred Wegener and Rasmus Villumsen

26. The Arctic sublime

27. Eskimo group

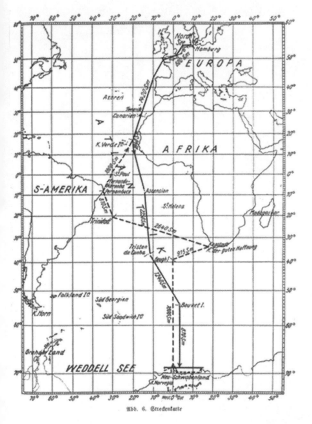

28. Map of the *Schwabenland* route

29. Alfred Ritscher

30. Glacier

31. Nazis in Antarctica

to practical problems. When ice prevented them from running a dredging line beneath the keel of the ship in order to take samples from the ocean bottom, Ludwig Ott, the second officer, suggested the implausible notion of attaching a line to an emperor penguin. After two tries, the bird actually succeeded in conveying the line from one end of the ship to the other.[53] A great deal of effort was devoted to arranging a wind-powered generator to light the ship with electric lights, which, though successful, produced such disconcertingly glimmering and unsteady light that they were discontinued in favor of oil lamps. The men used cinders and garbage, scattered over the ice, to absorb the sun's heat and open a channel to a nearby lead.

The varied and abundant shipboard cuisine may have contributed to the maintenance of morale. Drygalski recalled that although the conserved soup seemed to lose its taste, the other provisions were excellent. Extensive hunting of emperor penguin and seals, whose livers were especially valued by the crew, provided a plentiful supply of fresh meat. For their part, the emperors must have been happy at last to see the backs of Drygalski and his men. Over a thousand of these animals, the largest of the penguins, were slaughtered by the crew, often simply to burn their oily bodies as fuel. Since a full-grown adult emperor stands roughly one meter tall and weighs close to 40 kilograms, it is possible that the *Gauss* crew consumed 50 tons of penguin—about 750 kilograms a week—during their Antarctic stay.

That stay drew to a close with the lengthening Antarctic summer of 1902–3. Thanks to its northerly position, rain and temperatures above the freezing point turned the ice around the ship into a quagmire, and by mid-December it was impossible to leave the *Gauss*. Drygalski and Ruser anticipated the breakup of the pack at any time, and it occurred on 2 February, when the ice field began to drift and then to fragment. After fifty weeks, the *Gauss* once again found itself in navigable waters. Drygalski hoped at this point to spend a second winter, as originally intended, in the ice. From February to early April, he and Ruser cruised westward, always in the midst of ice fields, hoping to find an approach to the mainland or a suitable wintering site. Neither presented itself. On 9 April 1903 Drygalski, fearing that an attempt to remain in the drifting ice "might risk everything, the existence of the expedition and every already attained success," made the decision to return to South Africa.

Back at the South African harbor of Simonstown, however, where the *Gauss* dropped anchor on 9 June, bad news and broken hopes awaited Drygalski. Tragedy had struck at Kerguelen Island. There Luyken, En-

81

zensperger, and Werth had gathered geomagnetic and meteorological observations according to the program of the International Polar Year. They also planned to carry out zoological and biological research on the island itself. This did not go well. Accounts of life at the station are permeated by a sense of depression at the unrelieved monotony of the rain, snow, mist, and fog that enveloped the island, although there were no serious setbacks for the first several months. Then, in mid-June, Werth began to sicken. Sleeplessness and enervation, followed by an irregular heartbeat and swelling in the legs and stomach, indicated the onset of beriberi. The illness reached an acute point in late August, when Werth became a complete invalid. Thereafter, he slowly regained some strength but never recovered sufficiently to carry on his research.

Much worse followed. On 12 October Enzensperger noted in his diary the appearance of similar symptoms. "When I rose this morning, I noticed, to my not exactly pleasant astonishment, that my legs are swollen from the ankles upward to the middle of the shins," he wrote, "and they clearly hold water, since impressions with the fingers remain in the skin for a time until they fill out again."[54] His sleeplessness and exhaustion increased, despite his abstention from beer and cigars, until at the end of the month his upper legs too began to swell. At the time, most scientists believed that the illness was infectious. "We had now to deal with the mysterious Beri-Beri," Luyken declared, "which had obviously been carried in by the sick Chinese of the steamer *Tanglin*. It was a portentous irony of fate that the antarctically pure and fresh air of the island, which wouldn't bring forth even a harmless sniffle, was now infected with the contagious matter of a still so unknown and, therefore, for us terrifying tropical illness."[55]

Enzensperger's creeping, agonizing death was a disheartening and frightening experience for his station comrades. A strong and athletic young man whose daring feats of alpine mountaineering were renowned throughout Germanophone Europe, Enzensperger fought heroically against the disease. His descent into mortal illness, set down with heart-rending clarity in his diary, began with his own early recognition of the symptoms. He at first hid this knowledge from his comrades. Though he had privately criticized Werth for refusing to rest and for treating the disease with morphine, Enzensperger too tried to persevere at his work. Until well into December, he refused to permit others to take his observations or relieve him of other duties. Thereafter, he could no longer protest.

Enzensperger's awareness of his decline and his refusal to succumb to despair lend a particularly poignant cast to the diary for the later reader, who knows how the story will end. With unwavering hope, he clutched eagerly at illusory signs of recovery. "The edema in the legs seems to have abated somewhat or at least to have remained stationary," he wrote in mid-October. "On the other hand, now I have constant slight headaches, as if a strong arterial pressure were in the brain. The pulse is generally normal, but the breathing often not; at least, I have difficulty exhaling deeply. If I lie on the left side, I can hear and feel the heart beating very loudly, and breathing is difficult."[56] Neither suitable medication nor professional medical advice was available on the desolate and remote island, another serious oversight in the planning of the expedition. "It is atrocious that we have no doctor here. The thing may stem from the heart or from the nerves, from the liver and every other possibility, and I have no idea where."[57]

Enzensperger spent a good deal of time with the Siberian dogs that Drygalski had left behind, noting the distinctive personality traits of each and making plans to bring at least one home to Germany. Despite his illness, Enzensperger was still able to hunt seal in November, recording his success in graphic detail:

> I hurried to the beach with the small-caliber rifle; the animal came right to me, here and there lifting its mighty head out of the water and showing its back. At twenty meters distance I put a well-aimed bullet through its head. The powerful beast threw its colossal body a meter into the air and spun, whipping the water with its tail. It appeared to have been mortally hit immediately, since it did not hurry into the deep water. In any case, I gave it two more shots in the head and one in the body for safety, whereupon after three or four minutes it ceased thrashing and lay quietly in the still water, out of which its body projected twenty centimeters. For over half an hour, the blood sprayed out of the bullet holes, especially in the head, breaking into the water in thick jets and shooting up ten centimeters out of the water like a fountain. The entire bay was dyed a gorgeous red.

Despite his hunting success, Enzensperger was not recovering. Within a week, he was no longer able to hide his condition from the other men. The frequency of his diary entries fell off, with gaps now of a week or even two between notes. "Unbelievable, how the time passes!" reads Enzensperger's final entry on 6 December. "I only wish that the three months separating me from Australia and the doctor would pass so quickly . . . The time now passes horribly slowly, just the opposite of the last three quarters of a year; my work has come to a complete standstill."[58]

Luyken reports that his comrade's swollen body had to be turned every half hour, that he suffered constant pain, and that even a diet of the freshest rabbit, geese, vegetables, and rice stimulated no improvement. On the contrary, the swelling eventually spread to Enzensperger's entire body. He began to sense approaching death and to speak out in his dreams. "As he awoke from such fantasies on the evening of the second of February—from which we could clearly hear that his spirit was with his parents and siblings in his homeland—he spoke out clearly that he felt the end was near." He died within the hour and was laid to rest the next day in a coffin draped with the imperial flag.

Drygalski learned of the Kerguelen tragedy at Cape Town. More bad news awaited. On 2 July he received orders from Berlin not to plan for another winter in the ice but to return home. The mission of the *Gauss* was over. Even before Drygalski arrived back in Germany in November 1903, he and his expedition were condemned as failures. The survivors of the Kerguelen station arrived in Sydney in April, for example, with the news of Enzensperger's death and with Werth still desperately ill. The German consulate reported that the Australian media were harshly critical of the mission and of the grossly inadequate medical arrangements made for the Kerguelen men.[59]

Though Drygalski tried to convey the image of a successful expedition through the media, the results of the voyage were dismissed both publicly and privately.[60] No crowds waited to welcome the *Gauss* home, the kaiser was said to be angry, and media and political circles were either dismissive or, worse, sharply critical. "The geographical results have remained far beneath our cherished expectations; indeed, the expedition ship *Gauss* barely made it over the southern polar circle, therefore hardly brushed the actual Antarctic zone," declared the *Kölnische Zeitung*, ignoring the efforts of Drygalski, Richthofen, and others to argue that the mission was a success. "This apologetic declaration aimed at the wider public confirms the miscarriage, which occurred through the determination of the spot at which the expedition was to penetrate into the Antarctic."[61]

At home and abroad, Drygalski was accused of poor judgment, lack of industry, and failed nerve. The expedition suffered greatly from comparison with Scott's highly successful English mission and the recently completed, dramatic Arctic adventures of Otto Sverdrup, to which audiences throughout Europe had thrilled. For the Germans, the contrast was most unflattering. The *Deutsche Rundschau für Geographie und Statistik* (German review of geography and statistics) summarized public judgment of Drygalski in early 1904:

> The overflowing abundance of scientific material cannot obscure the fact that the expedition has not closed with the successes that one might have wished for in the interest of the continuation of Antarctic exploration. These require striking results, primarily, an expansion of our spatial knowledge of Antarctica. Efforts in this direction were certainly part of the program but have produced nothing substantial. If the leader of the expedition had left Kerguelen earlier, to account for the time he spent upon oceanographic research in the Atlantic, he would have won longer freedom of movement in his actual field of exploration and perhaps the chance to unveil a greater portion of the Antarctic coast. It was a stroke of luck in any case that despite the late season he could still make a landfall and overwinter in its vicinity. This land then provided the opportunity for sledding journeys, but unfortunately little priority was given this. With the English expedition to Victoria Land, it was completely different! The German expedition was able to contribute little to the solution of the interesting question whether a great connected land mass—an Antarctic continent—exists at the South Pole.[62]

Privately, the Ministry of the Interior condemned Drygalski even more severely. Critical newspaper articles were circulated from office to office with bitter anonymous notes in the margins, suggesting that Drygalski lacked judgment and nerve: "Had one (1) not permitted the Geographical Society to prescribe to Drygalski where to advance, such a disgrace had not occurred, and (2) not permitted a *scholar* (Drygalski) to be leader and commander of the expedition but instead let either a naval officer possessing long years of experience in polar journeys—like Sverdrup—or a whaler or captain have command."[63]

Official and public disgust with Drygalski's seemingly paltry achievements found expression in the immediate decision not to retain the specially constructed *Gauss* but to sell it for $75,000 to Canada, where it was rechristened *Arctic*. Abroad, judgments were slightly less critical. The American *National Geographic* magazine noted that Drygalski was experienced, that the expedition had been well planned and well financed (to the tune of

$400,000), and that "bad luck alone" explained what happened, but it still considered the journey "practically a failure."[64]

This may not have been fair. Drygalski and his team of scientists made a respectable contribution to knowledge of Antarctica, filling in a previously unknown portion of the coastline and laying to rest the myth of Wilkes's so-called Termination Land. They collected scientific data in such profusion that over one hundred contributors and editors labored for two decades to publish all the results, which finally filled twenty-two volumes.[65] Furthermore, the Germans had achieved this despite getting the worst of the concentric attack on the mainland. Neumayer's misguided conception of Antarctic geography was as unfortunate for Drygalski as Petermann's Arctic delusions had been for Koldewey. The English, for example, were able to sail twelve degrees of latitude nearer the Pole before hitting land, and, with their far more elaborately manned and outfitted expedition, they were able to make extensive sledding journeys over land rather than unreliable sea ice.

Nonetheless, the first German Antarctic venture was a bitter defeat for the publicists, scientists, and politicians who had given such enthusiastic support to the mission. Posadowsky, Baudissin, Richthofen, nationalists in the Reichstag, the kaiser, and many more—these men wanted great discoveries and enhanced scientific prestige for Germany. Drygalski returned with neither. Even his balloon flight, a bold and enterprising stroke, was eclipsed by the British under Scott, who used a balloon to beat the Germans aloft in Antarctica by eight weeks. "Our time," Gazert noted ruefully, "wants the sensational, wants tales of dangers and adventures. But we did not set out to seek those and then entertain the world but to track down the secrets of the Antarctic."[66] Such modest achievements were not enough. For its supporters, the legacy of the Drygalski mission was disappointment, recrimination, and death.

Meltdown: Wilhelm Filchner and the Collapse of Wilhelmine Exploration

The *Gauss* failed to win glory, but in at least one important respect, Drygalski's voyage was a success. The harmony of the expedition's personnel held together, threatened neither by the breakdown of individual participants nor by social conflict among the three castes of shipboard life—officers, scientists, and crew. This was no mean accomplishment. Despite plentiful food and drink, a full schedule of work, and the relative comfort of their ship, the polar winter could generate explosive psychological tension. When the *Belgica* froze in the Antarctic ice, for example, three years before the *Gauss*, one man ran mad and another died of heart failure. The pressure, danger, and deprivation of polar research threatened the cohesion of every expedition. Precisely such tensions, erupting out of control, shattered imperial Germany's final attempt at research in the Antarctic, the mission led by Wilhelm Filchner from 1911 to 1913.

For several years after Drygalski's return, German interest in Antarctic exploration waned. While Norwegian, British, and French expeditions busied themselves with new areas of the southern continent, German public and scientific opinion seemed to be recovering from the rebuff of Drygalski's failure. Though the book-buying public exhibited a "brisk demand" for stories of polar adventure, Germany itself had little direct engagement with the Antarctic for several years.[67] Germans, for example, were notably absent from the deliberations of the International Polar Commission in these years.[68] National attention was redirected to the Antarctic in the spring of 1910, however, when a Bavarian army lieutenant named Wilhelm Filchner proposed an ambitious expedition to the Berlin Geographical Society.

Just thirty-two years old, Filchner was already a dashing popular figure. Raised in refined surroundings at Bayreuth (he painted, and Wagner and Liszt occasionally called on his family), the restless, high-spirited boy entered the Munich Cadet Corps as a teen. He first won fame in 1900 for a solo journey from Russian Turkestan across the Pamirs into British India. This rugged and lawless region was little known to Europeans at the beginning of the twentieth century, and despite contracting a severe case of malaria that lingered for years, Filchner survived. His colorful memoir of the adventure, *Ein Ritt über den Pamir* (A ride over the Pamirs), was widely read and earned him an honorary medal personally presented by Emperor Franz-Josef of Austria-Hungary.

In 1903 he set out again, this time leading an exploring party through northeastern Tibet and into China. The journey became a real-life H. Rider Haggard novel, featuring all the elements of European exotic romance— dangerous carnivores, saber duels with hostile tribesmen, and hairbreadth escapes in native dress and darkened skin. Filchner's fame grew, and this time he was presented to American president Teddy Roosevelt. When not traveling, he trained in surveying, cartography, and geomagnetic studies with the Prussian Ordnance Survey (Preussische Landesvermessung). In

1908 the Albertus University at Königsberg conferred an honorary doctorate upon Filchner, making him, at thirty-one years of age, the youngest holder of such a degree in the German Empire. Success and fame, however, failed to satisfy his energetic nature. After a few years in Berlin, eager to travel again, his interest naturally turned to the scene of so much contemporary exploration, the Antarctic.

Filchner had been pondering an Antarctic expedition since the middle of 1909, and before presenting the idea publicly, he gained a number of influential supporters. The imperial Ministry of the Interior, now headed by Dr. Delbrück, was enthusiastic at the prospect of a Filchner-led expedition for the same reasons that had inspired support for the earlier Antarctic effort led by Drygalski. The ministry held both the man and his scheme in high regard: "Filchner is a man of such great energy, and his plan, approved by Privy Councilor Penck and to be discussed with Professor Drygalski, is admirable. One can only recommend that he be supported as far as possible. Germany has doubtless been surpassed by other nations in recent decades when it comes to great geographical discoveries. It is very much in the national interest to wish that the kind of prestige bound up with such successes might also once again redound to Germany's benefit."[69]

Filchner rallied still more influential supporters to his cause in the winter of 1909–10. His superior at the Trigonometric Section of the General Staff (Trigonomische Abteilung des grossen Generalstabs), General von Bertrab, backed his ambitious young officer's project, in turn persuading Germany's most powerful soldier, Count Helmuth von Moltke, chief of the General Staff (Grosser Generalstab) of the army, to support the idea. Moltke arranged a special private meeting at General Staff quarters so that Filchner could present his ideas to a high-powered audience, including Schmidt-Ott from the Prussian Ministry of Culture, Deputy Secretary von Lewald of the Interior, Hugo von Lerchenfeld, the Bavarian ambassador to the Reich government, and many others. Filchner contemplated a bold plan but made it clear that he did not anticipate being granted imperial funding to support the project. In the discussion after his presentation, a lottery was suggested instead.[70]

The most important backer whom Filchner's zeal won at this time was Albrecht Penck. At a time when the generation that had fostered earlier German polar ventures was passing away (Ratzel died in 1904, Richthofen in 1905, Koldewey in 1908, and Neumayer in 1909), Filchner needed academic legitimacy with the German geographic community. Penck provided this in abundance. Born in 1858, Penck trained in paleontology and geological mapping at Munich and won distinction with a doctoral treatise on alpine glaciation. In his late twenties, he went to the University of Vienna (Universität Wien) as professor of physical geography, a prestigious appointment for one so young, where he helped pioneer the subdiscipline known as regional geography.

Penck's position as Germany's leading geographer was established in 1906, when he was called to the chair of geography at Berlin upon Richthofen's death.[71] Here he also assumed the directorship of Richthofen's Museum of Oceanography, using his position to foster public interest in exploration through the museum's exhibits and lectures. Over the next thirty years, Penck became the national patron of polar exploration, serving as consultant to nearly every expedition mounted in Germany.[72]

With Penck's blessing, Filchner took his plan to the people in March 1910. His daring proposal, rivaling the audacity of Drygalski's mission, was to resolve the most pressing questions about the Antarctic mainland by crossing the continent at its "waist," the narrow stretch where the Weddell Sea on the Atlantic coast and the Ross Sea on the Pacific coast reach toward one another deep into the continent. No such crossing had been made, and this gave rise to widely varying speculation about the continent's formation. Some, like Shackleton and the Scottish explorer Bruce, believed the continent to be a single landmass. Others, among them Fridtjof Nansen, viewed Antarctica as a series of ice-covered islands.

A third school, of which Penck himself was the most famous proponent, conjectured that the continent was divided in two by an ice-filled oceanic strait stretching from the Weddell to the Ross Sea. This strait would divide the continent's mainland into a larger "East Antarctica," in which the geographical Pole would be located, and a smaller "West Antarctica." "Such an interpretation of our geographical knowledge of Antarctica is naturally of a purely hypothetical nature," Penck declared in response to Filchner's address, "but it is not in the least more arbitrary than the usual interpretation, according to which a single Antarctic land complex exists."[73] Filchner made it clear that his own plan had been made in consideration of Penck's theories and that he believed that only a well-financed and large-scale expedition was worth making. "This may only be attempted, of course, if means can be found to undertake two expeditions simultaneously, one from the Weddell Sea and one from the Ross Sea."[74]

Though Filchner's argument for two ships and two expeditioning parties was reasonable, it meant an inflation of cost to around 2 million marks. This was a very great deal, especially since Filchner expected no state funding. He did, however, suggest that the kaiser might perhaps be moved to use some of his private funds to support the project.[75] This was most improbable. Wilhelm's hostility to such an undertaking was well known. The humiliation of Drygalski's failure was still fresh in his mind, and he had high hopes for a zeppelin expedition to the Arctic that was being planned at the time.

In the spring of 1910 Ambassador von Lerchenfeld arranged a dinner for the kaiser, hoping to give Filchner a chance to win the mercurial monarch to his cause. The kaiser would not hear of it. Though Filchner had the tact in his memoirs to say that Wilhelm listened "benevolently" before turning him down, other accounts described the kaiser's behavior as less courteous. " 'So, you want to go to the South Pole?' he hectored Filchner. 'Wait, if you please, till Zeppelin gets that far with his airship. He'll do in a couple of days what takes you three years. You will not make this expedition—understood?' Filchner replied, 'Majesty, I have resolved already to lead the expedition.' The kaiser turned his back and left the hall."[76]

Filchner's plan had no chance of obtaining public funds in the face of Wilhelm's opposition, and that meant two things: costs had to be scaled back, and alternative funding had to be found. Both objectives were attained by the most obvious expedients. Knowing that Robert Falcon Scott and William Bruce were each outfitting Antarctic expeditions directed to the Ross Sea, Filchner traveled to London and Edinburgh in the summer of 1910 to assure the Britons that he viewed himself not as their competitor but as their colleague. Filchner got on well with Bruce and Scott, the latter as gracious now as he had been in smoothing the way for Drygalski's arrival in Cape Town years earlier, and both men were well disposed toward the German undertaking. Filchner agreed with Scott to try to coordinate his own projected sledding excursion from the Weddell Sea with Scott's, coming from the Ross Sea across Antarctica.

The decision thus to proceed with one ship halved projected costs, but around 1.2 million marks still had to be found. The idea of a lottery was sensible but depended upon approval by the governments of the various German states. Such approval was likely, Filchner felt, only with the assistance of some distinguished patron. The kaiser was obviously out. The German Empire was still bursting with titled aristocrats, however, many looking for something useful to do. They retained considerable prestige and power, safeguarded by the German social values of the day and the federalistic arrangement of the Reich.

Filchner turned to Prince Regent Luitpold of Bavaria. Traveling to Munich the day after his failed dinner with the kaiser, Filchner found the aged Luitpold—who acted in place of his mad Wittelsbach nephews, Kings Ludwig II and Otto—willing to assume the role of "honorary patron" of the expedition. Luitpold formed a national committee of 209 bankers, professors, nobles, and bureaucrats, winning approval for the plan in most of the German states and raising, by the spring of 1911, over 1.4 million marks without the benefit of official state support.[77]

Filchner, after initiating the fund drive, paid it little heed. Instead, during the summer of 1910 he took the sensible precaution of mounting a "practice expedition" to Spitsbergen, where he and six members of his Antarctic team spent August learning polar overland travel.[78] Upon his return, Filchner in the winter of 1910–11 procured the vitals of his expedition: a ship, personnel, provisions, and a detailed plan. The vessel was obtained in Norway. Filchner purchased the ship, initially christened the Bjorn and built in 1905 as a sister ship to Shackleton's Endurance, for an economical 260,000 marks and rechristened it the Deutschland.

Appointed with a greenheart "ice skin" and an engine upgraded to 300 horsepower, Filchner's ship was similar to the Gauss. Both were three-masted vessels, intended to be wind-powered but equipped with a steam engine as well. Both were constructed of wood, conforming to the popular opinion that "only wood had the necessary resilience and elasticity for ice navigation."[79] Like the Gauss, the Deutschland possessed private cabins for scientists and officers, while the crewmen shared common bunking rooms. The Deutschland was slightly shorter than the earlier vessel, however, and, with its deeper draft and less rounded hull, was somewhat more seaworthy in rough weather.

As in earlier German expeditions, painstaking care was devoted to provisions. Experts at the Urban Hospital in Berlin, the Nutritional Research Office of the province of Brandenburg, the German Marine Observatory, and other institutions crafted a diet of considerable diversity. Food and drink for the crew and a separate, high-calorie dietary program for the members of the planned sledding expeditions were divided into a series of "provision groups," each intended to last thirty-two men about two months. Filchner reproduced the contents of a typical provision group in his memoir of the expedition (see table 1).

TABLE 1. THE MEAT CONTENTS OF A TYPICAL PROVISION GROUP

MEAT AND FISH	AMOUNT IN KILOGRAMS
Salt beef	50
Salt pork	54
Corned beef and pork	40
Smoked ox tongue	60
Conserved Holstein beef	80
Chicken stew	40
Veal stew	40
Mock turtle stew	40
Salt pork ribs	40
Mutton with cabbage	15
"Emergency food"	1
Blood sausage	12
Tongue sausage	15
Smoked cervelat	10
Meat extract	6
Goose liver pâté with truffles	2
Liver pâté	15
Ox tongue pâté	2
Bacon	30
"Breakfast sliced bacon"	15
Jellied eel	5
Anchovies	1
Baltic sprat	3
Lamprey	2
Lobster	2
Salted herring	5
Sardines	12
Herring in oil	10
Bismarck herring	10
Jellied Baltic eel	6
Smoked salmon in oil	1
Smoked salmon	1

This voluptuous smorgasbord of artery-hardening meats is but a fraction of the contents of an entire "provision group," which contained an equally impressive array of preserved fruit and vegetables, chocolates, tea and coffee, crackers and breads, dried soups and condiments, juices, jellies, and alcoholic beverages. Each provision group, Filchner reported, weighed approximately five and a half metric tons. Clearly, as on the *Gauss*, none of the *Deutschland*'s carnivorous crewmen would want for nourishment, and one is not surprised at Filchner's remark that the provisions "earned the applause of all the expedition participants."[80]

The German government also provided essential assistance, even if not directly funding the expedition. Though some materials were donated by private firms (Alfred Nobel's company supplied free dynamite), government aid was indispensable. The German Geodetic Commission, the Magnetic Institute in Potsdam (Meteorologisch-Magnetisches Institut), the German Marine Observatory, the Meteorological Institute in Berlin (Meteorologisches Institut Berlin), and a host of other agencies loaned the expedition telescopes, theodolites, thermometers, chronometers, sounding machines, condensers, wireless telegraphic equipment, and many other costly devices.

The German state also smoothed the way diplomatically, gaining the goodwill of the Argentine government, for example, and offering to pay harbor fees for the *Deutschland*'s planned stop in Buenos Aires. A late effort to economize by requesting a donation from the Argentine government was quashed by Germany's Argentine ambassador with the observation that "people here would be amazed that such a rich and powerful country as Germany has to go begging for a trifling sum."[81]

As he readied ship and supplies for the journey south, Filchner also finalized detailed goals, which he made public in 1911. The *Deutschland* would leave Germany for Buenos Aires in the spring. The ship would pursue a four-month oceanographic research program during this first leg of the journey. With December's onset of the southern summer, Filchner would proceed to South Georgia and then to the Weddell Sea, sailing as far southward along this inlet's eastern coast as conditions would permit. At a suitable landing point, the crew would erect a prefabricated wooden station house. This was intended to serve for at least a year as home to a scientific research team of seven men and as a sledding base for a team of four who would push as far south as possible. To this end, Filchner shipped eight Manchurian ponies, seventy-five Greenland sled dogs, and two motorized sleds. After landing the two teams, the *Deutschland* was to return to South Georgia for coal and to carry on coastal and oceanographic research. In the event that the ship was frozen in the ice before making land, the Deutschland itself would serve as the expedition's base.[82]

The plan was judicious. Barring unusually bad luck, the Deutschland ought to be able to penetrate the Weddell Sea during summer to a landing point at a fairly high latitude. Given proper shelter and fuel, a team of well-fed, trained, and motivated men ought to be able to lead a productive winter on the Antarctic ice cap. The Achilles heel of the Filchner expedition, however, had nothing to do with provisions, equipment, or a poorly chosen landing site. The expedition fell victim instead to human failure, stemming from poor personnel choices and a flawed command structure aboard ship.

Filchner's five-man scientific complement was fine. Since the beginning of German polar expeditioning, the nation's commitment to scientific research had been more sincere than was the case with adventurers like Shackleton, Peary, Scott, and Amundsen, who had no interest at all in the scientific aspects of their journeys. Despite his adventurer's reputation, Filchner was a well-trained man of science, and he chose his experts carefully. As with the Gauss expedition, these men were products of the German university system, all in the early stages of their careers. They included friends of Filchner, like the astronomer and physicist Erich Przybyllok and the geologist Fritz Heim, as well as a trained alpinist, Felix König.

With the selection of the naval crew, however, and with his own position on board ship, Filchner made serious mistakes. He planned at first to recruit a Norwegian captain. This affronted the sensibilities of the German naval establishment, according to Filchner, who, upon the advice of Drygalski, instead took on as captain Richard Vahsel. This appeared to be a sensible appointment. Vahsel had been second officer on the Gauss and thus had a great deal of experience in Antarctic waters. He had not shied away from participation in the grueling sledding expeditions undertaken by Drygalski's crewmen, he had worked in the meantime as a respected captain for the Hamburg-America line, and Drygalski himself clearly had no doubt of Vahsel's fitness or he would hardly have recommended him to Filchner.

Nonetheless, Vahsel turned out to be a very bad choice indeed. He was quarrelsome, boorish, and dictatorial. He had a drinking problem and was ill with an advanced case of syphilis. His behavior later in the expedition suggests that he was not only a destructively vindictive liar but a coward as well. He also insisted on bringing aboard many officers and men of his own choice, like the ice pilot Paul Björvik and the ship's cook and carpenter, who had journeyed with him on the *Gauss*. These men formed a clique, and, as a result, Filchner comments, from the beginning of the expedition "I was opposed by a closed majority."[83]

Filchner in fact got a taste of the new captain's attitude before leaving port, when, "in his cups . . . laughing and swaggering, Vahsel boasted that in his role as captain he was unrestricted master aboard ship and would be entirely within his rights even to clap the expedition leader in irons if he didn't fall into line. I took his expression for a tasteless slip."[84] Vahsel's expressions were not slips at all. He seems, in fact, to have deeply resented Filchner's role as leader, an attitude with several possible sources. His experience of Drygalski's failure may have convinced him, as it did some in the German government, that the successful leadership of an expedition could be entrusted only to a genuine sailor, not a scholar or a polar adventurer. He was also aware that, in the course of 1910, a group of the expedition's backers had incorporated themselves as the League for the German Antarctic Expedition (Verein "Deutsche Antarktische Expedition"). This step, taken to free Filchner from the burden of attending to the financial aspects of the journey, also made Filchner into an "employee of the league," as he put it, which may have further undermined his authority with Vahsel.

On 7 May 1911, a brisk, blustery North German spring day, the *Deutschland* left Bremerhaven for its four-month journey to Buenos Aires, cheered on by Penck and many of the voyage's backers.[85] Filchner was not aboard, busy instead cleaning up leftover business in Berlin. He would follow by steamer. Scientifically, the *Deutschland*'s voyage to Argentina was a great success: ten thousand nautical miles (18,500 kilometers) were covered, and nearly a hundred oceanographic observation stations were completed.

The workload for the ship's scientists was heavy at each of the stations. Water temperature readings were taken at various depths; soundings were made; plankton was fished out; salinity, oxygen content, evaporation, and water color were assessed; and customary meteorological observations, including wind speed and direction, temperature, atmospheric pressure, and so on, were taken. Off the South American coast particular attention was given to investigating the zone of transition between the warm Brazil Current and the cold Falklands Current. This kept the entire ship's complement very busy, of course, and as Filchner related in later accounts, the comforting routine of life on board ship was soon adopted by everyone.

Ominous interpersonal frictions were already developing in this early leg of the expedition, however. The ship's geographer, Heinrich Seelheim, reported that "the long sea voyage certainly had about it something exhausting, enervating. A certain excitability had also developed on board, which led easily to discord, bickering, and quarrels among the participants."[86] In Filchner's absence, Seelheim acted as scientific director of the expedition, and he quarreled a great deal with Vahsel.

En route to Buenos Aires to join the expedition, Filchner received a message by radio telegraph that Vahsel was resigning his post. He persuaded Albert Kling, the first officer on board Filchner's passage ship, the *Cap Ortegal*, to take over for Vahsel. Arriving in port at Buenos Aires, however, Filchner found the quarrel resolved. Seelheim left the expedition to join the German consular service in Brazil, and Vahsel remained as captain. Kling, now committed to the expedition, was taken on board the *Deutschland* as a member of the naval staff.

With the unpleasantness apparently smoothed over, Filchner and his crew spent a month in Buenos Aires, from 7 September to 4 October 1911. Here the sled dogs were taken aboard, while the Manchurian ponies would be brought later, accompanied by Kling, to rendezvous with the expedition at the harbor of Grytviken on South Georgia. Filchner now decided that the motorized sleds, which he had intended to modify, would not be as useful as hoped. To conserve precious cargo space, the bulky machines were left behind.

As with the stay of the *Gauss* in Cape Town a decade earlier, the *Deutschland* was received with genuine international good fellowship, a kind of comradeship in the face of danger that transcended national rivalry. One could hardly turn around without bumping into Antarctic explorers in the southern spring of 1911, and a week after reaching Buenos Aires, another polar vessel docked alongside the *Deutschland*. This was the *Fram*, just back from dropping Amundsen on the coast of the Ross Sea, from where he would make history three months later. Filchner had a good many Scandinavians aboard, and, far from seeing any rivalry, the crews of the two vessels hit it off famously. The Argentine government was also extremely forthcoming with assistance, providing radio and coaling facilities for the expedition and dispensing with normal harbor fees for the *Deutschland*'s stay.[87] When Filchner and his men sailed out in the first week of October, the *Fram* saw the Germans out of the harbor with three cheers.

These were just about the last good feelings anyone aboard the *Deutschland* would experience. The passage to South Georgia was rough, and some of the planned oceanographic program had to be scratched. Ludwig Kohl, one of Filchner's two doctors, suffered an attack of appendicitis and could not continue past South Georgia. Arriving at Grytviken in November, the *Deutschland* stayed for two weeks, collecting the post and German newspapers and taking on coal and ponies. During the stay, Walter Slossarczyk, the ship's popular third officer, vanished while rowing a dinghy in the harbor. The death troubled Filchner, who was fond of Slossarczyk and who deemed his disappearance a bad omen. On 11 December, seven months after leaving Germany and on the eve of the Antarctic summer, the *Deutschland* set out southward from Grytviken.

Filchner meant to sail to the edge of the ice, then follow it eastward along the mouth of the Weddell Sea in search of a gap that might be used as an entry point. His ship was now densely crowded. In addition to the thirty-five members of the expedition and a hold crammed to bursting with masses of provisions and implements, the deck of the *Deutschland* resembled a floating barnyard. Ponies in wooden stalls, scores of Greenland sled dogs (whose numbers began to increase with newly thrown litters from the very day of departure), two oxen, two pigs, and several sheep all vied for space and created a deafening noise. The Manchurian ponies were a particular nuisance. Reportedly wild until captured for the expedition, several had run away on South Georgia, eluding their captors for days. Unwary handlers were in constant danger of painful kicks and bites.

Three days after leaving Grytviken, the first drift ice was encountered. Feeling its way through this, the *Deutschland* hit a belt of heavier pack ice on 17 December. Progress was slow and arduous, and the ship found itself on several occasions frozen into large ice fields. Compelled to drift with the tide and current, the *Deutschland* forced its way still slowly southward, despite occasional northward backtracking of the ice.

Filchner's great opportunity seemed to be within his grasp on 28 January 1912 after drifting south for more than a month. On that day the ice opened to reveal clear water stretching out to the horizon. "We were all very astonished, since no one had expected an open Weddell Sea behind a pack ice girdle of roughly 1,100 nautical miles [2,037 kilometers]."[88] On the following morning, a greater shock: land, indicated by light surf, was seen in the southeastern distance. This was truly terra nova, a stretch of the Antarctic coast previously unknown, and Filchner christened it "Prinz-Regent-Luitpold Land." The next day Filchner discovered the towering ice shelf, the counterpart of the Ross Ice Shelf, that fringes much of the coast of the Weddell Sea and that still bears Filchner's name.

97

The Antarctic ice shelves, some of which rival European states in size, are unique features of the southern polar world. Fed by accumulated snow, glacial discharge, and freezing seawater, they vary in thickness from 183 meters to as much as 1,219 meters at their junction with the land. Though they develop gigantic rifts up to 96.5 kilometers long, they survive without fragmenting thanks to their flanking arms of land and, it is generally believed, by being grounded at some point on the seabed. The tabular icebergs noted by Drygalski aboard the *Gauss* were likely products of the ice shelves, which produce bergs of this characteristic shape, sometimes of enormous dimensions. The largest recorded was over 160 kilometers long.[89]

This seemingly fortunate discovery, however, brought to a head simmering differences between Vahsel and Filchner. While both men had agreed to sail in navigable waters beyond the point that Weddell had reached in 1823 (that is, beyond 74.3° south latitude), Vahsel held to the view that this basically navigational task was the primary objective of the expedition. Given the preparations for the journey, in which extensive work on land was clearly foreseen, Vahsel's interpretation of his mission is inexplicable. However, Filchner made it clear that the sledding effort to scout the Antarctic mainland between the Weddell and Ross Seas was for him the primary goal, as it had been for the venture's supporters.[90] These were radically divergent conceptions of the ship's mission, and their reconciliation may well have led to conflict even between men of two more similar tempers. As it was, differing viewpoints were complicated by a sharp personality conflict, making an amicable solution to the disagreement almost impossible.

The Filchner who comes through his memoirs seems a bit stiff, something of a cold fish—undoubtedly upright and honorable in his dealings with his comrades but distant, with little sense of humor and lacking the common touch, so evident in Shackleton and Scott, that inspires devotion in subordinates. In England he might have been called a prig. He drank little, for example, and had a hard time hiding his disdain for those who indulged. He was further separated from his comrades by his censorious dismissal of the vice of tobacco, a trusted comfort of seamen whose use was ubiquitous and beloved aboard the *Deutschland*.[91] He tried to exercise leadership (giving what was meant to be an inspiring speech about the *Deutschland*'s great opportunity to win the kaiser to the polar cause on the occasion of Wilhelm's birthday, for example), but his words and accounts in his diary give the impression of one for whom such comradeship was a great effort.[92]

Vahsel, on the other hand, was not only a sea captain of the old school, hard drinking and touchy about naval hierarchy, but also a man of dubious integrity, perhaps sensitive to Filchner's code of gentleman's honor and made even more irritable by the steadily advancing health complications— colds, rheumatism, exhaustion, heart problems—arising from his syphilitic infection. He was clearly unfit for the job he had undertaken, and he himself suspected, correctly as events turned out, that he would not survive the journey.[93]

Filchner's published memoir mentions little friction aboard ship. His private diaries, however, and statements composed after the return to Germany by Kling and Przybyllok, the expedition's astronomer, portray the *Deutschland* as a floating powder keg of explosive hostility. While the ship followed the coast of the Weddell Sea westward, Filchner repeatedly sought a suitable landing site at which to construct the station house. Kling's testimony suggests that Vahsel was extremely timorous about continuing in search of a landing site. On separate occasions on 2, 3, and 4 February alike, Vahsel urged Filchner not to make a landing, allegedly because he feared the ship being frozen into the ice. A small bay in the ice shelf, christened the Vahsel Bay, was encountered, but "Captain Vahsel didn't dare to investigate the possibility of landing therein."[94]

As the ship probed the Antarctic coast, a rift widened steadily between the scientific and naval personnel. Alcohol was clearly a problem. "Heim is always drunk but friendly," Filchner writes on Christmas. "[Wilhelm von] Goeldel completely drunk, threatening with firearms," he writes later, citing the ship's doctor again and again for drunkenness and abuse of his fellows. Even the scientists fought in an immature fashion particularly likely to break down shipboard discipline. "König used a wet sponge this morning to wake Przybyllok," Filchner recorded late in January, "who then angrily beat König's door in with climbing boots. He acted afterward as if nothing had happened."[95] Sensing the hostility of the captain and his retinue and unequal to the task of rebuilding the group's cohesion, Filchner gradually withdrew from active leadership.

Despite these warning signs of building tension, Filchner continued during early February to plead with Vahsel to land a party for station work and a sledding journey. After days of frustrating wrangling over whether or not a landing might be attempted, Filchner convinced Vahsel to try to disembark the station house, sledding equipment, and work party upon an iceberg that was imbedded in the shelf ice. Filchner recognized this was a dangerous proposition should the iceberg break free, and before making a final decision he requested the opinion of the captain and of Björvik, the ice pilot. According to several accounts, Vahsel claimed to have consulted the pilot and determined that the iceberg was, in fact, aground, thus a safe spot for landing. Accordingly, on 9 February, Vahsel with the greatest caution maneuvered the *Deutschland* to the lip of the ice to begin landing men and equipment.

Initially, all went well. Vahsel and a skeleton crew kept the *Deutschland* under steam for a possible emergency evacuation, while the rest of the ship's personnel feverishly unloaded wood, nails, roofing materials, glass, and all the other items necessary to the assembly of the station house. Despite bad weather, they made rapid progress. In four days the roof raising was celebrated with cigars, chocolate, and beer, and on Saturday, 17 February, the house was completed.

Their triumph would not last twenty-four hours. That very night, while Filchner and the work crew slumbered in the newly completed structure, the watch reported an explosive boom, "as if a dozen cannon were fired simultaneously."[96] The sound was caused by the spring flood tide of the new moon, an enormous surge of water that heaved the barrier ice upward two to three meters, ripping free a six-hundred-square-kilometer chunk. Filchner and his men woke to find their house and "secure" base drifting and turning with the retreating tide.

The calving of the "station iceberg," as they had already begun to call it, was a catastrophic blow from which Filchner's expedition did not recover. The disaster seems to have been caused by the deliberate lying of Vahsel. In his private diaries, Filchner reports that he later learned that Björvik, the ice expert, had in fact advised against using the iceberg as a base. A few days after the landing on the iceberg, Filchner approached Björvik, commenting, "It's a fine spot, isn't it?"

> Björvik replied angrily, "Very bad. I have always had the opinion that you should build no station on a floating iceberg but only on the inland ice and, if possible, a couple of kilometers inland." The bos'n said that was his opinion too and accused me of not wanting to listen to the advice of the experienced Björvik. Björvik was so angry about it that he had no more pleasure in the whole thing! I told the bos'n and Björvik that I had asked Björvik through the captain and that at the time he had told the captain that it was all right. The

spot was very good! Björvik answered that he *never said that* and that the captain had in any case *never asked his opinion about it!!!*[97]

Confronting Vahsel with Björvik's charge, Filchner wrote that the captain angrily attacked him for relying on the word of a crewman, all of whom, he insisted, were liable to change their stories constantly.

Both the naval officer Kling and the astronomer Przybyllok later composed statements confirming the essentials of Filchner's diary account. Kling, clearly horrified by what was happening aboard the *Deutschland*, wrote a detailed account of his version of Vahsel's perfidy shortly after the end of the expedition. "As Dr. Filchner asked the captain for Björvik's opinion, Herr Captain Vahsel answered that Björvik also had no objections. *It turned out later that Captain Vahsel had never even asked Björvik, which led later to a fateful catastrophe, since Björvik had actually said that it would have to be a stupid boy who would try to erect a station on the iceberg.*"

Przybyllok confirmed this story in notes that he composed while still aboard the *Deutschland*. He claimed to have warned Filchner of the dangers of both the iceberg and the tides but that Vahsel insisted both he and Björvik felt the iceberg was grounded and safe. "Filchner, however, dismissed me with the justification that he had to rely on the proper authorities, in this case the ice-experienced captain." Przybyllok also noted that Björvik used the expression "stupid boy" to dismiss anyone who would build on an iceberg and observed that "one would actually expect that a ship's captain would have information on the tidal ebb and flood."[98]

Whatever Vahsel's motivation might have been for deceiving Filchner and deliberately undermining the expedition, his action and the consequent catastrophe had two consequences: the expedition's hope of realizing its overland program was ruined, and shipboard morale was utterly destroyed. When the ice barrier split, seven men, an entire provision group, seven horses, and seventy-five dogs were stranded on the iceberg. All were safely recovered, though the station house itself was lost. Vahsel took the *Deutschland* north, but the southern winter was fast approaching. On 15 March, after battling increasingly dense fields of ice, the ship was frozen in and would remain so until the end of November.

An effort was now made to use the *Deutschland* as a floating base, much as had been done with the *Gauss*, and to a certain extent a scientific program was pursued. But smoldering anger was poisoning shipboard life. Vahsel, according to Filchner, "wants to shove all the blame for not landing on me," and his men reported that Vahsel spread "slanders" and "lies" about Filchner. Vahsel tried systematically to draw the naval officers into a united front against Filchner, in which he had a great deal of success. While Vahsel indulged in "abundant consumption of whiskey," he insulted Filchner openly at table, verbally abused his scientific subordinates, and encouraged his officers to do the same.

The captain set an example of open drunkenness on board: "This drunkenness is a cancer. The captain is always in the thick of it." Both von Goeldel and the ship's first officer, Wilhelm Lorenzen, were especially hostile to Filchner. "The captain opposes me wherever he can," Filchner wrote. "He is a sly fox." By April, Filchner and Vahsel were no longer speaking to one another, and Filchner "shut [him]self off entirely from them."

At the beginning of August, Vahsel succumbed to illness and drink, dying of pericardial effusion. Far from improving shipboard harmony, as might have been expected, this event heightened tensions. Filchner turned command over to Lorenzen, the ranking naval officer. This, however, led to even more open hostility between the two camps on board when Filchner objected to Lorenzen's signing the log with the title "captain." Filchner clearly feared for his life. "I sleep nights on a bench in my room so that von Goeldel can't shoot me through the wall. I'm locked in and have a rifle and cartridges ready," he wrote on 17 October. "Dr. von Goeldel attempted to bump off König with a gun. He has also considered an attempt at poisoning. I strongly suspect Lorenzen to be an accomplice."[99]

While the ship seethed with such homicidal feeling, little of scientific value was undertaken. Filchner, König, and Kling left on a sledding journey at the end of June as much to escape life on board as to find anything new. They covered 150 kilometers in a week, a respectable distance considering that none of them had experience in sledding with dogs. The only notable scientific achievement of the sledding journey was the determination that the site of the supposed Morrell Land was actually covered by at least nine hundred meters of ocean. On 26 November 1912 the ice around the *Deutschland*, which had shown signs of thawing for weeks, finally broke up. The ship immediately set sail north, tying up in the harbor at Grytviken on 19 December.

With the arrival in port, open violence burst out aboard the *Deutschland*. A punching and shoving match between Filchner's supporters and the naval officers, enlivened by shouted insults and accusations against Filchner, was ended only by the arrival on deck of the British local chief of police. When Captain Larsen, the harbormaster, arrived, Lorenzen told him he wanted Filchner off the boat: "I am the commander. He has no more say on board this ship," Lorenzen declared. The crew, among whom had spread an unfounded rumor that they would not be paid, supported the naval officers, declaring, according to Larsen, "We don't want to have anything more to do with Dr. Filchner." Privately, Lorenzen broke down in tears at the stress of the last weeks of the voyage, declaring that he had been "crazy." Larsen's efforts to arbitrate a reconciliation failed: the naval officers wouldn't go near his house with Filchner present, avoiding it "like the plague."[100]

This was effectively the end of the expedition and of Filchner's career of polar exploration. The officers and Filchner returned to Germany aboard separate ships, broke and disheartened. The Siberian dogs, left behind on South Georgia, were shot for lack of food. The horses starved.[101] König made an effort to return to the Antarctic the following year and had both funds and the ship ready to sail from the Adriatic port of Pula. His plan to proceed again from the Weddell Sea now provoked tension with Shackleton and the British, who pointed out that they had declared the region a dependency of their Falkland Islands possessions in 1908.[102] The point became moot when war was declared. Austria confiscated the *Deutschland*, which ended up as a minesweeper in the Austro-Hungarian navy during the World War. Though some significant discoveries had in fact been made (the discovery of "Prinz-Regent-Luitpold Land" above all), none of Filchner's hopes had been realized. And, once again, from the point of view of its backers, another polar foray brought Germany not the anticipated scientific prestige of a successful expedition but only shame and recrimination.

Filchner, Drygalski, and the Legacy of Wilhelmine Exploration

Filchner's failure ignited an acrimonious public debate over Germany's repeated polar embarrassments. Though some foreign observers praised the "very important contribution to our map of Antarctica" made under Filchner's leadership, for most Germans it seemed yet another national disgrace.[103] The miscarriage of two highly publicized expeditions within a decade was made even worse by the disastrous outcome of what was planned as a training expedition to Spitsbergen, led by Herbert Schröder-Stranz a year after Filchner and his men left Germany. Of fifteen participants who set out in the summer of 1912, eight eventually perished, prompting an outburst of anguished hand-wringing in the German popular media.[104]

In January 1914 Penck published a short essay entitled "Antarktische Probleme" (Antarctic problems) in which he blamed Vahsel for the expedition's shortcomings. "All these geographical discoveries of the German Antarctic expedition are all the more noteworthy since the commander of the ship—the single personality of the staff who was familiar with navigation in ice seas—had joined the expedition with infirm health and finally in the ice sea succumbed to death."[105] Penck's suggestion that the deficiency lay with the naval leadership of the expedition provoked a sharp attack by the head of the Hamburg-America line, Director Polis, who had been a supporter of the expedition and who came to the defense of his deceased former captain. Speaking to merchant and naval officers at the German Maritime Congress (Deutscher Seeschiffahrtstag) in Berlin, Polis placed the blame squarely with Filchner:

> I agree with the previous speaker, that the success of a polar expedition does not depend on whether the leader is a scholar or a sailor but much more on whether an expedition is well prepared, organized, and carried out with conviction. Further, however, that above all the leader is a truly *manly personality, who by his abilities, experience, and character* enjoys the general regard of the naval as well as the scientific participants. That we Germans in recent years, as you all know, have been able to show such meager success in exploratory expeditions is certainly due in the first degree to the fact that these preconditions have not been met . . . The geographical discoveries of the expedition are, on the contrary, solely Vahsel's credit, who pursued the goals cited for him with the greatest energy, steadfast loyalty, and devotion, never sparing his own body from ice, storm, or weather.[106]

Filchner, in his own defense, declared publicly that the station had been built on the iceberg "at the explicit advice of the ice experts and after thorough common discussion" and that following the disaster it was Vahsel's reluctance that frustrated attempts to land.[107] This controversy endured for some time, prompting Rear Admiral Behm, director of the German Marine Observatory, to call for a permanent commission to oversee future ventures and avoid the "misfortune of German expeditions that affects not only scientific circles but the entire German nation."[108]

Penck, whose reputation was closely involved with the Filchner expedition, attacked Behm's plan, insisting that existing advisory institutions, like the Berlin Geographical Society, were sufficient and that it was in any case wrong to judge the Filchner expedition a failure. "The German Antarctic Expedition indeed failed to attain the expected," he wrote at the beginning of June 1914, "but had nonetheless good success. Nothing illustrates the success of the Filchner expedition better than the fact that now two expeditions, that of the Austrian König and of the Englishman Shackleton, intend to pursue the route pointed out by the German expedition."[109] Despite the active defense mounted by Filchner, Penck, and others involved with the *Deutschland* expedition, however, the public perception of failure could not be erased.

Many of the participants in the two imperial Antarctic expeditions shared the fates of Enzensperger and Vahsel very shortly after their journeys. Philippi died in 1910, Lorenzen died in early 1914, and Bidlingmaier and Vanhöffen perished in the Great War. Surprisingly, perhaps, failure ended the careers of neither Filchner nor Drygalski. Quite the opposite, in fact. Drygalski lectured to good crowds for a decade after his journey and went on to become perhaps the most revered geographer in Germany after the war, a scholar whose works were widely published and for whom in 1944 the Munich Geographical Society (Geographische Gesellschaft zu München) named its highest award for distinguished achievement, the Drygalski Medal.[110] Filchner's later career was filled with unexpected turns. He served on the Western Front, then in German naval intelligence in Norway, where he was wrongly accused of negligence with German secrets. At the end of the war, he helped arrange the kaiser's flight to the Netherlands—the two later became good friends—and afterward wrote successful espionage novels, resumed his travels in China, Tibet, and India, and finally metamorphosed under Nazism into an Aryan hero.[111]

Filchner represented Germany's contribution to what was undoubtedly the high tide of glamorous Antarctic exploration, the annus mirabilis of 1912, a year in which Scott, Amundsen, Shirase, Mawson, and Filchner were all busy mapping uncharted wastes. Unlike most of the other nations involved, which could show either Arctic or Antarctic heroes, living and dead, for their efforts, Wilhelm's Germany gained little in the way of national prestige. Despite scientific achievement, particularly in the Drygalski expedition, the German explorers were soon forgotten both at home and abroad. It is difficult to attribute their failure to lack of planning—these expeditions were meticulously prepared, amply funded, and led by reasonably competent men. Overly ambitious goals may be partly to blame (Filchner's dream of a trans-Antarctic sled journey wasn't realized for two more generations), but simple bad luck and human emotional breakdown, upon which the Germans certainly had no monopoly, were at least as crucial to the fates of the *Gauss* and the *Deutschland*.

The agony of Wilhelmine frustration was not entirely devoid of positive consequences for the future of German exploration. A rising generation of polar scientists and explorers, including Alfred and Kurt Wegener, Ludwig Kohl-Larsen, and Alfred Ritscher, cut their teeth on Wilhelmine expeditions in Antarctica, Spitsbergen, and Greenland. And, for better or worse, the postwar German government would agree with the suggestion that greater direct involvement by the state was a necessity for successful exploration. Many Germans on the eve of the war, however, must have agreed with Filchner's rueful judgment upon his own endeavor, written many years later: "Today I know that polar expertise can't be acquired in a couple of months or years but can only be commanded by a researcher or seaman aged in the ice who has passed his entire life in the white tracts of the north or south."[112]

4. THE SEARCH FOR POLAR REDEMPTION

There is a cape on Franz Josef Land where Nansen spent a winter with a comrade. They lay in a snow hut, eating polar bear meat and wondering whether the Arctic would release them. The Graf Zeppelin flew over this cape recently and radioed "A Thousand Words on the Arctic" to the Berlin Midday News. Times are changing.

ALBRECHT HAUSHOFER, 1931

When imperial Germany collapsed at the end of World War I, many Germans felt that an entire world had been swept away. Barely six years separated Armistice Day and the return of the *Deutschland* from the Weddell Sea, but little seemed left of the confident society that had dispatched Drygalski, Filchner, and their compatriots on ambitious polar journeys. The mighty kaiser was a refugee in Holland. The colonies were gone. The proud High Seas Battle Fleet of Admiral Tirpitz, the intended symbol and guarantor of Germany's place among the first rank of world powers, rusted in the depths of the British naval station at Scapa Flow, scuttled by its own commander.

The new government, the so-called Weimar Republic, was a weakling, forced by the peace settlement to disband German armies, surrender German territory, and deliver a significant portion of the German people into foreign rule. The age of German aspiration to world-shaking deeds, among them polar exploration, seemed to have passed for good. "When I read back over the things I said in December 1913," Albrecht Penck conceded sadly after the war, "it sounds to me like an echo from past ages."[1]

Most Germans had little enthusiasm for the new regime. Weimar was unable to replace the stability and economic vitality that, despite its faults, the Wilhelmine system had provided. The Republic, born a sickly child, expired in adolescence of a variety of ills. The specters of unemployment, hyperinflation, and poverty haunted its middle class. And the political culture that grew up in such conditions was fragmented and volatile. Strikes and street fighting, assassinations and attempted coups crippled the new government. Far from attracting the allegiance of Germans, the new state was identified with the one thing to which Germans of every political stripe objected: the hated Treaty of Versailles. The Republic "arose from revolution. And the revolution arose from betrayal. And the betrayal arose from stupidity," wrote Moeller van den Bruck. "It will be difficult, it will be perhaps completely impossible, once the people feels itself a nation, to ever extinguish these connections from the memory."[2]

The break with the German past was less complete, however, than it may have seemed to those who lived through the upheaval. Germany after the war retained much from Wilhelm's state. Economically, for example, the prewar cartels still dominated German industry. The ideological trends of the Wilhelmine era—anti-Semitism, imperialism, socialism, and pan-Germanism—remained influential in Weimar public life. Bureaucrats, judges, professors, priests, and journalists still adhered to values and ideas that had shaped the defeated nation. Among them were a group of scientists and public figures who preserved a commitment to exploration of the polar world. The Poles after the war seemed to them more vital than ever, providing a site where German technology, science, and discipline could show the world that, even in defeat, Germany remained a power of global importance.

Stunt: Germany and the Flight of the Graf Zeppelin in 1931

Many Germans believed that nothing embodied their nation's technological achievement more emphatically than aviation, and, like others in the West, they looked to flight to transform polar work. Explorers would now vault the defenses behind which nature had quarantined the polar world and, as the kaiser observed to Filchner, unveil all its secrets at a stroke. Dogs and sleds were declared obsolete. "The future of polar exploration," even the South Pole conqueror Amundsen conceded, "lies in the air."[3]

The dream of an aerial assault on the Poles was an old one, much older than the technology that made it feasible. Balloonists contemplated floating to the Poles as early as the eighteenth century, and in the 1860s a German schoolteacher named Meissel prepared detailed plans for a gas balloon flight to the Arctic.[4] In 1897, with powered flight still years away, the Swedish balloonist Salomon Andrée tried to take the *Eagle* to the Pole, only to vanish without trace within a week. Even in failure, however, Andrée's effort sparked interest in aerial exploration.

The turn-of-the-century German vision of aerial polar exploration focused upon the rigid, powered airship called the zeppelin, a craft that seemed to possess an unprecedented utility. Count Ferdinand von Zeppelin's first successful flights in the summer of 1900 introduced entirely new possibilities to the polar endeavor. The huge airships, whose ungainly shape contrasted with their fascinating, stately progress through German skies, matured slowly. A succession of forced landings and crashes marked their first years. By 1908, however, Zeppelin had founded an airship construction works, and influential Germans were considering the possibilities that a floating, maneuverable platform seemed to offer in the high latitudes.

The count himself, a popular figure whose walrus-mustached image was as well known as the kaiser's, took the lead in pointing out the potential of his creation. "I leave not to fantasy but to the practical consideration of all what utility such vehicles must bring to world travel of every kind," he told an audience of engineers and aristocrats in 1908. "The post, maritime navigation, the conduct of war, the exploration of the globe into the heart of yet unreconnoitered regions, to the very ice-encrusted Poles, to the depths of the seas, since the view from above penetrates even there."[5]

Germans enthusiastically agreed. When Cook and Peary assailed each other's claims to being first at the North Pole in 1909, a popular German postcard showed the count stepping over the antagonists to plant the German flag atop the globe:

> Cook and Peary in heated fight
> over who has really reached the Pole,
> never notice that in the meantime
> ZEPP has slipped past to the goal.[6]

Postcard doggerel was about as close to reality as German dreams of polar flight came before the war. In 1908 Zeppelin and the Trigonometric Section of the army's General Staff (where Filchner was posted) planned an aerial research expedition and eventually settled upon Spitsbergen as a likely venue. Under the patronage of Prince Heinrich of Prussia a preparatory mission was carried out in the summer of 1910, led by Zeppelin himself, accompanied by members of the Ministry of the Interior, Drygalski, and others.

The expedition investigated whether dirigibles could land, anchor, and maneuver over glaciers and ice fields. "Undoubtedly, the Arctic and Antarctic regions of the globe are among the areas that offer the greatest resistance to the explorer because of their hostile climatic and other conditions," wrote the prince. "So the thought occurred to overcome this resistance with the aid of the airship."[7] The venture seemed a great success. While Zeppelin regaled the participants with tales of his part in the Franco-Prussian War forty years earlier (he also fought with the Union in the

American Civil War), work went so well that Zeppelin built an airship hangar on Spitsbergen in 1912 to prepare for more ambitious polar flights.

The summer of 1914 snuffed any chance that the zeppelin would be put to such pacific uses. Germans hoped that the great airships would be their nation's "superweapon," able to rain bombs at will upon Paris, London, and other hostile capitals. Instead, the zeppelins were military disasters. With their colossal size and lumbering pace, they were easy prey for the fast and agile fighters of the Allies. Nonetheless, the war stimulated German airborne exploration of the Poles in two important ways. First, the desperate struggle for air superiority spurred a great leap forward in aviation technology. Aircraft became more durable, their engines more reliable and powerful (of particular importance for the progress of the underpowered early zeppelins), and their range greater. A burst of dramatic polar flights shortly after the war illustrated just how far the struggle had pushed aviation. Amundsen and Ellsworth's highly publicized failure to fly to the North Pole in 1925 was followed the next year by the successful flight of the American naval officer Richard Byrd, who set out from Kings Bay in Spitsbergen, near the site of the prewar zeppelin mission. Byrd's aircraft, the Fokker-designed *Josephine Ford*, was equipped with three powerful, air-cooled engines that were able to propel plane, crew, and 1,500 liters of fuel at speeds over 190 kilometers per hour. Three years later, in an identical machine, Byrd repeated his exploit, this time at the South Pole.

While aviation's war-inspired technical progress could be seen in all the states involved in the war, the conflict also heightened a specifically German sensitivity to the political value of polar exploration. Germany's sprawling colonial empire was a bitterly mourned casualty of the war, and some Germans, conservative and liberal alike, looked to polar territories to make good the loss. Given the ease of aerial transport in the region, the unclaimed polar world might open rich new lands to compensate for the lost colonies. The high latitudes were virgin territory, many believed, hiding valuable resources, and Germans had to hurry not to miss out on the scramble for the Poles as they had almost missed out on the scramble for Africa. "The division of the Arctic world, and probably soon the Antarctic as well, until now unruled because regarded as entirely worthless, is in full swing," wrote the geographer Richard Hennig in 1928. "The wish to secure a favored position within the Arctic air travel net is undoubtedly one of the chief motivating factors for this surprising and unique tendency in the geopolitical picture of the present day."[8]

The nearly forgotten prewar heritage of the Drygalski and Filchner failures was now trundled out by journalists who exhorted Germans to raise their "just claims" to regions explored by the two missions.[9] "The South Pole has become English on the sly," they warned, and colonial revanchists like Wilhelm Külz, a liberal minister of the interior, emphasized the importance of exploration to German "economic and cultural renewal."[10] The sector theory found increasing application in the 1920s, and German observers were sure that this was prompted by flight. "The states interested in the still-unclaimed regions of the high latitudes have sensed immediately with the development of aviation that a clear separation of 'mine' and 'yours' is becoming necessary in these zones."[11]

Germans thus sought a place at the table when the polar pie was carved, but they also looked toward the polar heavens for other reasons. With the German nation seemingly humiliated in defeat, the prospect of demonstrating German technological achievement to the world by means of the zeppelin was very attractive. A spectacular polar flight might represent a propaganda victory for the nation that had been beaten on the Western Front. The most influential proponent of this view, and the man most responsible for the eventual realization of a zeppelin flight to the Poles, was Hugo Eckener, who became chairman of the zeppelin works in Friedrichshafen after the count's death in 1917.

Born in 1868, Eckener earned a doctorate with a dissertation in what today would be known as experimental psychology. He was writing for the Frankfurter Zeitung when he first covered the count's flights in 1900. Eckener's initial skepticism about the utility of the strange vehicles turned to enthusiasm, and by 1908 he had found a place as one of Zeppelin's advisors. Taking over the plant in Friedrichshafen as the war drew to its disastrous close, Eckener struggled after Germany's defeat to keep the zeppelin program alive. By convincing the American government to accept a new airship in reparations and then engineering a wildly successful publicity campaign to cover the transatlantic flight of the ZR III (christened Los Angeles by the U.S. navy) in 1924, Eckener revived German interest in the zeppelin.[12] Gustav Stresemann, at the time German foreign minister, celebrated the transatlantic voyage and congratulated Eckener, whom he said had "achieved the highest possible success of technology and science and thus has fostered Germany's renown and visibility in the world."[13]

If the Allies would lift the ban on airship construction, Eckener told Germans, their nation could once more stand at the forefront of global technological advance. By the late 1920s, Eckener believed that dramatic zeppelin flights, circling the globe or reaching unexplored wastes, would best serve the purpose of keeping the airship before the public eye. With Arctic skies swarming with airborne adventurers, a polar flight seemed an obvious means to this end. "I believe the Entente will not refuse its consent when it is approached for permission to construct a large exploration airship in Germany," he told a Friedrichshafen audience on the silver jubilee of the first zeppelin flight in 1925. "That is why we have formulated our plans to realize Count Zeppelin's final great idea and to dispatch a scientific expedition to the polar regions by airship."[14] The zeppelin had always been seen as an emblem of German power, and Eckener was sensitive to the prestige that such flights garnered for his homeland. By a successful exploratory journey, he insisted, the airship could become the "symbol and measure of German greatness and hope."[15]

His activities over the years between such early statements and the eventual polar flight make clear, however, that for Eckener the airship program itself was the paramount concern. He was as willing to fly across the Atlantic or to central Asia as to the Poles to rally support for the zeppelins. But his expressed interest in polar flight sparked the dreams of other Germans. Zeppelin's own nephew, the Freiherr von Gemmingen, argued in 1919 that his uncle's prewar polar plans needed to be pursued and that "exploratory flights in the polar zones would deliver valuable results," proving the airship's continued utility.[16]

Other airship enthusiasts took up the polar cause. A retired zeppelin captain named Walther Bruns promoted the construction of a network of transpolar airship routes as the most practical way of reducing travel time between Europe and the Pacific. During the early 1920s Bruns petitioned German professional organizations, mounted a media campaign, and urged the value of polar exploration by airship upon the German scientific community. His activity and public clamor over the flight of the ZR III led in October 1924 to the formation of the International Society for the Study of the Arctic with the Airship (Internationale Studiengesellschaft zur Erforschung der Arktis mit dem Luftschiff), which became better known by its shortened name of Aeroarctic.

Aeroarctic, under whose auspices the *Graf Zeppelin* would eventually fly northward, arose from the commitment of a multinational group of scientists. The "manifesto" of the group,*Das Luftschiff als Forschungsmittel in der Arktis. Eine Denkschrift* (The airship as a research tool in the Arctic: a memorandum), listed eighty-three signatories representing nearly twenty nations.[17] Germans predominated, accounting for fifty-three of the signatures, some from very distinguished figures. Hugo Hergesell, a veteran of the prewar Spitsbergen expedition, Albrecht Penck, Bruns, and others took part, but the greatest publicity coup was in securing Fridtjof Nansen, one of the world's best-known explorers and a recent Nobel Peace Prize laureate, as president of the organization.[18] The prestigious Royal Swedish Academy of Sciences also supported the society. German scientists and politicians were determined to emphasize the international aspect of Aeroarctic, for fairly obvious reasons. When the organization was founded in 1924, Germany was a pariah. Officially blamed for starting the war, excluded from the League of Nations, with important internal and economic affairs subject to oversight by suspicious representatives of the Allies, German elites welcomed any opportunity to cooperate with other states as a step toward the ending of German isolation.

Aeroarctic held its first official congress at Berlin in November 1926.[19] One German speaker after another celebrated the occasion as a demonstration of the unbroken international brotherhood of science. Speaking in the ceremonial hall of the Prussian state legislature, Külz reminded his listeners that the "bold spirit of exploration" could not stop at the borders of the Arctic. "The impulse to explore the North Pole is supported by time-tested scientific experience and the important technology of airship construction, embodied in Germany in the name 'Zeppelin,'" Külz said. "The assembly is therefore obligated to again unite the science of the various nations." The mayor of Berlin, Gustav Böss, welcomed the assembly with the reminder that they had gathered in his town in a great multinational project, one "in which all peoples are concerned in equal fashion."[20] These were noble sentiments, and Aeroarctic would soon devise detailed plans to give them life. In the meantime, however, the society faced two serious hurdles: it had no money and no airship. The funding dilemma was never solved. The warm support that German ministers expressed for Aeroarctic's plans was more than mere lip service, but it did not extend to providing money for the flight. The Weimar Republic was a financial house of cards, and its government was chronically strapped. This militated strongly against the funding of projects that were uncertain to promise a quick and tangible return and produced a natural reluctance to commit too heavily to ventures in which Germans might not have the guiding hand. The government was more interested in the success of Eckener's company and in revising the

Versailles ban on airship construction than in the dreams of Aeroarctic's polar idealists. As a result, Aeroarctic faced a chronic financial crisis. The Ministry of the Interior, so crucial in the support of Drygalski and Filchner, gave Aeroarctic a mere 1,500 marks for 1927, a sum so small as to be almost useless. Insurance quotes for a polar flight alone could run as high as 1 million marks. Other governments normally gave even less—the United States, for example, consented to provide a mere $300 in 1928.[21] Occasional significant contributions came in, as when Canada donated $10,000 in 1928, but money was always short.[22] After December 1929 the German government withdrew its support entirely.

That the polar airship flight eventually became a reality despite Aeroarctic's financially moribund state was due to the complicated interplay of many factors. As Bruns, Nansen, and Aeroarctic agitated in 1924 and 1925 for the construction of a polar research airship, Eckener, sensing considerable popular support for the idea, decided to resort to the now traditional expedient of the impoverished German polar explorer: public charity. The move displayed Eckener's genius for adroit public relations ploys. In the late summer of 1925, he stole the thunder of Aeroarctic and gave a great impetus to his own dreams of a continued German airship program with the proclamation of a national fund-raising campaign. The goal of the campaign, he told Germans, was "to dispatch a scientific expedition to the polar regions by airship."[23] In fact, Eckener's chief motivation was to raise money for a new zeppelin by any means possible, including the use of Aeroarctic's polar vision.

Eckener's choice of a patron for his national zeppelin fund drive was equally shrewd. He solicited the aid of Friedrich Schmidt-Ott, Prussian minister of culture before the war and now president of a new government cultural agency called the Notgemeinschaft der deutschen Wissenschaft (Emergency coalition of German science), which was founded in 1920 and had the financial support of universities, the government, and an alliance of industrial backers headed by Carl Friedrich von Siemens. Schmidt-Ott himself sat on the board of Germany's most powerful industrial cartel, I. G. Farben, and exploited valuable connections in the German business world. Though genuinely concerned with science, Schmidt-Ott also appreciated the cultural propaganda value that a successful zeppelin venture could hold.[24]

With Schmidt-Ott's help, Eckener rallied German schoolchildren (a constituency naturally prone to enthusiasm about zeppelins and polar adventure) to stand on street corners and go door to door on behalf of the nation's airship future.[25] This drew in 2.5 million marks, an amount sufficient to begin construction but far short of the roughly 7 million that he had hoped to obtain. Eckener turned then to the government, using his initial collections as leverage to gain state funding. With the support of the Ministry of Transport (Verkehrsministerium), the zeppelin project received 1.1 million marks from 1927 to 1928.[26] In August 1929 Eckener flew the new *Graf Zeppelin* around the world, profiting from the sale of newspaper rights, winning the Special Gold Medal of the American National Geographic Society, and drawing huge crowds in Tokyo and Los Angeles, where the airship docked en route.[27] If any German could make a polar airship flight fiscally feasible, it was the technocrat, entrepreneur, and showman Eckener.

The entire operation was nearly destroyed, however, by a simmering feud between Eckener and Aeroarctic. This had deep roots in the world of postwar German airship construction. In the early 1920s, Bruns and Aeroarctic had contacted an airship designer named Johann Schütte, who ran the only serious German rival to Eckener's firm. Schütte proposed a polar airship of his own design. Eckener, naturally enough, saw Bruns as a meddler and the so-called Schütte-Lanz polar airship as competition that endangered efforts to keep the zeppelin works in operation.[28] It cannot have helped relations between Eckener and Aeroarctic that at the same time Nansen began putting out propaganda brochures promoting a polar flight using the *Graf Zeppelin*.[29] Aeroarctic, to make matters even worse, several times denounced Eckener to the Foreign Office, complaining that his excessive nationalism was delaying the flight.[30] This was unfair. Eckener was certainly unscrupulous in his exploitation of the polar cause, about which he was never really enthusiastic, but his reservations about the genuine risks involved in a polar flight were legitimate. As a publicity stunt, it was in some ways unnecessary, since the recent global flight had vindicated the airworthiness of the zeppelin. Byrd had already reached the Pole in an airplane, and the *Graf Zeppelin*, were it to attempt the same feat, would not even be the first airship there, since the *Norge*, an Italian craft, had reached the Pole in 1926. Nor was the flight devoid of the potential for disaster. In the summer of 1928, the airship *Italia* went down during its return from a polar flight. Eight men died, while nine more, including Roald Amundsen, perished in the course of rescue attempts.

Even members of Aeroarctic worried that the zeppelin was obsolete for purposes of exploration, and Hans Krüger, a German explorer famed for travels in Africa and Greenland, publicly declared that the dangers of airship exploration far outweighed any benefits to be gained.[31] The remains of Andrée's flight, including the corpses of Andrée and his two colleagues, were also discovered in 1930, providing another graphic warning of the threats to lighter-than-air Arctic aviation.[32] Many others argued that the airship was too vulnerable to the play of wind and storm, making a polar venture "with the current state of the technology a thoroughly uncertain affair."[33] Aeroarctic also nurtured grandiose plans for the *Graf Zeppelin*. Eckener favored a quick stab into the Arctic world, fulfilling scientific goals, to be sure, but aimed equally at what he called "the prestige gain it would have represented for Germany."[34] Aeroarctic, on the other hand, viewed the Arctic flight as the mere beginning of a standing polar commitment for Eckener's zeppelin. The group wanted a three-stage circumpolar airship excursion, from Murmansk westward to Nome, from Nome out over the Pole, and returning to Murmansk from Nome by way of Siberia. Bruns himself, at the society's second international congress in Leningrad, called the Arctic flight only the "first step" and exhorted his comrades to remember the long haul: "The society must always keep in sight that only systematic investigations over a series of years, carried out by a network of observation stations to be secured by airships and airplanes, will be able to lift the veil that hangs over the Arctic."[35]

Coming from an insolvent, airshipless passel of beggars like Aeroarctic, such elaborate schemes must have struck Eckener as exaggerated at best. The polar project consequently languished until 1930, caught between the ambitious but penniless organization and the more practical man who held the trump card of the only German dirigible. Death and money, the great transformers, then intervened. Nansen died in May 1930, and the directors of Aeroarctic, desperate to make some reality of their dreams, swallowed the bitter pill and offered the organization's presidency to Eckener. Hesitant at first, he eventually accepted, fully aware of the significance of his move: "It was clear that as president of Aeroarctic I would have the moral duty to employ the airship, the use of which I determined as quickly as possible for the goals of the society."[36] The very next month, an Australian polar adventurer named Sir George Hubert Wilkins chartered an obsolete American submarine, which he renamed the *Nautilus*, for an attempt to sail underwater and surface at the North Pole. William Randolph Hearst bought the rights to the story and then offered $150,000 to Eckener if he would fly the *Graf Zeppelin* to the Pole for a hazardous rendezvous with Wilkins's submarine. Since such a flight would cost roughly $25,000, the stunt promised a handsome profit, and Eckener accepted.[37] Wilkins, however, setting out in April 1931, failed to get farther than 81° north latitude and was unable with his elderly vessel to pierce the ice. He abandoned his plan, and Hearst backed out of the project.

Hearst's change of heart failed to torpedo the polar airship dream, since help surfaced from an unexpected source. The German Ullstein press chain now offered to buy the rights to an Arctic airship journey at the bargain basement rate of about 40,000 marks. Through the offices of Aeroarctic's Russian members, especially the geologist Rudolf Samoilovich (a polar veteran who led rescue operations in the *Italia* disaster), it was now arranged that instead of meeting an Australian submarine at the Pole, Eckener and his airship would rendezvous with a Russian icebreaker somewhere near Franz Josef Land. Eckener was still interested, but clearly, even more financial support would be needed. Eckener turned again to the public. The German postal service agreed to issue special zeppelin North Pole stamps in the spring of 1931. They could be used to mail letters and postcards that would be canceled with a unique North Pole cancellation mark in a postal station aboard the *Graf Zeppelin*. The mail would be passed on to the Soviet icebreaker *Malygin*, returned to the U.S.S.R., and then sent back to eager philatelists in Germany. The response was enormous. Transatlantic mail was still a rarity, and exotic postmarks were very popular with collectors. The North Pole seemed the ultimate in such postal novelties. Stamp sales raised about 200,000 marks, accounting for 75,000 letters and postcards. As his predecessors had done, Eckener called upon patriotic German manufacturers to supply provisions and equipment free of charge.

The *Graf Zeppelin*'s adventure also inspired German diplomats. The Foreign Office pressed Eckener throughout the 1920s not to lose sight of the craft's intended polar purpose.[38] This became particularly important to German statesmen when it seemed probable that the project would be a largely German-Soviet venture. Weimar Germany looked to Soviet ties to offset its isolation from the West, and friendly cooperation with the Soviets characterized the Republic's diplomacy. As Germany succeeded in entering the League of Nations in 1926, German policy makers exploited ties with the Soviets in order "that Germany might be the bridge to create a balance between East and West in European affairs."[39] Well into the early 1930s, Weimar diplomats remained "most positively disposed" toward cooperation with the Soviets.[40] The *Graf Zeppelin*'s venture promised to extend this cooperation into the field of science, and so the turn toward a German-Soviet coloring of the polar zeppelin flight delighted German diplomats. They recalled the smashing public relations success of a zeppelin flight to Moscow in September 1930. Internal memoranda cited the "powerful impressions" that the aircraft made upon huge crowds in Moscow and declared that "the airship provided the best evidence for the brilliant achievements of German technology in the nation-binding area of air travel."[41] Even more importantly for both the diplomats and Eckener, the trip sparked Russian interest in developing a Soviet airship program, with technical help, and possibly the lion's share of the construction, provided by the Friedrichshafen zeppelin works. Embassy officials in Moscow reported to Berlin "confidentially that, on the basis of the powerful impression of the zeppelin visit in Moscow, all provincial newspapers have been directed to make propaganda for the development of Soviet airship construction with German aid and to introduce fund drives."[42] In Eckener's opinion, the talks, if successful, could produce extremely profitable contracts netting several million marks for the German zeppelin operations.

With means at hand and urged on by such powerful incentives, Eckener turned in the spring of 1931 to the problems of outfitting and staffing. These were serious. The *Graf Zeppelin* was designed as a long-distance conveyance for a handful of passengers, a few packages, and a bit of luggage. Normally, the airship served twenty or so well-heeled travelers who enjoyed unforgettable scenery in luxury and comfort intended to rival first-class passage on elegant ocean liners. It was an apparently gargantuan vessel. Constructed with over 16 kilometers of Duralumin girders, the *Graf Zeppelin* measured 236.5 meters from tip to tip and 29.8 meters in diameter. Five 250-horsepower, reversible engines propelled this huge mass at a cruising speed of 105 kilometers per hour. That such an enormity should fly practically defied belief, and the airship entranced spectators. No one who glimpsed the "fabulous silvery fish, floating quietly in the ocean of air," ever forgot the sight.[43] Despite its immense exterior proportions, however, usable space in the gondola was in very short supply. The salon, writing room, and ten passenger cabins were elegantly appointed but quite compact. Wealthy patrons endured the hardship of using only two shared bathrooms and had to forgo bathing entirely. The ship's accoutrements and capacity made it more like a yacht than a liner of the sky.

The conversion of the *Graf Zeppelin* from flying yacht to flying laboratory required substantial innovation. The scientific aims of the expedition were geographic and meteorological. While the public believed, and was told, that the North Pole was the goal, this was untrue. Thanks to insurance restrictions, Eckener could not take his vessel farther than 82° north without risking a complete loss in the event of a crash. Under these circumstances, the fantasies of Aeroarctic were moot. The ship had to do what was possible and productive within the limits set by financial prudence. Eckener's program, devised in collaboration with Samoilovich, was a flight to Franz Josef Land to meet the *Malygin*, then eastward over the top of Russia to the Taimyr Peninsula, returning home by way of the Siberian coast, Novaya Zemlya, and Arkhangelsk. The chief technical tasks of the flight would be photographic mapping, geomagnetic recording, close observation of wind and weather conditions, and the use of sonic depth finders to map the Arctic Ocean floor. Samoilovich was appointed scientific director of the flight.

Even this very modest agenda entailed radical alterations to the zeppelin. In the cavernous hangar at Friedrichshafen, workmen hauled out mattresses and bunks to save weight. A sleeping cabin at the rear was converted into a temporary geomagnetic laboratory, using equipment donated by the Carnegie Foundation. The floor was ripped out of another cabin, and laborers installed a specially designed "panorama camera," one of the chief mapping tools used by the expedition. Mounted vertically in the floor of the gondola, the panorama camera possessed nine objectives, eight peripheral lenses arranged around a larger central lens. Every few seconds throughout the flight, a single, shared negative was exposed to the entire series of lenses simultaneously. The result was a comprehensive photographic image made of nine pictures that fit together at their edges, embracing a landscape of several kilometers and "completing in hours a job that would take years for the land surveyor."[44] In the same chamber, installed so that it could be aimed to either the starboard or port sides of the ship, was a Zeiss double serial surveying camera. This device took overlapping photos of the landscape from the airship to the horizon that were used to create stereoscopic images as a basis for more accurate isobaric maps.

The meteorological specialists aboard the *Graf Zeppelin* required yet more complex additions to the vessel. In order to record atmospheric conditions at altitudes beyond the operational ceiling of the airship, the Soviet electrophysicist Pavel Molchanov designed an ingenious remote sensing probe. This consisted of a small hydrogen balloon that carried instruments to measure altitude, wind speed, temperature, and humidity as well as a radio transmitter. A special shaft had to be built into the airship hull behind the gondola. After being inflated with hydrogen from the ship's gas cells, the weather probe would be released from this shaft. Weighted with a sandbag, the balloon would descend for approximately one minute until it was clear of the airship, after which a self-release mechanism detached the ballast. The balloon would then shoot upward to heights of anywhere between 13,700 and 16,500 meters. The transmitter was designed to relay measurements to the ship at three-minute intervals. As the balloon ascended, the German meteorologist Ludwig Weickmann would lower a stabilized probe from another hull opening, taking similar readings from the *Graf Zeppelin* downward to nearly the ocean surface. A comprehensive atmospheric profile would thus be obtained.

While the ship was remodeled, the provisioning for the projected forty-six-member trip proceeded under the direction of Ludwig Kohl-Larsen, an experienced polar traveler who had participated in the early stages of Filchner's expedition and who led a small German mission to South Georgia in 1928. Crated goods poured into Friedrichshafen by the ton, all donated by patriotic manufacturers: dried fish and biscuits, watertight overalls in the expedition's uniform brown, reindeer-skin sleeping bags, wine, hurricane lamps, frost-proof fountain pens, and menthol-flavored, plastic imitation cigarettes to keep nicotine cravings at bay in the smoke-free environment of the *Graf Zeppelin*. Kohl-Larsen also prepared measures for the worst-case scenario of a forced landing on the ice. Crimson tents, sleds, inflatable rescue boats, harpoons for seal hunting, and, incredibly, lassos to catch polar bears were all stowed away with emergency provisions. True to the airship's luxury traditions, privation was not anticipated. "The rations were so abundantly measured that they came to 855 grams per man per day," Kohl-Larsen later noted. "As Ellsworth reported, he had at his emergency ice landing at 87° north only about 300 grams per day, so that, without being an optimist, one could have gotten by for four months and longer with our 2,760 kilos for the forty-six men."[45] Kohl-Larsen was referring to the American polar aviator Lincoln Ellsworth.

The journey of the *Graf Zeppelin* would be Ellsworth's second airship flight into high latitudes—he had been aboard the *Norge* in 1926 and was already an international polar celebrity for his role in Amundsen's 1925 polar flight.[46] Ellsworth was part of the small non-German contingent of the expedition, which included four Soviets; another American; the Hungarian Arthur Koestler, along as correspondent for the Ullstein newspapers; and a token Swede, Professor G. Ljungdahl, representing the Royal Academy of

Sciences. The remainder of the crew and the scientific complement were Germans, including Aeroarctic general secretary Bruns, finally to see his dream realized; Ernst Lehmann, a veteran of perilous wartime zeppelin missions; and Max Pruss, who would pilot the Hindenburg to its fiery date with disaster in 1937.[47]

The effort to give the expedition a multinational flavor failed to obscure its Russo-German character. Germans provided the bulk of the personnel and scientific equipment, while the Russians provided the largest non-German contingent, the icebreaker, and mooring and fuel facilities at Leningrad. Anticipation was high at the Foreign Office on the eve of Eckener's Arctic flight. This in part reflected the influence of Herbert von Dirksen, former director of the Eastern Section of the Foreign Office and in the early 1930s German ambassador to the Soviet Union. Even after relations between the U.S.S.R. and Germany had cooled somewhat from the early 1920s, Dirksen remained an influential advocate of close German military and civil ties with the Soviets.[48] Other German officials also expected great things from the flight, including a potential colonial-style land grab. A Rear Admiral Kahlert urged the Foreign Office to remember that "the zeppelin may, if it comes upon previously uncharted land in the Arctic, occupy it, to demonstrate that Germany has not renounced the acquisition of possessions outside its borders."[49]

And the general outlook in Germany, notwithstanding the cavils of a few pessimists, was that the flight would be a triumphant success. Observers who had followed polar exploration since the turn of the century characterized Eckener's undertaking as a "reconnaissance flight" for the future that would determine just how teams of researchers might best be resupplied by air.[50] Eckener himself, never particularly noted for tact or humility, was caustic when asked why he would succeed where Umberto Nobile, who had piloted the Italia to disaster, had failed. "Because he is, as we say, a nervous jackass. Such people should keep away from flying!"[51] After indicting Nobile for clumsy handling of his airship, Eckener declared that the Italia disaster was "no argument against the use of airships in the Arctic." He also waved off concerns that the airship would take on ice and become dangerously heavy, insisting that the zeppelin's heavy, multilayered cotton skin was too poor a conductor of heat to create icing conditions.

At dawn on 24 July 1931, the three-hundred-member ground crew of the Graf Zeppelin gingerly walked their gigantic airship out of its hangar at Friedrichshafen. The ship spent that evening in Berlin after circling the city several times to give the enthusiastic urban masses a good last look before departure. The next day Eckener and his crew proceeded to the actual jumping-off point for the expedition, Leningrad. An escort of fighters rose to meet the zeppelin at the border of Soviet air space, guiding it past sensitive coastal defense installations to the mooring mast at the Commandant Aerodrome, four kilometers outside the city. The Russians received their guests in style. After a committee of local apparatchiks and military officers met Eckener, Soviet and German technicians topped off the airship's stores of gasoline and hydrogen while Soviet scientists stowed their equipment on board. After a round of speeches, Eckener and his comrades were whisked off to a lavish vodka-and-caviar Russian banquet, where they toasted the scientific cooperation of the two great peoples. The feast, Eckener noted cynically, was a culinary Potemkin village, given the food shortage prevailing in the U.S.S.R.

On 26 July the *Graf Zeppelin* started out late, groggy from "the previous night's celebrating," as Eckener recalled, and to do proper justice to the caviar and bacon sent by the Russians for breakfast. Making their final good-byes about 9:00 A.M., crew and ship set course northeastward for Arkhangelsk. This was passed in a few hours, after which the route continued more directly northward for Franz Josef Land and the rendezvous with the *Malygin*. The original program for the flight called for a passage over Novaya Zemlya first, but an atmospheric depression above that island forced a change in plan. This bit of bad weather was exceptional. The elements throughout seemed to smile upon the *Graf Zeppelin*. Clear skies and manageable winds were the rule, providing magnificent visibility and photographing conditions. The expedition's members recalled the trip as a dream. Modern air travelers, crammed into metal tubes and peering through tiny windows at the distant landscape speeding by at a near-sonic rate, can only imagine the experience. Aboard the *Graf Zeppelin*, passengers enjoyed the breathtaking view through windows more than a meter wide. Skimming the earth's surface at a normal cruising altitude of five hundred meters, travelers were thrilled by an exhilarating impression of proximity to the scenes beneath, passing by at a pace so deliberate and measured that they felt they were floating. Even the temperature seemed to wish Eckener success—the coldest reading on the entire trip was 5°C, enabling the crew to move about the gondola and attend to business in their normal clothing.

The Arctic voyage of the *Graf Zeppelin*, in fact, is unique in the annals of polar exploration, standing without rival as the most comfortable expedition ever made. Gliding effortlessly over lands that had claimed scores of lives in recent decades, scientists and crew alike remarked the "wonderful silence" of their ship in its passage, quieter than "any compartment on an express train." In their comfortable cabins, seated at tables before bright windows that revealed a succession of passing wonders, the men "could read novels or poetry in complete rest and comfort."[52] For many, including Eckener, the journey took on the aspect of a sightseeing trip through the glories of the polar world. Noting "the wondrous clarity and visibility of the air," he was struck by the paradox of comfort in the midst of polar wastes. "A strange experience, to float in ease over a sea that inhabited the imagination as hostile and malicious and that now revealed itself in pure light and color and beauty!"[53] The luxurious appointments of the vessel impressed everyone. "In their electrically heated cabins, they passed over glacier and iceberg as in a salon."[54] The airship's flight demonstrated the extent to which the West's technological achievement was transforming polar exploration, turning the experience of life-threatening struggle into something between a comfortable scientific jaunt and a tourist trip, sufficiently risk-free to include bookish interlopers like the media agent Koestler.

Disaster always loomed, of course, as the tons of emergency supplies and the recent experience of the *Italia* testified, but it loomed at a reassuring distance. The only real drama of the voyage occurred on the evening of 27 July, when the airship reached the bay on Hooker Island where it would rendezvous with the *Malygin*. The icebreaker radioed Eckener of its readiness in the morning, and just after 5:00 P.M. Greenwich mean time the airship cleared the rugged hills ringing the bay and hove into view of the ship and its cheering crew. Conditions initially appeared to be ideal, with very light winds and a bay that looked from altitude to be free of ice. Eckener brought the zeppelin through a slow circle for its descent, touching the surface of the bay on rubber pontoons five hundred meters from the *Malygin*. The five mighty engines came to a stop. After stabilizing the airship, nose into the breeze, with a parachute-like "water anchor" that kept the bow and stern of the gondola level, the postal exchange was ready to go forward, 300 kilograms of mail from airship to icebreaker and 120 kilograms in the opposite direction, all canceled with the bogus North Pole postmark.

At sea level, however, the benign aspect of the transaction suddenly turned threatening. The wind at the zeppelin's top, nearly thirty meters above the gondola, was clearly stronger than at the level of the water's surface, causing the ship to drift despite the water anchor. A worse danger soon appeared. "As invisible as the ice had seemed from a height, it was nonetheless on hand," Kohl-Larsen reported. "One could tell that the fragments, as one neared them, would grow to colossi of unpredictable thrust."[55] Under such hazardous conditions, Eckener was taking no chances. "The danger existed that the gondola on which the ship rested might be pierced by these floes. A substantial leak could indeed have become dangerous." As the boat from the *Malygin* neared, Eckener commanded that the transaction be carried forward with all possible dispatch. Aboard the *Malygin*'s launch, with a dozen or so Soviet naval officers and meteorologists, was Nobile himself. Haunted for life by his failure with the *Italia*, he had offered his services to Eckener before the voyage, only to be turned down, since, as Eckener put it with typical asperity, "we had no intention of collecting experience on ice floes." Now the general approached the airship again in the High North, smiling and waving ("he would no doubt gladly have come aboard the zeppelin"), only to suffer a second rebuff. With Eckener watching the transaction "as if on hot coals," pleasantries were stifled, the mail was exchanged, and the airship ascended immediately, leaving Nobile and the "disappointed and somewhat amazed *Malygin* people beneath us."[56]

As icebreaker, bay, and gaping Russians receded, the airship set out north and eastward again to pursue more seriously its scientific agenda. Six hours later, the *Graf Zeppelin* attained its highest latitude, 81°9′ north. At this point, nine hundred kilometers from the North Pole, the airship passed Cape Fligely, the northernmost point of Franz Josef Land. Here, at the prescribed insurance limit, the nose of the zeppelin collided sharply with the invisible wall of financial security, recoiling "as if we were attached to a rubber string whose other end was held by earnest businessmen in Berlin."[57] Aerial photography on this stretch of the trip revealed a number of minor cartographic corrections to the outline set by Julius Payer's Austrian expedition in 1874 but, on the whole, Payer showed himself to have achieved a remarkably accurate map under the most trying conditions. More substantial gains were made as the airship continued eastward the next day. A number of previously uncharted islands were discovered east of Franz Josef Land, and the next morning the *Graf Zeppelin*'s scientists made their first sighting of "Northern Land." Now called by its Russian name of Severnaya Zemlya, this island, as it was believed to be, was charted for the first time in 1914 by a Russian icebreaker. Its extent, outline, and topography were completely unknown. The zeppelin now established that the island was in fact two islands and that the larger northern island was mountainous and glaciated. Eckener had brought along a packet of books, newspapers, strawberries, "and other goodies," sent by the wife of Professor Nikolai Urvantsev, to be delivered to the professor at his weather station on the northern coast of Severnaya Zemlya. Fog made the delivery impossible, even by parachute, to the showman Eckener's great regret.

Passing over the islands in a great zigzagging pattern at a variety of altitudes in order to give the greatest opportunity for the use of the photographic equipment, Molchanov's radio probe was also sent aloft with great success. After bringing the airship to a halt to prevent the air current passing over the exterior from driving the balloon into the propellers, the specially constructed chute was opened, and the balloon plunged downward, then shot aloft. The instrumentation functioned perfectly, transmitting its data at the prescribed three-minute intervals for the next fifty minutes. The zeppelin next passed southward over the Taimyr Peninsula, the eastern half of which was almost entirely uncharted, before beginning the swing back westward at about 74° north latitude. The afternoon and evening of 28 July were spent in passing westward over Taimyr, and at 2:00 A.M. on the twenty-ninth, the Graf Zeppelin crossed the northern cape of Novaya Zemlya. Though well known, these two islands had been little explored, and Samoilovich particularly was interested in photographing their glaciers, mountains, and other topographical features. With the fine weather holding, the airship reached Arkhangelsk on the evening of 29 July and at 3:00 A.M. on the thirtieth passed over the Commandant Aerodrome once more, a mere ninety hours after leaving on its polar tour. Thinking of fuel considerations and dreading the vodka binge being prepared by the Leningrad city authorities, Eckener returned directly to Tempelhof Field in Berlin.

The tired aeronauts of the Graf Zeppelin could congratulate themselves on a journey that was an unqualified scientific success, in some ways the most successful German polar undertaking of the entire era from 1870 to World War II. For a relatively small financial outlay and with no threat to the lives of any of the participants, the expedition reaped a bountiful scientific harvest. "The flight lasted 105 hours and 17 minutes, and in this time covered a stretch of 10,700 kilometers," Samoilovich noted. "The numbers speak for themselves and show what a superb means an airship of the type LZ 127 is, not only for scientific observation but for transportational goals in Arctic regions."[58] Penck noted in a private report to government officials that "the Eckener polar flight has produced unexpectedly rich geographic results . . . [with] a surprisingly informative picture of a previously completely unknown coast."[59] The general feeling was that the voyage laid to rest any doubts about the utility of airships in the Arctic created by the *Italia* disaster, which was now attributed to that airship's "much too weak" engines and "special circumstances."[60] German and foreign observers alike shared Lincoln Ellsworth's assessment that the journey had gone "like a dream."[61]

Despite such scientific gains, however, the *Graf Zeppelin*'s voyage in retrospect seems to have been a journey to nowhere, an inconsequential stunt more than the start of any new age. Dreams of a lucrative Soviet contract for German assistance in the construction of an airship progressed no further after Eckener's return from Leningrad. Diplomatically, the entire landscape in which the German Foreign Office operated was radically altered eighteen months later, when Adolf Hitler came to power. The "easterners" in the German diplomatic corps who had hoped to use the zeppelin to advance their vision of German-Russian solidarity would see their influence diminish rapidly. Even scientifically, the zeppelin's flight was a dead end, an exploratory freak, in the evolution of polar research. No lighter-than-air craft again ventured into the Arctic.

Eckener himself gave one of the most sober evaluations of the flight that recognized both its achievements as well as the limitations of the airship. "The journey in fact proved what a valuable and extraordinarily productive instrument the great, distance-conquering airship can be in the service of polar and general geographical exploration," he wrote. "It showed in what a comfortable fashion and with what rich results it can carry scientists over distant regions that remained until now practically closed." He recognized the unusually clement climatic conditions prevailing during the *Graf Zeppelin*'s flight, however, and doubted that airships could regularly be used to land on the polar ice cap. But, basking in the immediate afterglow of the mission's success, Eckener was ebullient about the future of polar airship exploration, a method that made the once-dangerous work almost too easy. "But why belittle that which effortlessly produces the fruits that until now were attained only by the heroic risk of life and limb? Technology could make human life so much easier. Yes, it could."

Tragic Greatness: The Martyrdom of Alfred Wegener

While the Arctic remodeling of the *Graf Zeppelin* entered its final stage during the last days of May 1931, grim news of the outcome of a different German foray into the Arctic reached Europe: Alfred Wegener had died on the Green-land ice cap. Wegener was a geologist of global distinction, and all Germany mourned the dead scholar. Popular magazines lamented "The Tragic Fate of Professor Wegener," while German science recognized in Wegener's death the passing of a titan. "Nansen and Amundsen, Scott and Shackleton are dead. Since its great 'Africans,' Germany has been able to show few names that could stand in their ranks," wrote Albrecht Haushofer. "Alfred Wegener was one of these few."[62] Wegener perished in the course of the German Greenland expedition, a daring and otherwise highly successful scientific undertaking. Like the zeppelin flight, the Wegener expedition set out in part to maintain German scientific prestige and to keep Germany in the front ranks of the exploring nations. The great irony of the German Greenland venture is that Wegener's death made a crucial contribution to the attainment of the nonscientific goals of the expedition.

When he died atop Greenland's ice sheet in the autumn of 1930, Wegener had for decades been a prominent member of the German scientific com-munity. Born in the bustling heart of Berlin in 1880, he came from a long line of scholarly Protestant pastors and priors. Wegener's father directed a middle-class orphanage, a religious refuge for the sons of clerics, doctors, bureaucrats, and businessmen. Neither Alfred, his older brother, Kurt, nor his older sister, Tony, possessed any affinity for the family's theological tradition. While Alfred and Kurt studied mathematics, astronomy, and the natural sciences, Tony became a painter. Completing his studies in 1904, Alfred the following year joined his brother as an assistant at the Royal Prussian Aeronautical Observatory (Königlich Preussisches Aeronautisches Observatorium). From the first, Wegener was drawn to research involving an element of physical risk. The observatory, located on the northern outskirts of Berlin in Tegel and later south of the city in Lindenberg, focused on the study of atmospheric physics and meteorology. In the course of pursuing these disciplines, the observatory developed into a center for lighter-than-air aviation. Wegener took to the field immediately. In 1905 he made his first balloon flight. Arthur Berson, his guide and companion, had established a world altitude record of over ten thousand meters in 1901 and would later become a founding member of Aeroarctic. A year after Alfred's first ascent, the daring Wegener brothers set a new ballooning endurance record, remaining aloft over fifty-two hours. Despite the most negligent preparation (Alfred and Kurt ascended clad in light summer jackets, provisioned with cold cuts, a pocketful of chocolate, and two bottles of water), the brash young scientists successfully demonstrated the value of the spirit-level clinometer for aerial navigation. Just as important, Kurt noted, was the fact that the two raw lab assistants were able to keep their balloon aloft "seventeen hours longer than France's most distinguished airshipman."[63]

Wegener's weather research during these flights provided an entrée to polar exploration. In 1906 he won the post of meteorologist on the Danish northeast Greenland expedition, led by Ludvig Mylius-Erichsen, a journalist who had guided the so-called Danish Literary Greenland Expedition, when artists and writers ventured out to record impressions of Greenland's nature and inhabitants.[64] The northeast Greenland expedition was sent to chart large areas of the island's unmapped upper reaches. Wegener, the only German participant, was working at the time with Wladimir Köppen, director of the Meteorological Department of the German Marine Observatory (Meteorologische Abteilung der deutschen Seewarte). Köppen would eventually become Wegener's father-in-law, and his influence seems to have helped the young adventurer. Mylius-Erichsen's *Danmark* expedition, as it became known, introduced Wegener to polar exploration and inspired an enduring fascination with Greenland's mysterious and wild interior. For two years, from June 1906 to August 1908, Wegener explored, mapped, and collected atmospheric readings on the eastern coast of Greenland. The expedition's twenty-seven members included a small contingent of artists and writers as well as some, like Peter Freuchen and the Danish captain, Johann Peter Koch, who would gain fame on later polar journeys. The wastes of northern Greenland killed Mylius-Erichsen, who died on a sledding journey, but they gave Wegener his polar apprenticeship, initiating the novice into the technique of Arctic icecraft. Athletic, ambitious, and diligent, Wegener was inexhaustible in his conduct of kite and cabled balloon ascents. He led prolonged sledding trips inland, making one of the expedition's most startling discoveries, the ice-free valley of plants, rocks, and fossils called "Queen-Luisa's Land." Along the way, he acquired a sense of mission, a feeling that his service with the Danes was preparing him for his life's work. "I have had a series of small but valuable experiences," Wegener wrote in his diary. "How one repairs a broken sled, the quickest way to unfoul the dog lines, how to prevent the dogs from tangling the lines after stops, and so on. The Arctic technical experience I am collecting alone is worth the two years."[65]

Wegener was dreaming of new polar adventures even before his return.

The humiliation of Drygalski's failure stung the patriotic scientist, and he longed to redeem German national honor in a successful thrust at the Poles. "It's strange how the thought of a South Polar expedition preoccupies me," he wrote. "Will it really prove impossible for Germans to carry out a successful polar expedition? I believe that the resolution to take part in this expedition will prove decisive for my entire life."[66] In the long run, Wegener's feeling that his destiny would take its course through Arctic research proved correct. For the time being, however, he returned to Germany in 1908, taking a post as lecturer in astronomy and meteorology at Marburg. During the next few years, Wegener's scientific creativity won enduring fame. Contemplating a bathymetric world map in 1910, he was struck by the congruency of the continental margins, which he found especially pronounced between Africa and South America. He eventually arrived at the conclusion that the slow movement of the continents over a malleable stratum of the earth's crust was the most reasonable explanation for the phenomenon. In 1912 he published two short articles arguing that the continents had gradually drifted apart. This was not the first exposition of such an idea (an American geologist named Frank Taylor had arrived independently at similar views a few years earlier), but Wegener's proposal was by far the most thoroughly elaborated, and it touched off a global scientific controversy. Though his conception of the precise mechanics of continental drift proved faulty, Wegener's work, published in 1915 in *Die Entstehung der Kontinente und Ozeane* (*The Origin of Continents and Oceans*), laid the foundations for modern plate tectonic theories.[67]

The sleepy, picturesque university town of Marburg soon proved too confining for Wegener's restless energy. He had already discussed another Greenland expedition with Koch, and in June 1912 the two set out to attempt what had never been done: an overwintering on the Greenland ice cap, followed by a crossing of the island at its broadest point. Relying upon Icelandic ponies rather than dogsleds, the four-man expedition team found abundant danger and hardship. They were nearly wiped out by calving glaciers while attempting to ascend the fringe of the inland ice cap, temperatures plummeted to an incredible -50°C, Koch fractured a leg falling into a glacial crevasse, and the unanticipated intensity of the blistering, high-altitude Arctic sun "burned the skin from our faces" during the march across the island. Every horse perished. The last, Grauni, a pet and mascot of the small band, was shot after being hauled on a sled for miles.[68] Here, too, however, Wegener acquired invaluable technical expertise in Arctic survival and transport, including ice climbing, ice skiing, and the use of sail sleds atop the windswept ice cap. The trip was a milestone in Arctic travel, and an older Wegener recalled it as his "most successful and fortunate undertaking."[69]

Returning as Europe stumbled into war, Wegener, a reserve lieutenant, found himself called up into the III. Garde Grenadier Regiments Königen Elisabeth (Queen Elizabeth grenadier guards). The Western Front proved even more perilous to the young explorer than had the Arctic wilderness. He was shot twice during the German advance into Belgium, first through the arm and a few weeks later through the neck. Thereafter deemed unfit for active duty, he served the remainder of the war in the field meteorological service. With the armistice, Wegener, now approaching forty, found professional success. In 1919 he took over Köppen's position at the German Marine Observatory and in 1924 was appointed professor for meteorology and geophysics at Graz in Austria. Though he had planned a third Greenland trip with his old friend Koch, the latter's health deteriorated steadily until his death in 1928. Wegener settled into a staid cycle of teaching and research, prolific scientific publishing, weekend trips into the mountains, and winter skiing. The future seemed to hold little more than productive but uneventful academic living. "In lovely Graz," recalled his wife, Else, "we were very close to sinking into bourgeois complacency."[70]

In the spring of 1928, however, several forces came together to propel Wegener once more into the Arctic. He himself had never entirely abandoned the notion of returning to the field, hoping to measure the depth of the Greenland ice sheet. Although these dreams had taken a blow with the infirmity and eventual death of Koch, his intended comrade, the longing to see Greenland once more still slumbered within Wegener. It was roused in January 1928 by a proposal from Johannes Georgi, a former student and subordinate of Wegener's at the marine observatory. Georgi had recently returned from a state-sponsored project in Iceland, where he conducted some of the first research on the wind currents known as jet streams. He hoped to pursue related work on the Greenland ice cap. Submitting his plan to Wegener, who was generally regarded as "the man among all living Germans who had the most extensive polar experience," Georgi found his old mentor wistfully toying with the idea of going back to Greenland. "This is, to be sure, an old plan of Freuchen, Koch, and myself. If the war hadn't come along, the plan would probably already have been carried out. In the meantime, though, Freuchen has lost a leg, Koch is too old and in the hospital, and I have lost a little something and am no longer a youngster."[71]

Although Georgi's scheme was not quite sufficient to lure Wegener from his academic idyll, scientific and political authorities of greater persuasive power began about the same time to rekindle Wegener's Greenland ambitions. In May 1928 he received a visit from Wilhelm Meinardus, a distinguished meteorologist a generation older than Wegener who had worked before the war in Spitsbergen and later edited the results of the Filchner expedition. Meinardus proposed a new journey. A geophysicist named Emil Wiechert, working at the Göttingen Geophysical Institute (Institut für Geophysik), had devised a new technique for the measurement of ice depth. An artificial earthquake could be created by detonating explosive charges buried in the ice. The resultant vibrations could be recorded by distant seismographs. Measurements of the time that elapsed between detonation and the reflection of the seismic shock from the ground beneath the ice could accurately determine the ice cap's depth. Recent tests in the Austrian Alps had shown the method to be successful. Would Wegener be interested in leading a small summer expedition to apply the same techniques for the first time in the interior of Greenland?

The proposal was attractive. Meinardus, an important figure in the German scientific community, already had financial backing: Schmidt-Ott had committed the emergency coalition to funding the trip. Wegener at the time was a director of the Austrian section of Aeroarctic and was busy preparing a paper for presentation in Leningrad during the coming June. Inspired by Meinardus, however, and by the prospect of ample funding, he composed instead a memorandum for a far more elaborate and systematic Greenland undertaking that was presented to, and approved by, the emergency coalition during the summer of 1928.

Schmidt-Ott assembled a Greenland commission of scientists and bureaucrats, rallying Germany's polar subculture to the cause of a Wegener-led expedition. In composition and aims, the commission demonstrated the important links between the prewar and postwar German polar scientific communities. Schmidt-Ott himself, nearly seventy years old, had been an outspoken supporter of Drygalski and Filchner. His commission united men with a broad range of polar expertise, including Hugo Hergesell, the veteran of zeppelin research in Spitsbergen, Drygalski, Meinardus, and the ubiquitous Penck, among others. Albert Defant, head of the Berlin Institute for Oceanography, and Admiral Dominick, director of the German

Marine Observatory, were also active members of the commission, as were representatives of the German navy, the Transport Ministry, the Ministry of the Interior, and the Foreign Office. A decade after the World War, academia and government were united again in a German polar endeavor.[72]

Wegener presented an audacious scheme to the commission. Using prefabricated housing, three research stations would be erected at intervals along the seventy-first degree of latitude, like beads on a string stretched across the very waist of the great island. The primary station would be located on the western rim of the ice sheet. Meteorological and geological data would be collected here simultaneously with stations operating at the eastern edge of the ice and, in the expedition's boldest stroke, at Ice Central, a station to be located hundreds of meters above sea level, four hundred kilometers from each coastal station, in the frozen heart of the inland ice. Comparative readings for an entire year, for a complete cross-section of the island, would thus be obtained for the first time. The most daunting obstacle facing the expedition would be to move 120 tons of equipment—provisions, fuel, scientific instruments, building materials—across the bare Greenland coastal strip and up the edge of the ice cap to altitudes of nearly three thousand meters. A mission on such a grand scale would not be cheap, Wegener warned, but Schmidt-Ott and the German government were open-handed, promising up to 150,000 marks for the expedition and eventually covering costs considerably in excess of this amount.[73] This was an extraordinary commitment. The winter of 1929–30, in the aftermath of the global economic crisis initiated in October on the New York Stock Exchange, was a moment of unparalleled financial need for the Weimar government. Despite their desperate straits, however, scientific ideals, nationalism, and cultural values convinced Weimar officials to back the Greenland expedition. The generosity toward Wegener contrasts strangely with the niggardly reluctance to aid the Eckener flight, perhaps due to Eckener's dubious status as a scientist and his evident ability to obtain funds from other sources.

Scientifically, Wegener's plan promised valuable advances in a number of fields. The great blanket of ice covering Greenland was still a mystery. It was avoided by the natives of the island, to whom it seemed the home of evil spirits, and was known only in small fragments to European scientists and explorers. As a lingering remnant of the last ice age, the ice cap is a unique environment that, at over 1.5 million square kilometers, is several times the size of any European state west of Russia. Unlike the Antarctic ice cap, most of the ice cap in Greenland does not reach the sea, preventing scientists from studying its edge. Set in a ring of coastal mountains, the ice cap rises to around three thousand meters, and, where it does meet the sea, it discharges a steady stream of icebergs into Atlantic shipping lanes. Near Jacobshavn on the southwestern coast lies the most fertile glacier of the Northern Hemisphere, calving a new berg on average every five minutes and sending out annually 20.8 cubic kilometers of ice. European meteorologists were already realizing that the intense cold of the ice cap, where temperatures of -70°C have been recorded, helped generate the high and low pressure cycles that created their weather fronts.

The Greenland commission found these to be persuasive scientific grounds for the Wegener trip. In a lengthy presentation to the commission in November 1929, Meinardus tempted his colleagues with the promise of the journey. "Greenland's inland ice is a great ice reservoir that fills the polar currents with ice masses," he noted. Gravitational and magnetic readings, coupled with measurements of ice depth, would provide insight into the elasticity of the earth's crust, valuable not least for what it might reveal about Wegener's theory of continental drift. Oceanographers would benefit from greater knowledge of how Greenlandic cold currents influenced "the varying nutritional content of the polar currents." Greenland offered the geologist "a classic example of the formation, maintenance, and movement of a continental ice mass." Meteorology, above all, would benefit, since "the high pressure region over the inland ice is the most important action center of the atmosphere in the northern hemisphere," and research here would "determine the existence or nonexistence of the 'glacial anticyclone.'"[74] In speaking to the commission, of course, Meinardus was preaching to the choir, but for good measure he noted a range of economic benefits. A year-long observation of the expansion and contraction of the ice cap would provide new insights "in which the enterprise of the northern seas (fisheries, whaling, etc.) is particularly interested." Climatic research promised valuable results for "transatlantic air travel, whose northern line on its shortest route from Europe to North America goes directly over the Greenland inland ice." More timely iceberg alerts for North Atlantic shipping might also arise from such an expedition, as would a better understanding of the geophysics of Germany itself, "since the soil of North Germany is the ground moraine of a great inland ice . . . The best way to an understanding of our native soil is to go where an inland ice is still available and to study it there."[75]

The commission was also acutely sensitive to the matter of German scientific prestige. As Meinardus pointed out, Germany had achieved a great breakthrough with the seismic reflective method of depth measurement, but there was no guarantee its lead would last.

> The question of ice thickness measurement is also being tackled with great energy by the Americans. Last year, before his departure to the Antarctic, where he is now preparing new flights, the American aviator Byrd asked in Göttingen if he could get the instruments that Wiechert has invented for this. His wish could not be fulfilled, because only *one* instrument has been, and is, constructed. German science, therefore, disposes today of a monopoly on the measurement of ice depth, but it is very likely that this will be lost if the apparatus is not soon employed on the inland ice region.[76]

Wegener, too, wanted to display German technological achievement. When the question of waiting for a more favorable financial moment was broached in the winter of 1929, Wegener argued passionately against delay, pointing out that Germany had a chance to take the lead in the use of propeller-driven sleds, "a completely different technical aid to the conquest of distance."[77]

> Delay creates the danger that foreigners will precede us in the use of ice depth measurements on the inland ice, and that the new insights that are to be anticipated precisely in the first application of this new research method will be lost to German research. Likewise, it would naturally be regrettable if by postponement the first attempt to use propeller sleds on the inland ice came from another venue, and German technology would suffer a loss of prestige if we are not first to have our cargo driven over the inland ice by Siemens motors.[78]

Privately, Wegener was exasperated with questions about the value of the mission. "I already hear, 'what does Greenland matter to Germans?'" he wrote to Schmidt-Ott. "I am of the opinion in regard to the question if Germany should participate in the noble competition of the nations or stand aside that the public educational side of polar research should be considered. We give out lots of money for sport, and rightly so, I believe. But isn't the crossing of unexplored territory more than an athletic victory?"[79] For Schmidt-Ott too the expedition was vital, to ensure that "Germany should not be shut out of the international competition of the nations in polar exploration."[80]

Wegener's age and physical condition also lent urgency to the timing of the mission. The great man would turn fifty in the course of the expedition, an advanced age for pioneering Arctic work. Nansen was in his twenties when he first crossed the inland ice, and neither Drygalski, Filchner, Shackleton, nor Amundsen had yet reached forty when they made their greatest polar journeys. Wegener noted his declining physical powers to Georgi, seemingly in jest, but when the question of postponing the expedition was raised before the commission, he faced the issue of age with his typical candor. "Through my increasing age, I am becoming less and less capable . . . It is easily possible that in two years I will not feel able to take on the leadership of this huge task with full responsibility."[81] Penck, Schmidt-Ott, and others agreed that the expedition had to be undertaken soon so that Wegener's hard-won Arctic wisdom would not be lost. "For this expedition we have in the person of the applicant an excellently suited man at our disposal who by his participation in several Arctic projects offers the best guarantee for a happy completion of the undertaking," Penck argued. "We now still have the opportunity to use the experiences united in him and to pass them on to the next scientific generation, which will be lost in the postponement of the expedition even for only a year or two."[82]

These arguments carried the day, and preparations went forward for launching the main expedition in the spring of 1930. The combination of motives that sent Wegener out to his eventual death—his ambition for and fascination with Greenland, the lure of scientific and economic gain, German national prestige—suggests that the revival of German polar exploration in the 1920s was an expression of a deeply held and widely shared nationalist view of the cultural activity of scientific research. Just as when, decades earlier, Germans first began to reach out to the Arctic in the days of Koldewey, the deliberations of the Greenland commission were permeated by a sense that German national pride demanded continued participation in the great Western cultural work of opening the polar world. To Schmidt-Ott and the commission, German absence from the polar "competition"—a word they use on a number of occasions—meant surrendering the nation's place among the great peoples.

In April 1929 Wegener and the three men who would be his closest associates on the expedition, Georgi, Fritz Loewe, and Ernst Sorge, reconnoitered the western coast of Greenland. Loewe and Sorge, both in their early thirties, were meteorologists whom Wegener had recruited to his plan during the summer of 1928.[83] All four men came from the same scientific milieu. Loewe, a native Berliner like Wegener, had studied in Switzerland and was working in Wegener's former position at the Prussian Aeronautical Observatory when invited to make the Greenland trip. Sorge studied at the University of Berlin and did graduate work under Albrecht Penck. In Greenland the team prospected sites where the main expedition could ascend the inland ice the following year. After cruising the island's western coastal waters and mounting two sledding trips, Wegener resolved to scale the ice cliffs by way of the Kamarujuk glacier. This site would provide a sheltered landing site at Kamarujuk Bay, in the district of Umanak, at very nearly the chosen latitude of 71° north. The men also practiced ice climbing and tested the use of black flags, set at intervals of five hundred meters, to mark easily followed routes on the icecap.[84]

Wegener spent the winter and spring of 1929–30 in the usual preexpedition frenzy. For a time, his life was a dizzying carousel of travel between Berlin, Copenhagen, Munich, and Graz, where, amazingly, he contrived to maintain his normal schedule of lectures while directing preparations. Permission had to be obtained from Danish authorities for the importation of fuel and other prohibited items into their Greenland possession, though this was little more than a formality, since Wegener's relations with the Danes had been excellent from the time of his prewar expeditions. He traveled to Finland, where the two 112-horsepower propeller sleds for which he had such great hopes were being designed by and constructed at the Finnish National Aircraft Factory in Helsinki. He promoted the cause, presenting slide shows on his 1929 expedition. And he took care of business. In Berlin he once more urged the economic benefits of his plan to the financial backers of the emergency coalition. This violated his deeply held beliefs: "for the researcher the discovery of the environment with its laws must be the Holy of Holies to which he devotes his existence . . . If he squints about for practical uses, he misses this Holy of Holies and ceases to be a scientist."[85] Still, he bent the knee before Mammon and was rewarded with an additional 300,000 marks.

Photographs of Wegener from these days show a man in youthful middle age, usually with a cigar or pipe. His mouth and eyes seem always on the verge of a wry smile, but his visage conveys an overall impression of resolve, composure, and calm. Though outwardly unruffled, he must have spent some anxious nights. Expenses, for example, were mounting steadily. The cost for scientific and photographic instruments ran to 50,000 marks, provisions were more than 37,000 marks, the two propeller sleds cost a combined 30,000 marks, the prefabricated housing and feed for the horses and dogs came to around 25,000 marks each, and on it went.[86] Georgi arranged extremely elaborate photographic preparations, including special microphotographic apparatus for the study of ice crystals, devices to capture the northern lights, cameras to record cloud formations of meteorological significance, special lighting equipment, and more.[87]

Wegener, Loewe, and Georgi tried taking a page from Hugo Eckener's book, seeking funds by peddling their story to the media. German publishers, still reeling from the shock waves of the stock market crash, were not in a mood to take risks. "The awful thing on such research trips is that there is never anyone around who understands how to photograph with a proper journalistic eye," the Ullstein press told Loewe. "It's always the same boring pictures of dogs running around on the snow, icebergs, and men standing in front of tents. If we could somehow get a guarantee that good picture material in our sense was to be had—like on the Byrd expedition, in which sixteen of the best American press photographers participated—we would probably have an interest."[88] Other publishers turned down queries with similar remarks.

In the spring of 1930 Wegener completed preparations for an April departure. Working with the commission, he selected a scientific complement of eighteen. His choices reflected the expedition's sober scientific devotion. No soldiers, sailors, journalists, or adventurers would take part. Although Georgi hoped to film parts of the expedition, there was no hint of the showmanship that attended Eckener's zeppelin stunt. Nor was Wegener, a tolerant and cosmopolitan man, distracted by efforts to make some "internationalist" political gesture. All the members of the team were German. All were trained scientists and technicians. Most held or were close to attaining doctorates in meteorology and geophysics, while the remainder were engineers and mechanics.[89] Though Sorge, Georgi, and Loewe had some experience in Iceland and in their brief scouting jaunt to Greenland, the expedition members apart from Wegener were polar neophytes in the sense that they had never had to deal with the Arctic winter. The personnel of the western and central stations would proceed together to Umanak, while the three-man team for the eastern coast, under the leadership of Walther Kopp of the Prussian Aeronautical Observatory, would travel independently to their station. On 1 April Wegener and his companions set out from Copenhagen aboard the *Disko*, a vessel of the Royal Greenlandic Company. A week later they stopped in Iceland to take on ponies and three Icelandic assistants, traveling then through the Davis Strait to the port of Holstenborg in southwestern Greenland, arriving on 19 April. Here the men, animals, and goods of the expedition were transferred to the *Gustav Holm*, a vessel specially designed to forge through drifting ice. On 4 May Wegener and his companions reached Umanak, eager to tackle the task of moving onto the Kamarujuk glacier.

At Umanak the expedition encountered its first and most important setback, one that in retrospect may be seen as Wegener's initial step on the path to his doom seven months later. The Kamarujuk fjord was filled with ice. After being dropped by the *Gustav Holm*, the smaller boat with which the bulk of the expedition's equipment was to be brought up the fjord was unable to penetrate the dense pack choking the route. Wegener and his men could do little more than wait for the ice to break up. A case of dynamite was detonated in small parcels set at five-meter intervals to blast open a route, but to no avail. For nearly six weeks they waited, until mid-June. These were precious summer days, every hour of which would be needed to transport goods up the inland ice and to build the essential station houses in time to meet the arrival of Greenland's brutal winter. Each day's passing lessened their chances of success.

Wegener's reports back to the Greenland commission are filled with reassuring accounts of his team's activity in the face of the setback (the erection of a radio station, some gravitational measurements, astronomical and cartographic work), but his worry and frustration show through. "Who wishes to practice patience goes into polar ice," he wrote. "It grows cold again, eight days pass, fourteen days pass, and the ice is still firm. The complete indifference with which nature ignores our accomplishments threatens to drive us crazy."[90] Privately, his assessment of the delay was somber. "The program of our expedition is gradually becoming seriously endangered by the stubbornness of the ice," he wrote in his diary. "What we could do here is too pitifully little, and we're too few as well. And time is running out—it's already the middle of June! The affair is developing catastrophically. In this perhaps most important question of fortune, we are pursued by ill chance."[91]

Despite this frustration, the spirits of the expedition team remained high, thanks in large part to Wegener's leadership skills. From his first days in the Arctic, he had attracted the notice of those around him. Remembered by his comrades on the *Danmark* expedition of 1906 as "a quiet man with the most charming smile on his face," he had matured into an experienced Arctic leader who inspired his men by his selfless work ethic and scientific idealism.[92] His quiet, collegial approach to command and his unquestioned personal courage produced a passionate loyalty in his subordinates. "And like me, Wegener's personality attracted all my comrades as well," Georgi wrote in his memoir of the expedition. "It produced our steadfast admiration, which through his unprecedented confidence and his comradely demeanor soon evolved into the strongest feeling that bonds men to one another. It was impossible to escape the charm of his direct, open, natural personality."[93]

After thirty-eight days of frustration, the ice finally opened on 17 June, and the expedition began the backbreaking work of bringing men, equipment, and provisions hundreds of meters up the glacier and onto the inland ice. The transport onto the ice and to Ice Central was the greatest technical obstacle facing the expedition and constituted a logistical challenge that dwarfed anything attempted in polar regions before. Over ninety metric tons of goods had to be taken up the Kamarujuk glacier and 10 kilometers into the ice to an elevation of over 900 meters, where the western station, Scheideck, would be erected in the vicinity of a prominent nunatak. Roughly ten metric tons more would be taken from Scheideck to Ice Central, 400 kilometers farther inland and 2,100 meters higher. Here, Wegener hoped, the propeller sleds would justify their high cost by easing the expedition's daunting transport mission across the ice cap. Wegener spent a week at this time visiting the local villages, buying up sleds, dogs, and foodstuffs— macaroni, smoked bacon, conserves, and dried apples and apricots. All of it, due to the general poverty of the region, he found "expensive and difficult to procure," unsurprising in light of the fact that most of what he purchased came from the stored reserves of the locals.[94]

The work of moving supplies up the fractured and treacherous rim of the glacier began on 22 June. Wegener recruited thirteen Greenlanders, swelling his work force to thirty-three, and the twenty-five hundred cases of goods were gradually taken up in three stages, with Loewe, Sorge, and Georgi leading the final stage. Wegener described the scene: "The visitor can already see at a distance the small tent village, with the German flag fluttering above. Behind that, on the glacier itself, a distant bright spot can be seen, higher up a second, and at the top a third. Those are the transfer sites, where the red and brown crates are lying."[95] The work was done mostly at night, since the sun over the ice was too hot for men and animals in daytime. "We had never dreamed in Europe that we could sweat so much in Greenland," recalled Georg Lissey, one of the expedition's technicians. "To such polar novices, it didn't seem very expedition-like."[96] All the expedition's members became stevedores and teamsters for weeks, using the ponies to help muscle crates through a steady station-to-station relay on the route to the glacier's top. Wegener was particularly pleased with the work of the Greenlanders. "All thirteen worked the whole day without a break, except for the midday pause, and they worked hard. It was a true joy to see. European workers would not have done so much; they would have moved more slowly."[97] The work was hazardous as well as strenuous. Horses, men, and dogs all fell into glacial crevasses, and two of the dogs died of heart failure.

Bulky equipment, such as the awkward, automobile-sized propeller sleds and their engines, proved especially difficult to move. The men referred to the sleds as "the heavyweights" and had to rely on cables and laboriously anchored winches to haul the machines nine hundred meters upward, sometimes over vertical ice walls. Wegener described the procedure for his backers in Berlin. "Slower than a snail, the great sled begins to press its front against the wall and to creep upward. The four broad but short runners, each independently suspended, snuggle themselves into all the irregularities of the ground with almost exaggerated precision, and the whole thing looks as if a giant salamander, slowly, very slowly, were climbing up the glassy mountain. With fascinating poise, the monster gains meter by meter, and before one realizes it, the thing has reached its new position . . . a mere 50 meters higher."[98] In his diary, however, he vented his smoldering impatience at the pace. "Our organization works with peculiar lack of economy! Naturally, it's the work with the propeller sleds that sabotages the order of the labor again and again, because they suddenly need more people. It's a misery."[99]

Already, as the first crates of tents, gasoline, food, and instruments reached their depot at the Scheideck station, preparations were made to continue inland to Ice Central. There was no time to be lost. Meteorological readings from Scheideck, the most western station, were under way by late June, and it was known that the team at East Station on Scoresby Sound would be starting at any time (Wegener in fact received news that they began at the start of August). The sooner the crucial central station was up and running, the sooner a complete set of data for an entire year could be collected. The summer days on the ice cap, furthermore, had to be exploited to their fullest before autumn's darkness, frigid temperatures, and heavy new snowfalls made sledding difficult and, eventually, impossible.

Accordingly, the first of four sledding parties to Ice Central set out on 15 July. Georgi led Loewe, another German, and ten Greenlanders with a dozen dogsleds. This pioneering group blazed a well-marked trail for subsequent teams to follow. The team erected snow pyramids topped with directional indicators every five kilometers. Between these, at half-kilometer intervals, the sledding party planted the black pennants tested the year before. Along the way, at kilometers 25 and 200, way stations were established as supply dumps and to ease some of the burden on tired sled dogs. Loewe, as prearranged, turned back at kilometer 200, while Georgi and his comrades reached their goal of kilometer 400 on 30 July. Georgi began to collect meteorological readings, living for the time being in tents. On 2 August he began digging into the firn, or layer of perpetual snow, to construct a shelter to house scientific instruments and in which to inflate balloons with the hydrogen gas that was produced onsite. The geophysicist Karl Weiken led the return trip, and his Greenlandic comrades were received as heroes, the first of their people to go so far into the inland ice.

Wegener did not celebrate. The first provisioning trip took most of a month to get to and from Ice Central at a time when the weather was at its most favorable. The sleds had conveyed only 769 kilos of supplies, well short of a ton, and Wegener reckoned that at least ten tons would be needed to ensure the operation of Ice Central through the winter. It would be difficult, perhaps impossible, to ferry sufficient provisions to the station before winter curtailed further sledding. With a sense of mounting desperation, the other scientists threw themselves into an all-out effort to provision Ice Central. On 6 August Loewe set out with another ton of supplies, which his team carried across the four hundred kilometers in a record twelve days, setting out for the return trip on the very day of their arrival. Another ten-man team led by Sorge made it to Ice Central at the start of September with 1.3 metric tons of supplies. Still, this was far short of what was needed. The materials for the station house had not yet been transported, and though Wegener feared privately for the mission's success, publicly he remained undaunted. He encouraged Georgi, now living as a hermit at Ice Central, not to panic. The motor sleds were on their slow but persistent way up to the Scheideck station, "and then it won't be long until they come."[100] With good reason, however, he harbored private reservations about the untried technology. "I am still worried," he wrote. "August will bring the decisive battle, and I have to confess that I view the prospect with concern in regard to the central firn station."[101]

The great day came at the end of August. Finally arrived at Scheideck, the propeller sleds were stocked with half a ton of supplies and tested for the first time. Wegener was ecstatic, convinced that he was witness to the dawn of a new age. "Now the dream has become reality. I have traveled over the inland ice sitting comfortably in an enclosed cabin, smoking my pipe. The whole thing is an unheard-of luxury and strikes me as completely unreal . . . I have a strong feeling that we stand before a new epoch of polar exploration that will be characterized, now that it has worked, by the application of new technological means in a rational manner."[102]

Wegener's euphoria was short-lived, however. The two sleds, Polar Bear and Snow Sparrow, soon proved to be extremely limited in their capabilities. The motors were too weak, failing to generate sufficient thrust on inclined terrain. The broad runners froze into the surface whenever the sleds came to a halt. The vehicles progressed much more slowly than Wegener had hoped and were very difficult to control. A week after the first tests, Wegener's ardor had cooled. "On the smooth ice, the drivers seemed to lose control over the sleds, which skidded left and right and were not to be stopped . . . The crevices were snowed over, the snow was lower than the surface of the ice. It was impossible to turn about, since the sleds would have slid into them sideways. Only one thing to do: step on the gas! It went well, but it was a dangerous affair."[103]

Wegener's levity could not disguise the peril in which Georgi and Sorge now found themselves at Ice Central. Ferrying most of the freight by motor sled was a crucial component of the expedition plan. The frustrating delays—waiting for the ice to melt in the fjord, then the excruciatingly slow progress of the sleds up the glacier so that they were only ready much later than anticipated—sabotaged the schedule. The sleds were put to work in September moving goods steadily closer to Ice Central, but strong prevailing head winds with new snow, dry and fine as grains of sand and falling at times to depths of thirty centimeters, slowed their advance. They could get the freight no farther than the depot at kilometer 200. "The use of the propeller sleds is coming to naught," Wegener wrote his wife on 11 September. "They are only comparable in speed with automobiles, not with aircraft. Once one has accepted that fact, they are very useful, and our movement of freight over the ice until now (2,400 kilos were taken to the depot at kilometer 90 in a couple of days) surpasses what has been done before on the inland ice." For Wegener, the situation was a "catastrophe," which admitted of only one, very hazardous solution: "There will be a great shortfall for the central firn station, and we must make yet a fourth dogsled trip, and it must be larger than any of the others."[104]

Wegener had realized by 6 September that a fourth sled trip was needed. Conditions at Ice Central seemed desperate. Giving up hope for receiving the station house materials, Georgi and Sorge had gone to earth, digging out tunnels and rooms in the firn. This was an entirely feasible alternative (Nansen survived a winter on Franz Josef Land essentially buried in the snow, though he had local sources of nourishment denied the inhabitants of Ice Central), but it depended on food and heating fuel, both of which were scarce, particularly the latter. Eventually reaching down eighteen meters, the station gave its inhabitants the feeling of being "entombed in a crypt. The last remnants of the day's light shimmered through from above, magically blue."[105] The surreal beauty of their icy burrow, however, could not hide the fact that supply shortfalls made work conditions extremely difficult. "The overwintering is far more primitive, hence physically and spiritually far more wearing, than we had thought and than is usually the case in overwinterings," Georgi wrote, noting that "the shortage of petroleum forces us to work in room temperatures of -10°C or to vegetate in our sleeping bags and naturally impedes our work uncommonly."[106]

Frustration and anxiety began to wear on Wegener's psyche. He dreamed of Adriatic vacations and confessed to his brother that "even paradise, after a time, loses its ability to make one happy." Determined to overcome the crisis at Ice Central, however, he planned to lead a massive relief effort in person. "The whole thing is a serious catastrophe, and it does no good to try to hide the fact," he wrote. "It is now a matter of survival." The plan to bring the housing materials was dropped, and only food, fuel, and vital scientific equipment would be delivered. Wegener, Loewe, and the thirteen Greenlanders would convoy fifteen dogsleds across the ice. With luck, Wegener thought the team could make the trip to Ice Central and back in thirty days. Mushing dogs over the inland ice in October, when the Arctic autumn can turn savage in a matter of moments, was extremely risky, and Wegener's integrity would permit no one else to lead the venture. "I have resolved to participate in this sled journey in Weiken's place, because I would very much like to get to kilometer 400 yet before the winter sets in," he wrote his wife. "Besides, I also feel that my presence will exert a moral pressure on the Greenlanders to stick it out and not to turn back because it is too cold."[107]

On the morning of 21 September, the very start of the northern autumn, Wegener and his team set out. Just as they departed, the third provisioning party arrived back from Ice Central. They brought a letter from Georgi, declaring that he and Sorge did not believe they could survive the winter and that, should no further provisioning with petroleum and instruments be forthcoming, they would depart the station on 20 October on foot for the coast. To an experienced Arctic hand like Wegener, the letter was a declaration of intent to commit suicide. An attempt to pull sleds for four hundred kilometers over the Greenland ice cap in late October, as Kurt Wegener put it later, could result only in "the destruction of Georgi and Sorge."[108] Though coming after Wegener had already decided to sled to Ice Central, the letter must have strengthened his resolve to make it through to the beleaguered team before their October deadline, whatever the cost might be.[109]

Just three days of sledding showed that Wegener had been grossly overoptimistic. With the benefit of excellent weather, the team made only fifty kilometers of progress, averaging little more than sixteen kilometers per day. They had to average nearly twenty-seven kilometers per day to complete the round trip in the hoped-for thirty days. Heavy snow was encountered from 27 September on, slowing progress even more, and temperatures plunged to -27°C. On this day, too, the team passed the Snow Sparrow, a victim of mechanical breakdown, abandoned by its crew. The sight did not raise spirits.

The question of the team's morale was an important one, because the Greenlanders seemed to be losing heart. Though Wegener wrote his wife on 25 September that "it has been very warm . . . so our Greenlanders have more courage," in fact, Wegener's local recruits had already begun to defect.[110] One departed on the second day out, at kilometer 40, after his sled was damaged, returning with the Polar Bear, which was on its way back from a run to one of the depots. Three days after Wegener wrote to his wife of his confidence in the Greenlanders, the remainder declared that they were going to turn back. Wegener persuaded four to push on, bribing them with a higher rate of pay for the balance of the trip, but the situation was bad. "It was hard to get the other four to stay with us," he wrote. "And whether they will stick it out to kilometer 400 remains to be seen. Today it's -28°C with scouring snow and a head wind . . . charming conditions."[III]

Conditions in fact only worsened. Though temperatures varied, they were increasingly cold and would soon become bitterly so. Worse was the soft, deep, new snow the team encountered on the route that swallowed up the sleds and left the dogs floundering. By 7 October the last Greenlanders had had enough and turned back. One alone, Rasmus Villumsen, determined to press on with Wegener and Loewe. By this time, the team had sledded only to kilometer 160 and on many days made no more than five kilometers of progress. Temperatures sank to -40°C, and the small band wasted entire days huddled in their tents, enduring the frigid winds. Reaching the depot at kilometer 200, halfway to their destination, the three men took an entire day to adjust the registering instruments and load the deposited kerosene and gasoline.

This was on 13 October, and Wegener now clearly realized there was no hope of reaching Ice Central before the twentieth, the date Georgi had set as his team's deadline for resupply. Accordingly, Wegener, Villumsen, and Loewe agreed to go only as far as kilometer 230, drop there what supplies they could to aid the returning team from Ice Central, and then march back westward themselves. This resolution was abandoned, however, after a spell of relatively favorable weather that permitted the three to exceed their travel expectations and make about fifteen kilometers per day. Once they continued past kilometer 250 or so, however, the option of returning disappeared. As the members of the relief party diminished, it became necessary to lay aside more and more of the supplies intended for the station, and by kilometer 300 the "rescuers" were transporting to Ice Central little more than themselves and forty liters of kerosene. They were past the point of no return, increasingly driven by their own need. With insufficient supplies to risk a return trip, they were in effect fleeing forward to what shelter and food Ice Central might provide. With temperatures hitting -50°C, the toes on both Loewe's feet began to show signs of frostbite.

On the morning of 30 October the team ditched even the last of the kerosene. Feeling their way forward through dense fog at temperatures of -52°C, they covered the last few kilometers and stumbled into the station, numb and empty-handed, just before noon. Here they were shocked to find a situation considerably less urgent than they had anticipated. In early October, long after sending their letter to Wegener, the two men in Ice Central began a series of expansions and improvements. Using planks from provision crates and the tent in which they had originally camped upon the ice, they insulated parts of their cavern. They added new rooms and passages and began to realize that, with roughly nineteen months' worth of stored provisions, they might make it through the winter after all. Showing a good deal of resourcefulness, they used blocks of excavated snow and ice to construct an outdoor scientific station, and Sorge devised a special indicator to warn if the firn over the rooms sank to the point where it might threaten collapse. When no relief party had arrived a week after their 20 October deadline, they decided to stick it out until spring. The ice burrow into which Wegener, Loewe, and Villumsen crept on 30 October was not very comfortable, but it was undoubtedly bearable for a few months at least. Thanks to blowing snow building up at the entrance, the men eventually had to descend into their home through a vertical shaft a few meters long. Deep in their chilly dugout, they busied themselves with work and with diversion, celebrating Sundays and holidays, engaging in long talks, playing games, and even creating a handwritten newspaper, "The Inland Ice: Newsletter for Greenland Travelers," complete with classifieds.[112]

"Yesterday another very lovely Sunday," Georgi recorded later in a diary entry. "Sorge made coffee and observations in the morning; we conversed for hours over philosophical questions on Schopenhauer. Afternoon evaluated readings, a very fine dinner (a sort of rissole), and evening chocolate."[113] The newly arrived Loewe had a difficult time. His toes had to be amputated, and here another oversight showed itself—Ice Central was ill prepared for emergencies. "No medical expertise, no book with directions for the problem, no surgeon, instruments, anesthetic, a minimum of bandages and disinfectant—it was a desperate situation."[114] Ultimately, the frozen digits were removed with metal shears and a pocketknife.

While Loewe obviously had no choice but to remain at Ice Central, Wegener realized that he and Villumsen had no choice but to leave, and soon. Where three men might eke out the provisions at the station, five men might starve. His place as expedition leader, furthermore, demanded that he return to the primary station near the west coast. And, far from being exhausted, Wegener claimed to feel invigorated by the nearly six weeks of struggle it took to get to kilometer 400. Accordingly, the day after arriving, on Wegener's fiftieth birthday, he and Villumsen departed Ice Central. With two dogsleds they took food and a can of fuel. Neither man was seen alive again. Their prospects were bleak from the start, as Wegener must have realized. At this late season, they had only a few hours of travel time each day. The approaching Arctic winter sharply reduced daylight, and the darkness, by obscuring the flags marking the trail, would have made it impossible to travel for all but a fraction of each day. Neither of the stations was in a position to send help. The radio transceiver planned for Ice Central had been abandoned in the course of reducing provisions to the barest essentials, so there was no means of getting messages in or out from November to May. The scientists back at Scheideck therefore assumed that Wegener, alert to the danger of a return trip, must have decided to overwinter at Ice Central. The three-man team at Ice Central likewise presumed he made the return as successfully as he had negotiated his way to them.

Months later, when the two overhauled propeller sleds finally broke through to Ice Central on 7 May, Wegener's comrades realized his fate. Sorge recorded the men's shock and dismay as the propeller sleds arrived and the truth became clear. "They stop and climb out. I recognize Kraus, and we fall into each other's arms. Both ask together, 'Is Wegener there?' and both turn away, pale and mute. What neither seriously believed has occurred: Wegener and Rasmus have not arrived."[115] A search team found their leader's body at kilometer 189, several days out of Ice Central, buried beneath a half meter of snow in a grave marked by his skis. He had been carefully sewn into two sleeping bags and lay in apparent peace, the ghost of a smile still hovering on his face. Investigation showed no sign of freezing and suggested that he probably died of heart failure while lying down in his tent. Rasmus Villumsen, just twenty-one years old ("little Rasmus," as Kurt Wegener and the others affectionately recalled him), had gone on alone, making it at least as far as kilometer 155, where the remains of a dog camp were found.[116] There his trail ended without further trace. Presumably he died, alone, in a glacial crevasse, and with him Wegener's final diaries were lost.

The Zenith of German Polar Exploration

The news of Wegener's death, radioed from Greenland on 8 May, transformed the significance of the expedition. The tale of his heroic martyrdom unleashed a wave of popular interest and bitter private recrimination and ultimately obscured his team's scientific achievements. Wegener's men continued their work to its appointed end in August 1931, as their fallen leader would undoubtedly have insisted. Schmidt-Ott sent Kurt Wegener out to the ice fields that summer to oversee his brother's work to its conclusion, and, in scientific terms, it was a hugely successful undertaking.

By the time the men began returning to Germany in August, seismic readings had been taken over the course of the year at thirty-four sites, providing the first picture of the incredible thickness of the inland ice, over three kilometers deep in places. Greenland's form, it was discovered, resembles a gigantic trough, ringed by mountains that retain a convex mass of ice nearly half the size of the island. Hundreds of kite and balloon ascents conducted at all three stations provided pioneering data on wind and cloud movement, air temperature, moisture, atmospheric pressure fluctuations, and a host of other meteorological statistics. Compiled and evaluated, this information painted the first comprehensive portrait of the cyclical changes in Greenland's climate. Finally, the team collected valuable data on the movement of glaciers and the accumulation and evaporation of frozen precipitation in the island's interior. This was field research of the very highest caliber, and the emergency coalition was elated at the Greenland expedition's haul.[117]

The human drama of Wegener's fate, however, overwhelmed the pedestrian pursuit of science, no matter how brilliantly conducted. Geophysics, geology, and glaciology meant little to the average German. Death, on the other hand, has a universal fascination. Previously famous only in scientific circles, Wegener's heroic death made him an instant international celebrity and "elevated the German Greenland Expedition to tragic greatness."[118] The Danish Geographical Society awarded him its gold medal, posthumously of course, in a highly publicized ceremony held at the end of 1931, attended by most of the expedition team and the Danish crown prince. "He had, after all, spent three years as a member of a Danish expedition," his brother Kurt observed, "and the Danes considered him one of their own."[119] Having lived and taught in Austria for years, Wegener was also claimed by the Austrian media, who lamented "the tragic death of the Austrian scientist."[120] In his hometown of Berlin, Wegener was mourned at a combined public wake and welcome home ceremony for the survivors in early 1932, where he was eulogized by Schmidt-Ott as "a selfless leader and comrade" who had advanced international science and given Germany "once more a tribe of polar researchers."[121] His old ballooning companion Berson commemorated him for the members of Aeroarctic as "one of the greatest of polar explorers," a man who loved the challenge of "surmounting the greatest obstacles," while he was recalled at the Congress of German Natural Scientists and Doctors (Gesellschaft deutscher Naturforscher und Ärzte) as a leader "who died as a hero, for science and for his friends."[122] Nor was the loyal Rasmus forgotten. The young man had been his family's sole support, and at the suggestion of Kurt Wegener the emergency coalition endowed a pension fund in his memory.[123]

The public clamored for details. Members of the expedition were immediately celebrities, deluged with solicitations from radio talk shows, the Reich League for Jewish Settlement (Reichsbund für jüdische Siedlung), the Locomotive Drivers League (Lokomotivführrerverein des Deutschen Eisenbahnvereins) of Bielefeld, high school clubs, charitable societies, and German cultural groups as far away as Bulgaria.[124] Death also worked its magic on jaded German publishers, who, having dismissed the expedition prior to Wegener's heart failure, now couldn't get enough of the drama. Akademia, a scientific news bureau, paid 10,000 marks to the emergency coalition even before the expedition had returned for the right to market photos and news from the story, and the Brockhaus publishing firm, which put out the scientific results and memoirs of the trip, promoted the most sensational aspects of Wegener's fate.[125] Full-page ads trumpeted "the race against the threatening winter night, the struggle against storm, snow, and cold. It is as though the unexplored land demands tribute, and the life of the leader and his loyal companion will be the price of victory." The campaign worked, with sales figures for the popular account of the journey in the thousands per month.[126] Publicly, therefore, Schmidt-Ott and the Greenland commission had achieved all they could hope for, apart from the loss of Wegener and Villumsen. The Greenland expedition was not only a great coup for German science, it was also, thanks to Wegener's death, a huge public relations success.

Privately, however, the expedition erupted into emotional chaos once back home. The loss of the beloved Wegener cast an enduring pall over their scientific achievements, and several members of Wegener's team, led by the engineer Kurt Herdemerten and Kurt Wegener himself, blamed their leader's tragic demise on the crew of Ice Central, in particular on Johannes Georgi. Their accusations precipitated years of litigation, bitter recriminations, and unbelievably acrimonious bickering. Kurt Wegener and Herdemerten, among others, accused Georgi of causing Alfred Wegener's death through his inexperience, overweening ambition, and loss of nerve. Alfred's brother, in fact, maintained that Georgi, well known for belligerence, would not even have been included in the expedition but for powerful friends at the German Marine Observatory, a charge given substance by the fact that later the director of the observatory, Admiral

Dominick, was one of Georgi's most influential private defenders.[127] In his account of the expedition published in 1933, Kurt Wegener charged that Georgi chose the goods to be taken by sled to Ice Central, that he chose very badly, and that he erred disastrously in relying on the untried propeller sleds to make good his oversights in later trips.[128] "Unfortunately, the false ambition of a few expedition members contributed to my brother's misfortune," Wegener declared. "The leader of the station, for example, claimed complete freedom of disposition there, though he had never yet overwintered in the polar ice. Through lack of necessary experience he had items brought to the station that weren't even used in the first year. Finally, as all became clear, he let it be known that he could not overwinter and that he would begin the march home on the twentieth of October."[129] In support of his argument, Kurt publicly cited passages from his brother's final diary entries, particularly a passage from 3 September: "If only Georgi and Sorge had brought fewer instruments and more food and the house! I fear it will avenge itself that I left the thing, at Georgi's insistence, to him." Even worse was Georgi's rash letter, which Wegener passionately believed to be the proximate cause of his brother's death. He became practically uncontrollable when discussing what he regarded as Georgi's cowardice, according to Alfred's wife, Else, and he actually discussed with Schmidt-Ott the possibility of bringing a charge of negligent homicide against Georgi.[130]

Others also blamed Georgi for Wegener's untimely end. Lecturing a Berlin meeting of the Nazi Kraft durch Freude (strength through joy) program in November 1934, Herdemerten charged Georgi with a litany of evils, including moral and physical cowardice, failed judgment, and lack of integrity. First, he argued, Georgi ignored Wegener's warnings about provisioning Ice Central. In the place of kerosene, Georgi took too many and unnecessary scientific instruments. He accused Georgi of "the unheard-of," meaning cowardice, for permitting Wegener to make the return trip, arguing that Georgi or Sorge ought to have volunteered to go in their older chief's place. Herdemerten insisted that the idea of a cardiac defect in Wegener had been invented by the inhabitants of Ice Central to absolve themselves of blame for his death, Georgi had tried against all legal agreements to seize command of the expedition after learning of Wegener's death, and he had conspired with Sorge upon return to Europe to misrepresent the course of the expedition.[131]

For a few years, the building hatred between members of the expedition team remained a private affair, though Georgi was perfectly aware of the feelings against him. Albrecht Penck, who saw Georgi as soon as he returned to Europe, noted that the young scientist "tortures himself with the idea that he may be in part to blame for Wegener's death."[132] Publicly and privately, both Schmidt-Ott and Else Wegener worked to smooth over disagreements. "My husband so much hoped that his expedition would remain free of the wrangling that has unfortunately been typical with other German expeditions," Else Wegener lamented. "It is so bitter for me that this wish is now being disregarded." Hoping to head off public recrimination, she wrote to members of the Greenland commission expressing her admiration for the brave crew of Ice Central. The commission agreed, worrying that the strife could "smear German scientific prestige."[133] Schmidt-Ott worked hard to make peace, declaring publicly that Wegener's "heartrending fate is to be ascribed alone to the most unfortunate chain of circumstances, particularly the weather conditions, which delayed the main expedition for six weeks."[134] Privately, he was clearly exasperated with what he viewed as Georgi's feelings of persecution. "At his first reception, I expressed my admiration and characterized his complete blamelessness for Wegener's death as a settled question," he wrote. "In very difficult negotiations in Copenhagen, I got all the expedition members to agree to the formula that his death was fate . . . Georgi ought to be satisfied. I cannot leave unsaid confidentially that this thoroughly complicated and perhaps also somewhat psychopathic man makes the greatest difficulty in other regards."[135]

These accusations against Georgi burst into the open in 1933 and 1934 in many venues. Kurt Wegener expressed his feelings about the Ice Central team in a presentation to the Geographical Society of Vienna in October 1933, and in the following year Herdemerten gained wide coverage for what the newspapers called his "Sensational Revelations about the Death of Greenland Explorer Dr. Wegener." Georgi, for his part, struck back vigorously, both in the courts and before the court of public opinion. He published lengthy rebuttals of books or articles that he felt were unfair to him, arguing that in fact Wegener knew in the most exact detail what supplies were at Ice Central and that Wegener's decision to make the journey had been based not on Georgi's letter but on Wegener's own awareness of the dire position of the station. He brought suit for defamation against Herdemerten, a suit that was eventually dropped. He argued that all the other accounts of the expedition used false comparisons, like that with Nansen's overwintering on Franz Josef Land, to misrepresent and minimize the extremely harsh conditions of life at Ice Central and that they ignored the trauma of the amputations performed upon Loewe. He conceded that he may have made mistakes but charged that others in the planning stages of the expedition had done likewise. And, he argued, it was not he, Georgi, but Kurt Wegener and Herdemerten who, by their "public breaking of the fortress peace," were disloyal to Wegener's own desire for what Wegener himself had called "expeditions without an aftertaste!"[136]

Georgi spent the thirty years after the expedition in a successful campaign to absolve himself of guilt. He published a good deal, helped initiate the Second International Polar Year in 1932, and managed to obscure the old debate over the tragedy on the inland ice. Modern German accounts of Wegener's last days carefully avoid the issue of blame for the hero's death and typically ignore the subsequent orgy of bickering and accusation.[137] This historical delicacy may derive from a deep reverence for Wegener's scientific achievements or from a desire to spare his reputation the consequences of too searching an investigation into his judgment. There is certainly no shortage of blame for the tragedy. Much of it belongs to Georgi. He made mistakes in provisioning on the first sledding expedition to Ice Central. Despite Georgi's claims, Wegener may very well not have known of this thanks to the fact, as Kurt Wegener later pointed out, that his brother was not at Scheideck for part of the time this provisioning took place. Nerve and judgment also failed Georgi at a crucial time when he sensed a nonexistent emergency and sent the ill-advised letter. This message did not initiate Wegener's march to death on the ice cap, but it created pressure not to turn back with his Greenlanders when the trip became ever more hazardous. The deadline of 20 October convinced Wegener that Georgi and Sorge were intent on marching out to certain doom, and for a man of his integrity there was no choice but to try either to stop or to aid them. In light of the fact that three men later survived on what Georgi declared was insufficient for two, Kurt Wegener's anger at Georgi seems justified. He had helped cause the death of Alfred.

Kurt Wegener could also have attached some blame to his brother, however. There can be no question either of Alfred Wegener's courage or of his moral integrity. He gave his life for his men, and he is undoubtedly the most heroic figure in the annals of German exploration. His judgment on his last expedition, however, was poor. He failed to ensure the provision of even rudimentary medical supplies at Ice Central, for example, a lesson that every German explorer ought to have learned from Enzensperger's death decades earlier. He placed too much faith in untried technology—the propeller sleds—and too little in that which was proven—the airplane. Bad weather and stubborn ice can hardly be blamed, unless one indicts Wegener even further, for these are the stock in trade of polar exploration and must always be taken into consideration. But his reliance on the propeller sleds, an unproven and even untested method of transport, soon showed itself to be misguided. At the same time, he neglected the entirely feasible opportunity to fly materials to Ice Central during the early provisioning stages in the midsummer of 1930. He feared that such flights would capture media coverage and deflect attention from the scientific aspect of the expedition, according to Fritz Loewe, and that they might discourage the men forced to continue sledding to and from Ice Central.[138] These were serious blunders, though Georgi's letter probably helped render them fatal.

Despite Wegener's death and the ensuing bitterness, the Wegener and Eckener expeditions look in retrospect like the very zenith of German polar exploration in its classical age. In these two Arctic undertakings, the German polar endeavor of the era claimed its greatest success and began at the same time to decline. Both expeditions were scientific victories, and Wegener's was truly epochal, achieving great breakthroughs in Arctic meteorology, geophysics, and glaciology. Both exploits attained a level of international acclaim for German polar research that had neither precedent nor successor. Wegener and Eckener were honored outside Germany, Wegener especially being memorialized abroad, as an American popular work put it in 1940, as a "Martyr to Science."[139] Commemorated afterward in monuments from Greenland to Austria and at many sites in Germany, Wegener more than any other German has left a lasting impression on the global image of the polar explorer. Every story needs a hero, and Wegener, in the narrative of German polar endeavor, is the genuine article.

At the same time, much began to end in German polar exploration in the early 1930s. The generous internationalist impulse that helped drive the Eckener zeppelin flight was very real, however self-serving some of its ends may have been. Eckener and the other zeppelin enthusiasts, such as Aeroarctic's Walther Bruns, were idealists who saw the Poles not as venues exclusively to prove Germanic virtue but as sites where a new brotherhood of international science might also be constructed.[140] A grim age was dawning in Germany in the early 1930s, however, and the nation's new masters would share neither Eckener's sober patriotism nor Wegener's moral probity and scientific idealism. Eckener, in fact, would see his airship program discontinued by the Nazis and his beloved *Graf Zeppelin* scrapped. And the

New Order that dawned in 1933 would have different uses for exploration, and explorers, than the scientific ends pursued by Wegener.

An age ended with these two expeditions in more than an ideological sense, however. A new era was dawning, and Eckener was its herald in Germany. The classical age of polar exploration was giving way to its modern age. Expeditions dependent upon the whims of weather and relying on wind, dogs, horses, and human resolve were becoming relics. The future would belong to permanently manned research stations rather than expeditions, relying not upon man and beast but upon the mechanical miracles of flight and the internal combustion engine. In the shadow of Eckener's zeppelin over the Arctic, this age could be dimly perceived. The dawning era would have no place for the deeds of an Alfred Wegener. "The heroic age of geographical exploration is over," wrote Albrecht Haushofer in elegy to Wegener. "Technical progress has swept it away."

5. THE GERMAN IMAGE
OF THE POLAR WORLD

Nature there is too strong and demanding. She demands hard men, men who can face this strong nature with an equally strong personality.

JOHANNES KOLL, 1934

By the time Germans celebrated Eckener and mourned Wegener, their nation had been engaged in the opening of the Poles for most of a century. Yet few Germans (or citizens of any state, for that matter) participated directly in the great polar adventure. Instead, the nation experienced the Poles vicariously, in a steady stream of memoirs, histories, articles, and popular accounts of polar travel produced for decades by German publishers. Using this literature, Germans created a polar world at home, a world drawn from the genuine travails of German adventurers but expressing as well the values and interests of the vast majority who would never set foot in the high latitudes. Like other exploring peoples, Germans wove memory, history, and fantasy into an imagined polar world that was as much a part of their encounter with the Poles as were the actual deeds of scientists and sailors.

Germany's polar world was as complex as the nation that created it. Unknown, unclaimed, largely uninhabited, the polar regions made handy conceptual tabulae rasae upon which Germans sketched out their thoughts on many contemporary issues. These thoughts were rarely unequivocal. New ideas and perspectives emerged over time, and they often endured side by side with apparently contradictory imagery. Nonetheless, certain recurrent themes dominated German perceptions of the polar world for decades.

One of these was the notion of purification through struggle with the hostility of nature. By pitting the polar elements against the resources, bravery, and imagination of German explorers, expeditions served as proving grounds for Germanic manhood. The struggle to master the last unconquered wilderness, many believed, brought out the best in Germans and validated German social and cultural norms. In their encounter with the Eskimo and other peoples of the polar world, Germans also refined their ideas about race and non-Western cultures. And a persistent strain of fantasy and mysticism tinged the German polar experience. For Germans fascinated with the occult, the Poles were the ultima Thule, a region thought since ancient times to be a fount of supernatural forces, concealing at its center verdant meadows that had been the ancient home of the Aryan "race."

Nature, Nationality, and Character

German accounts of polar adventure consistently stressed the positive impact that the struggle with nature exerted upon human beings: exploration was good, many insisted, because it forced young men to face the unique environment of the Poles. The values that Germans drew from the purifying struggle with environmental extremes varied in different historical settings, however. From the days of Petermann to the turn of the century or so, Germans thought of the Poles as sites where masculine honor could be forged and tested, where men pursued scientific progress in the name of pure idealism, and where the struggle of the nations, while never entirely absent, was less important than the international brotherhood of science. From the turn of the century, however, and climaxing in the National Socialist era, the polar experience was progressively nationalized. The Poles became one more field of vital international competition whose environment evoked specifically German, rather than general human, qualities of character.

This evolution is predictable. While the high latitudes remained beyond the West's reach, they were also beyond the struggle of nations. In isolation, the Poles transcended enterprise and empire alike, testing courage, discipline, and the human character in ways that made national competition seem irrelevant. As technology and scientific progress facilitated intrusion into the polar environment, however, and as the scramble for Africa intensified Western competition for territory, the polar environment became an inviting political and economic vacuum. By the eve of the Great War, the once nearly extraterrestrial regions in the high latitudes had become the objects of a veritable rush to the Poles, partly in the defense of national interest.

The idea that struggle with the danger of polar environments contributed to healthy character development drew on very old traditions. German romantics since at least the days of Goethe, for example, extolled the impact of nature on human character.[1] Environmental determinism was strong throughout the West in the late nineteenth century, and its influence in Germany lasted through the Nazi era. American optimism, African "primitivism," and German technological innovation were all explained as products of nature's impact upon human personality and culture.[2] In the setting of the Poles, this cultural conceit endowed the struggle against nature with particularly edifying qualities. "How much human sacrifice has been brought before the Moloch of the North Pole!" wrote one German commentator. "How much determination and presence of mind, courage, and resilience were already present in the medieval daredevils who sought the way to India and China, the lands of gold, by way of the North Pole. And today, in the age of science, what steely resolve, perception, and knowledge, what stubborn self-discipline it takes, after the great example of Fridtjof Nansen, to make a great cultural deed of mere adventure or sport. Truly, the polar regions have been the scene of a great portion of human heroism."[3]

Similar declarations on the benefits of suffering through polar misery echo through the era's literature, often flowing, perhaps unsurprisingly, from the pens of armchair polar adventurers.[4] Throughout the period up to World War II, one current of German polar writing continued to stress the universal quality of the virtues nurtured in the struggle between the "hot will of the human spirit" and the "threatening claws of the Arctic beast... Noble is the struggle for knowledge, its history rich in adventures and sacrifices, and so it profits to write it down."[5] Observers deplored the German inclination to find flaws in polar heroes, who deserved to take their rightful places with Polo, Magellan, and Columbus. "Polar explorers are only too rarely given unqualified praise... [they are] too often taken only for skilled sportsmen or bold adventurers. And yet they are no less brave heroes than the earlier explorers."[6]

From around the turn of the century, however, polar environments began to be seen as sites that drew out specifically German qualities. This is most strikingly evident in accounts of the wreck of the *Hansa*. The refreshing humility of Buchholz, who in 1871 conceded that the *Hansa* party survived thanks to "unusual luck," yielded by century's end to a chest-thumping inclination to see the crew's survival as proof, like the victory over the French, of "German tenacity, German discipline."[7] Similar sentiments and words turn up with striking regularity in the discussion of German work at the Poles after the 1890s. "Energy and courage, stamina and tenacity, bravery and enthusiasm" were needed by all in "the struggle with the disfavor of the elements," wrote Paul Zeidler in the 1920s, and "the deservedly renowned thoroughness and reliability of the Germans" fitted them particularly well for such work.[8] The *Hansa* crew's survival was proof of Teutonic virtue: "Despite the fearful situation, discipline never wavered for a moment, and the *Hansa* men proved themselves true Germans who knew how to obey."[9]

After World War I, the imagined benefits of the polar experience acquired new urgency for Germans. With their territory reduced by the Treaty of Versailles, deprived of the "geopolitical school" of colonial empire, Germans saw continued polar engagement as vital for the development of healthy character: "In one respect, the polar lands will always remain great and ideal: they demand from the individual everything of which his physical and mental vigor is capable. . . . Here the gauntlet is thrown down to the entire man: spirit and courage, will and energy, self-sacrifice and loyalty to the last breath. Resolute constancy at scientific readings, on marches, fulfillment of duty in every smallest detail despite ever new, recurrent torment, that is a categorical imperative."[10]

The tendency to romanticize suffering was not unique to Germans. The British did the same thing with the Scott and Shackleton expeditions.[11] Nonetheless, the impact of national chauvinism on German stories of polar endeavor is marked. Nor should the glorification of suffering be taken for a natural development. There was, in fact, a kind of minority counter-tradition that held that far from ennobling humanity, the unforgiving stringency of the high latitudes forced men to revert to barbarity. Decrying polar zones as "vast wastelands," a handful of observers warned that the polar environment was one that reduced men to the level of beasts, surviving on raw flesh, where "only miserable nomads wander or barely less miserable fishermen lead a beastlike existence."[12]

The demurrals of this sensible minority were generally lost in support for the belief in the ennobling qualities of suffering. This idea itself may or may not be a perversity. Applied to the experience of the West at the Poles, however, it is unquestionably the product of a perversely selective reading of polar history. Polar hardship is as likely to corrupt as to ennoble the human spirit. From the age of Hudson through the *Hansa* to Robert Falcon Scott, expeditions in extremity usually witnessed at some point a collapse of human valor and dignity. Heroism is certainly part of the West's encounter with the Poles, but so, in equal part, are mental and emotional breakdown, cannibalism, suicide, mutiny, madness, and murder.

As Germans over the decades selectively reinterpreted the experience of suffering at the Poles, they also recast the importance of polar environments to the German state. From the beginnings of German polar exploration to the turn of the nineteenth century, polar spaces were seen as having little intrinsic value. Polar zealots in the 1870s complained that Germans were too skeptical of the polar endeavor, too likely to ask "Why these travels into unprofitable regions[?] . . . How can one call the journeys to the North Pole national undertakings?"[13] As late as the turn of the century, some Germans denounced the often fatal ventures into the "desolate, ice-covered, useless polar world," while explorers wrung their hands at the public's lack of proper commitment.[14]

During these decades, less effort was made to convince Germans of the practical value of polar lands than to provide lyrical descriptions of the desolate and imposing majesty of the polar environment. Thus polar literature dwelt upon the spiritual impact of the icy landscape's aesthetic qualities, the "indescribable impressions" created by "the lonely land and desolate sea" of the Far South or North.[15] This was very much the sentimentalized nature of the romantics. Drygalski's discussion of his exposure to the polar world, written prior to his *Gauss* journey, is typical. "The nature of the polar regions possesses powerful beauties that have never yet failed to impress their viewer," he wrote. "The stark contrast between the soaring cliffs, water, and ice, the intermittent, unexpectedly rich display of life forms, the colorful splendor of the ice clouds, which in the pure clarity of the air glow from the farthest distances—all this leaves impressions that one never forgets."[16]

Drygalski, Filchner, and many others recalled the feeling of being dwarfed by the "superhuman size" and isolation of their environment. "Solemn silence hung over the sublime landscape of cliff, ice, and water. Dead silence, torn now and again by the cries of the auks." The dramatic composition of its elements, the vast scale, the emptiness and danger of the land gave to Arctic nature the macabre fascination of a Friedrich painting, the somehow uplifting desolation of the Victorian English "Arctic Sublime."[17] "The strange, horrible beauty of Arctic nature exercised its attraction upon humanity for centuries," but for some, the emptiness of the land produced an eerie sensation of liberation: "It's a strange feeling to be able to roam hemmed in by no law, in an uninhabited and unowned land, in which no one has anything to order or to prohibit. Here one is merely a human being, here one may be a human being."[18] Many who had once encountered the polar world, like Drygalski and Wegener, remarked again and again upon its persistent magnetism, and their inability to forget the polar landscape once back in warmer climes may have had to do with this liberating sense of being beyond the verge of Western propriety.

The haunting fascination of the landscape was intensified by the eerie visual contrast, frequently noted in the literature, between the land's literally blinding whiteness and the disconcertingly brilliant colors of the atmosphere. "The complete antithesis of darkness" that is encountered in the polar world, the pervasive, enveloping luminosity that permits no contrast to which the optic nerve may respond, is as impenetrable to the human eye as is total darkness.[19] "Gray on gray. Bare, naked cliffs . . . all life seems to have perished here," Wilhelm Ehlers recalled of Spitsbergen. "We stop at a safe distance from the jostling, cracking, roaring, glowing, and glistening ice formations. A grandiose sight, heightened by the bluish shimmer cast over the unique, grotesque scenery. . . . The phenomenon is all the more wondrous because over us the sky is covered, and the sun, from our perspective, is invisible."[20] Memoirs of German polar journeys are filled with accounts of the unnerving experience of snow blindness, common even on cloudy days if the eyes are not protected. "Without any kind of resting point, the gaze swept over the exhausting uniformity of the white waste," Hegemann recalled of the *Hansa*'s trip. "If one wandered far from the house, buried deep in the snow, all visible characteristics disappeared."[21] The disorienting "gray on gray" of the land, however, only intensified the impact created by the play of light on ice formations and moisture in the polar heavens. "In the sunshine, the snow crystals glitter like a million diamonds. The rose of sunrise and sunset turned the white plains pale green. The nights were magnificently bright. The radiant firmament and the light-receiving and -reflecting snow glowed so brilliantly that one could read the finest script without effort and spy far into the distance."[22]

The purity of their beauty was at first complemented by the economic and political sterility of the polar environments. The published records of Koldewey's second expedition, for example, which concluded during the war with France, deliberately juxtapose the "tumult of war" on the Continent with the "peaceful endeavors in the fields of science" far to the north.[23] Again and again in these years, scientific and popular accounts insist that the polar endeavor is "a magnificent scientific task, supported by all the world."[24] German scientists were exhorted to share with the scientists of other lands, "in joint scientific labor without any national rivalry," "the laurels for gallant struggle with the terrors of polar nature in the service of that lofty idealism that has already driven so many enlightened predecessors on the dark path out into the threatening ice, bearing the torch of the ceaselessly striving intellect."[25]

By the eve of World War I, however, the Poles were seen less frequently as

builders of character or theaters of international cooperation and more often as fields of political competition and reservoirs of untapped resources.
Though lamenting the public's sometime indifference to the practical
value of the Poles, geographers noted with approval that books on polar
exploration enjoyed growing sales.[26] Drygalski and others saw the Poles
as inviting fields for German expansion and framed this image in explicit
terms of "the international competition" with other states.[27] The Poles were
at last being engulfed in the matrix of the European global order. The fine
network of economic, cultural, and political ties that had long been drawn
over other extra-European regions was finally covering the Poles, changing
German conceptions of the high latitudes as it did so.

German intellectuals worked hard to alert the public to the importance
of the polar environment. "Polar land" displays and dioramas sprouted up
at turn-of-the-century German museums. The Berlin Institute for Oceanography opened a museum of its own in 1906 as a means of "enlivening the
understanding of the oceans and of maritime affairs in the German people."
Lifelike dioramas, filled with specimens of South Polar life, displayed "the
penguins and seals, on icy fields, brought home by the German Antarctic
expedition."[28] By 1912 an elaborate permanent exhibit occupying an entire
chamber detailed for the museum's 100,000 annual visitors the German
contribution to the opening of the Arctic and Antarctic and the importance
of these regions to Germany.[29] At almost the same time, the Berlin Museum
of Natural History (Museum für Naturkunde) unveiled its own Antarctic
diorama, featuring the fauna of "Kaiser Wilhelm II Land," displayed before
a re-creation of the *Gauss* at work in the distance.[30] Popular polar literature
drove home the point that though as yet not much used by Europeans, the
Poles were increasingly important in the "budget of the earth."[31]

Defeat in 1918 lent new urgency to calls to exploit the Poles. Declaring
that "Polar travel is necessity!" German polar enthusiasts cheered on
Wegener and Eckener. Trips like Wegener's would not only unveil the
mysteries of Europe's weather ("Up on the roof of the world the winds
and storms brew, which then move southward to the lands where men
live") but also tap a rich store of yet-to-be-exploited natural wealth: "The
Arctic appears to be of particular value to our economy not only by virtue of
its natural forces but through its abundance of resources—coal, iron, and
other metals—as well as its lush whaling, sealing, and fishing grounds."[32]
Polar litterateurs reminded Germans that with the land lost in the peace
settlement, Germany was "crammed into the cauldron of central Europe,

bound in on every border, without access to world seas," as a result of which "we see polar spaces assuming a greater role in state politics and the polar lands drawing upon themselves the competition of peoples."[33]

Attention to the value of polar lands grew in predictable ways under National Socialism. The changing German image of the Poles in the years from Koldewey to Wegener and, finally, to Hitler reflected the progress of Western technology, the tensions generated by international conflict, and Europe's dawning awareness of the globe as a closed system. The competition for Africa left the West, after centuries of imperial growth, with the Poles as the last venues of new acquisition. Nature at the Poles in the days of Koldewey could be the sites for character formation and the high-minded pursuit of scientific progress because they were hardly part of this world. Remote, dangerous, and barren, the Poles inspired awe rather than cupidity.

As technology evolved, the Poles drew nearer to the West. A state system that had reached its limits in other regions now generated a "race for the territorial distribution of the heretofore totally undervalued Arctic and Antarctic regions."[34] The same goes for the economic value of the Poles as the industrialized states drew more of the globe into their grasp. This was clearly evident in the mood of paranoia and anarchic competition immediately preceding World War I. The "expedition mania" that seized Europe (and Japan) reflected a widespread feeling that the Poles were the last sites of easy material gain. The great modern economic generator of tourism was already extending its poisoned hand toward the Poles by the time of the Great War. "Spitsbergen is developing more and more into a great tourist land," Otto Nordenskjöld noted in 1909, "where thousands of people for the only time in their lives can cast a glance into this strange world."[35] Even before the war, a short-lived hotel catering to tourists had been erected there, and the business of Arctic tourism, which would boom in the 1920s, was already established by the North German Lloyd line by the 1890s.

In all the attention to the beauty and riches of the polar lands in these years, however, there are just a few signs of what might be considered an ecological sensibility. Germans lyricized the beauty of the polar environment, the awesome splendor of its auroras, the fantastic shapes and unearthly hues of its icebergs, and the clarity of its atmosphere: "It is an air that permits no anxiety! Besides, the powerful impressions prevail of the unrestricted enjoyment of the sublime, of the original, of the novelty of the entire surroundings, of the formative power of nature."[36] They frequently anthropomorphized the polar environment, endowing it with human qualities of malice, treachery, or magnanimity. Only very rarely, on the other hand, did polar chroniclers perceive the fragility of this environment. The notion that the polar biospheres are essential but fragile global properties, where human beings may be intruders at best and vandals at worst, would not emerge for some decades.

The lone exception to the disregard for the impact of man upon polar nature, and it is not without significance, concerned the fauna of the polar regions. While adventurers like Enzensperger recorded their hunting kills with a pornographic attention to bloody detail, other Germans sometimes evinced a dawning awareness of the vulnerability of beasts. Drygalski noted the plentiful, indeed "overabundant fauna" of the Antarctic and the fatal innocence of polar wildlife.[37] "It was particularly delightful in these excursions to observe animal life in its original state quite uninfluenced by contact with human beings," he wrote after the *Gauss* voyage. He was most impressed with the emperor and Adélie penguins, who quite understandably learned to fear his rapacious crewmen and canines. "Both showed the same unsuspiciousness of man, and only on our return voyage through the pack were they at all shy of us."[38]

The occasional observer noted with revulsion the wanton slaughter of Arctic wildlife, marine mammals in particular, as well as its invariable consequence—the depletion, in many cases to near extinction, of these species. In 1896, for example, Ludwig Herz visited Spitsbergen on a tourist steamer in the company of Wilhelm Bade, former second officer of the *Hansa*, now working for the Lloyd line. Herz recounted that the men were permitted to go shooting for water fowl in the cliffs and rookeries of the islands. After rebuking a "somewhat sentimentally inclined young lady" for her empathy with the birds, Herz concedes the scene's repugnance: "The hunters were once more disembarked and maintained a murderous fire on the birds swarming about; the brooding were even knocked down from their clefts and holes, careless of whether the slaughtered bird could even be reached; rarely has the 'noble passion' of hunting seemed so hateful to me and appeared so identical with nauseating blood lust as here."[39]

The passion of the day's tourists for senseless destruction was noted a few years later by Nordenskjöld as well. "The butchery that unreasonable tourists carry on at their pleasure among reindeer and half-tame eider ducks must be halted."[40] Even this regard for the ecology of the region, however, was often followed with the hope that new, more fertile marine hunting grounds might yet be opened.

The years around the turn of the century were nonetheless a period in which a German environmental sensibility began to emerge, and this may have affected perceptions of polar animal life. The first proposals for German national parks were put before the Reichstag in 1898, driven in part by the conviction of many early German environmentalists that there was an essential link between German landscapes and Germanic character.[41] The belief that the natural environment shaped culture also affected the ways in which Germans understood the untamed nature of the Poles. Friedrich Ratzel, who seems to be everywhere in the sciences of culture in these years, illustrates the links between belief in the character-shaping qualities of land and nature, on the one hand, and the extension of this same view to the Poles, on the other. Ratzel was an early defender of nature preservation because of his insistence on the relationship between the German land and the German national character. His convictions led him to view exposure to the polar environment as a matter of German character formation and helped spur his support for greater German polar activity at the German geographic congress in 1883.[42] Many German explorers and polar adventurers shared Ratzel's beliefs in the impact of environment on character, though they often discussed this in terms of "race." For these men, and for Germans in general, the outstanding example of the impact of environment on race and character was not to be found in the resolve of stranded Germans, however, but in the native inhabitants of the Arctic, the Eskimo.

First among Savages: The German Romance of the Eskimo

The curious German who consulted popular reference works about the peoples of central Africa during the 1880s could have learned the following. The "character of the Negro where it is preserved in its originality" was "indolent and childlike" and, where it had come in contact with the slave trade, "greedy, horrible, and malicious." A black father "would swap mother and child for a colorful loincloth or string of beads." Insensible even of the most oppressive conditions, black Africans retained an "abandoned gaiety . . . the Negro passes his nights in song, dance, and music, heedless of the next day, in which he lets himself be slaughtered or led into slavery with dull indifference." The African was both strangely repugnant, with an oily skin that emitted a "peculiar odor," and habitually lethargic, so that the black male avoided arduous work by using his woman as "slave and beast of burden."

Consulting the same source to learn about the Eskimo, however, the reader would have found a surprisingly different appraisal of the peoples of the Far North. The fourth edition of *Meyers Konversation-Lexikon* gushes over the guileless character, keen intelligence, and political egalitarianism of the Eskimo lifestyle. "Simplicity without stupidity and cleverness without calculation are the essentials of their mental outlook. The Eskimo are truth-loving, honorable, and brave; the fact that they learn dominoes and board games (even chess) very quickly speaks for their sharp intellect. They performed essential services for ancient and modern mariners in the theater of the Northwest Passage . . . They live in complete equality, without government or even chiefs."[43]

This laudatory assessment of the Eskimo, not at all unusual in the German polar literature of the time, surprises modern sensibilities attuned to the commonplace racism of late-nineteenth-century Europe. Judgments upon the Eskimo presented a stark contrast not only to German evaluations of other extra-European peoples at the time but also to similar appraisals in the English-language literature of the day, which were typically given to tut-tutting at the "uniformly filthy and disgusting" character of Eskimo personal and domestic hygiene as well as their "extreme absence of morals and their utter want of shame" in sexual matters.

That the Eskimo, now called Inuit, enjoyed such a positive press in the German literature of the polar golden age is also surprising when considered in the cultural setting of the era. The tribes of the circumpolar Arctic world were known to educated Germans long before their nation began to take an active part in the exploration of the Far North. The earliest known European pictorial representation of an Eskimo was printed in Germany in 1567, and as early as the 1730s, some of the works of Hans Egede, a Norwegian missionary in Greenland, began to appear in German.[44] At about the same time, German missionaries of the Moravian Brethren began to evangelize among the Eskimo of southern Greenland. One of them, David Cranz, published a *Historie von Grönland* after a thirteen-month inspection of the missions in the 1760s. Cranz provided an extended and very positive portrayal of the life of Greenland's natives and introduced such words as "kaiak" and "umiak" into European usage.[45] Generations later, in the wake of the Napoleonic wars, the aristocratic young adventurer Adelbert von Chamisso traveled among the Chukchi of Siberia with the Russian expedition of the Rurik. His account of his travels, including descriptions of Chukchi customs, was published in three volumes in 1821. 46

When German explorers thus began, some decades later, to record their impressions of the peoples they encountered in the northern high latitudes, they built upon a slight but significant tradition of nonscientific cultural observation. At the same time, German accounts of the Arctic's native inhabitants were influenced by two more recent trends. One of these was represented by the emerging scientific disciplines of ethnology and anthropology. A second increasingly potent intellectual force, overlapping the first, reflected the popular Social Darwinist racialism of the late nineteenth century.

Hierarchies of culture dominated German perceptions of the non-European world from the middle of the century at the very latest. Imperialism was revealing an ever more complex kaleidoscope of human variety to the West, and German scholars, like intellectuals in other nations, sought a theoretical framework to help them classify and order human cultural diversity. Innovators in the German sciences of culture, beginning with Gustav Klemm and Theodor Waitz in the 1850s, had distinguished between the advanced Kulturvölker (cultural peoples) and the primitive Naturvölker (natural peoples). Their approach, based upon certain standards of cultural achievement, endured in ordinary usage through World War II. Relying upon technological, social, and political criteria, such schemes of cross-cultural ranking were popularized in the widely read works of litterateurs like Ratzel. The Kulturvölker used machines, ran complicated nation-states, and built empires. Peoples of nature did not. "No primitive people has ever built a great state," Ratzel wrote in typically apodictic fashion.[47]

The notion of classifying cultures in this way may have been initially untainted by biological racism. It is also possible to argue, hypothetically, that such rankings do not intrinsically and necessarily culminate in racial hierarchies. In practice, however, the distinction between "cultural" and "natural" peoples soon became conflated with racist concepts. This is not surprising. The idea of race, and speculation that racial differences had a relationship to the environment, already had a long history in Germany, stretching back to Kant's lectures on physical geography delivered at Königsberg in 1765.[48]

The reception of Darwin's ideas—often appallingly ethnocentric in their own right—and their propagation by disciples like Ernst Haeckel gave a pernicious twist to racial theory, adding malignant, biologically conceived racial hierarchies to the already troubling concept of cultural hierarchies.[49] Haeckel, for example, divided humanity into thirty-six races, with the "wooly-haired" of the "lowest tribes" at a level "very little above the mental life of the anthropoid apes."[50] Over the last decades of the nineteenth century, such views gained a wide popular hearing.[51]

Given the widespread presumption of European racial superiority, the German image of the Eskimo is striking for its extraordinarily positive tone. From the era of Koldewey onward, German explorers and popular polar writers characterized the Eskimo in tones of admiration rather than denigration. Though this admiration sometimes patronized northern peoples, it presents nonetheless a striking contrast to views of other non-Europeans. While many related but distinct groups populate the Arctic in Siberia, Alaska, Canada, and Greenland, nonscholarly German accounts in general focused upon the so-called Central and Greenland Eskimo of Greenland and the Canadian Arctic. And it is clear that the positive German image of the Eskimo was due primarily to a single fact: Germans admired the Eskimo ability to survive in the Arctic environment.

German respect for Inuit skill in exploiting the resources of their unique natural setting is evident from the earliest days of organized German exploration. A year after Koldewey returned from Greenland, for example, Georg Hartwig treated the Eskimo at length in *Der hohe Norden im Natur und Menschenleben* (The High North in nature and human life), a popular work of "natural history" that went through many editions. Hartwig traced the range of Eskimo settlement, described the characteristic Eskimo physique (short of stature, broad of face and shoulder, delicate of hand and foot), and portrayed their outlook and physical comeliness in glowing terms: "Cheerfulness, benevolence, and confidence are typically reflected in the faces of the young Eskimo—and the women, who are by no means inclined to suppress their laughter, reveal two bright rows of white pearls, such as many a European beauty cannot claim." Conceding that they wash infrequently, Hartwig nonetheless observes that their skin color "approaches the white," and the women, especially, might display "a perfectly charming complexion."[52]

While remarking the folkways and appearance of the Eskimo, Hartwig presumed that his readers were far more interested in the vital and practical issue of their success in defying the elements. "It is not their more or less fortunate efforts to beautify themselves, however, that primarily interest us in the Eskimo," he writes. "We see man here transplanted into the apparently most unfavorable conditions, and we ask with interest how he succeeds in preserving his existence in the struggle with the rigors of such a climate, such a nature."

Hartwig ascribed Eskimo success to an adaptability and resourcefulness that he related in the most superlative terms. Their parkas, underclothes, and gloves "allow them to defy the most biting cold," as do their "masterful" sealskin boots, finished by the Eskimo women "with a delicacy that would honor the finest shoemaker in Europe." Hartwig admired the "amazing craft" with which the Eskimo construct their summer huts and winter igloos, which, in their ability to be warmed with simple oil lamps, stood as "the triumph of Eskimo architecture." The kayak—"undoubtedly the most admirable and unique invention of the Eskimo"—and its use as a hunting device likewise drew praise. Hartwig enthused at the agility of the Eskimo hunter in his frail vessel, noting his ability to capsize and right himself, and related the unflattering story that Eskimo men, who disdained rowing in the open umiak as a woman's means of transportation, mistook rowing English sailors for bearded women.

This same tone of enthusiasm for Eskimo aplomb in the struggle for survival dominates the first really lengthy German-language discussion of Inuit life, Heinrich Klutschak's *Als Eskimo unter den Eskimos* (As Eskimo among the Eskimos), published in Vienna in 1881. Klutschak, a German native of Prague, traveled in the Canadian Arctic from 1878 to 1880 with an expedition led by the American soldier Frederick Schwatka. The venture was yet another of the era's innumerable quests for the truth about Franklin's debacle (this one was a qualified success), but the expedition was more noteworthy, in retrospect, for another of its aspects: Schwatka and his team attempted to live as fully as possible in the manner of the Eskimo, as Klutschak's title indicates.[53]

The team's efforts paid off. Immersing themselves in Eskimo nature-craft, living at close quarters with Eskimo guides and in frequent contact with various groups of the Inuit of the region, Schwatka's band crossed thousands of kilometers overland, much of it in the dead of the Arctic winter, without loss of life or serious illness. Although the slightly later work of Franz Boas on the Central Eskimo is far better known in the Anglo-American world, Boas was neither widely read nor particularly influential in Germany, either in popular or scholarly milieus. Klutschak, on the other hand, enjoyed a wide audience throughout Germanophone Europe.[54]

His memoir is hardly free of defects. Klutschak was deaf to the nuance and richness of Inuit language, and he dwelt at inordinate length upon the violent antipathy that marked relations between some Inuit bands. The overall tenor of his account, however, is thoroughly positive, amplifying the natural virtue and savvy survival skills of the Eskimo. Klutschak "abandoned every civilized item of clothing," adopting the "advantages" of the lighter, more flexible, and water-resistant native garb. He praised the "primitive yet ingenious" Eskimo igloos that sheltered the expedition's members, conceded the "weaknesses of the whites" in comparison with the Eskimo in the region, and praised the home comforts of the Eskimo village in the Far North: "It appeared most beautiful on a dark night; the round shapes of the houses, here and there half covered by snowdrifts, gave the appearance of mounds of earth thrown up by gigantic animals, and yet a light glowed through the slabs of ice from the well-lit interiors, transposing the amazed observer into a labyrinth of little crystal palaces . . . This was life, indeed a world of its own."[55]

As these observations suggest, Klutschak did not, in general, condescend to the Inuit. Their domestic arrangements struck him as admirable. Polygamy, he argued, was rare, and Eskimo women seemed to enjoy considerable status, though he reserved his most ardent admiration for their willingness to work. "She is the first up and the last in bed, the true and unmistakable picture of a good housewife and mother." He took a generally respectful interest in their religious practices and entertainments, sketching vignettes on Eskimo music, dance, gymnastics, and string games. Hunkered down against the Arctic cold in a snug igloo, he paid perhaps the highest compliment of which a European adventurer was capable, admitting that "the first builder of such a house, and the inventor of the sleeping bag of the northern world, has probably rendered just as great a service as the one to whom the civilized world is now indebted to the invention of the steam engine."[56]

Klutschak was not the only German to write with familiarity of the Central Eskimo. Decades later, in 1914, a German businessman named Rudolph Franke published his diary of months spent in the Far North, first with a wealthy American sportsman named John Bradley and then as the lone white companion of Frederick Cook during the latter's now notorious effort to reach the North Pole in the spring of 1908. Unlike Klutschak, Franke lived for a time as the only white in an Eskimo group, thoroughly immersed in their lives. His diary is in some ways a more noteworthy and perhaps more revealing portrait of German popular attitudes toward the

Eskimo since he was, as the introduction to his memoir states, "neither ex-plorer nor scientist" but a simple German man of business who entered the Arctic world "unprepared and free of every traditional view, of preconceived notions and opinions."[57]

Franke spent a great deal of time traveling with Eskimo guides and living in Eskimo settlements, and his admiration for their way of life went far beyond utilitarian admiration for their ingenious survival techniques. He paid close attention to Eskimo sexual mores and childrearing, for example, and found them closely in accord with his own values and superior in many ways to those of Europeans. The Eskimo, he noted, "display each spring an intensive love life, which flourishes barely more voluptuously in southern zones. But the sexual drive alone is not the only basis for this but instead the joy in the product, the limitless love of the Eskimo for their children." Franke considered the intense parent-child bond vital to the maintenance of the Eskimo population, given the high mortality rate in Arctic zones. He also found that nature itself produced childrearing practices among the Eskimo that might be a model for whites. "I have never seen the Eskimo chastise their children, and I am convinced that this is not necessary, since the hard conditions of existence, the dangers of the High North lurking everywhere, produce caution, quiet consideration, and self-discipline to a certain extent involuntarily, even naturally. Just as, on the other hand, unhealthy influences—it may be, now and then, those of the white man—are completely excluded."[58]

He also noted that the powerful Eskimo sexual appetite seemed hygienic, that is, safely heterosexual. "Though the Eskimo sex drive may be very lively, I have never observed an anomaly, let alone a perversity." The men, he claimed, were somewhat jealous of their women and not inclined to share them, whatever popular myth might say about the Eskimo. Like Klutschak, he greatly admired the Eskimo women, whose ideas of domesticity seem to have suited German men of the time. Though they were inclined to let their sexual morals "slip out the peep-hole of their igloos" when the men were away for extended hunting trips, Eskimo women were in every other respect the economic and moral backbones of their communities, careful with the household budget, hard-working, and resourceful: "Thus must one credit the Eskimo woman with diligence, dexterity, thrift, and loyalty!"[59]

Far from seeing Western society as a model for the peoples of the Far North, Franke on several occasions, as in his reference to their childrearing practices, implied that whites in fact corrupted the Eskimo. Commenting, as others had, on their consistently happy disposition, for example, Franke noted that "the Eskimo tribes of the High North, in contrast to their southern Greenlandic tribal relatives who live under Danish protection and Danish administration in permanent settlements on the coast, are completely free nomads and heathens, and despite that, or perhaps precisely because of this, are good-natured, reliable children of nature, full of trust and free of tricks and malice!"[60]

Germany's romance with the Eskimo peaked at the turn of the century, with the West eagerly tracking the heated and sometimes fatal last sprint for the Poles, when a spate of popular articles and books echoed Franke's extravagant praise of the North's native tribes. Unlike many other indigenous peoples, the Eskimo were not clearly in demographic decline after contact with the West, proving "that physically and mentally they are at a much higher level than the North American Indian or the Australian Negro," occupying in fact a special place among the globe's natural peoples: "Their aptitude is in many cases positively astonishing. In many respects this gallant people occupies the first place among the so-called savages . . . In their style of living one sees immediately a certain superiority to the other natural peoples."[61]

The qualities of the Eskimo personality—friendliness, good cheer, contentment, and hospitality, even to enemies—are again and again contrasted favorably with the shifty and melancholy "Red" Indian tribes of the Canadian North. Many note their facility at chess, which was clearly viewed as a reliable cross-cultural measure of analytical intellect. Popular books and magazine articles portrayed the Eskimo as "a true ideal example of adaptation to hard living conditions" and characterized the superiority of Eskimo naturecraft to that of the Europeans in extravagant terms. German Arctic travelers, following in the footsteps of Klutschak, advised others to go native. "I took neither tent nor sleeping bag but got a roof over my head with the natives. And I had good experiences this way," wrote Oscar Iden-Zeller of a trip among the Chukchi. "In any case, I hold to the view that, on journeys that take one into the regions of the polar peoples, one ought to exploit the experience of the native inhabitants as far as possible." Recommending that only weapons, a few provisions, and scientific tools be brought from home, he warns German readers that "all other European gimcrackery is superfluous and only makes the journey harder."[62]

Many popular German notions about the Eskimo—their love of children, their "healthy" sex life, the danger of corruption by contact with whites—were the standard fare of European "noble savage" ideology. Still, noting the ways German construction of Eskimo identity fits into a tradition of sentimentalizing non-Western peoples begs an important question. Why, in an era when theories of European racial superiority often produced extremely negative popular stereotypes of Africans, indigenous Americans, Australian aborigines, even of European Jews, would the German image of the Inuit and other northern peoples have diverged so widely from the pattern?

There might be several reasons. Most obvious of these is the simple fact that Eskimo techniques of Arctic survival worked so well. Many European expeditions that were successful in overland exploration, particularly from the turn of the century onward, relied extensively upon methods that originated with Eskimo practice. Nansen's success in Greenland and Peary's final drive for the North Pole were made possible by close study of Eskimo icecraft, and much of Wegener's transport and clothing technique derived from Eskimo models. This did not go unnoticed in the era's polar literature. It was difficult to deny at least some measure of natural genius to the Eskimo when the success of their innovations was so tangibly manifest.[63] Eskimo mastery of the hazardous North impressed nearly all German observers.

Germans could also be generous in their appraisal of the indigenous peoples of the Arctic because of the nature of German intrusion into the region. The European image of the "noble savage" often developed where interaction between Europeans and non-Europeans was most fleeting and economically disinterested.[64] The long Western romance with the supposed primeval innocence of Tahitian society, for example, was based largely upon images derived from the most superficial and incidental contact between Tahitians, European sailors, and a couple of artists. Where Europeans had money to make and land to take, on the other hand, as with the slave trade in central Africa or with the native tribes of North America, more negative images often emerged.

Germans had no need to vilify the Eskimo, since they had no claims on Eskimo land and little to interest them economically in the Eskimo. As active participants in the West's African colonial venture, a different and most unflattering image of the "Negro" races was more useful in Germany. It is worth noting, in this regard, that the image of the "Red Indian" in Germany was often very positive as well, as in the enormously popular *Winnetou* novels of Karl May, deriving once again from an intercultural contact in which Germans had few material interests at stake.[65]

Indeed, it is symptomatic of the general development of European images of non-European peoples that in the years after World War I, as the apparent economic value of the polar regions grew, a new note entered German writing on the native peoples of the Far North. German polar literature began to describe the Eskimo and other northern peoples as fated to racial extinction. Germans had debated this matter for decades, since the turn of the century at least. Nansen raised the issue in Germany in 1903, for example, predicting their gradual retreat and eventual extinction in the face of European intrusion. At the time, the general consensus of most German observers seems to have disagreed, insisting that both the Greenland Eskimos and other northern peoples displayed considerable demographic resilience since contact with whites.[66]

After the war, as Weimar and Nazi era German nationalists trumpeted the urgent necessity for access to resources at the Poles (and in Africa, where similar arguments were used by colonial revanchists), German polar writers saw the chances for the region's natives beginning to dim. A Nazi era guidebook to Arctic science and culture, put out in 1939 by Leonid Breitfuss, for example, concluded that despite their many virtues, most of the peoples of the North had a very slight long-term prospect of survival. "Many of these peoples, among whom the Eskimos of the ice-bound coast may today be seen to a certain extent as Ice Age men, are distinguished by their cleverness, tenacity, and dexterity as well as by their sharp observation of and love for nature. Despite such qualities, not all these peoples with their primitive culture are in a position to withstand the hostility of polar nature in the long term, and they are therefore, with the exception of the peoples of Taimyr, the Greenland Eskimo, and a few Indian tribes, fated to extinction."[67]

Even the scientific results of the Wegener expedition, written from a point of view quite sympathetic to the Eskimo of Greenland, who had performed such signal services to the undertaking, concluded that the Eskimo might survive only at the expense of their cultural existence. "Europeanization is in any case so far advanced that we really have before us in no regard any longer the genuine life of a polar people," read the expedition's official scientific records. "The Eskimo must pay for southern civilization with ideal values, with the gradual loss of his own culture, and that is certainly an unavoidable process that in this case proceeds without damage to the health of the people. We must be glad, from a humane standpoint, and yet we are painfully touched, because here something completely unique expires: the culture of the Arctic."[68]

The erosion of Eskimo populations and culture was widely perceived to be natural—"hardly avoidable"—by German observers who also after the war linked the Eskimo's dwindling numbers to their declining racial "purity" as a result of their intermarriage with southern peoples. "A fearful disruption has already occurred in the life and race of polar man; the population has sunk by more than half, half-breeds of every kind, even between Eskimo and Negro, have taken the place of the pure, robust children of nature."[69]

Thus, despite their undoubted virtues, the peoples of the North were ultimately fated to vanish, some through extinction and some through absorption by the stronger culture of the South. This prognosis, in fact, may have been both realistic and ultimately accurate, despite the discomfort it causes the cultural pluralist, but it also holds the key to many of the crucial cultural assumptions that underpinned the German view of the Northerner throughout the polar golden age. Though ingenious, loveable, and better than most nonwhites, the Eskimo in German eyes was still inferior to the white, and precisely those cultural attributes that adapted him so admirably to his unique environment also helped define his difference and, implicitly, the true nature of the German.

The very cheerfulness of the Eskimo, for example, was often seen as evidence of his primitive tendency toward living solely in the present and failing to envision, plan, or long for a better future. His infamous gorging sessions were proof of this: "A beastly voracity often oversteps the bounds of need, and in excess the frivolous savage forgets all too often the requirements of the coming morning."[70] Klutschak too noted the "lack of any energy" or any desire for betterment that characterized the more abject of the bands he encountered.

Nor did the northern peoples show evidence of higher intellectual activity in their response to their world, despite their facility at European games. Germans who praised the material achievements of the Eskimo as evidence that they possessed "some of the prerequisites of civilization" then tended to dismiss these pragmatic achievements, reflecting that the Eskimo still "thought through no scientific problems."[71] Even those accounts that were most sympathetic to the Eskimo noted their extreme superstition ("of course, like all natural peoples, they part from the age-old only with difficulty") and endorsed the work of Christianity in ridding the North of its primitive customs.[72]

Their adherence to environmental determinism also convinced German observers that the Eskimo and other northern peoples were confined to a lower level of cultural development through the very rigors of an environment that focused all their energies upon mere survival. Stimulating an advanced material response, their unique surroundings also retarded further progress for the Eskimo. As the "remnants of Stone Age men," they lived without state, religion, or leaders "under the most primitive conditions, in constant struggle with the most barren environment of the globe."[73] Germans explained the "retreat of the polar peoples," which began to be commented upon around the turn of the century, in Social Darwinist terms that emphasized a development paradoxically promoted and then stunted by environmental pressures.

> It is never one cause alone that determines the fate of the culturally poor nations, but many always work together; and they derive on one hand from the natural surroundings, on the other from the national character and, not least, from contact with Europeans. It is mutual support that first frees man from the manacles of nature; therefore, he is that much more its slavish subject the lower his level of culture and the slighter his numbers. The Eskimo has tried very well to exploit with cunning the advantages of his surroundings in the effort to overcome hardships through the adoption of a carefully adapted lifestyle, through simple and nonetheless useful huts and similar vessels. He has established himself in districts where other tribes cease to exist and accomplished astounding things with the simplest means, where great expeditions maintain themselves only through complex outfitting. Obviously, he will hardly be able to force himself to higher attainments. His homeland presents him with such insurmountable hindrances, and his struggles directed exclusively to the maintenance of his existence prohibit the concentration of population and the development of the intellectual systems that are promoted only by mutual stimulation.[74]

On the eve of World War I, Otto Nordenskjöld published in Germany a work called *Die Polarwelt und ihre Nachbarländer* (The polar world and its neighboring lands) that captured perfectly the kind of qualified admission of virtue that typified popular German attitudes toward the Eskimo. Nordenskjöld's uncle, Nils Adolf Erik Nordenskjöld, was the first to traverse the

Northeast Passage, and the younger Nordenskjöld had himself taken part in expeditions to the Antarctic. For Nordenskjöld, as for many others, the remarkable material culture of the Eskimo constituted one great exception to a level of cultural development that was in most ways far closer to the savage than to the civilized. "One might at first expect," Nordenskjöld writes, "that a people living isolated among such difficult external circumstances would stand at a very low level of cultural development. In social respects, this may perhaps be said of them. With the exception of the sorcerers and shamans, the 'Angekok,' they have neither leaders nor chieftains, no tribal coalitions, no legislation, and also no adjudication."[75]

Despite these deficiencies, Nordenskjöld, like many in Germany, was willing to concede that the Eskimo were certainly capable of learning (he cites their satisfactory performance in Danish colonial schools rather than their skill at chess) and that their environmental adaptation was unparalleled. "What nonetheless arouses the admiration of everyone who has come to know this curious people is their highly developed material culture, which is adapted in wonderful fashion to the nature in which they live. The evidence for this is ready to be seen in the fact that the Europeans who are compelled to live under the same conditions adapt themselves to this culture in very many things." Here, he readily concedes along with Klutschak, that the Eskimo far surpass the Europeans. "The progress of modern polar exploration rests to a great extent in the fact that they have learned from the Eskimo how man must live in the polar regions."[76]

Recognition of native ways by Western explorers like Nordenskjöld, Klutschak, Nansen, and Peary was only fitting. At a time when European technology was not yet able to defy the polar elements, the environmental adaptations pioneered by the Eskimo and other indigenous northern peoples represented the best means of carrying on human activity in the high latitudes. While conceding the debt owed to northern peoples by exploring Europeans, however, the era's prevalent anthropological conceits required that the technical prowess of the Eskimo not be allowed to obscure their place in the hierarchy of cultures, a place very different from and inferior to that occupied by civilized Europeans and Germans.

At the same time, Germans accounts of indigenous northern peoples did more than simply gaze passively at yet another exotic product of the imperial experience. They also modeled in their image of the Eskimo an implicit vision of themselves and their society. Consider most obviously the virtues that German travelers and explorers claim to find in the Eskimo. Their women find their greatest fulfillment in domesticity. The Eskimo of both sexes work hard with good cheer, despite the most trying environmental conditions. They are contented with life and uninterested in political contest. They are somewhat free in their sex lives but also free of sexual "perversity." They are, in short, good bourgeois by nature, confirming the values of the Western middle class in their spontaneous social and moral response to their environment.

At the same time, this reading of what Germans derived from this intercultural encounter—a flattering image of their own values—does not go quite far enough in understanding the unusual charm that the Eskimo exerted upon their German interpreters. A close reading of German testimony cannot fail to note a tone of wistful envy that pervades much of this evidence, an awareness that in their simpler condition they are somehow permitted—or have retained—things denied or lost to Germans. The respectful and usually sensitive treatment of Eskimo sexual mores, the reluctant concessions that the passing of Eskimo mysticism is probably for the best, above all the emphasis upon their egalitarian politics suggest that Germans who looked at the Eskimo saw not only what they themselves were but what they missed in themselves sometimes as well. "They are many things that we cannot be" is an implicit part of the German romance with the North's peoples.

This awareness of the ways in which the experiential quality of Eskimo life surpassed that of modern Germans is yet another manifestation of the environmental determinism of the era, for many Germans who noted this aspect of Eskimo existence also linked it to their unique natural setting. Noting the Inuit love for their homeland, Germans remarked "how much sublimity and sorcery must live in a land that despite such fearful stringency so binds men to it that in the friendly South they languish and die off?"[77] This very stringency set the Far North beyond and above ordinary judgments of culture, creating and justifying the free and harmonious society of its indigenous peoples. They were liberated by the very hostility of their environment in a way that Germans could not be.

This sentimentalized image of the innocent and virtuous child of nature, ultimately doomed in his struggle with the more complex cultures of the West, was a fantasy of the time that reflected the peculiar characteristics of German interaction with the polar world and its inhabitants. Where an earlier time of missionary activity had focused upon the squalor and violence of Inuit life, the self-satisfied imperial Germany of the polar golden age could permit itself a more magnanimous view of Eskimo defects, romanticizing their virtues while keeping them at a distance from equality. Both images, of course, were tinged by fantasy. But that too was appropriate, since fantasy had always taken a prominent place in German thought about the polar world and its occupants.

A World Clothed in Fantasy

It was natural that before their final unveiling in the twentieth century the Poles should attract the speculation of dreamers. Much as the heavens, with their visible but unattainable and unknown bodies, served since ancient times as a focus of human myth and legend, so the great blank spaces that framed the known portions of the globe were filled in by armchair polar enthusiasts. "Both end points of the earth's axis, like the peaks of the highest mountains, have been goals of human yearning since time out of mind," wrote the popular geographical writer Richard Buschick in the 1930s, "and fantasy has clothed them with its magic. Some have even gone so far as to maintain that paradise lay here."[78]

Speculation about what might be found at the Poles, or what may once have existed there, took many forms throughout the West. Conjectural geography, naturally, was a part of polar fantasizing, producing such phenomena as the open polar sea obsession of Hayes, Petermann, and others. Nordenskjöld called the atmospheric dust that collected atop the Greenland ice cap "cryoconite," or cosmic dust, and speculated in the face of all empirical evidence that the center of Greenland was ice-free.[79] Other Western dreams about the polar world exhibited more remote connections with reality. Greeks in the age of Pythias imagined temperate oases hidden in the ice of the polar lands, Spaniards claimed that Columbus reached Icelandic settlements, and nineteenth-century Americans were titillated by Capt. John Cleves Symmes's descriptions of a world concealed within a hollow earth whose gateways would be found at the Poles.[80]

In Germany, turn-of-the-century fantasies about the wonders hidden in the high latitudes revolved around the alleged origins of the "Aryan" or "Indo-Germanic" race. The terms were synonyms for tribes that many believed to be the racial ancestors of northern Europeans. Coined by the philologist Friedrich Max Müller, the term "Aryan" was conceived as an alternative to the more cumbersome "Indo-German." Müller always insisted that "Aryan" had no reference to ethnic or "racial" traits, denoting only a family of languages, but his term was soon conflated with the notion of the Germanic branches of the European "race." Mingling with occultist racial fantasy, the Teutonic mysticism of Wagner, and a tradition of scholarly speculation about Indian migration to Scandinavia and the Arctic, the idea of "Aryan" or "Indo-German" racial ancestry grew popular with the German Right.[81]

Internal evidence in the writings and art of ancient Near Eastern cultures, according to this strain of polar mysticism, suggested that "the Indo-Germans must have inhabited a now-frozen land or island region at the North Pole several millennia ago." Many circumstances reinforced such assumptions. "The earlier cultural flowering on the Nile and Euphrates suggests, as does the heavy clothing of Assyrians and Persians on monuments, that at that time a temperate climate prevailed in those now hot lands, and in our latitudes perhaps the last glaciation neared its end," wrote Georg Biedenkopp in 1906. "It is also easily conceivable that, perhaps in consequence of warm oceanic currents, the Indo-German homeland at the North Pole enjoyed mild skies, while glaciers lay over northern and central Europe. The advance and displacement of the Ice Age permitted the glaciers to win the North Pole and drive the Indo-Germans from their place."[82]

The notion that the ancestral founders of Germanic culture had come from the North Pole was long-lived, surviving both the Great War and the actual attainment of the Pole itself. This stubborn polar fantasy was able to defy reality thanks to a number of contemporary cultural factors.[83] First and foremost, the creation of an Arctic home for "Aryans" served the needs of racial pride by freeing Germans from their debt to an "Indo-Germanic" culture (and race) that arose in Asia and hence could not be really seen as "white." In fact, locating the beginnings of the Indo-Germans at the Pole permitted a reversal of cultural debts. "The ancient astronomical achievements of the Chinese, Assyrians, and Egyptians are more easily understood if we imagine Indo-German culture-bearers or culture-slaves coming from the North, amid the symmetry of the fixed-star heavens, all stars circumpolar stars, the Pole coincidental with the zenith!"[84]

Polar mysticism in Germany was also aided by science, especially geology, climatology, and archaeology. Although scientific rationalism may seem to be at odds with the erratic fancies of polar mystics, the discoveries of science provided fodder for speculation. By selectively citing new discoveries, polar dreamers could draw upon the immense prestige science enjoyed in Germany and add seeming credibility to their arguments for the mysterious connection of the polar regions to the Western past. Science proved, for example, that the polar regions were not always frozen. The recently discovered "gigantic, herbivorous animals, which could certainly have devoured an entire tree crown for breakfast, could never have lived in an ice desert; they needed a luxuriant swamp vegetation, like the Indian jungles. And the devastating global catastrophe must have broken over the inhabitants of this antediluvian paradise with extreme suddenness."[85]

During the turbulent era of the Weimar Republic, German polar speculation often bordered upon the lunatic. Theosophy, sun-ray therapy, and all the fringe epistemologies that flourish in unsettled times embraced the opportunity offered by the still little known Poles. For some, the North Pole was an umbilical cord connecting humanity with the power of the universe. "The North Pole forms the immediate connection of the earth with the surrounding universal space, with the Ur-radiation," insisted G. A. Hoenerssen. "The North Pole forms the gate through which the earth maintains uninterrupted its life force, 'from heaven above,' the material in energy form that it requires for its existence. . . . The North Pole is the navel of the world, through which it receives its life force, the Ur-radiation, which lets all be."[86] Others argued for a hidden Pole-to-Pole axis that concealed a Valhalla-like home of gods and mythical heroes.

> I say that it can only be the polar regions of the globe, as the last remaining earthly regions not yet embraced in their entirety by human exploration, that may be considered as the eventual divine home . . . Mankind! Do you seek still today, perhaps, after paradise in this world? Look, you have been standing amid it since the dark, dawning days of an earthly human race! Whether you adorn it or not, I would not like to say, considering your contemporary conception of life! Therefore, mankind, guard yourself before certain great and mighty pincers, easily embracing and crushing you, whose one blade is hidden in the divine Arctic and the other in the divine Antarctic![87]

Such flights were unusual, but the general sentiment that the Poles possessed a kind of ominous and compelling power was common. Even sober, legitimate scholars and scientists conceded that the polar lands cast a mystical spell. Some ethereal attraction in the high latitudes exerted a powerful impact upon men and women, whether they were mere visitors or natives of the region. Thus Ludwig Kohl-Larsen noted in a memoir penned shortly before he joined Eckener in the *Graf Zeppelin* that the "wild, menacing landscape" at South Georgia awoke strange sensibilities and made even his consumption of raw meat on a long sledging journey seem natural.[88]

At Wegener's lonely East Station on the Greenland coast in 1931, while busy gathering Eskimo remains, Hermann Peters felt it too. To him, the impact of their eerie land explained the traditional religion of the Eskimo—their "superstition"—and made it seem somehow natural, fitting for their environment. "The modern Eskimo is perhaps nearer to us mentally; we have a common basis, that is, our civilization," he reflected. "But the old shaman, the Angekok, who attained communion with the spirits in the ecstasy of the drum dance, he came much closer to the essence of the Arctic in his attitude toward the supernatural since this land with its great lonelinesses knows no gods, only demons."[89]

The fact that the Eskimo were irresistibly drawn to the polar homeland, despite the many hardships it imposed, was also taken as evidence of its mysterious power over those who drifted into its orbit. It may have been that his "existence could hardly be called happy," trapped in the "dubious atmosphere of his snow huts," enjoying the "seal meat that he gobbles by the pound," but the "Hyperborean is contented with his lot." He loved his land "above all else" and would "exchange it with no other . . . How much sublimity and sorcery must live in a land that, despite such fearful stringency, can so bind men to it that in the friendly South they languish and die off."[90]

Throughout the classical polar era, Germans seeking the mysterious and inexplicable would continue to look to the Poles, but by the eve of World War II the world of polar fantasy was plainly under siege. As polar lands became more and more accessible, obviously, they became better known, and the range of unknown global surface territory within which fantasy could be given free reign became more and more constricted. Even the willingly gullible, if they are indeed sane, demand of their imaginings that they have some degree of credibility. As the Poles were repeatedly attained, by land and by air, the range for credible speculation on the mysteries they might still conceal steadily diminished. The success of exploration left the Poles, in a word, demystified.

Or perhaps not quite entirely. Even as the polar regions were being definitively mapped, Germans found new ways of using the Poles to frame both the hazards and the opportunities of "modernity." Alfred Döblin in 1924 made the unexplored wastes of Greenland the setting for his popular fantasy novel about the dangers of technology run amok, *Berge, Meere* und *Giganten* (Mountains, seas, and giants), in which maniacal Faustian scientists unwittingly unleash ogres concealed within the ice cap.[91] German geographers at the same time prophesied the emergence of a busy Arctic and Antarctic air travel net and warned German policy makers that the nation's chances of remaining among the leading states depended upon the exploitation of this future "Arctic global travel network."[92] Even to the present, the German engagement with the Poles continues to fascinate the credible and sprout at times the most exotic notions. A global subculture obsessed with Nazism began in the 1970s to argue that Hitler's followers continue to maintain clandestine submarine and "flying saucer" bases in Antarctica, a myth kept alive in dozens of sites on the Internet.[93]

By the middle of the 1930s, however, a different language of polar fantasizing began to supplant the enthusiasms of the polar mystics. National Socialist Germany would construct its own imagined polar world, but it was one in which there was little time for dreams of Valhalla, even less for wistful regret at the passing of indigenous northern cultures. Instead, as the darkness began to fall upon Germany and thence over Europe in the late 1930s, the new German state would find in the Poles sites where the struggle to build a better race, and a more powerful Germany, might be advanced. In this regard, perhaps, the National Socialist polar exploration grew from strains of an older German approach to the Poles.

For if one theme may be said to link the many images Germans created around the Poles over these seven decades, it is that of struggle. The crude Darwinism evident in so many aspects of German popular and elite culture in these years—in German conceptions of "race," of social structure, of international politics, of colonial and military affairs—decisively shaped and reshaped interpretations of the Poles. It was as a site for the struggle of man with nature at its most hostile, and with his own weaknesses in the face of that nature, that the image of the polar world received its most characteristic form in the early years of German polar adventurism. Later, as Germany was united and rose to world power, it was the struggle with competing powers that gave the polar environment its most salient characteristics in German polar literature. In the golden age of its exploration, the polar world took shape for Germans, as Erich von Drygalski described his own transformation at the hands of the polar environment, "out of the struggle with vast nature."

6. ARYAN AURORA

We see most recently how polar spaces play a role even in international politics and draw to themselves the rivalry of the nations—a sign of how the last, small potentials of the globe are seized in the struggle for existence, the struggle for space. These last opportunities are doubly important for the restless, high-energy civilization that the West has developed . . . Trivial as the particular instance may seem, be it the opening up of Alaska, be it the settlement of Spitsbergen, the more fundamentally impressive is the emerging overall picture of the Europeanization of the earth precisely in this most extreme direction: toward the Poles.

L. MECKING, 1925

In September 1935 Wilhelm Filchner set out through Tibet on his last great journey. His days of polar exploration were long since passed, and he returned now to the central Asian setting of his youthful exploits, leading a geomagnetic mapping expedition funded in part by the Emergency Coalition of German Science. The years by this time had caught up with even the energetic Filchner (he was nearly sixty when he set out), and the venture did not go particularly well. Kidney stones and broken bones complicated all the natural difficulty of research among the rugged terrain and primitive infrastructure of the Tibetan mountains, and the old man was happy when, after two grueling years, he at last reached the Indian border in September 1937. To his astonishment, Filchner was met in the hills outside Srinagar by the German consul at Calcutta, Count von Podewils, who had ridden out to greet the returning explorer with happy news: the führer had awarded Filchner the German National Prize for Art and Science (Deutscher Nationalpreis für Kunst und Wissenschaft), a newly created honor that carried with it a hefty monetary award of one hundred thousand marks.[1]

Filchner was struck dumb. "I had returned to Germany many times without applause or honors," he remarked, summarizing with delicate understatement a career that included public snubbing by the kaiser and national disgrace after his polar failure. Disdained, ignored, even vilified during and after the war, Filchner suddenly found himself a hero the New Order could use, as he further discovered on his return to Berlin two months later. There he was lionized by the regime's official organ, the *Völkischer Beobachter*, as a "Viking of the twentieth century" and was reminded that the

183

Third Reich knew better than its predecessors how to honor its great men: "For the first time in his life, Filchner has found recognition." After cordial visits with Hitler and Goebbels and a ceremonial presentation of the award at a black-tie dinner in the Reich capital, Filchner paid grateful tribute to the values of the new Germany with an essay entitled "Deutscher Landvolk— Arbeit an Grund und Boden adelt" (German peasantry—ennobled by labor on land and soil). Finally, he set off to bring his story to the German masses on a speaking tour sponsored by the popular Nazi Kraft durch Freude (strength through joy) program.[2]

Filchner's memoirs, written after World War II in India, where he had been interned by the British, mention neither his article nor his speaking tour, but they do make it clear that a great deal had changed. His elevation to the status of honorary Viking indicated that National Socialism was prepared to put scientific exploration to the service of the state in new ways. The signs of the government's new relationship to science were all around him. The old Weimar emergency coalition had changed, taking in 1937 a new name, the Deutsche Forschungsgemeinschaft (DFG, German Research Society), and a new director, Rudolf Mentzel, a thoroughgoing Nazi. And even as Filchner thanked the Nazis for the honors bestowed upon him, the groundwork was being laid for Germany's most ambitious effort to exploit scientific exploration in the service of politics: the National Socialist Antarctic expedition of 1938–39.[3]

Blitz over Antarctica: Technology, Exploration, and Autarky

The imperial aims that guided German foreign policy under Adolf Hitler are well known. They may be simplified as territorial expansion on the European Continent—the acquisition of Lebensraum—in order to create a self-sufficient Germany able to play a dominant role in global affairs. Eventually, this would include the rebuilding of the colonial empire that had been lost after World War I.[4] The essentially barbaric Nazi approach to international relations was complemented by a change in diplomatic style. Nazi foreign policy was expressed in a truculent and assertive nationalism that contrasted sharply with the generally internationalist tone of Weimar foreign policy. The new belligerence was clearly evident in "reborn" Germany's attitude toward polar exploration.

Hitler and his followers transformed the German polar endeavor. Under the Nazis, the array of motives that drove German activity in the high latitudes—scientific idealism, national pride, hunger for fame and fortune—was reduced to an essential, utilitarian minimum. Imperial expansion in the name of military and economic might would now provide the rationale for German work at the Poles. Weimar Germany made only one, very small scale research expedition in the High South, led by Ludwig Kohl-Larsen to South Georgia in 1928. Under the oversight of Hermann Göring, Hitler's highest subordinate, Germany in 1938 adopted a much more aggressive posture, launching one of the era's most straightforward attempts to parcel polar lands out among the European powers.

It would be a mistake, however, to blame the Nazis for the growing polar political competition that preceded World War II. While Hitler's Germany certainly aggravated the friction the West was generating at the Poles, a new tendency to squabble over polar claims was emerging entirely independently of the Nazis. The United States, Canada, and Norway all bickered in the 1920s over Arctic claims, and though tensions declined somewhat after the Second International Polar Year in 1932, Norway and Denmark had to resort to the Permanent Court of International Justice to resolve their conflicting interests in eastern Greenland (Denmark won). The Soviet Union grew more assertive of its rights in the Arctic Circle, and the United States reflected the increasingly acrimonious tenor of the times by its formal withdrawal from further participation with Aeroarctic in 1933, by which time the society had in any case become a practical nullity.

In Antarctica increased tension between the World Wars was caused by the expansion of one industry: whaling. From the founding of the Dutch North Sea Company in 1614 to the middle of the nineteenth century, the right, gray, and other species of whales inhabiting Arctic whaling grounds had been hunted to near extinction. At about the same time, Wilkes, Ross, and the seafaring explorers of the "Age of Navigators" were returning from the southern polar reaches with reports of the region's teeming marine mammal population. These accounts drew the eager interest of the Norwegians, who had been watching their profits in northern whaling grounds steadily dwindle. They initiated the modern Antarctic whale-harvesting industry in 1904, when Carl Larsen established the region's first shore-based whaling facility in the harbor at Grytviken on South Georgia, the same site where he parted the quarreling members of Filchner's homebound expedition in 1912.[5]

Larsen's station inaugurated a new global era of whale hunting, leading to yearly kills of unprecedented size that peaked on the very eve of World War II. By 1930 6 shore stations, 41 factory ships, and 232 whalers were active in Antarctic waters. Germany, with no real national whaling tradition, was not yet involved in the industry. Depletion seemed to threaten here as it had in the Arctic, and though the whalers were theoretically limited by the International Agreement for the Regulation of Whaling, signed by nine states in 1937, the year 1938 saw a new record slaughter of an incredible 46,039 whales. These yielded half a million metric tons or so of oil and other goods. Germany imported one fifth of the annual whale harvest's by-products, turning them into margarine, cosmetics, medical ointments, fat and meat extract, high-protein animal fodder, and many more high-profit items.[6]

The extremely lucrative character of Antarctic whaling, naturally enough, stimulated a rash of territorial claims. The United Kingdom, as already noted, in 1908 claimed Graham Land and a number of island groups in the continent's Atlantic sector, claims the British steadily expanded over the next two decades to embrace the coast of the Weddell Sea. Amundsen in 1911 claimed for Norway a large territory on either side of his route to the Pole as well as the region around the Pole itself. Though the Norwegian government did not make official claims at this time, its nation's rights in the area were widely viewed as proprietorial, and in 1928 it seized Bouvet Island for use as a whaling and fueling station. France already controlled Kerguelen Island and the Crozet group and in 1927 likewise expanded its claims to include Adélie Land in the Indo-Pacific sector. The increasingly grasping and exploitative attitude evident throughout the West complicates the expected picture of Nazi villainy in the region.

German observers certainly noted the growing profitability and political complexity of the Antarctic, however. Even before the Nazi accession to power, many were urging government action to prevent Germany's exclusion from polar resources. Noting recent English and French Antarctic expansion in 1933, Hans Härlin warned Germans that "political developments in the Antarctic show with emphatic clarity that the glaciated continent no longer strikes the great seafaring nations as worthless."[7] The thirties witnessed a burst of popular treatments of the polar exploits of other nations, particularly the Soviets, accompanied by continued admonitions from homegrown polar hands like Drygalski that Germany must not fall behind in reaping the Antarctic "treasures of the seas."[8] Other Germans appealed to their compatriots with less subtlety. The whaling captain Carl Kircheiss opened his Nazi era memoirs with the inscription "Whale! Whale! Germany requires again its own whaling!"[9]

National Socialism, bent upon German autarky, wholeheartedly agreed. The Nazis found their dependence upon the importation of such valuable materials intolerable, and their response was to build a whaling fleet of their own. Newly founded German whaling companies in 1934 and 1935 refitted an old freight and steerage liner, the *Württemberg*, at the Blohm and Voss yards in Hamburg. Rechristened the *Jan Wellem*, this factory ship was sent to Antarctic waters on its maiden whaling voyage in the winter of 1936–37, accompanied by six smaller whaling vessels. "For the first time, the swastika flag fluttered over a whaling ship and thereby announced Germany's claim to an appropriate share of the economic products of the southern polar seas."[10] This very modest first expedition proved a resounding success, bringing home nearly thirty thousand metric tons of oil, sufficient to cover roughly a tenth of Germany's annual needs at the time.

This promising start was eagerly pursued. Within two years a German whaling flotilla of five factory and thirty-eight whaling vessels (supported by chartered Norwegian ships) was harvesting thousands of whales and returning with nearly ninety thousand metric tons of oil. The fledgling German fleet grew at a rate that panicked neighbors, trailing only England and Norway in its yearly harvest by the winter of 1939. Nationalists exulted at the success of "Germany's struggle for nutritional and resource freedom!" Linking the whaling fleet with their reborn navy, Germans defied the claims of their rivals to special rights in Antarctic waters: "The sea is free! Wherever our fleet travels is a German hunting preserve, is a German colony, is German *Lebensraum!*"[11]

More to the point, German production helped drive the per-ton price of whale oil down sharply from its 1937 high of twenty-two English pounds to an immediate prewar low of only fourteen English pounds. Even sober German scientific journals gleefully noted that "the times in which the Norwegians could dictate the price of whale oil to importing nations are no more."[12] German government agencies worked hard to maintain a keen public appreciation of German polar interests, sponsoring popular volumes and reference works on the Poles, like Leonid Breitfuss's *Arktis*, while now-heroic adventurers like Filchner continued to urge the cultivation of polar awareness in Germany.[13]

The National Socialist Antarctic venture was conceived against this backdrop of increasing political and economic exploitation of the Antarctic. It was in many ways a unique endeavor and as such a fitting conclusion to the golden age of German polar exploration. In contrast to earlier German expeditions, for example, the impetus for the Nazi Antarctic mission arose almost entirely from the German government. None of the traditional sources of Teutonic polar inspiration, neither loose-cannon geographers set on verifying wild polar hypotheses like Petermann nor ambitious amateur explorers like Filchner nor academic societies, played any significant role in the events leading to the 1938–39 voyage. Nor was the slightest effort made, in a striking departure from earlier practice, to generate popular support for the voyage. Quite the contrary—German authorities struggled to maintain the strictest secrecy around the mission until well after its departure for the Far South. And finally, the Nazi expedition differed from its predecessors in its motivation. Science was to be incidental to territorial expansion and preparation for war.

The first proposals for renewing German continental exploration in Antarctica came from Helmut Wohlthat, a high-ranking bureaucrat in Hermann Göring's Four-Year Plan staff. The plan, proclaimed by Hitler himself at the Nuremberg party rally in 1936, was a program intended to free Germany from dependence upon foreign suppliers of raw materials, including oils and lipids. Göring was appointed deputy for the Four-Year Plan and given extensive powers to use legal sanctions and state funds to remodel the German economy for wars of conquest. Wohlthat, an ambitious and active forty-two year old, wasted no time, assembling a team of ministers in November to plan a follow-up to Filchner's debacle nearly a quarter century earlier.[14]

From the very beginning, as Wohlthat made clear later, the Nazi Antarctic expedition had both economic and territorial goals. Convening representatives of the German navy, the Foreign Office (Auswärtiges Amt), the Ministry of Economics (Reichswirtschaftsministerium), and others, Wohlthat prepared a plan that, "in combination with the expansion of German whaling, should also justify German claims to Antarctic possession."[15] As approved by Göring in the summer of 1938, the plan certainly entailed an ambitious slate of scientific activities, including coastal mapping, atmospheric measurements, oceanic depth sounding, and the collection of meteorological data. That the admirable research program was window dressing—Göring was utterly indifferent to scientific idealism—is clear from the content of his confidential orders approving the expedition: "In addition to the purely scientific mission of the expedition, which shall last for two to three months, the order is also given to research the Antarctic mainland and in part to survey it cartographically by airplane. The goal of this part of the entire mission is to create the conditions for the territorial establishment of Germany in the region."[16]

Göring's Four-Year Plan staff not only inspired and planned the expedition but also provided the funds, amounting to several hundred thousand marks, to make it possible. The vision for the expedition clearly fit into the long-term strategy making of a nation preparing for war within the year, and there can be no doubt that the decision to make a strike for Antarctic resources and territory was integrated into economic planning for the coming war. The territorial goals of the mission were classified, and efforts were made to preserve both the secrecy of the entire expedition prior to its embarkation and, in accord with Göring's wishes, to conceal the role of the office of the Four-Year Plan. Wohlthat accordingly approached other German scientific institutions seeking a "front." When Carl Bosch, head of the Kaiser Wilhelm Society (Kaiser Wilhelm-Gesellschaft), turned him down, the next logical choice was the emergency coalition's successor, the DFG. It had supported Wegener's Greenland foray, and its new president, Mentzel, shared none of Bosch's ambivalence about the Nazis. Wohlthat sweetened the request, assuring Mentzel that in return for the support of the DFG, Göring's office might make funds and equipment more readily available to research expeditions in the future. Mentzel readily assented, and the mission went forward disguised as a scientific endeavor of the DFG.[17]

The few weeks of a single Antarctic summer provided a very narrow window of opportunity, and both expert personnel and advanced equipment were essential if the ambitious scientific and political aims of the mission were to be realized. Fortunately, these were at hand. Anticipating Göring's approval during the summer of 1938, Wohlthat confidently began assembling men for his mission. As overall commander, he and his advisors chose a naval aviator, Capt. Alfred Ritscher.

At the time, Ritscher was fifty-nine years old and suited by experience as perhaps no other German for the leadership of a polar aviation mission. In December 1912 he had made his way on foot across more than two hundred kilometers of Spitsbergen, traveling by moonlight, alone and without food for over a week, in an effort to gain help for comrades stranded in the ill-fated Schröder-Stranz expedition. To this day, Ritscher's survival of the ordeal defies comprehension, and it reflected both stalwart courage and enormous stamina. He flew for the imperial navy during the war and worked after Germany's defeat for the Lufthansa, where he led the firm's department for aerial navigation. On May Day 1933 he joined Hitler's National Socialist party. Devoting himself thereafter to scientific essays and naval handbooks, Ritscher was vacationing in the hills and forests of the Harz when, at the end of July 1938, he received a letter offering him leadership of the secret expedition, beginning on 1 August 1938.[18]

Ritscher was supported by personnel nearly as qualified as himself. Alfred Kottas, an experienced mariner employed by the Lufthansa to support the transatlantic service of its flying boats, would captain the expedition's ship. As ice pilot, Wohlthat secured the services of Capt. Otto Kraul, the most experienced whaling captain available in Germany. Kraul was a veteran whaler of more than twenty years' experience who led the first voyages of the German Antarctic whaling fleet in 1936.[19] Twenty-five more scientists and technical experts were enrolled for the expedition. Many of these already had relevant experience as well, including two veteran pilots, Rudolf Mayr and Richard Schirmacher, and the geographer Ernst Herrmann, who spent the summer of 1938 testing German reconnaissance aircraft in Spitsbergen and, ironically, brought back newly discovered relics of the Schröder-Stranz venture.

Fifty-four sailors, provided by the North German Lloyd line, rounded out the expedition's complement of eighty-two. One of them, Adolf Kunze, had sailed into the Antarctic with Filchner a generation earlier. It was a choice crew ("I could not suppress my pride at daring a spring into the white wilderness of the Antarctic with such men," Ritscher later recalled), and their zeal for Germany's polar cause was fired by a 50 percent "polar supplement" pay raise and the presence on board of Karl-Heinz Röbke, a Nazi "political officer" (or domestic spy), sent along to ensure that all maintained the proper attitude.[20]

Blessed with able and experienced human resources for the polar mission, National Socialist Germany was just as fortunate in having at hand the ideal means for completing a rapid inventory of a great swath of Antarctic territory: long-range seaplanes, launched by catapult from floating "aircraft support vessels," using the most advanced photographic equipment available. From the outset of planning, Wohlthat had intended "to liberate the undertaking from the customary elaborate and time-consuming form of polar research with dogs and sleds and to employ in their place the modern aids of science and technology, in other words, the airplane, particularly in the exploration of the interior."[21] He naturally turned to Germany's air travel monopoly, the German Lufthansa, which had been created in 1924 by a forced merger of smaller airlines and thereafter pioneered regular transatlantic service.

In 1929, in collaboration with North German Lloyd shipping lines, the Lufthansa outfitted the passenger liner *Bremen* with a pneumatic catapult so that seaplanes carrying mail could be launched in mid-Atlantic. Five years later, this same technique was used to implement regular service from Berlin to Buenos Aires. Using Dornier Whale flying boats, the ocean crossing was made at the Atlantic's narrowest point, between British Gambia on the west coast of Africa and Rio de Janeiro. Refueling stops were conducted midflight at the ship *Westfalen*, a Lufthansa-owned "floating island" in the mid-Atlantic.[22]

To meet the dangers of potentially ice-filled waters and to fulfill the scientific requirements of the planned mission, Wohlthat and Ritscher convinced August von Gablenz, one of the directors of the Lufthansa, that extensive refitting of the *Westfalen* would be required. The *Westfalen*, however, was based in Rio, and in the late summer of 1938 Ritscher realized, as he put it later, that in a Brazilian shipyard it would be impossible to maintain the "necessary secrecy of the undertaking, pursued with all means and largely maintained in Germany to the very end."[23] This prompted Gablenz to offer the use of one of the Lufthansa's other air support vessels, the *Schwabenland*, which was responsible for refueling the Lufthansa's North Atlantic aviation from its base in the Azores.[24]

The *Schwabenland*'s specifications, like the new prominence of aviation, reveal the extent to which technology had revolutionized polar exploration. A mere thirty-five years earlier, Nansen went into the Arctic with the *Gjoa*, powered by a simple 13-horsepower steam engine. Twin diesel engines generating 1,800 horsepower apiece drove the *Schwabenland*. Four auxiliary diesel motors supplied power for shipboard needs. Twenty-five years earlier, the *Antarctic* kept Filchner incommunicado for months, until his return to the telegraph station at Cape Town. The *Schwabenland* carried long- and short-wave radio transmitters, with reception equipment, capable of ranges up to a thousand kilometers and providing in coastal regions almost instantaneous relayed communication with the fatherland.

The explorer's infatuation with wooden vessels was also a thing of the past. The *Schwabenland* had an up-to-date steel hull and was further modernized in a refitting noteworthy for its thoroughness and efficient rapidity. Displacing around 7,250 metric tons, it was an exploratory behemoth, over ten times the size of the craft commanded by Filchner, Shackleton, and the legends of earlier days. The *Schwabenland* reached Hamburg on 27 October, with roughly six weeks to meet its 15 December deadline for trials and departure. Wohlthat put a small army of engineers, welders, and machinists to work. The ship would be conveying to Antarctica twice the human cargo it normally carried in the North Atlantic, so cabins and messes had to be redesigned and expanded. Most of the officers and flight personnel received comfortable private accommodations. The crew went three to a room. On the advice of Kraul, the ship's internal frame was strengthened to resist ice pressure; the bow was reinforced; a steel belt, or "ice girdle," was bolted around the waterline; and the bronze propellers, vulnerable to deformation under ice pressure, were replaced with cast steel. New fuel and water tanks, laboratories, and housings for depth-sounding equipment and radio balloons completed the *Schwabenland*'s transformation into a polar research vessel.

The most crucial tools of the expedition, of course, were the two Lufthansa-owned Dornier flying boats—*Boreas* and *Passat*—with which Mayr and Schirmacher would survey the Antarctic mainland. These were four-man craft, designed as transatlantic mail carriers. Each was propelled by two BMW engines, powerful 690-horsepower, 12-cylinder machines that straddled the center of the single elevated wing in a push-and-pull arrangement behind and above the cockpit. They were of a type commonly known as Whales, and the name fit very well. Each one weighed nine metric tons. Slow and low-flying craft, they couldn't be driven to go much faster than 220 kilometers per hour, and they were unable to operate effectively at altitudes above 4,500 meters or so, a height to which they could struggle only after half an hour or more of laborious ascent.

These defects were more than offset, however, by a number of virtues that fitted the Whales very nicely for polar work. For one thing, they were spacious, capable of carrying very substantial loads, including nearly four and a half metric tons of fuel, men, and equipment over ranges of hundreds of kilometers. For another, they were rugged and durable aircraft whose metal alloy frame and sheet metal body could endure open ocean landings, long-distance flying in turbulent, icy weather, and the stress of catapult launchings at velocities of 150 kilometers per hour.

The *Passat* had proven the durability of these aircraft in December 1936, when its rear propeller fell off four hundred kilometers from the African coast. Forced to land on the open ocean, the craft survived more than a day of bobbing on the South Atlantic swell before it was retrieved, outfitted with a spare prop, and sent back to work.[25] With their enormous fuel capacity, these aircraft could remain aloft up to fifteen hours if they had not been overloaded. In the summer of 1925, the Whale had been the first metal-skinned airplane taken into the Arctic, when Amundsen and Lincoln Ellsworth took two of them north of Spitsbergen. If no one was likely to mistake the craft for a flying thoroughbred, it was nonetheless a superb piece of functional aeronautical design and without question a dependable mechanical draft horse.

In early December 1938, while the *Schwabenland* in its Hamburg dock was a buzzing hive of round-the-clock labor, the Whales were modified for polar research. Skids were installed as preparation for a possible forced landing upon the Antarctic ice. Each airplane was also tailored to its task in a more unusual manner. Special bays containing racks for the release of metal "dart-bombs" were installed beneath the tail at the rear of each plane's fuselage. The dart-bombs were one-and-a-half-meter fléchettes, designed, along with their release apparatus, by engineers at Dornier. Each metal shaft was tipped at one end with a steel point and at the other with three stabilizing fins, as at the back of a throwing dart or aerial bomb. One fin on each dart was embossed with the swastika.

Tests over Alpine glaciers conducted in November 1938 showed that, when dropped from heights of five hundred meters, the points of these devices would generally penetrate the ice to depths of thirty centimeters. Released over the Antarctic by the Whales at intervals of twenty to thirty kilometers during their flight, these "sovereignty emblems" would define the limits of German territory. The idea of confirming a valid claim to sovereignty by casting darts at the vast Antarctic ice sheet was less ridiculous then than it seems today. Byrd, for example, had tried to establish American precedence in Antarctic territory by dropping flags from his airplane a decade earlier.[26]

In keeping with the commitment to secrecy, both the personnel and equipment for the third Antarctic expedition were drawn from state agencies or corporations with close ties to the government. The Lufthansa, for example, founded at the insistence of the state, subsidized by the state, and with many of its personnel soon to be absorbed into the Luftwaffe, was in the late 1930s an arm of the German government in all but name. Dornier was accustomed to cooperating with German authorities, as was the North German Lloyd line, responsible for supplying provisions as well as crewmen. Scientific specialists for the trip came from a range of government offices, including the Naval High Command, the Reich Office for Meteorology, the Reich Ministry of Nutrition and Agriculture, the Reich Ministry for Economics, and the German Marine Observatory in Hamburg.[27]

Just as in Germany's other great venture in aerial polar exploration, the flight of the *Graf Zeppelin*, sophisticated photographic technology provided by Zeiss was expected to survey in hours an area that would take weeks to reconnoiter by land. A specially built double serial survey instrument was mounted behind the fuel tanks of each aircraft in what had been the mail room. Focused downward at twenty-degree angles, these cameras provided from an altitude of three thousand meters a detailed topographical image to a range of twenty-five kilometers on each side of the plane and would take in imagery with less clarity at extreme ranges of up to a hundred kilometers. Each image, captured on a gargantuan eighteen-by-eighteen-centimeter negative, would have a 60 percent overlap with the images immediately preceding and following on the film spool.

After six weeks of round-the-clock remodeling by more than a hundred craftsmen, the *Schwabenland* was ready. On the morning of 15 December, high-ranking representatives of all the ministries, agencies, and institutes that had contributed to the preparations appeared on board for a day-long test run of the ship's new equipment. Led by Wohlthat, the delegation of visitors came aboard from the starboard literally as the last mechanics and craftsmen scurried down the port gangway. The day was bitterly cold, appropriately, but Ritscher remembered later that the honored guests were reluctant to seek shelter, preferring, after their dinner of "hearty stew" in the mess, to take their coffee and liqueur on the bridge and promenade deck.

Wohlthat had a few hortatory words in private with each of the officers and scientists. He concluded the day by addressing the ship's entire company as well as some carefully selected and briefed members of the press. "I congratulate you on being a member of the German Antarctic expedition of 1938–39, which will once again attempt, after a pause of twenty-six years, to accomplish valuable scientific work in the still least known continent. I wish you and your seasoned expedition leader the best health and achievement. Come back safe and sound, and bring back good results. Heil Hitler!"[28]

Two days later, on a sunny and bitterly cold Saturday afternoon, the *Schwabenland* left Hamburg for the Antarctic.

Lines on the Ice

Great pains had been taken to conceal the nature of the *Schwabenland*'s mission and its departure. The leaders of the ship's various scientific and technical units were discouraged from too much loose talk with one another, and instead, by Göring's orders, all were to refer directly and only to Ritscher. Flying the flag of the DFG, a blue-and-yellow affair created especially for the mission, the *Schwabenland*'s departure went virtually unreported in the media. A week after Ritscher and his crew sailed, a few scattered and easily missed notices, usually grouped in news tidbits sections and never more than a sentence or two long, appeared in a handful of German newspapers and geographical journals.[29] In general, it went unnoticed abroad as well, at first. The journal of Britain's Royal Geographical Society, for example, didn't publish its first reports that the expedition had even taken place until September 1939, months after the *Schwabenland* had returned and after the war had broken out. A comprehensive account, even then only a few pages long, did not appear in England until 1940.[30]

The veil could not be drawn completely over the expedition, however. Secrets are hard to keep along the waterfront, and the Hamburg docks were full of rumors, some of surprising accuracy. "So, are you really going to the South Pole?" a dockworker asked Herrmann. A local vegetable seller, who claimed her son was one of the crew, had told the worker the story.[31] Some of Germany's rivals, perhaps more alert than the British geographical establishment, noticed as well. Four weeks after the *Schwabenland* departed, on 14 January 1939, the Norwegian government took the decisive step of declaring the portion of the Antarctic coast between 20° west and 45° east longitude a Norwegian sovereignty zone.

This was a preemptive strike at precisely the region toward which the *Schwabenland* was directed. Ritscher's orders were to map the coast and inland regions in the area due south of Bouvet Island, between 5° west and 15° east longitude. The *Schwabenland* covered the roughly 4,000 nautical miles (7,400 kilometers) between Germany and the Antarctic coast in just under four weeks, making 220 to 240 nautical miles (410 to 450 kilometers) most days, a respectable if not spectacular pace. Ritscher reported that progress was slowed by chronic breaks in the cooling system of the port engine, apparently caused by excessive vibration of the engine block.

No such breakdowns bedeviled the ship's social structure. Recalling perhaps the disgraceful collapse of shipboard harmony under Filchner, Ritscher noted that his men displayed admirable discipline in avoiding "the formation of clique, group, and faction that has been the death of so many an expedition."[32] Shipboard life passed in much the same way as in earlier German expeditions. The empty hours when work was finished were filled with tobacco; chess and skat; choral music; a quartet of violin, zither, accordion, and flute; and a fair amount of drinking. Food was richly provided, and in a bow to National Socialist egalitarianism, there was no distinction in the fare provided officers and crew.

Two or three nights a week, selected expedition members lectured their comrades on their field of expertise: hygiene and the prevention of frostbite by the ship's doctor, handling of boats in drift ice by the ice pilot, preparation of the catapult and aircraft recovery by the flight personnel, and so on. Collegial feeling, fortified by male camaraderie, reigned. "We go into a land where the men don't have to blow themselves up like roosters," Herrmann noted, paraphrasing Byrd, "because there are no chickens there. But, to anticipate the story, when the first 'chickens' turned up after eleven and a half weeks, then they may perhaps have seen some things."[33]

Accounts left by the participants show the *Schwabenland* mission as an unmistakable product of the Third Reich's official values. Both the command structure instituted during the clandestine preparations and the informal social practices of the expedition faithfully reflected the National Socialist ethos. In keeping with the Nazi *Führerprinzip* (leadership principle) during preparation, subordinate agencies were discouraged from working directly together, ostensibly in the name of secrecy. Channeled instead through the leader, the system generated a certain degree of administrative inefficiency, as it did in the Third Reich at large. And the faux egalitarian posture of the New Order, so important to the popular appeal of Nazism, was manifested aboard the *Schwabenland* in the widely noted lack of distinction between the provisions for officers and men.

Christmas was observed in particular style. The crew's mess was decked out on Christmas Eve with trees and wreaths, and an impromptu chorus accompanied by the quartet provided appropriate music. Each crewman received Yuletide fruits and nuts and three bottles of special beer, with ham and asparagus dished up on an all-you-can-eat basis. The ship's electrician rigged loudspeakers in the mess to take in Christmas broadcasts from home as the ship passed by the Canaries. Afterward there were festive trinkets for all (tobacco implements, pocketknives, knickknacks, carved penguins), and Röbke, justifying his presence on board, led a round of "Sieg Heils" for führer and Reich. To conclude the evening, officers and fliers regaled their fellows with tales of adventure in whaling, the Arctic, and flight. Ritscher's account of his solo journey across Spitsbergen, which also fell across the Christmas holidays, impressed the entire crew. "It was certainly good," Herrmann noted, "that every expedition participant could once more be assured that his expedition commander was no neophyte in ice and snow, that each heard once more from his own mouth the experiences in which he had had to prove himself in the most bitter fashion."[34]

The ship's scientists set to work as soon as the Schwabenland cleared the English Channel, and they pursued their research with devotion throughout the four-week voyage to the edge of Antarctica. The meteorologists, directed by Herbert Regula of the German Marine Observatory and Heinz Lange of the Reich Ministry for Science and Education (Reichsministerium für Wissenschaft, Erziehung und Volksbildung), were especially active. From Ushant on the French coast southward, they gathered data on wind speed, cloud cover, air temperature, precipitation, and other meteorological phenomena to compile detailed daily weather charts.

An important part of their mandate, and one with obvious application to military aviation, included the launching at regular intervals of high-altitude radio weather balloons. The balloons, one and a half meters in diameter and filled, like the Hindenburg, with hydrogen, were launched from a specially crafted circular shaft in a cargo hatch on the afterdeck. Each one carried a battery-powered radio transmitter weighing about .75 kilograms. Upon release, the transmitters relayed a steady stream of data on wind direction and speed, relative humidity, temperature, and air pressure. Though none of the balloons reached the hoped-for altitude of thirty thousand meters, for which a special prize had been offered, they were very successful in collecting data at heights up to twenty-eight thousand meters, and the radio transmitters proved both highly efficient and reliable.

On 9 January, after twenty-four days at sea, crewmen spotted the first albatross seen from the deck of the Schwabenland. Icebergs followed. By the afternoon of 16 January, Ritscher counted fifty-three of them, some up to a kilometer in length, surrounding the ship. The Schwabenland was nearing its goal. On 17 January, Ritscher and his crew rendezvoused at 63° south latitude with a tanker called the Ana Knudsen, a support vessel for German whalers operating in the area. Herrmann used one of the ship's boats to ferry replacement radio tubes to the tanker, returning with a gift of whale fillets, which the *Schwabenland*'s men at first sampled with suspicion and then consumed with gusto. Now at the edge of the Antarctic summer pack ice, Ritscher cautiously maneuvered his ship as far south as possible, near the target longitude of 5° east. On the night of 19 January, the ship faced an unbroken front of pack ice at 69° south latitude and 4° east longitude. Here the crew set to work making Germany's Antarctic claim.

Preparations for the first flight of the *Boreas* commenced during the night, and the craft was launched with Teutonic punctuality, precisely on schedule, at 4:40 A.M. on 20 January. The heavily laden aircraft was carrying over five metric tons, a half-ton overburdening that was dismissed as trifling at the time. Each of the surveying cameras was a bulky colossus, at over 150 kilograms the equivalent of two additional crewmen. Tons of fuel and scientific instruments and hundreds of kilograms of emergency provisions and supplies were also included. Parachutes (naturally), sleds, rifles, skis, tents, food, first-aid supplies, kerosene, and other polar necessities were packed into the Whale's fuselage to be used in the event of a forced landing on the Antarctic inland ice.

The flight plan laid out for Schirmacher (and for the *Passat*) was simple. The plane was to carve out a great rectangle, flying due south from the *Schwabenland* for 880 kilometers, completing a ninety-degree left turn and continuing 30 kilometers east, then making another turn for a return flight on a line parallel to the outward-bound route. The *Boreas* and *Passat* would alternate such flights, each to begin 50 kilometers eastward of the last. En route, their flight crews would cast out their fifty territorial markers and ten swastika flags at regular intervals, thus delimiting the bounds of the eventual German claim.

This was admirably rational planning. Theoretically, if a constant elevation around three thousand meters could be maintained, the Zeiss cameras would produce on each flight detailed photographic images of roughly two hundred thousand square kilometers of Antarctic territory. In reality, as the interior of the continent rose before the advancing aircraft, it would prove impossible for the Whales to hold such an elevation. The continental interior reached altitudes of thousands of meters above sea level, and the Whales, loaded as they were, would not, at their maximum, climb above four thousand meters. Growing closer to the land they photographed as the planes advanced toward the south, their cameras would take in a smaller range of territory, so that in fact each flight would compile a photographic record of only about sixty-five thousand square kilometers, less than a third of their theoretical optimum.

This was a significant achievement nonetheless. The *Schwabenland* had, in its coastal sector, advanced farther toward the mainland than any previous ship, and the land to be mapped was for the most part entirely uncharted. The launching of the *Boreas*, in the excellent weather that favored the expedition for much of its Antarctic sojourn, went without a hitch. Slung from its slide, the first German aircraft over the Antarctic slowly ascended as Schirmacher circled the *Schwabenland*. The eyes of nearly the entire crew, Herrmann noted, followed the *Boreas* until it finally vanished on its course to the south. "Then, with heavy thoughts, we returned to the bridge," he wrote. "It's not the soldier in the field who worries but always those who remain behind."[35]

While the crew of the *Schwabenland* waited anxiously for news of this, their first attempt to perform their real mission, the *Passat* was mounted on the catapult launcher for immediate departure in the event of an emergency. The first radio messages began to arrive from the *Boreas* about an hour after departure. Though the Whale performed reliably, the flight soon proved to be far from an unqualified success. About four hours after takeoff, Schirmacher had overflown a coastal mountain range and then encountered a steeply climbing inland plateau. Eventually this reached an altitude of nearly four thousand meters, and the *Boreas*, unable to struggle to much higher altitude, was skimming the surface at an elevation of a mere two hundred meters. At this point, only six hundred kilometers south of the *Schwabenland*, Schirmacher made his turn to the east to complete the short side of his flight rectangle and return to the ship.

Two hours later, the flight photographer reported that the starboard camera had ceased functioning. The *Boreas* was ordered back to the ship, and the first flight came to an end after completing 1,100 of its intended 1,790 kilometers. During the course of the flight, furthermore, Ritscher was compelled to violate the expedition's ironclad rule against sending one of the aircraft aloft before the other had returned. While the *Boreas* was still over the inland ice, pack ice, "hard as granite," Ritscher noted, had begun to close in on the *Schwabenland*. Ultimately, it became necessary to launch the *Passat* as an airborne ice pilot, guiding the ship through leads to a stretch of fairly open water.

Despite these setbacks and irregularities, later at the nightly debriefing the mood was a happy one. The flight had gone without a serious hitch, and it seemed to vindicate the potential of the new method of exploration. "This first flight was the first test of material and equipment," Herrmann noted. "It is important to establish that further flights can go forward in the same fashion."[36] The ship's technicians immediately went to work on the faulty photographic equipment. The men dined with the appetite of the healthy (the *Schwabenland*'s crew were looked after with daily supplements of vitamins C, D, and A), and then the pilots reported to their colleagues on the splendors that they had been the first of humankind to view. This was a heady notion for all aboard upon which the crew reflected before gathering in the salon to hear broadcasts from Berlin. "Strange thought! Here we sit on the icy coast of the Antarctic continent and hear a man speak who is standing in Room 137 of the Radio House in Berlin. And how it all interests us! The political part naturally but also the local news."[37]

Back in Wohlthat's Leipziger Strasse offices in Berlin, one and a half kilometers or so from the broadcaster to whom the *Schwabenland*'s men were listening, more good feeling was going around. Now styled ministerial director for special employment, the spiritual father of the expedition passed the news of the safe arrival and successful start of the Antarctic mission to his boss, Göring, and to colleagues in half a dozen government agencies. "The scientific results are very satisfactory," he assured the project's backers on 24 January. "The mood and health on board the *Schwabenland* are excellent." He claimed that over eighty thousand square kilometers had now been photographically mapped and proposed that steps be taken without delay to arrange publication of the expedition's results and to work out a strategy for naming new landmarks. "Since the question of nomenclature for the just-mentioned geographical discoveries can become very urgent under certain conditions, I beg you for a prompt consideration of this question."[38]

Others in Berlin's government quarter shared Wohlthat's urgent desire to get appropriate German names onto the Antarctic map as quickly as possible. Naming was seen as an important political deed, reflective perhaps of a naive faith in the permanence of such acts—one evident too in the satisfaction of Petermann at seeing German names on maps— that was bound to be cruelly disappointed. Wohlthat's circular to his colleagues sparked an exchange of bureaucratic notes and meetings over the next three weeks that involved high officials from the Foreign Office, Goebbels's Propaganda Ministry (Reichsministerium für Volksaufklärung und Propaganda), the Reich Ministry for Science and Educational, the DFG, and many other agencies. The question of names might seem incidental or even trivial in retrospect. Nothing could be further from the perspective of the Berlin bureaucrats at the time, however. Mentzel, speaking for himself and several ministers in other agencies, put the issue squarely at the heart of the führer's dreams for the new Germany's global position:

> Proceeding from the supposition that Germany is in the process of pursuing its already raised claim to the restitution of its colonies with heightened emphasis before the world, particularly since the last Reichstag speech of the führer, it appears desirable to so choose the names of those portions of the Antarctic mainland ex-plored by the *Schwabenland* and to be taken into possession that they can make self-evident reference to our current economic-political and colonial-political situation. The assembled representatives of the just-named ministries thus suggest as first choice of a name for the new German overseas possession "Necessity Land." As a second choice the name "Schwabenland" was suggested, with reference to the research journey carried out by the ship *Schwaben-land*.[39]

Ignoring Mentzel's plodding bureaucratese and the appallingly pedes-trian name brought forth by the labors of his clerks' panel, his words suggest that the government was very serious about beginning its quest for extra-European *Lebensraum* at the South Pole. Here they found a *Raum ohne Volk* ready for the representatives of the *Volk ohne Raum*.

While the memoranda flew in Berlin, the *Passat* and *Boreas* continued their photographic flights over the ice, despite being grounded by bad weather between 23 and 29 January. The topography of the land and the technical limitations of the Whales, however, combined to impose a change in the underlying photomapping strategy of the expedition. The series of three photographic flights conducted between 20 and 22 January before the onset of storms had revealed a broad, ice-covered foreland, largely free of landmarks and not particularly promising as a subject for aerial mapping. This foreland was bordered, at a distance of roughly forty kilometers inland, by an impressive range of mountains running apparently over one hundred kilometers toward the east. Beyond this again appeared a steadily rising but largely featureless ice plateau. Given this situation, Ritscher resolved that the most fruitful course upon the return of clement weather would be to pursue the mapping flights on an east-west axis along the mountain range and the coastline.

In the meantime, evenings were passed as they always were aboard expedition vessels. Classical music performances (Praetorius made a particular impression on the crew), games and cards, radio broadcasts, and the celebration of birthdays helped pass the time. The ship even radioed birthday greetings to Göring on 12 January, which he acknowledged with a brief message to the crew a few days later. On 30 January the crew assembled in the swastika-bedecked common room to hear National Socialist District Group Leader Röbke commemorate the sixth anniversary of Hitler's dictatorship, or what Ritscher called the "seizure of power." There is no recorded evidence of the depression and irritability that plagued so many German expeditions. This, of course, may be due simply to the tendency of all official accounts to strive for the best possible presentation of proceedings. It may also reflect the fact that alcohol consumption, in contrast with earlier ventures, was strictly limited. Herrmann notes that a full glass of schnapps was seen as a considerable indulgence aboard the *Schwabenland*.

With clearing weather, a second series of long-distance flights began on 29 January. Despite enjoying unusually fine flying weather, both aircraft had shown trouble maintaining altitude, particularly the *Passat*. The problem, described as a "ballast difficulty" in the accounts of the expedition, was probably more straightforward: the planes were simply overloaded. This recurrent problem led to the expedition's one serious brush with tragedy and to Ritscher's decision to curtail long-distance flights.

By the morning of 3 February, the *Schwabenland* had worked its way eastward to a point near 15° east longitude. The *Passat* was launched southward just after 7:00 A.M. in clear weather that, the ship's meteorologists informed Ritscher, would not last more than twenty-four hours. The ship was to perform photomapping over the eastern reaches of what became known as the Wohlthat Mountains, a range whose highest peaks topped three thousand meters.

At 9:00 A.M. the radioman, Herbert Ruhnke, reported "engines grumbling." Within the hour, this had become more serious: "Engines sneezing back and forth, since the fuel mixture is too cold. External thermometer apparently not recording accurately, since it has not changed. Must be at least -30 Centigrade." This message alarmed the entire ship's crew. Ritscher ordered the *Boreas* cleared to start in case emergency support was required. Inspections were begun on the sixty reserve parachutes to be used for supply drops in case the aircraft was stranded. An hour later, Ruhnke reported again: "4,150 meters. Strongly gusting. Machine barely controllable. Very tail-heavy. Flying to east edge of mountains, then return to ship." Later, cut off by a frontal system that Ruhnke reported as "black as a bear's ass," the *Passat* altered course once more. Finally, at just past 2:00 P.M., the flying boat touched down beside the *Schwabenland*.

The return of the *Passat* closed the expedition's one episode of really hair-raising danger. Had Mayr and his crew indeed been forced down on the ice, their survival, even if they had made it through a forced landing, was unlikely. The *Boreas* could perhaps have located them, though this is by no means certain, but repeated low-level flights by both craft had shown that a landing on the ice without special equipment was unlikely to be successful or to permit the Whale to lift off again. It would have been up to survivors of a crash, in other words, to make their way out of the inland mountains and to the coast. With the momentary Antarctic summer already showing signs of turning toward its typically savage autumn, their chances would not have been good. These considerations were present in Ritscher's mind and in those of the flight captains. With the *Passat* safely back and in agreement with his fliers, Ritscher curtailed long-distance flight. On 4 February one more short flight was made, and two days later the *Schwabenland* began the long voyage back to Germany.

The Passing of "New Schwabenland"

The *Schwabenland* anchored outside the mouth of the Elbe on 10 April, entering the harbor at Hamburg the next day. Wohlthat and Mentzel led a welcoming delegation of officials from civilian and military agencies, who celebrated the return of Ritscher and his men first aboard ship and then with a formal ceremonial dinner at Hamburg's posh Four Seasons hotel (Hotel Vier Jahreszeiten). Speeches, telegrams, and hugs and kisses were exchanged, and the mood was triumphal. Hitler's laconic personal telegram, conveyed to Ritscher and his comrades at dinner, was a highlight of the welcome home. "I thank the members of the German Antarctic expedition 1938–39 for the message of their return to the homeland. With it I convey my heartfelt congratulations on the successful completion of the tasks confided to the expedition. Adolf Hitler."[40]

The *Schwabenland*'s brief Antarctic foray certainly seemed to have been a triumphant scientific success. Ritscher and his team brought home to Germany a bountiful harvest of data. In more than 11,000 aerial photographs, the *Boreas* and *Passat* had reconnoitered 250,000 square kilometers of previously uncharted territory. They viewed, without systematically photographing, another 350,000 square kilometers, thus exploring an unknown region whose total size was larger than Germany in its borders of 1937. Their findings were of greatest importance to geographers, able for the first time to gather an overview of a large region of Antarctic topography without the arduous necessity of land expeditions. Though certain inaccuracies due to navigational misreadings crept into German charts, the fliers established the general nature of what they christened New Schwabenland: it consisted of a slowly rising, ice-covered coast, broken inland by a series of mountain ranges, some near 3,600 meters. German names, in fulfillment of Petermann's dreams, now dotted the cartographic face of Antarctica: Wohlthat Mountains, Petermann Range, Ritscher Upland, Penck Trough.

These noteworthy geographic achievements were by no means the scientific limit of the *Schwabenland*'s success, a great deal of which was accomplished on the voyages to and from Antarctica. Only 19 days of the entire 117-day mission had been spent on the edge of the Antarctic ice. The meteorologists had sent 184 radio balloons aloft (a fifth of them south of the Antarctic Circle), gathering a valuable series of data sets covering a broad expanse of the South Atlantic. Electro-acoustic sounding equipment aboard the *Schwabenland* produced a new and more accurate picture of the ocean floor, particularly of the South Atlantic Ridge. Leo Gburek, of Leipzig Geophysical Institute (Institut für Geophysik), made valuable contributions to the German tradition of geomagnetic mapping in the course of four journeys onto the coastal ice off New Schwabenland. German science viewed the mission as an unqualified success. "The German people look with great pride on its sailors, fliers, and scientists, who in a great historical moment have accomplished bold acts of discovery and have brought honor to the German name in the distant, ice-armored Antarctic."[41]

But, like the earlier South Polar ventures of Filchner and Drygalski, the mission of the *Schwabenland* had been about a great deal more than mere science. For most of those concerned with its planning, it is safe to say, scientific considerations were little more than a convenient veil for far-reaching political aims. Was the mission a political success? Wohlthat believed so, as did Göring and others in Berlin. The *Schwabenland* had not been home three months when Wohlthat, striking while the iron of his success was still hot, began detailed planning with the military and other civilian agencies for a new and more elaborate Antarctic expedition to be carried out within a year. Three days before the invasion of Poland, Wohlthat circulated a memorandum, with Göring's support, that proposed for the new mission the use not only of the *Schwabenland* and its aircraft but also a Fiesel Stork reconnaissance plane (which Herrmann had taken to Spitsbergen) and a large Junkers 52 trimotored transport as well.[42]

Ritscher also believed he had succeeded. Writing three years later, as his nation slowly succumbed to the Allied coalition called forth by Hitler's mania, Ritscher boasted of his crew's political triumph: "By the exploration, mapping, delineation, and possession of New Schwabenland, Germany has made the first step in international law toward a declaration of possession in this district. It may now be established that through the activity of the expedition the Reich has acquired an entirely valid right to codetermination in the impending apportionment of the Antarctic by the interested powers. For its right to participation in the whale catch in Antarctic seas, which is of the utmost value for our fat supplies, the expedition will also be of the greatest significance."[43] Many others in Germany agreed, citing the expedition to argue that exploration of an Antarctic region was a prerequisite to a declaration of sovereignty and to refute Norwegian claims to the area (which were not, in any case, well grounded).[44]

Herrmann also defended the political rights of Germany in a chatty, popular work on the *Schwabenland*'s journey that he put out in 1941, preceding in print the scientific results of the expedition. Incidentally, this account nearly mired Herrmann in trouble with the government. His book, with the innocuous title *Deutsche Forscher im Südpolarmeer* (German researchers in the South Polar sea), is not nearly so sober as it sounds, relating political views, the practical jokes of the crew, and sentimental stories of common seamen in a uniform and ultimately annoying tone of sophomoric levity. It clearly annoyed his contemporaries, too. In February 1942 Herrmann was denounced in an anonymous letter to the Reich Chamber of Culture (Reichskulturkammer):

> The book *Deutsche Forscher im Südpolarmeer*, by Ernst Herrmann, which recently appeared with Safari Publishers and which in the introduction is characterized as a "popular work about the German Antarctic expedition," exists for the most part of *idiocy*, which is concerned with the ship's crew and does not shy away from vulgarity. As a German, one feels shame that such stuff concerning an expedition carried out with state means can be printed and promoted by public presses. The taste- and tactlessness of the author produces such scenes as the following, on page 81: "We got along very well. First with 'Good morning! Heil Hitler!' That made

little impression." The one thus greeted with Heil Hitler! is a young *penguin!!* If you did that at the zoo, you'd be locked up. Where is the office that today watches over German literature? Heil Hitler!

The denunciation became a part of Herrmann's party record. Authorities in the Chamber of Culture wrote him a calm, chilling note, observing with regret that, "unfortunately, the complainant did not sign his name, and I thus have no occasion to pursue the matter further. But I recommend you privately to draw the necessary conclusions for yourself."[45]

In retrospect, the work of the *Schwabenland* was clearly a dead end and an utter political failure. Hitler's war, by antagonizing naval powers far better able to control marine routes than Germany, quashed German Antarctic ambitions and permanently discredited any claim that might have arisen from the success of Ritscher, Mayr, Schirmacher, and the other members of the expedition. Many of the expedition's members didn't even live to see its results published. Gburek died in air combat over Scotland; Erich Gruber, the flight radio officer of the *Boreas*, died in a plane crash on the French coast; and the vessel's oceanographer, Karl-Heinz Paulsen, was killed leading a machine-gun company in Estonia, all before 1942. All, in Ritscher's elegiac note in his account of the expedition, were sacrificed to "the freedom fight of Greater Germany."[46]

The political success of the *Schwabenland*, in contrast with its record of solid scientific achievement, lasted only a few months. As soon as war broke out, German vessels in the region were reduced to the status of fugitives fleeing from more powerful Allied naval units. German whaling, of course, disappeared. The *Jan Wellem* was destroyed in the invasion of Norway, and Germany made no wartime whaling ventures, although the raider *Pinguin* seized a fourteen-boat Norwegian whaling fleet in 1941, successfully guiding it through the blockade to Germany.

This was an isolated polar victory, however. German weather stations operated in the Arctic under conditions of extreme privation throughout World War II, but Hitler's land grab put an end to German activity in the Antarctic for a generation.[47] By 1942 polar regions apparently existed for Hitler only as part of his vengeful racial obsession, wastelands to which he threatened to deport stiff-necked subject peoples.[48] Association with Hitler's war discredited, in a few years, close to a century of German activity in the high latitudes. Even the Germanic nomenclature concocted by the bureaucrats in Berlin largely vanished. New Schwabenland, thanks to a more careful postwar Norwegian land survey, soon became Queen Maud's Land on most Western maps, although Wohlthat's name and a few others survive in the mountains scouted by *Boreas* and *Passat*. Once again, the political dreams that had drawn Germans toward the Poles proved elusive, and their seeming fulfillment was no more substantial than the auroras that entranced German explorers in the high latitudes.

EPILOGUE
Elusive Glory

As the twentieth century drew to its close, Germany's leading polar science foundation, the Alfred-Wegener-Institut für Polar- und Meeresforschung (Alfred Wegener Institute for Polar and Oceanic Research), organized an elaborate exhibit looking back at 125 years of German exploration. Curious visitors wandered among artifacts dating from the age of Koldewey and Petermann to the new millennium, including many of the devices that made the German presence at the Poles possible: sleds and tents, Eskimo-style garments, theodolites, telescopes, diaries, ships' logs, and all the material apparatus of polar legend. Stripped of the aura of hardship and extremity lent by their intended setting, however, the glamour of these objects fades, much as carnivorous beasts appear diminished when seen through bars at the zoo. Fascinating as they may be to the historian or polar enthusiast, some essential quality of the polar experience eludes museum exhibits. Perhaps retrospective displays of polar materiel seem incomplete because they seldom convey a sense of where a nation's polar episode fits into its larger history.

Germany in the late nineteenth and early twentieth centuries was clearly a nation striving to prove itself at the Poles. Just as clearly, it failed to do so. A succession of Germans went forth for decades to do battle with polar nature, driven by the quest for fame, scientific achievement, and political gain. Usually they returned with those hopes unfulfilled. An unlucky star seems to have hovered over most of the German scientists and adventurers who took their nation's flag into the high latitudes. Time and again, meticulously prepared ventures set out with buoyant confidence, only to have their dreams dashed by shipwreck, disease, nervous collapse, bungled communication, or death. The story of Germany's encounter with the polar world is largely a story of failed aspirations.

This is not to say that German work in the high latitudes was without successes. Germans could congratulate themselves upon a number of achievements. Their scientific record during the era of the race for the Poles compares well with that of the states who won the race. While Amundsen, Scott, Peary, and Shackleton focused the attention of their nations on the glory-hunting march to the earth's axes, Germans helped organize the productive, sober research of the First International Polar Year. The Drygalski and Wegener expeditions collected immense quantities of scientific data while missing the fame so eagerly pursued, and won, by the other Anglo-Saxons. In the sounding of the polar oceans, analysis of the polar atmosphere, application of aerial photography, and exploration of the Greenland ice cap, German explorers nurtured a valuable tradition.

It is also possible that much more than mere scientific data was salvaged from the ineffectuality of the German polar quest. A dawning appreciation for the ingenuity and folkways of non-European peoples, however limited and flawed by later standards, can be perceived in the respect evoked in Germany by some of the native cultures of the Far North. Just as significantly, an emerging awareness of the global environment as something more than the object of political or economic acquisition might be seen in the occasional protests raised by German observers against the wanton slaughter of polar wildlife. Contemporary Germany's admirable sensitivity to both global cultural diversity and the fragility of the natural environment may be vaguely discerned in the ways Germans interpreted their polar experience.

Nonetheless, considered in its historical setting, the German polar endeavor miscarried badly. This failure is most striking from the perspective of the political aspirations of the state. These took many forms. For the German elite before World War I, exploration of the Arctic and Antarctic was an exercise intended to reap international prestige and to ensure that Germany not be omitted from consideration as a nation with legitimate polar interests. For the Nazis, obviously, the political aims of polar work were more tangible: the occupation of Antarctic land and the guarantee of access to polar resources. German explorers failed, for a variety of reasons, to attain any of these goals. Ironically, it was only the Weimar Republic, derided by its enemies, with some justice, as a weak, divided, and ineffectual regime, that actually succeeded in using polar exploration to attain its political ends, the enhancement of the nation's scientific prestige, and the advancement, even if only very temporarily, of cooperation with its mighty eastern neighbor.

Not only did most of the German expeditionaries fail to fulfill their intended political function, they also failed to achieve even their scientific aims. As critics of Drygalski's Antarctic foray noted, the wealth of data brought back could not obscure the fact that the ship never reached its target destination and was unable to explore properly or to carry on its geological researches. Most of the other German expeditions also fell short of their scientific goals. Filchner's journey was an utter scientific dead end,

Eckener spent most of his flight over lands that were already well known, and much of the mapping carried out by the *Schwabenland* had to be redrawn by Norwegians in the 1950s. Both the *Passat* and the *Boreas* had deviated in a northwesterly direction from their projected flight paths, leading to a faulty interpretation of their photographic images and the inaccurate replication of mountain chains and other features. Only in Greenland, under Koldewey and Wegener, were the scientific results of German expeditions close to commensurate with expectations, and of course the success of Wegener's Greenland mission was obscured by the death of its leader.

The sources of Germany's long frustration in the high latitudes were many. In part, they were brought on by a tradition of grossly errant geographic surmise, which inspired misleading and unattainable expectations of German expeditions. For all the glory of Germany's tradition of scientific geography, its great men repeatedly championed wildly misconstrued notions of the geography of the high latitudes. Petermann's mania for the "open polar sea" deceived Koldewey. Neumayer's conviction that nonexistent warm currents south of Kerguelen Island must open a great embayment in the Indian Ocean sector of Antarctica helped stymie Drygalski when he struck land much farther north than expected. And Penck's notion of the frozen, sleddable trough separating the two "halves" of Antarctica misguided Filchner. The expeditions that sailed forth based on the polar fantasy of these scientists were, inevitably, disappointments.

Taken as a whole, however, it is hard to avoid the conclusion that German efforts came in for more than their share of simple bad luck. Misjudgment in planning, failures of leadership, even simple mechanical breakdown of course helped to undermine German efforts. But Germans hardly had a monopoly on polar vicissitudes of this kind. While men like Drygalski, Filchner, Koldewey, and even Wegener certainly committed errors, they were easily the equal in competence and bravery of their counterparts from other lands. And it is easy to imagine history judging men such as Ernest Shackleton quite differently if a few things had gone slightly differently during their voyages. The Germans may, after all, have been too modest and sober in their goals. If more of their failures had occurred in the course of ballyhooed efforts to actually reach or fly over the Poles, perhaps they would retain a greater aura of heroism in the popular mind.

German explorers also had the misfortune to come from the nation that produced Hitler, and in part their relative obscurity is his legacy. Forcing the German tradition of polar scientific idealism into the Procrustean bed of his savage diplomacy, Hitler here, as with so many other aspects of German culture, brought lasting discredit upon a history in which his countrymen could once take justifiable pride. Thanks to World War II and its origins in Hitler's aggression, German exploration also failed to secure either a permanent German presence at the Poles or even much of a place in the West's polar memory.

When Germans finally resumed polar scientific research in the late 1950s, it was as participants in expeditions led by the Cold War superpowers. Not until the 1960s would Germans once more mount independent, and quite small-scale, expeditions, and not until the very end of the 1970s, more than three decades after the war's end, would the two German states erect in Antarctica the kind of permanent research stations that by then had long been in use by the other powers. Political ambition for Germany became, in a sense, its own nemesis in the polar world. German explorers who were willing to gamble "a few lives," as Petermann put it at the founding of the German polar adventure, brought much back from their ventures into the high latitudes. Rarely, however, did they return with those things they had set out to gain.

NOTES

Introduction

1. The Arbeitsgemeinschaft für Geschichte der Polarforschung (Work Group for the History of Polar Research) publishes articles and monographs, and the Alfred-Wegener-Institut für Polar- und Meeresforschung (Alfred Wegener Institute for Polar and Oceanic Research) has a historical section. More typical, however, are popular works like Salentiny's *Dumonts Lexicon der Seefahrer und Entdecker* (Dumont lexicon of mariners and discoverers) that entirely ignore important German explorers such as Karl Koldewey. At the same time, works on the Anglo-American tradition continue to proliferate.

2. Reinke-Kunze, *Aufbruch*, 359–70, 375–77.

3. Not until 1895 did Carsten Borchgrevink become the first human being to actually tread upon the mainland. Maxtone-Graham gives the year as 1893 (*Safe Return Doubtful*, 190), but most other sources say 1895 (see, e.g., Cameron, *Antarctica*, 129). John Davis, an American whaler from Connecticut, apparently walked upon the Grahamland Peninsula in February 1821, but the claim to be the first is disputed as well by partisans of Dumont D'Urville of the French navy, James Clark Ross of the Royal Navy, and Charles Wilkes of the United States Navy.

4. Shackleton cited in Courtald, *From the Ends of the Earth*, 316.

5. Goethe, *Goethes Werke*, 930. Craig notes nineteenth-century Germany's infatuation with science in "The End of the Golden Age" (19).

6. Bremischen Comite, ed., *Die zweite deutsche Nordpolar-Expedition*, 27.

7. Victor, *Man and the Conquest of the Poles*, 111.

8. Enzberg, *Heroen der Nordpolarforschung*, 162–63.

9. On media manipulation of polar news and the use of the media by explorers, see Riffenburgh, *The Myth of the Explorer*.

10. The first women reached the South Pole in 1969. See Neider, ed., *Antarctica*, 8.

11. See Freuchen and Salomonsen, *The Arctic Year*, 3–15.

12. Verein für die deutsche Nordpolarfahrt zu Bremen, ed., *Die zweite deutsche Nordpolar-fahrt*, 1:xvi.

13. Houben, *Der Ruf des Nordens*, 8.

14. One lead, the so-called Big Lead of Peary, appears to be semipermanent, constituting a narrow channel north of the Lincoln Sea that is usually open, but this is unique. See "The Big Lead and Other Disasters," in Hempleman-Adams, *Walking on Thin Ice*, 146–69.

15. Smedal, *Acquisition of Sovereignty*, 11.

16. Levere, *Science and the Canadian Arctic*, 340–41.
17. McCannon, *Red Arctic*, 3–29.
18. See the review of some of these issues in Smedal, *Acquisition of Sovereignty*, 54ff., and later discussion in Lampe, "Versuch," and the acrimonious anonymous response, "Bemerkungen zu K. Lampe."
19. Hanessian, "National Interests in Antarctica."
20. Smedal, *Acquisition of Sovereignty*, 27–31; Fogelson, *Arctic Exploration*, 1–5.
21. Jones, "The Antarctic Treaty."
22. Data on the *Preussen* in Villiers, *The Way of a Ship*, 66.
23. Drygalski, *Zum Kontinent*, vii.
24. Bremischen Comite, ed., *Die zweite deutsche Nordpolar-Expedition*, 7.

1. Germany Discovers the Poles

1. German scientists, including Georg Wilhelm Steller and J. G. Gmelin, joined Russia's Great Northern Expedition in the 1730s. German missionaries and miners, including David Cranz and Karl Ludwig Giesecke, took part in the early European exploration of Greenland. It was also a German scientist, Georg Adolf Erman, who first recorded elephant and rhinoceros bones on the islands off the northern coast of Siberia.
2. Wichmann, "August Petermann," concludes that Petermann was essential to the revival of European interest in the North. More recently, Vaughan (*The Arctic*, 108–9) blames Petermann's "hare-brained" polar theories as the basis of the route of the disastrous *Jeannette* expedition of 1879–81 that resulted in several deaths, including that of the expedition's commander, George Washington De Long.
3. Franklin led an English expedition of two ships to seek the Northwest Passage in 1845. They disappeared in July of that year. Several rescue expeditions in the 1840s and 1850s failed to locate any trace of the missing explorer or his crew. A series of piecemeal discoveries between 1854 and 1952 eventually turned up artifacts and bodies from the expedition, which came to disaster on the northwestern coast of King William Island.
4. Wichmann, "August Petermann," 797. Petermann was clearly well known to popular audiences on the Continent. Early in Jules Verne's best-selling and pioneering science fiction novel, *Twenty Thousand Leagues under the Sea*, the narrator mentions the journal to show how well known the story of Nemo's submarine has become.
5. Petermann, "Die Eisverhältnisse," 136.
6. Hayes, *Das offene Polar-Meer*.

7. Petermann, *Spitzbergen*, 9. His comments are quoted from Petermann, *Die deutsche Nordpol-Expedition*, 2, emphasis in original.
8. Petermann, *Die deutsche Nordpol-Expedition*, 1.
9. See the discussion of Petermann's views on this in Krause, *Zweihundert Tage im Packeis*, 247–48.
10. *Proceedings of the Royal Geographical Society* 9 (1865): 90, 114.
11. Wilhelm Freeden, one of the leading figures of German marine research and later founder of the North German Marine Observatory, observed sourly that such a journey would cost several thousand English pounds (an enormous sum), deliberately suggesting that the English were more likely to carry out such a plan than the Germans. Cited in Reinke-Kunze, *Aufbruch*, 20. See also Petermann, *Spitzbergen*, 12. Currency comparisons between economies and across time are notoriously tricky, but the Assembly estimates were undoubtedly high. A similar small-scale trip to Spitsbergen five years later by Theodor Heuglin cost 1,200 taler (Koldewey, *Die erste deutsche Nordpolar-Expedition*, v). See the *Amtlicher Bericht*.
12. Koldewey, *Die erste deutsche Nordpolar-Expedition*, iv.
13. Brinnin, *The Sway of the Grand Saloon*, 145–46.
14. Petermann cited in Hoheisel-Huxmann, "Die erste deutsche Nordpolar-Expedition," 7.
15. Litke cited in Petermann, *Spitzbergen*, 16.
16. This account is based on Werner's report to Petermann, reprinted in *Spitzbergen*, 16.
17. Werner cited in Petermann, *Spitzbergen*, 16, 22.
18. Koldewey, *Die erste deutsche Nordpolar-Expedition*, vi.
19. Krause, *Zweihundert Tage im Packeis*, 254–57.
20. Petermann, *Spitzbergen*, 24.
21. Koldewey, *Die erste deutsche Nordpolar-Expedition*, vi; the letters of both ministers to Petermann, "Die deutsche Nordfahrt," 146.
22. "Decret," signed Roon, 22 December 1865, and "Votum," 2 February 1866, both in GStA: HA I, R 90; Krause, *Zweihundert Tage im Packeis*, 261.
23. For the resolution of the deputies, see Petermann, "Die deutsche Nordfahrt," 77, and see the reproduction of Wilhelm's letter in Krause, *Zweihundert Tage im Packeis*, 265.
24. Petermann, "Die deutsche Nordfahrt," 144–62.
25. Petermann, "Nordseefischereien"; "Das nördlichste Land der Erde," 176–80; and "Der Walfischfang." He also published Spörer, *Nowaja Semlä*.
26. Petermann, *Die deutsche Nordpol-Expedition*, 2.

27. Koldewey, *Die erste deutsche Nordpolar-Expedition*, vi.
28. Koldewey, *Die erste deutsche Nordpolar-Expedition*, viii; see also Na'aman, *Der deutsche Nationalverein*.
29. Koldewey, *Die erste deutsche Nordpolar-Expedition*, viii; Petermann, *Die deutsche Nordpol-Expedition*, 6.
30. Petermann, *Die deutsche Nordpol-Expedition*, 3.
31. Breusing cited in Petermann, *Die deutsche Nordpol-Expedition*, 6, 7.
32. Koldewey, *Die erste deutsche Nordpolar-Expedition*, 4.
33. Geerken letter cited in Koldewey, *Die erste deutsche Nordpolar-Expedition*, 1, 3. In a footnote to Koldewey's account of the *Grönland* expedition, Petermann comments on the fine performance of the ship in ice and observes that "everyone with the slightest familiarity with the relevant literature who is not an old experienced sea captain knows."
34. See the "Instruktion für den Oberbefehlshaber der Expedition," in Petermann, *Die deutsche Nordpol-Expedition*, 8–12.
35. Petermann, *Die deutsche Nordpol-Expedition*, paragraphs 27, 23.
36. Petermann, *Die deutsche Nordpol-Expedition*, paragraph 34, emphasis in original.
37. See the account of this in Maxtone-Graham, *Safe Return Doubtful*, 39–40. See also Loomis, *Weird and Tragic Shores*; and for a heartrending tale of Eskimo quasi-abduction, see Harper, *Give Me My Father's Body*.
38. Koldewey, *Die erste deutsche Nordpolar-Expedition*, 8.
39. Koldewey, *Die erste deutsche Nordpolar-Expedition*, 15.
40. Koldewey, *Die erste deutsche Nordpolar-Expedition*, 21.
41. Koldewey, *Die erste deutsche Nordpolar-Expedition*, 48.
42. Koldewey, *Die erste deutsche Nordpolar-Expedition*, 54.
43. Krause, *Zweihundert Tage im Packeis*, 280.
44. See the analysis in Freeden, *Über die wissenschaftlichen Ergebnisse*.
45. Freeden, *Über die wissenschaftlichen Ergebnisse*, 13f.
46. Koldewey, *Die erste deutsche Nordpolar-Expedition*, 54.
47. Petermann cited in Reinke-Kunze, *Aufbruch*, 29.
48. Oscar Peschel, "Die deutsche Nordfahrt," *Ausland*, 8 October 1870: 983.

2. Persistent Dangers, Unusual Luck

1. Verein für die deutsche Nordpolarfahrt zu Bremen, ed., *Die zweite deutsche Nordpolar-fahrt*, 1:xvi.
2. Verein für die deutsche Nordpolarfahrt zu Bremen, ed., *Die zweite deutsche Nordpolar-fahrt*, 1:xvii; Krause, *Zweihundert Tage im Packeis*, 289.

3. On the committees, see Verein für die deutsche Nordpolarfahrt zu Bremen, ed., *Die zweite deutsche Nordpolar-fahrt*, 1: xviii–xx; Krause, *Zweihundert Tage im Packeis*, 292–94; for a comprehensive list of donations received to the end of 1869, see Bremischen Comite, ed., *Die zweite deutsche Nordpolar-Expedition*, 57–59; on Bastian, see Koepping, *Adolf Bastian*, 7–20, and Smith, *Politics*, 100–102, 116–20.

4. BAP: R 901, 37538; *Mitbürger!* 3 April 1869.

5. BAP: R 901, 37538; *Erste Quittung*, 1 April 1869.

6. See "Anlage 4: Abdruck eines Briefes von Petermann an Koldewey, Gotha, 14. Juni 1869," in Abel and Jessen, *Kein Weg durch das Packeis*, 78.

7. Krause, *Zweihundert Tage im Packeis*, 291.

8. Villiers, *The Way of a Ship*, 37–38.

9. The account of the outfitting of the *Germania* comes from many sources, most notably the following: Adams, *Recent Polar Voyages*, 385–88; Krause, *Zweihundert Tage im Packeis*, 298; Verein für die deutsche Nordpolarfahrt zu Bremen, ed., *Die zweite deutsche Nordpolar-fahrt*, 1: xxxiv–xxxviii; Bremischen Comite, ed., *Die zweite deutsche Nordpolar-Expedition*, 36–39; The comment on the book collection is recorded in the diary of Wilhelm Bade, second officer of the *Hansa*, reprinted in Krause, *Zweihundert Tage im Packeis*, 13.

10. The entire poem is recorded by Bade in his diary; see Krause, *Zweihundert Tage im Packeis*, 12.

11. Mosle cited in Bremischen Comite, ed., *Die zweite deutsche Nordpolar-Expedition*, 44.

12. Koldewey, "Die Fahrt der *Germania*," 3.

13. Koldewey, "Die Fahrt der *Germania*," 4; Börgen, "Kurze Bemerkungen," 15–16.

14. Koldewey, "Die Fahrt der *Germania*," 7.

15. Koldewey, "Die Fahrt der *Germania*," 6.

16. Verein für die deutsche Nordpolarfahrt zu Bremen, ed., *Die zweite deutsche Nordpolar-fahrt*, 1:350.

17. Koldewey, "Die Fahrt der *Germania*," 7.

18. Koldewey, "Die Fahrt der *Germania*," 7.

19. See the account of the settlement's remains in Verein für die deutsche Nordpolarfahrt zu Bremen, ed., *Die zweite deutsche Nordpolar-fahrt*, 2:594–606.

20. Verein für die deutsche Nordpolarfahrt zu Bremen, ed., *Die zweite deutsche Nordpolar-fahrt*, 2:359.

21. See the account in Löwenberg, *Die Entdeckungen und Forschungsreisen*, 83.

22. Verein für die deutsche Nordpolarfahrt zu Bremen, ed., *Die zweite deutsche Nordpolar-fahrt*, 2:458.

23. Verein für die deutsche Nordpolarfahrt zu Bremen, ed., *Die zweite deutsche Nordpolar-fahrt*, 2:458; Koldewey, "Die Fahrt der Germania," 6.

24. Cited in Adams, *Recent Polar Voyages*, 530.

25. Koldewey, "Die Fahrt der Germania," 12–13.

26. The following account of the *Hansa*'s stranding is drawn from several sources. These are primarily the two-volume official account of the expedition, Verein für die deutsche Nordpolarfahrt zu Bremen, ed., *Die zweite deutsche Nordpolar-fahrt*; other contemporary sources, especially the account by the ship's first officer, Richard Hildebrandt, "Fahrt der Hansa," 24–45; the account by the ship's naturalist, Reinhold Buchholz, *Erlebnisse der Mannschaft des Schiffes Hansa*; and, especially, the published diaries of Hildebrandt, the ship's captain, Friedrich Hegemann, and the second officer, Wilhelm Bade, which are reproduced in Krause, *Zweihundert Tage im Packeis*. This work is volume 46 of the series Schriften des deutschen Schiffahrtsmuseums. The entire adventure, some have speculated, would not have occurred had the *Hansa* been equipped with even a small steam engine. See the speculation of Abel and Jessen, *Kein Weg durch das Packeis*, 26.

27. Buchholz, *Erlebnisse der Mannschaft des Schiffes Hansa*, 14.

28. Hildebrandt, "Fahrt der Hansa," 27; Buchholz, *Erlebnisse der Mannschaft des Schiffes Hansa*, 14.

29. The best account of the construction is in Verein für die deutsche Nordpolarfahrt zu Bremen, ed., *Die zweite deutsche Nordpolar-fahrt*, 1:66–67. A good illustration of the elusive nature of historical accuracy can be gained by trying to determine, from contemporary accounts, the distance from this structure to the *Hansa*. It is variously recorded, by men who were all closely engaged eyewitnesses, as 450 paces (Verein für die deutsche Nordpolarfahrt zu Bremen, ed., *Die zweite deutsche Nordpolar-fahrt*, 1:66), 700 paces (Hildebrandt, "Fahrt der Hansa," 27), and simply "several hundred paces" (Buchholz, *Erlebnisse der Mannschaft des Schiffes Hansa*, 14).

30. Hildebrandt, "Fahrt der Hansa," 27.

31. Hildebrandt, "Fahrt der Hansa," 28.

32. Hildebrandt, "Fahrt der Hansa," 28–29; Verein für die deutsche Nordpolarfahrt zu Bremen, ed., *Die zweite deutsche Nordpolar-fahrt*, 1:69–71.

33. Buchholz, *Erlebnisse der Mannschaft des Schiffes Hansa*, 18.

34. Hildebrandt, "Fahrt der Hansa," 31.

35. Hegemann quoted in Krause, *Zweihundert Tage im Packeis*, 91.
36. Bade quoted in Krause, *Zweihundert Tage im Packeis*, 82.
37. Hildebrandt, "Fahrt der Hansa," 36; Buchholz, *Erlebnisse der Mannschaft des Schiffes Hansa*, 17.
38. On the fox, see Bade quoted in Krause, *Zweihundert Tage im Packeis*, 124; on the bear, see Buchholz, *Erlebnisse der Mannschaft des Schiffes Hansa*, 15, and Hildebrandt, "Fahrt der Hansa," 36.
39. Bade quoted in Krause, *Zweihundert Tage im Packeis*, 82.
40. Buchholz, *Erlebnisse der Mannschaft des Schiffes Hansa*, 32.
41. Bade quoted in Krause, *Zweihundert Tage im Packeis*, 110–11.
42. The best account of Buchholz's utter breakdown is in Bade quoted in Krause, *Zweihundert Tage im Packeis*, 144–45. On Laube, see Bade quoted in Krause, *Zweihundert Tage im Packeis*, 104, 136. Hildebrandt too records Buchholz's meaningless monologues and frequent efforts to throw himself into the water. See Hildebrandt quoted in Krause, *Zweihundert Tage im Packeis*, 142, 151.
43. Bade quoted in Krause, *Zweihundert Tage im Packeis*, 162.
44. Buchholz, *Erlebnisse der Mannschaft des Schiffes Hansa*, 32.
45. Bade quoted in Krause, *Zweihundert Tage im Packeis*, 116.
46. Both Hildebrandt and Bade record Böwe's insistence to the crew, for example, that precisely on 25 February the seals would return to begin mating. All knew Böwe's claim was not intended seriously. On the appointed morning, the other crewmembers fashioned a decoy seal from stuffed sealskin pants, placed it at the edge of the floe, alerted Böwe to the accuracy of his prophecy, and then as a group assaulted the dummy seal with clubs. Ponderous physical humor, perhaps, but a good deal better than despair. Hildebrandt and Bade quoted in Krause, *Zweihundert Tage im Packeis*, 135.
47. Bade quoted in Krause, *Zweihundert Tage im Packeis*, 164.
48. Hildebrandt, "Fahrt der Hansa," 43.
49. Buchholz, *Erlebnisse der Mannschaft des Schiffes Hansa*, 36. On the crew's reception in Friedrichsthal, see Verein für die deutsche Nordpolarfahrt zu Bremen, ed., *Die zweite deutsche Nordpolar-fahrt*, 1:145–46; Meier, "Aufzeichnungen über Grönland-Expeditionen."
50. Hildebrandt, "Fahrt der Hansa," 44.
51. Koldewey, "Die Fahrt der Germania," 14.
52. Reinke-Kunze, *Aufbruch*, 38–39.
53. Koldewey, "Die Fahrt der Germania," 2. The *Hansa* crew were astonished

to learn that the site where they initially became icebound was less than a day's journey from the *Germania*.

54. Abel and Jessen, *Kein Weg durch das Packeis*, 34.

55. Krause, *Zweihundert Tage im Packeis*, 312.

56. Bates, ed., *The German Arctic Expedition*; Gourdault, ed., *Voyage au Pole Nord*. A very lengthy account also appears in Adams, *Recent Polar Voyages*, 384–544, and a shorter one in Greeley, *A Handbook of Polar Discoveries*, 170–72.

57. On the popularity of histories of English exploration in Germany, see William Barr's introduction to Klutschak, *Overland to Starvation Cove*, xx.

58. Hildebrandt cited in Löwenberg, *Die Entdeckungen und Forschungsreisen*, 81–82.

59. Laube, *Reise der Hansa ins nördliche Eismeer*, 52. Nearly a century later, German accounts mentioned the "depression" suffered by Buchholz. See Abel and Jessen, *Kein Weg durch das Packeis*, 27.

60. Herz, *Tropisches und Arktisches*, 166–67.

61. Lindeman and Finsch, *Die zweite deutsche Nordpolarfahrt*, vii.

62. Enzberg, *Heroen der Nordpolarforschung*, 156, 163.

63. The conditions under which the survivors were ultimately rescued were the most horrifying imaginable—trapped within their collapsed tent, subsisting by consuming their clothing and bedding, bodies slowly corroding from frostbite. For the gory details, see Schley, *The Rescue of Greely*; Greely, *Three Years of Arctic Service*.

64. See the account of the rescue in Bartlett, *The Log of Bob Bartlett*.

65. Krause, *Zweihundert Tage im Packeis*, 310.

66. See Villiers, *The Way of a Ship*, xiv.

67. See, for example, Laube, *Volkstümliche Überlieferungen*.

68. Koldewey writes that while the expedition made many important scientific discoveries, it had also "thoroughly destroyed the illusion of the open polar sea of Kane and Hayes, which was no more than a lead in a channel swept by a strong current." See Verein für die deutsche Nordpolarfahrt zu Bremen, ed., *Die zweite deutsche Nordpolar-fahrt*, 1:698.

69. Löwenberg, *Die Entdeckungen und Forschungsreisen*, 72.

70. Osborn cited in Weller, *August Petermann*, 93n.

71. Weller, *August Petermann*, 208.

72. Weller, *August Petermann*, 27.

73. A cape and a mountain chain in Novaya Zemlya, mountains in Australia and New Zealand, a mountain and a fjord in Greenland, among other

sites, bear his name. He is characterized as "half-forgotten" in Weller, *August Petermann*, 212.

74. Verein für die deutsche Nordpolarfahrt zu Bremen, ed., *Die zweite deutsche Nordpolar-fahrt*, 1:x.

75. In March 1883, for example, the third German Geographical Congress (Deutscher Geographentag) passed a resolution urging the resumption of German expeditioning. On Neumayer and the two German stations erected as part of the polar year, see Neumayer, ed., *Die internationale Polarforschung*. The other participant nations were the United States, Denmark, Sweden, Norway, Austria, Finland, Russia, France, and the Netherlands.

76. Wichmann, "August Petermann," 804.

3. Imperial Failure in the Antarctic

1. Gauss's predictions appeared in C. F. Gauss, "Allgemeine Theorie des Erdmagnetismus," in Gauss and Weber, eds., *Resultate aus den Beobachtungen*, 1–57. The best summation in English of his work is Garland, "The Contributions." For an introduction to the state of geomagnetic theory at the time, see Good, "Geomagnetism."

2. On Neumayer, see Baughman, *Before the Heroes Came*, 13–14, 70–71.

3. He addressed the Conference of Natural Scientists and Physicians at Innsbruck in 1869, the International Geographical Congress in Rome in 1879, and meetings in London, Antwerp, Bremen, and Vienna.

4. Neumayer, "Polarexpedition oder Polarforschung," 211, in BAP: RMdI 1501, 16016; Neumayer, *Auf zum Südpol*, 57ff.

5. See the account of Ratzel's remarks to the German Geographical Congress in 1883 in Löwenberg, *Die Entdeckungen und Forschungsreisen*, 142–43. This author actually credits Ratzel with coining the word "Antarktis" to denote the South Polar landmass, though the term "Antarctic" had been common in English for centuries. On the polar year, see Barr, *The Expeditions*. On Ratzel and his influence on geography, see Smith, *Politics*, 219–29; Murphy, *The Heroic Earth*, 7–13. See also Buttmann, *Friedrich Ratzel*; Bassin, "Friedrich Ratzel." The German Geographical Congress lent its influence to Neumayer's crusade, resolving in 1883 that "the resumption of polar expeditions is in the interest of science and of the nation." See Löwenberg, *Die Entdeckungen und Forschungsreisen*, 35.

6. From the 1880s, for example, works such as Embacher, *Die wichtigeren Forschungsreisen*, and Stein, *Die Entdeckungsreisen*, can be cited.

7. Neumayer, "Polarexpedition oder Polarforschung," 238. On Virchow as politician, see Boyd, *Rudolf Virchow*.

8. Bismarck's name does not appear in the list of contributors that Petermann prepared in 1869 entitled "Erste Quittung über die bis zum 1. April 1869 eingegangenen Beiträge für die 1. und 2. deutsche Nordpolar-Expedition, 1868 und 1869/70" in BAP: R 901, 37538.

9. Reinke-Kunze, *Aufbruch*, 169.

10. See the comments on Bismarck's attitude in Smith, "Colonies and Colonial Society."

11. Lüdecke, "Die Routenfestlegung," 109–10.

12. See the tables in Kosack, *Die Polarforschung*, 335; see also Cameron, *Antarctica*, 245.

13. Löwenberg, *Die Entdeckungen und Forschungsreisen*, 150.

14. The list of subscribers provided by Oberhummer shows, in comparison with those compiled more than a generation earlier by Petermann, a much higher ratio of organizations (banks, scientific groups, manufacturers) to individuals. See the list and comments in Oberhummer, "Die deutsche Südpolarexpedition," 94–134, esp. 94ff. This report was published in 1900.

15. Reinke-Kunze, *Aufbruch*, 172. See the account of the fund-raising, and comparisons with contemporary English efforts, in Hassert, *Die Polarforschung*, 219.

16. Note the comments in Wichmann's account of Petermann's life.

17. On the naval program, in English, see Balfour, *The Kaiser and His Times*, 201–9. The standard work is Berghahn, *Der Tirpitz-Plan*, particularly 185ff.

18. Baughman, *Before the Heroes Came*, 69. See also Chun, *Aus den Tiefen des Weltmeeres*. Chun and the *Valdivia* rediscovered Bouvet Island, lost for a century and a half since being incorrectly charted by its first European visitors.

19. Drygalski, *Zum Kontinent*, 5–6. See also Schmidt-Ott, *Erlebtes und Erstrebtes*, 35.

20. Bruch, *Weltpolitik als Kulturmission*, 5–7.

21. Drygalski, *Zum Kontinent*, 6; Reinke-Kunze, *Aufbruch*, 186f.

22. Gröber cited in the introduction to Drygalski, *The Southern Ice-Continent*, viii. The entire speech, delivered on 1 March 1899, can be found in *Verhandlungen des Reichstages*, 166:247–49.

23. So, for example, Erich von Drygalski, a member of the commission and eventual leader of the Antarctic voyage, could write: "It has always been the glory of powerful seafaring peoples to expand and deepen knowledge of

the seas. And in the moment where Germany is now prepared to develop its naval might to an extent that was earlier unimaginable, an expansion of nautical knowledge in the one global region where it is still lacking would be a national deed worth the cost" (Die Ergebnisse der Südpolarforschung, 18). See similar sentiments, expressed almost identically, in the following: speech of Undersecretary Rothe in Nord-Ostseezeitung, 12 August 1901, 22, in BAP: RMdI 1501, 16122; speech of Posadowsky in Verhandlungen des Reichstages, 165:401–2.

24. Drygalski, Die Ergebnisse der Südpolarforschung, 17–18.

25. The words are those of Prince von Arenberg, head of the Berlin-Charlottenburg section of the German Colonial Society (Deutsche Kolonialgesellschaft), delivered to a demonstration in support of the Antarctic expedition in January 1899. See the account in "Gemeinschaftliche Sitzung." For further evidence of the close support lent the Antarctic mission by colonialist circles, see the account in Neumayer, "Zweiter Thätigkeitsbericht," 3–32, esp. 26–27.

26. Drygalski, Die Grönland-Expedition.

27. GStA: R 92 NL Schmidt-Ott, no. 33 (Sonderdruck, Erich v. Drygalski, 68).

28. Schmidt-Ott, Erlebtes und Erstrebtes, 50.

29. Drygalski, Zum Kontinent, 61. For an account of the ship's specifications and construction, see the chapter entitled "Der 'Gauss' und seine Ausrüstung," in Drygalski, Zum Kontinent, 57–81; see also Stehr, "Das Südpolarschiff Gauss."

30. Drygalski, Zum Kontinent, 2.

31. Lüdecke, "Die Routenfestlegung," 103–4.

32. Drygalski, Zum Kontinent, 8.

33. See the plans in "Dritte Denkschrift betreffend die deutsche Südpolar-Expedition," in BAP: RMdI 1501, 16123. See also Drygalski, "The German Antarctic Expedition."

34. "Rede zum Taufakt," in BAP: RMdI 1501, 16120.

35. "Even the special aids to polar exploration otherwise native to Scandinavia such as snowshoes, sleds, boats, fishing equipment, and sporting material of all kinds" were obtained from German firms. See "Dritte Denkschrift," 2; Direktor der KGI an Blumenthal, 30 October 1901, in BAP: RMdI 1501, 16138; Reinke-Kunze, Aufbruch, 181.

36. See the account in Täglichen Rundschau, 12 August 1901.

37. Drygalski, Zum Kontinent, 66.

38. Wilhelm Meinardus, a geographer, was denied a place because of his

marriage. Only unmarried men were permitted among the scientists and officers, although three married crewmen were included. See "Dritte Denkschrift," 2.

39. See a brief account of Ruser's sailing career in Becker, Unterwegs, 20–23.

40. See Drygalski's discussion of this later controversial aspect of the expedition in Drygalski, Zum Kontinent, 53–55.

41. Drygalski, Zum Kontinent, 79.

42. BAP: RMdI 1501, 16123, p. 148. This is from an article in the Weser-Zeitung, 5 November 1901. It should be noted in regard to power, however, that Douglas Mawson made an Antarctic voyage a decade later in the Aurora, which was equipped with only a ninety-eight-horsepower engine.

43. See Drygalski's notes of Ruser's opinions on the seaworthiness of the Gauss in Drygalski, "Erster Bericht," 423.

44. See the note of Lansdowne to the German ambassador in London dated 30 July 1901 in BAP: RMdI 1501, 16122, p. 15, and the note of von Schlözer in the Imperial Embassy, Paris, to Graf von Bülow, 10 August 1901, in BAP: RMdI 1501, 16122, p. 62.

45. Drygalski, "Allgemeiner Bericht," 8.

46. From the account in BAP: RMdI 1501, 16124, p. 129.

47. The account of the experience in the ice stems primarily from the following contemporary accounts: Drygalski, Zum Kontinent; Drygalski, Allgemeiner Bericht, with an afterword by Karl Luyken; Gazert, Die deutsche Südpolar-Expedition; Josef Enzensperger's diary account of his time on Kerguelen in Ein Bergsteigerleben; Dröber, Die Polargebiete; Braun, Die Erforschung der Pole.

48. Drygalski, Allgemeiner Bericht, 31.

49. A detailed account by the ship's mechanic can be found in Stehr, "Bericht über die Ballonaufstiege."

50. Gazert, "Gesundheitsbericht," 53.

51. Bidlingmaier cited in Härlin, Am Südpol, 14. As Härlin comments, "Is not that a cozy German small town, packed into the planking of a good ship?"

52. Drygalski, Zum Kontinent, 378. The prescribed drinking regimen was not heavy—wine twice a week, grog or brandy two or three times a week, according to Gazert's account. Apparently, some crewmen modified this moderate and sensible program. See Gazert, "Gesundheitsbericht," 51–52.

53. This episode is recounted in Gazert, "Gesundheitsbericht," 279–80.

54. Enzensperger, Ein Bergsteigerleben, 283. The volume including the diary was edited by the Akademischer Alpenverein of Munich. As late as the 1950s,

NOTES TO PAGES 82–88

this death was still being attributed in popular German works to infection from the Chinese rather than to the nutritional deficiency that is its true origin. See, for example, Hassert, *Die Polarforschung*, 217, whose words are almost identical to those of Luyken.

55. Luyken's report in Drygalski, *Allgemeiner Bericht*, 47–48. Richthofen noted the same belief in his introduction (iv).

56. Enzensperger, *Ein Bergsteigerleben*, 285.

57. Enzensperger, *Ein Bergsteigerleben*, 286.

58. Enzensperger, *Ein Bergsteigerleben*, 293.

59. Kaiserlich deutsches General-Konsulat für Australien an v. Bülow, 18 April 1903, in BAP: R 901, 37556. The lack of medical preparation at Kerguelen was particularly noted. See also the news of the death at Kerguelen in "Kleine Mitteilungen aus allen Erdteilen."

60. For Drygalski's insistence that the expedition was a success, see the account from *Wolff's Telegraphisches Bureau* on 10 June 1903 from BAP: R 901, 37566, and the report of Drygalski's views in kaiserlich deutsches General-Konsulat für British Süd-Afrika an v. Bülow, 10 June 1903, in the same folder.

61. Clipping from *Kölnische Zeitung*, 2 September 1902, in BAP: RMdI 15957, vol. 10. See also the coverage in a popular venue such as the *Berliner illustrirte Zeitung*, 6 December 1903, which ran a picture of Drygalski and crew but gave no story other than a brief caption.

62. "Über die deutsche Südpolexpedition," 92–93.

63. See the anonymous marginalia appended to the *Kölnische Zeitung* article cited above. Emphases and parenthetical comment in the original.

64. "German South Polar Expedition."

65. The scientific merit of the expedition was recognized, for example, in contemporary works such as the popular account of Mill, *The Siege of the South Pole*, 424.

66. Gazert cited in Venzke, "Die deutsche Südpolar-Expedition," 68.

67. Lampe, "Erdkundliche Interessen," 33. Books like the account of the Nansen expedition or of the *Valdivia* voyage, Lampe noted, "always turn a profit." Accounts from other European lands were also popular (e.g., Schmiedgen, *MacClures Nordpolarfahrt*), as were translated accounts such as Cook, *Meine Eroberung des Nordpols*.

68. Internationale Polar-Kommission, *Protokoll*, 41–44.

69. Memorandum, signed Lewald, 19 January 1910, 1–2, in BAP: RMdI 1501, 16293.

70. Filchner, *Ein Forscherleben*, 94–95.

71. The appointment generated controversy, since many expected it to go to Richthofen's student, Drygalski.

72. Meynen, "Albrecht Penck"; Dickinson, *The Makers of Modern Geography*, 100–111. Examples of the museum's promotion of the polar cause include lectures like that presented by Otto Baschin in November 1909, "The Struggle for the North Pole." See "Der Kampf um den Nordpol," 1790, in GStA, HA I, R 90, or the lectures delivered by Drygalski on ice navigation noted in the same folder.

73. See the comments labeled "Geheimrat Penck" in "Plan," 157.

74. See the comments labeled "Oberleutnant Wilhelm Filchner, kommandiert zum grossen Generalstab," in "Plan," 153.

75. Memorandum, signed Lewald, 19 January 1910, 1–2, in BAP: RMdI 1501, 16293.

76. *Berliner Lokal-Anzeiger*, 11 January 1938, 117, in BAP: 61 Re 1/120/Filchner.

77. Aufruf, 20–21, in BAP: RMdI 1501, 16293; Delbrück an Valentini, 28 April 1911, 38, in BAP: RMdI 1501, 16293. See the attacks on the government for its failure to support the voyage, and Delbrück in response, in *Verhandlungen des Reichstages* 265: 5683–85.

78. Filchner and Seelheim, *Quer durch Spitzbergen*; Philippi, *Ergebnisse*.

79. Filchner, *Zum sechsten Erdteil*, 29.

80. Filchner, *Zum sechsten Erdteil*, 16.

81. Filchner, *Zum sechsten Erdteil*, 18–21; Filchner an Reichsamt des Innern, 17 January 1911, 8–9, in BAP: RMdI 1501, 16293; Bussche an Bethmann-Hollweg, 29 March 1911, 50, in BAP: RMdI 1501, 16293 (copy).

82. "Denkschrift über die deutsche antarktische Expedition," 14–19, in BAP: RMdI 1501, 16293.

83. Filchner, *Ein Forscherleben*, 99.

84. Filchner, *Ein Forscherleben*, 100.

85. See the front-page account in *Weser-Zeitung*, 8 May 1911.

86. Filchner, *Zum sechsten Erdteil*, 44.

87. BAP: RMdI 1501, 16293, pp. 67–68.

88. See "Bericht von Alfred Kling," in Kirschmer, ed., *Dokumentation*, 59.

89. Swithinbank and Zumberge, "The Ice Shelves."

90. See Filchner on the aims of the expedition and Vahsel's attitude in Filchner, *Zum sechsten Erdteil*, 139–40.

91. See his comments on alcohol and his appraisal of the "barely comprehen-

sible significance" attached to tobacco by his crewmen in Filchner, *Zum sechsten Erdteil*, 17.

92. In fact, Filchner's own bizarre misjudgment of character in the case of the kaiser is remarkable. Remarking on the various opinions expressed about Wilhelm aboard the *Deutschland*, Filchner noted that "few know the truth: he is a deeply religious man, with a firm belief in himself, and extraordinarily good." See the entry for 27 January 1912 excerpted in Kirschmer, ed., *Dokumentation*, 16.

93. See the statement of Captain Larsen in BAP: RMdI 1501, 16293, pp. 153–55.

94. "Bericht," in Kirschmer, ed., *Dokumentation*, 60.

95. "Aus den Tagebüchern von Wilhelm Filchner," in Kirschmer, ed., *Dokumentation*, 90–91.

96. Filchner, *Zum sechsten Erdteil*, 245.

97. Kirschmer, ed., *Dokumentation*, 113.

98. Erich Przybyllok, "Handschriftliche Aufzeichnungen von Erich Przybyllok über Vorkommnisse während der Filchnerschen Antarktisexpedition," in Kirschmer, ed., *Dokumentation*, 53–54.

99. Kirschmer, ed., *Dokumentation*, 113.

100. See Larsen's statement in BAP, cited above.

101. Bobrik an den Reichskanzler, 26 November 1914, 183–84, in BAP: RMdI 1501, 16293 (copy).

102. "Albrecht Penck und die deutsche antarktische Expedition," *Berliner Tageblatt*, 11 March 1914.

103. See the article entitled "New Land: The German Discovery," *Sydney Morning Herald*, 17 January 1913, 100–101, in BAP: RMdI 1501, 16293.

104. See also a brief contemporary account of part of the expedition in Ritscher, "Wanderungen." On the rescue expeditions, see Hergesell and Wegener, "Die deutsche wissenschaftliche Station." For the bathos prompted by the fate of the expedition, see Raebel, "Was ist zur Rettung?"

105. Penck cited in "Polar- und Forschungs-Expeditionen," in *Hamburger Fremdenblatt*, 24 March 1914, 6, in BAP: RMdI 1501, 16022. See also Penck, "Antarktische Probleme."

106. Polis cited in "Polar- und Forschungs-Expeditionen."

107. Filchner cited in "Die deutsche antarktische Expedition," *Vossische Zeitung*, Abendblatt, 2 June 1914.

108. "Die deutsche antarktische Expedition."

109. For Behm's proposal, see BAP: RMdI 1501, 16022, pp. 61–62; for Penck's response, see Institut für Meereskunde an Königl. Universität, 64–65, in

BAP: RMdI 1501, 16022 (copy). For another defense of the expedition, see the second officer, Müller, *Einiges aus der Geschichte*, 13–17. See also Wichmann, "Der Stand."

110. He was a popular lecturer at the Institute for Oceanography, for example, and also lectured on his polar experiences all over Germany. See GStA: HA I, R 90, no. 1790, on his Institute lectures and the account of his lectures in *Jahresbericht des Frankfurter Vereins für Geographie und Statistik* (1905): 151–55.

111. Filchner, *Sturm über Asien*, which was sufficiently popular to be reissued in 1928 under the title *Wetterleuchten im Osten*. His image in the Nazi era will be discussed below.

112. Filchner, cited in Reinke-Kunze, *Aufbruch*, 188.

4. The Search for Polar Redemption

1. Penck, "Deutschlands Seeinteressen."
2. Arthur Moeller van den Bruck, *Das dritte Reich*, published in 1923. Cited in Michalka and Niedhart, eds., *Die ungeliebte Republik*, 98. On the universal German hatred for Versailles and the government's role in promoting it, see Heinemann, *Die verdrängte Niederlage*, 152–54.
3. Amundsen cited in Weickmann, "Die Polarfahrt," 88.
4. Reinke-Kunze, *Aufbruch*, 110.
5. "Zeppelins erste Luftschifferbekenntnis," *Tägliche Rundschau*, 14 July 1908, in BAK: NL Dörr, Mappe 14. Zeppelin was addressing the Württembergische Bezirksverein deutscher Ingenieure (Württemberg district league of German engineers) in a speech attended by the king of Württemberg and members of the court. On the enormous popularity of Zeppelin and on public effort to fund airships, see Fritzsche, *A Nation of Fliers*, 17–18; Robinson, *Giants in the Sky*, 40–83.
6. This is translated from the rhyme on the card illustrated in Hoheisel-Huxmann, "Die Arktisfahrt," 109.
7. For the comments of the Prince, see the foreword to Miethe and Hergesell, *Mit Zeppelin nach Spitzbergen*. See an assessment of the results in Drygalski, "Die Zeppelin-Studienfahrt," 13–14. An insightful discussion of the zeppelin as a tool of cultural propaganda is offered in Syon, "Technology as a Tool."
8. Hennig, "Geopolitische Wirkungen," 586. Note also the observations of Otto Baschin on the war and aviation: "The World War has been a great teacher here as well through the powerful advance it produced in the mastery of the air as a means of transport" ("Berichterstattung," 516).

9. The analogy with the scramble for Africa and the reference to just claims are in Fester, "Polarpolitik," 802. See also Hennig, "Geopolitische Wirkungen."

10. Quessel, "Kurze Chronik." See also the essay for *Der Auslandsdeutsch*, 108, in BAK: NL Külz, 25; Lampe, "Versuch."

11. Maull, "Erdumspannender Bericht," 199.

12. An account of Eckener's success in this may be found in Fritzsche, *A Nation of Fliers*, 138–39.

13. Stresemann cited in Meyer, *Airshipmen*, 155.

14. Eckener cited in Meyer, *Airshipmen*, 162.

15. "Unsere Zukunft liegt in der Luft," 100, in BAP: 61 Re 1/104/Eckener.

16. "Bericht von Gemmingen," 3, in BAK: NL Dörr, Mappe 7 (copy).

17. Aeroarctic, ed., *Das Luftschiff*.

18. Accounts vary on the date of the organization's founding. Arthur Koestler (*Arrow in the Blue*, 317) says 1925. Douglas Botting (*The Airships*), Douglas Robinson (*Giants in the Sky*, 277), and Rolf Italiaander (*Hugo Eckener*, 151) suggest 1926, the year of the first international congress of the Aeroarctic and the year recalled by Eckener (*Im Zeppelin*, 353) in his postwar memoirs, while Henry Cord Meyer (*Airshipmen*, 159) declares that the organization began immediately after the war and without the cooperation of Bruns. All three seem unlikely—if Eckener, Italiaander, Koestler, and Botting are correct, the organization published a memorandum before it came into existence, while Meyer's suggestion means the group waited eight years to hold its first international meeting. Walther Bruns, furthermore, was the first general secretary of Aeroarctic, a surprisingly important role if he really played no part in the organization's creation. The founding in October 1924, with the publication of the "manifesto," and the first international congress two years later seems most plausible and is the scenario suggested by Reinke-Kunze (*Aufbruch*, 118–19) and Syon ("Technology as a Tool," 12). One source (Hassert, *Die Polarforschung*, 12, 197) cites in the same work two different years (1924 and 1925) for the organization's founding.

19. Aeroarctic activists like Leonid Breitfuss had already been agitating for polar airship travel. See Mohr, *Zum Pol*, 36–37.

20. Külz and Böss comments in "Ausbau der Polarforschung," in BAK: NL Dörr, Mappe 14.

21. See the dismal financial report in "Kassenbericht."

22. Fogelson, *Arctic Exploration*, 155.

23. See the account in *Vossische Zeitung*, 22 August 1925; Meyer, *Airshipmen*, 162.

24. Schmidt-Ott, *Erlebtes und Erstrebtes*, 307. Schmidt-Ott's fascinating memoirs express the views of an uncompromising conservative, proud of his sons' service with the Freikorps during the postrevolutionary period of ferment, a man who himself patrolled the streets of Berlin against the revolution in 1920 and who, after World War Two, still publicly complained about the influence of the "Jewish powers" in prewar Germany (Schmidt-Ott, *Erlebtes und Erstrebtes*, 173). On his views of the Emergency Coalition's work, see Schmidt-Ott, "Die Not." On his personality and "linder Antisemitismus" (mild anti-Semitism), see Hammerstein, *Die deutsche Forschungsgemeinschaft*, 47.

25. Note the recollection of local pride in the airship hangar at Stolp and the popular interest in polar airship travel recounted in the memoir by Krockow, *Die Reise nach Pommern*, 9.

26. Meyer, *Airshipmen*, 164.

27. See the account of the flight and the speech in Eckener, "The First Airship Flight." This is a typically lavishly illustrated article, and the comments on page 661 on the durability of the airship are especially revealing.

28. For the story of this forgotten father of rigid airship aviation, see Schütte, ed., *Der Luftschiffbau Schütte-Lanz*.

29. See the eight-page pamphlet by Nansen and Breitfuss, *Die Erforschung*.

30. Meyer, *Airshipmen*, 163.

31. For internal criticism, see "Ist das Zeppelin-Luftschiff überholt?" *Stuttgarter neues Tageblatt*, 22 November 1926, in BAK: NL Dörr, Mappe 14; on Krüger, see Fogelson, *Arctic Exploration*, 155.

32. An engaging and reliable account of the Andrée expedition and the discovery of its remains can be found in Stefansson, *Unsolved Mysteries*, 168–270.

33. Mohr, *Zum Pol*, 30.

34. Eckener, *Im Zeppelin*, 357.

35. Bruns cited in "Bericht der zweiten ordentlichen Versammlungt."

36. Eckener, *Im Zeppelin*, 358.

37. This estimate is based upon Eckener's comments in *Im Zeppelin*, 360, and the amount later raised to support the flight reported in Koestler, *Arrow in the Blue*, 321. The proposal to sail a submarine to the Pole originated (apart from the stories of Jules Verne) in 1901 with the German engineer Hermann Anschütz-Kaempfe, one of the fathers of modern guidance technology and inventor in 1908 of the gyrocompass. He suggested the submarine

polar journey in a speech to the Vienna Geographical Society. See Knothe, "Moderne Polarforschung," 362; Gerlach and Sommerfeld, "Nachruf."

38. Meyer, Airshipmen, 162–64.

39. Stresemann cited in Michalka and Niedhart, eds., Die ungeliebte Republik, 194. The most illuminating discussion of this conception of Weimar foreign policy is in Krüger, Die Aussenpolitik, 217–18.

40. Akten zur deutschen auswärtigen Politik, vol. 14, no. 204. Schmidt-Ott also enthused over cooperation with the Soviets. See the discussion of his pro-Russian orientation in Hammerstein, Die deutsche Forschungsgemeinschaft, 75.

41. Deutsche Botschaft Moskau, "Besuch des Luftschiffes Graf Zeppelin in Moskau," 11 September 1930, 1, 3, in AA: R32994.

42. Deutsche Botschaft Moskau, telegram, signed von Twardowski, 11 September 1930, in AA: R32994.

43. The words are Eckener's, cited in Fritzsche, A Nation of Fliers, 23.

44. Koll, Der Kampf um die Pole, 146.

45. Kohl-Larsen, Die Arktisfahrt, 51.

46. A colorful account of the flight of the Norge may be found in "Navigating the Norge."

47. Lehmann's memoirs illustrate the virtues and liabilities of the zeppelin in military service. See Auf Luftpatrouille und Weltfahrt. Also aboard was Hans von Schiller, whose comments on airship navigation may be found in "Transozeanverkehr."

48. See the comments on his attitude and its variance from those of some of his superiors in Krüger, Die Aussenpolitik, 384–85. Also, for a closer inspection of Dirksen's impact, see Sütterlin, Die "Russische Abteilung" des auswärtigen Amtes, 223–27.

49. Aufzeichnung, signed Frohwein, 22 July 1931, in AA: R32994. Penciled marginalia, including exclamation points after the word "occupy," indicate the amazement of the Foreign Office officials.

50. Baschin, "Die Arktis-Expedition."

51. Eckener, Im Zeppelin, 368.

52. Kohl-Larsen, Die Arktisfahrt, 56, 103.

53. Eckener, Im Zeppelin, 376. Similar remarks were made by other participants. "The play of colors was unusually beautiful, since it was not night at this season," recalled pilot Hans von Schiller. "The ice flashed and sparkled in all colors, and we could observe seals, walruses, whales, and once even polar bears" (Zeppelin, 92).

54. Koll, Der Kampf um die Pole, 155.

55. Kohl-Larsen, *Die Arktisfahrt*, 130.
56. Eckener, *Im Zeppelin*, 378–79. The Russians thought Eckener boorish. See Sieburg, *Die rote Arktis*, 94–95.
57. Koestler, *Arrow in the Blue*, 319.
58. Samoilowitsch, "Die Flüge," 28. Samoilowitsch also praised the airship's capabilities in "Die Polarfahrt."
59. Penck an Schmidt-Ott, 21 October 1931, in BAK: R73, 249.
60. Weickmann, "Die Polarfahrt," 89.
61. Ellsworth cited in Kohl-Larsen, *Die Arktisfahrt*, 197. See also the assessment in Eckener, *Der Weg voran!* 115.
62. The headline is from *Berliner illustrierte Zeitung*, 23 October 1931. See Haushofer, "Alfred Wegener," 250.
63. K. Wegener cited in Wutzke, *Durch die weisse Wüste*, 25. Wegener was referring to the then-famous balloonist, the comte de la Vaulx.
64. See the brief account in Erngaard, *Greenland, Then and Now*, 142–44, 154–55.
65. Wegener cited in Voss, "Alfred Wegeners Weg," 82.
66. Wegener cited in Wutzke, *Der Forscher*, 45.
67. For discussions of this, see the following: Frankel, "Continental Drift," 118–36; Greene, "Alfred Wegener"; Wegener, *Die Entstehung der Kontinente und Ozeane*.
68. See the accounts of Koch and Wegener in Koch, "Unsere Durchquerung." See also Wegener's assessment of the expedition in Wegener, "Vorläufige Bericht."
69. Wegener cited in Voss, "Alfred Wegeners Weg," 85.
70. Wegener, *Alfred Wegeners letzte Grönlandfahrt*, 13.
71. Wegener cited in Wutzke, *Durch die weisse Wüste*, 161. The description of Wegener is by his brother Kurt, "Vortrag Kurt Wegeners," 7, in BAK: R73, 256.
72. For a complete list of the membership of the commission, see "Niederschrift über eine Sitzung, 27 November 1929," in BAK: R73, 243.
73. See also "Auszug aus der Niederschrift über die am 14. Dez 1929 in den Raümen der NG und des Hotels Prinz Albrecht abgehaltene Hauptausschutzsitzung," in BAK: R73, 243. Wegener estimated the main expedition would cost double this amount. See also "Aktennotizen der NDG für 30.11.29," in BAK: R73, 243.
74. Meinardus, "Betrifft Darlegungen zur Grönland-expedition im Anschluss, 27.11.29," and "Prof. Dr. Alfred Wegener, Graz, Inlandeis-Expedition nach

Grönland," apparently composed by Albrecht Penck, both in BAK: R73, 243.

75. Penck, "Prof. Dr. Alfred Wegener."

76. Meinardus, "Betrifft Darlegungen," 2. See also the assessment of Schmidt-Ott's sensitivity to German scientific prestige in regard to the expedition in Hammerstein, *Die deutsche Forschungsgemeinschaft*, 75.

77. Wegener cited in Wutzke, *Durch die weisse Wüste*, 162.

78. Meinardus, "Betrifft Darlegungen," 2.

79. Wegener to Schmidt-Ott cited in Wutzke, *Kommentiertes Verzeichnis*, 98.

80. Schmidt-Ott cited in Jacobshagen et al., eds., *Alfred Wegener 1880–1930*, 28.

81. Meinardus, "Betrifft Darlegungen."

82. Penck, "Prof. Dr. Alfred Wegener," 3.

83. Wutzke, *Kommentiertes Verzeichnis*, 91.

84. Wegener, *Mit Motorboot und Schlitten*.

85. Wutzke, *Durch die weisse Wüste*, 197.

86. Wegener an der NG, 05.12.29, in BAK: R73, 246.

87. "Grönlandex. 1930, 766–2: Besprechung in der NG am 16. und 17. Jan. 1929," 1–6, in BAK: R73, 243.

88. Verlag Ullstein an Fritz Loewe, 14 February 1930, and Presse-Verlag Dammert an Wegener, signed Rudolf Dammert, 17 February 1930, both in BAK: R73, 244.

89. "Besprechung mit Prof. Dr. Wegener und Stud. Rat Dr. Sorge in der Notgemeinschaft am 16.12.1929," in BAK: R73, 244.

90. "Reisebericht 3, 22.06.30," in BAK: R73, 244.

91. Wegener cited in Voss, "Alfred Wegeners Weg," 88.

92. The assessment of Wegener was made by the painter Achton Friis, a participant in the expedition, cited in Voss, "Alfred Wegeners Weg," 81.

93. Georgi, *Im Eis vergraben*, 22.

94. Handwritten report by Wegener without date or title, in BAK: R73, 244.

95. "Reisebericht 4, ein Tag auf dem Kamarujuk-Gletscher," BAK: R73, 244.

96. Lissey cited in Wegener, *Alfred Wegeners letzte Grönlandfahrt*, 37.

97. Wegener cited in Wutzke, *Durch die weisse Wüste*, 207–8.

98. "Reisebericht 4."

99. Wegener cited in Wutzke, *Durch die weisse Wüste*, 206.

100. Wegener an Georgi, 31 July 1930, reprinted in Wutzke, *Kommentiertes Verzeichnis*, 122.

101. Wegener cited in Wutzke, *Durch die weisse Wüste*, 208.

102. Wutzke, *Durch die weisse Wüste*, 211–12.

103. Wegener cited in Reinke-Kunze, *Aufbruch*, 68.
104. "Einige Mitteilungen aus Prof. Alfred Wegeners Briefen über seine letzte Schlittenreise. Mitgeteilt von Else Wegener," 1, in BAK: R73, 248.
105. Georgi cited in Wegener, *Alfred Wegeners letzte Grönlandfahrt*, 166.
106. Georgi cited in Reinke-Kunze, *Aufbruch*, 70.
107. "Einige Mitteilungen aus Prof. Alfred Wegeners Briefen," 2.
108. Wegener, "Die deutsche Grönland-Expedition," 27.
109. There is disagreement about exactly when Wegener received Georgi's letter and when he actually departed for Ice Central. Ulrich Wutzke, the leading expert on Wegener's life, maintains that Wegener received the letter on 21 September and set forth on the twenty-second. Every other source, to the contrary, states that Wegener actually set out on the twenty-first and received the letter from returning sled crews shortly after leaving Scheideck. The latter view seems more likely. It was represented by Kurt Wegener, who took over the expedition after Alfred's death, and also seems indicated in a letter written by Wegener to his wife, dated the twentieth, in which he writes: "Early tomorrow morning I leave with Loewe and the thirteen Greenlanders with dog sleds for Station Ice Central." Wegener was clearly determined to leave, letter or no, but the timing of the message from Georgi became important in later debates over the blame for Wegener's death. See Wutzke, *Durch die weisse Wüste*, 213; Wegener, "Die deutsche Grönland-Expedition," 27; Voss, "Alfred Wegeners Weg," 90–91; Reinke-Kunze, *Aufbruch*, 69; and "Einige Mitteilungen aus Prof. Alfred Wegeners Briefen," 2.
110. "Einige Mitteilungen aus Prof. Alfred Wegeners Briefen."
111. Wegener cited in Wutzke, *Durch die weisse Wüste*, 215.
112. "Ein Winter auf dem grönlandischen Inlandeis," in BAK: R73, 244.
113. Georgi cited in Voss, "Alfred Wegeners Weg," 91.
114. Georgi cited in Reinke-Kunze, *Aufbruch*, 70.
115. Sorge cited in Voss, "Alfred Wegeners Weg," 93.
116. Wegener, "Die deutsche Grönland-Expedition," 32.
117. See Penck's assessment of the importance of the data in Penck an Schmidt-Ott, 10 October 1931, in BAK: R73, 249 (copy).
118. Knothe, "Moderne Polarforschung," 363.
119. "Vortrag des Herrn Prof. Dr. Kurt Wegener, gehalten im Rundfunk am 21. Nov. 1931," 7, in BAK: R73, 256.
120. "Sensationelle Enthüllungen," *Neuigkeits-Welt-Blatt* (Vienna), 8 November 1934.

121. "Schlusswort," in BAK: R73, 269.
122. Berson, "Alfred Wegener," 1; "Naturwissenschaften," in BAK: R73, 256.
123. Schmidt-Ott an Daugaard Jensen, 7 September 1931, in BAK: R73, 247 (copy).
124. See the correspondence of Loewe, Sorge, Kurt Wegener, Else Wegener, and others in BAK: R73, 256; the letter from the director of the Royal Zoological Garden in Sofia to the Emergency Coalition, Peters an NDW, in BAK: R73, 257.
125. "Aktennotiz, NDG," signed Schmidt-Ott, 26 April 1933, and the use they made of materials from the story as early as June 1931 in Der Hausfreund mit Rundfunk Program. Einzelhandels dienende Wochenschrift, 12 June 1931, both in BAK: R73, 246.
126. "Börsenblatt für den deutschen Buchhandel," 2 May 1932, 19 May 1932, 26 May 1932, in BAK: R73, 254; sales figures in Fritz Loewe an K. Wegener, 14 February 1933, in BAK: R73, 250.
127. Der Präsident der deutschen Seewarte an Schmidt-Ott, 3 January 1933, in BAK: R73, 258.
128. See his account of the provisioning of the station in Wegener, "Die deutsche Grönland-Expedition," 26–27.
129. "Wegeners Grönlandexpedition und die Kontinentalverscheibung," Reichspost (Vienna), 7 February 1935, 3, in BAK: R73, 250 (copy).
130. "Nachtrag," signed Kurt Wegener, 7 January 1935, in BAK: R73, 250; Else Wegener an Schmidt-Ott, 29 November 1931, in BAK: R73, 249.
131. "Entgegnung auf die Klage des Regierungsrat Dr. Georgi," 1–4, in BAK: R73, 250.
132. Penck an Schmidt-Ott, 10 October 1931, in BAK: R73, 248.
133. Der Präsident der deutschen Seewarte an Schmidt-Ott, 3 January 1933, in BAK: R73, 258.
134. "Naturwissenschaften."
135. Schmidt-Ott an Senator Dr. de Chapeaurouge, 13 February 1932, in BAK: R73, 248.
136. See "Ich bitte ums wort," by Georgi, in BAK: R73, 258; Georgi, Im Eis vergraben, 21–22; and Georgi, Alfred Wegener, 84–91.
137. See, for example, Wutzke, Durch die weisse Wüste; Reinke-Kunze, Aufbruch; Voss, "Alfred Wegeners Weg"; and Jacobshagen et al., eds., Alfred Wegener 1880–1930.
138. Loewe, "Alfred Wegener," 1.
139. Wheeler, ed., Marvels of the Modern World, 73.

140. Bruns actually proposed to the United Nations after the war that all the territory above 80° north latitude be internationalized. See Bruns an L. P. Lochner, 19 July 1949, and Bruns an der Generalsek. der Ver. Nat., 11 July 1949, both in 21 AF Louis P. Lochner Papers, Box 2, Folder 24 (copies).

5. The German Image of the Polar World

1. See Hermand, *Grüne Utopien in Deutschland*, 50–58.
2. Germans argued that the American continent, for example, "created the red peoples." African nature gave blacks an "animalistic nature." The German setting, influenced by everything from cloud formations to climate, "had to make the German people that which they are today." See, respectively, Lissner, *Völker und Kontinente*, 40; Banse, "Über den Zusammenhang"; Ratzel, "Die Wolken"; and Kohl, *Ursprung und Wandlung*, 5. See also Murphy, "'A sum.'"
3. Houben, *Der Ruf des Nordens*, 11–12.
4. See, for example, Dröber, *Die Polargebiete*, 54–55; Miethe and Hergesell, *Mit Zeppelin nach Spitzbergen*, 188–89.
5. Züchner, *Der weisse Magnet*, iii.
6. Dröber, *Die Polargebiete*, 3.
7. Herz, *Tropisches und Arktisches*, 166–67, 162–63.
8. Zeidler, *Polarfahrten*, 7, 9.
9. Enzberg, *Heroen der Nordpolarforschung*, 156.
10. Mecking, *Die Polarwelt*, 19.
11. See Shackleton's comments in *South*, 373–74; Raban, "The Endurance Myth," 16; and Simpson-Housley, *Antarctica*, 18–37, 76–89.
12. Hartwig, *Der hohe Norden*, 3. See similar views in Hassert, *Die Nordpolargrenze*, 16–17, and in the description of the scientists of the Wegener expedition as reduced nearly to the condition of "hand workers, stable boys, and pack-bearers" by the glacier cliffs of Greenland in the Brockhaus promotional flier in BAK: R73, 252.
13. Bremischen Comite, ed., *Die zweite deutsche Nordpolar-Expedition*, 4.
14. Wichmann, "August Petermann," 804; Dröber, *Die Polargebiete*, 2.
15. Buchholz, *Erlebnisse der Mannschaft des Schiffes Hansa*, 5; Brehm, *Vom Nordpol zum Äquator*, 5.
16. Drygalski, *Die Ergebnisse der Südpolarforschung*, 17.
17. Filchner, *Ein Forscherleben*, 103; Loomis, "The Arctic Sublime."
18. Houben, *Der Ruf des Nordens*, 11; Herz, *Tropisches und Arktisches*, 182.
19. Henry, *The White Continent*, 38.

20. Ehlers, *In die Wunderwelt*, 63–64.
21. Enzberg, *Heroen der Nordpolarforschung*, 147. Gazert, Drygalski's medical expert, recounts the high incidence of snowblindness, even on overcast days ("Gesundheitsbericht," 48).
22. Gazert, "Gesundheitsbericht," 148. See almost the same words written decades later in Ehlers, *In die Wunderwelt*, 64.
23. Verein für die deutsche Nordpolarfahrt zu Bremen, ed., *Die zweite deutsche Nordpolar-fahrt*, 1:iii.
24. Neumayer, ed., *Die internationale Polarforschung*, 235.
25. Löwenberg, *Die Entdeckungen und Forschungsreisen*, 135, 150.
26. Lampe, "Erdkundliche Interessen," 33–35.
27. Drygalski, *Die Ergebnisse der Südpolarforschung*, 18. Precisely the same words appear in Müller, *Einiges aus der Geschichte*, 69.
28. Penck, *Das Institut*, 29.
29. GStA: HA I, R 208C, no. 7, p. 34.
30. Lynn K. Nyhart, "Creating a 'Public' Nature and a 'Professional' Nature: The New Museum Idea in German Natural History," paper presented at the Universities of Manchester and Cambridge, 24–26 February 1998.
31. Braun, *Die Erforschung der Pole*, 86–87.
32. Züchner, *Der weisse Magnet*, 204; Breitfuss, *Arktis*, 1.
33. Houben, *Der Ruf des Nordens*, 7; Mecking, *Die Polarwelt*, 3–4.
34. Hennig and Korholz, *Einführung*, 68.
35. Nordenskjöld, *Die Polarwelt*, 68.
36. Ehlers, *In die Wunderwelt*, 57.
37. Hassert, *Die Nordpolargrenze*, 2. The same phenomenon is remarked by Herz: "The tameness of the animals, who do not yet know the danger of man, is astounding; the numerous birds pay no notice to our approach, the crack of a shot barely suffices to hurry them off a short stretch, and as we came upon a couple of reindeer during a walk, they eyed us for a long while before they made away with solemn steps" (*Tropisches und Arktisches*, 182).
38. Drygalski, "The German Antarctic Expedition," 198.
39. Herz, *Tropisches und Arktisches*, 175.
40. Nordenskjöld, *Die Polarwelt*, 98.
41. See Andersen, "Heimatschutz."
42. Dominick, *The Environmental Movement in Germany*, 23; Löwenberg, *Die Entdeckungen und Forschungsreisen*, 135, 142.
43. "Afrika"; "Neger"; "Eskimo," in *Meyers Konversation-Lexikon*.

44. "Eskimo," in *The Encyclopedia Britannica*. See the discussion in Spufford, *I May Be Some Time*, 184–235, particularly the comments on pages 200–201.
45. Egede, *Des alten Grönland* and *Die Heiden im Eis*. Though often described as a Dane, Egede was in fact a Norwegian working for the Danes, according to Vilhjalmur Stefansson. See also Cranz, *Historie von Grönland*, 1:218–65; and Oswalt, *Eskimos and Explorers*, 166.
46. See Erngaard, *Greenland, Then and Now*, 56–57.
47. Chamisso's *Entdeckungs-Reise in die Süd-See und nach der Berings-Strasse zur Erforschung einer nordöstlichen Durchfahrt: Unternommen in den Jahren 1815, 1816, 1817 und 1818, auf Kosten Sr. Erlaucht des Herrn Reichs-Kanzlers Grafen Rumanzoff auf dem Schiffe Rurick unter dem Befehle des Leutnants der russisch-kaiserlichen Marine Otto von Kotzebue* was originally published in 1821. The work appeared in English as Adelbert von Chamisso, *A Voyage around the World with the Romanzov Exploring Expedition in the Years 1815–1818 in the Brig "Rurik," Captain Otto von Kotzebue*, ed. and trans. Henry Kratz (orig. pub. 1836, reprint Honolulu: University of Hawaii Press, 1986). See the perceptive discussion in Liebersohn, "Discovering Indigenous Nobility."
48. See the treatment of this concept in Smith, *Politics*, 50, 111. See also Ratzel, *Politische Geographie*, 155. This work originally appeared in 1897. Mary Louise Pratt has described the emergence of a "European planetary consciousness" in this era of which ethnology and anthropology were part. See Pratt, *Imperial Eyes*, 34–35; Adas, *Machines as the Measure of Men*. See also Waitz, *Introduction to Anthropology*.
49. See, for example, the notes on "Physische Geographie" in Kant, "Nachricht von der Einrichtung"; see also Kant, "Von den verschiedenen Racen" and "Physische Geographie."
50. Writing of his encounter with "primitive" peoples during the voyage of the *Beagle*, Darwin comments: "Of individual objects, perhaps no one is more certain to create astonishment than the first sight in his native haunt of a real barbarian—of man in his lowest and most savage state. One's mind hurries back over past centuries, and then asks, could our progenitors have been such as these? Men, whose very signs and expressions are less intelligible to us than those of the domesticated animals; men, who do not possess the instinct of those animals, nor yet appear to boast of human reason, or at least of arts consequent on that reason. I do not believe it is possible to describe or paint the difference between savage and civilized man" (*Voyage of the Beagle*, 375).
51. Haeckel cited in Hawkins, *Social Darwinism*, 139–40. See the discussion

on pages 138–45. See also Becker, *Sozialdarwinismus*; Gasman, *Haeckel's Monism*.

52. See Chamberlain, *Die Grundlagen*, a work that first appeared in 1898. See also Mosse, *Toward the Final Solution*, 79–81, 105–8.

53. Hartwig, *Der hohe Norden*, 230, 231. Chamisso also noted the cheerful nature of the Chukchi. See Liebersohn, "Discovering Indigenous Nobility," 756.

54. William Barr's outstanding translation of Klutschak, upon which this discussion relies, takes as its title, rather curiously, *Overland to Starvation Cove*.

55. On Boas, see Smith, *Politics*, 113–14; Knötsch, *Franz Boas*, 109–11. See also "From Physics to Ethnology," in Stocking, *Race, Culture, and Evolution*, 133–60; the introduction by Henry Collins in Boas, *The Central Eskimo*, v–xi.

56. Klutschak, *Overland to Starvation Cove*, 44, 33, 112.

57. Klutschak, *Overland to Starvation Cove*, 46, 47.

58. Volckmann, ed., *Erlebnisse*, 7.

59. Volckmann, ed., *Erlebnisse*, 82–83.

60. Volckmann, ed., *Erlebnisse*, 96.

61. Volckmann, ed., *Erlebnisse*, 78.

62. Dröber, *Die Polargebiete*, 55, 56.

63. Braun, *Die Erforschung der Pole*, 84; Sokolowsky, "Wie der Polarmensch lebt," 115; Iden-Zeller, "Die Organisation," 2028.

64. See, for example, Baschin, "Polar Katastrophen," 90.

65. See Urs Bitterli's remarks on contact between European and non-European societies, which he characterizes in three types: incidental contact, sustained economic or political relationships, and cultural "collisions" resulting in genocide or near-genocide. See Bitterli, *Die 'Wilden' und die 'Zivilisierten,'* 81–179; the essays in *Cultures in Conflict*, esp. 20–50. Where Europeans made a good deal off the resources of the polar lands, as in the Russian fur trade, popular attitudes toward the natives (as distinct from occasionally well meant official policies) were very negative. See Weiser, *Die Völker Nordsibiriens*, 16–17.

66. Austrian Germans also sympathized with native Americans. Johannes Brahms toasted Sitting Bull's victory at the Little Big Horn (Swofford, *Johannes Brahms*, 530).

67. Nansen, *Eskimoleben*, 288–89. See the critical remarks in Oehlmann, "Review"; Braun, *Die Erforschung der Pole*, 86; and Dröber, *Die Polargebiete*, 54, who writes: "Nansen maintains that the Greenlanders will perish through closer contact with European culture. To the contrary, new statistics

indicate a slight increase in the population, though dangerous epidemics and misfortunes claim considerable victims."

68. Breitfuss, *Arktis*, 21–22. See also his views in *Das Nordpolargebiet*. For similar views of the "natural peoples" of Africa that reflect a similar pessimism, see Heinrich Schnee (at the time president of the German Colonial Society), "Aufzeichnung betreffend koloniale Fragen," 24–66, in GStA: R 92 NL Schnee, dated 1930.

69. Peters, *Anthropologie und Zoologie*, 3.

70. Mecking, *Die Polarwelt*, 9.

71. Hartwig, *Der hohe Norden*, 237.

72. Dröber, *Die Polargebiete*, 56.

73. See, for example, Sokolowsky, "Wie der Polarmensch lebt," 118. One of the best-known writers of popularized Eskimo anthropology, Vilhjalmur Stefansson, made the same point in 1913. See *My Life with the Eskimo*, 295. See also Dröber, *Die Polargebiete*, 57.

74. Meyer, *Die Rätsel der Erdpole*, 22.

75. Hassert, *Die Nordpolargrenze*, 69.

76. Nordenskjöld, *Die Polarwelt*, 21.

77. Nordenskjöld, *Die Polarwelt*, 22.

78. Buschick, *Die Eroberung der Erde*, 325.

79. Maxtone-Graham, *Safe Return Doubtful*, 112.

80. A readable account of older polar myths is Stefansson, *Ultima Thule*. On Symmes, see Spufford, *I May Be Some Time*, 64–70.

81. For Müller's own views on the use of "Aryan" as a racial term, see Müller, *Biographies of Words*, 88–89. See also Stackelberg, "Racism," 812–13; Godwin, *Arktos*, 37–45; Mühlen, *Rassenideologien*; Poliakov, *The Aryan Myth*. For more respectable scholarly theories about Indian sources of Germanic/Scandinavian culture, see Schlegel, *Werke*, 221–29.

82. Biedenkopp, *Der Nordpol*, 165–66.

83. The best postwar examples are Wirth, *Der Aufgang der Menschheit*; Wirth, "Das Geheimnis von Arktis-Atlantis."

84. Biedenkopp, *Der Nordpol*, 167.

85. Houben, *Der Ruf des Nordens*, 9.

86. Hoenerssen, *Neue Erkenntnisse*, 39.

87. Würzner, *Das Mysterium*, 29.

88. Kohl-Larsen, *An den Toren*, 85–93, 114.

89. Peters, *Anthropologie und Zoologie*, 3–4.

90. Hassert, *Die Nordpolargrenze*, 16–17.

91. Döblin, *Berge, Meere und Giganten*.
92. Hennig, *Weltluftverkehr und Weltpolitik*, especially the section entitled "Der kommende Luftverkehr in arktischen und antarktischen Gebieten" (The coming air travel in the Arctic and Antarctic regions), 51–58; Hochholzer, "Zur Geopolitik des Flugwesens."
93. See Friedrich, *Germany's Antarctic Claim*.

6. Aryan Aurora

1. Filchner, *Ein Forscherleben*, 336–37; *Berliner Lokal-Anzeiger*, "Zwei Stunden schlaf genügt den Forscher," 11 January 1938, in BAP: 61 Re 1/120/Filchner, Reichslandbund. The "National Prize" was established in 1937 and awarded thrice yearly. Alfred Rosenberg, among others, joined Filchner as recipient. See Brinkmann, *Orden und Ehrenzeichen*, 24.
2. Filchner, *Ein Forscherleben*, 336–37; "Was bedeutet Filchners Forschung für uns?" *Nationalsozialistische Landpost*, 18 February 1938; "Wikinger des 20. Jahrhunderts," *Völkischer Beobachter*, 19 January 1938; and "Die Reichshauptstadt ehrt Dr. Filchner," *Völkischer Beobachter*, 14 February 1938, all in BAP: 61 Re 1/120/Filchner, Reichslandbund. On the Nazi manufacture of heroes, see the epilogue to Baird, *To Die for Germany*.
3. See the introductory notes to the *Findbuch* in BAK: R73.
4. The literature on Nazi foreign policy is enormous. See Rich, *Hitler's War Aims*; Weinberg, *The Foreign Policy of Hitler's Germany*. A reliable recent consideration of Hitler's goals in this regard can be found in Stackelberg, *Hitler's Germany*.
5. Cameron, *Antarctica*, 130.
6. Cameron, *Antarctica*, 130; Lampe, "Versuch," 110; Hassert, *Die Polarforschung*, 253–54. See the account in Mawer, *Ahab's Trade*.
7. Härlin, *Am Südpol*, 74.
8. See Drygalski, "Die Entwicklung" and "The Oceanographical Problems"; Baschin, "Berichterstattung aus der Arktis" and "Berichterstattung aus der Antarktis"; Knothe, "Moderne Polarforschung"; and books such as Heinze, *Der weisse Tod*; Sieburg, *Die rote Arktis*; Wodopjanow, *Die Eroberung des Nordpols*.
9. Kircheiss, *Polarkreis Süd—Polarkreis Nord*, 2.
10. Paas, "Der deutsche Walfang," 161.
11. Paas, "Der deutsche Walfang," 162.
12. "In Kürze," *Polarforschung* 9 (1939): 6.
13. On government support for polar publishing, see BAP: 49.01–2621/Leonid

Breitfuss, 1939–44, 6–7, and the memorandum from 1939 signed by Filchner and others entitled "Ein deutscher Standardwerk über Polarforschung," 26–29.

14. On the Four-Year Plan, see Volkmann, "The National Socialist Economy," and Petzina, *Autarkie-Politik*. On Wohlthat's role in planning, see his foreword to Ritscher, ed., *Deutsche antarktische Expedition*, ix–x, and BDC: Personalakten Wohlthat.

15. Ritscher, ed., *Deutsche antarktische Expedition*, viii.

16. "Vermerk," signed Mentzel, 8 December 1938, in BAK: R73, 242.

17. "Vermerk"; "Geheim—Wohlthat an den Herrn Präsidenten der deutschen Forschungsgemeinschaft E.V.," 8 December 1938, in BAK: R73, 242. See also Macrakis, *Surviving the Swastika*; Johnson, "Kaiser Wilhelm/Max Planck Societies"; on Bosch, see Holdermann, *Im Banne der Chemie*; Hammerstein, *Die deutsche Forschungsgemeinschaft*, 142–49.

18. See Ritscher, "Wanderungen"; Georgi, "Polarforscher Kapitän Alfred Ritscher"; Vetter, "Alfred Ritschers Beiträge"; Ritscher, "Instrumente und Methoden"; BDC: Personalakten Ritscher.

19. Kraul, *Käpt'n Kraul erzählt*.

20. Ritscher, ed., *Deutsche antarktische Expedition*, 8, 13; Herrmann, *Deutsche Forscher im Südpolarmeer*, 27.

21. Ritscher, ed., *Deutsche antarktische Expedition*, 3.

22. Irving, *The Rise and Fall of the Luftwaffe*, 353 n.; Deutsche Lufthansa, ed., *Die Geschichte*, 47–48; Reinke-Kunze, *Aufbruch*, 225–26.

23. Ritscher, ed., *Deutsche antarktische Expedition*, 4–5.

24. The ship was originally constructed in 1925 as the *Schwarzenfels*, intended for use as a freighter in the Indian trade. It was acquired in 1934 by the Lufthansa, remodeled, and rechristened. At the time, the Lufthansa also deployed a third such vessel, the *Ostmark*. See Fritzsche, *A Nation of Fliers*, 175–76; Deutsche Lufthansa, ed., *Die Geschichte*.

25. See the discussion of the innovations on flying boats a decade earlier in Hochholzer, "Grundzüge."

26. Hassert, *Die Polarforschung*, 252.

27. Ritscher, ed., *Deutsche antarktische Expedition*, 6–10.

28. Herrmann, *Deutsche Forscher im Südpolarmeer*, 14.

29. See, for example, the almost incidental first mention in "Südpolargebiet," *Geographische Zeitschrift* 45 (1939): 147 and "Südpolargebiet," *Geographischer Anzeiger* 40 (1939): 41.

30. "The *Schwabenland* in the Antarctic."

31. Herrmann, *Deutsche Forscher im Südpolarmeer*, 14.
32. Ritscher, ed., *Deutsche antarktische Expedition*, 44.
33. Herrmann, *Deutsche Forscher im Südpolarmeer*, 18.
34. Herrmann, *Deutsche Forscher im Südpolarmeer*, 30.
35. Herrmann, *Deutsche Forscher im Südpolarmeer*, 60.
36. Herrmann, *Deutsche Forscher im Südpolarmeer*, 65.
37. Herrmann, *Deutsche Forscher im Südpolarmeer*, 65–66.
38. "Betr.: Deutsche antarktische Expedition 1938/39," signed Wohlthat, 24 January 1939, 10, in BAK: R73, 242.
39. "Geheim," Mentzel an Wohlthat, 13 February 1939, 25–26, in BAK: R73, 242.
40. Ritscher, ed., *Deutsche antarktische Expedition*, 114.
41. Rüdiger, "Geographische Nachrichten," 193. See "Die deutsche antarktischen Expedition 1939/40."
42. "Geheim: Richtlinien für die Vorbereitung und Durchführung der deutschen antarktischen Expedition 1939/40," 28 August 1939, 46–49, in BAK: R73, 242.
43. Ritscher, ed., *Deutsche antarktische Expedition*, 81.
44. Rüdiger, "Geographische Nachrichten," 193.
45. See the notes in BDC: RKK 2100, Box 0141, File 09.
46. Ritscher, ed., *Deutsche antarktische Expedition*, 28.
47. See Farnes, *War in the Arctic*; Barr, "Wettertrupp Haudegen," 143–58, 323–33.
48. Hitler declared, after the assassination of Heydrich, that the Czechs might be resettled beyond the Arctic Circle. See Koning, "Germania Irredenta," 30.

BIBLIOGRAPHY

Manuscript Sources

Berlin Document Center (BDC)
    Personalakten Herrmann
    Personalakten Ritscher
    Personalakten Schirmacher
    Personalakten Spiess
    Personalakten Wohlthat
    RKK 2100
Bundesarchiv Koblenz (BAK)
    NL Dörr
    NL Külz
    R73 (Deutsche Forschungsgemeinschaft), 242, 243, 244, 247,
    248, 249, 250, 252, 256, 257, 258, 269
Bundesarchiv Potsdam (BAP)
    R 901 (Auswärtiges Amt), 37538, 37556, 37566
    RMdI 1501 (Reichsministerium des Innern), 15957, 16016,
    16022, 16120, 16122, 16123, 16293
    49.01–2621/Leonid Breitfuss, 1939–44 (Reichsministerium für
    Wissenschaft, Erziehung und Volksbildung)
    61 Re 1/104/Eckener
    61 Re 1/120/Filchner
Geheimes Staatsarchiv preussischer Kulturbesitz, Berlin-Dahlem (GStA)
    HA I, R 90 (Förderung der Polarforschung, 1788; Förderung
    der Meereskunde, 1790)
    HA I, R 208C (Institut für Meereskunde)
    R 92 NL Schmidt-Ott
    R 92 NL Schnee
Politisches Archiv des auswärtigen Amts, Bonn (AA)
    R32993–98, 9 Fahrten mit dem neuerbauten Luftschiff
Wisconsin State Historical Society Archive, Madison
    21 AF Louis P. Lochner Papers, Box 2

Published Sources

Abel, Herbert, and Hans Jessen. *Kein Weg durch das Packeis. Anfänge der
    deutschen Polarforschung (1868–1889)*. Bremen: Carl Schünemann
    Verlag, 1954.

Adams, William H. D. *Recent Polar Voyages: A Record of Adventure and Discovery*. London: Thomas Nelson and Sons, 1880.

Adas, Michael. *Machines as the Measure of Men: Science, Technology and Ideologies of Western Dominance*. Ithaca NY: Cornell University Press, 1989.

Aeroarctic, ed. *Arktis. Vierteljahrsschrift der internationalen Gesellschaft zur Erforschung der Arktis mit Luftfahrzeugen* 1 (1928): 15–117.

————. *Das Luftschiff als Forschungsmittel in der Arktis. Eine Denkschrift.* Berlin: Aeroarctic, 1924.

"Afrika." In *Meyers Konversation-Lexikon. Eine Enzyklopädie des allgemeinen Wissens.* 4th ed., 1:148–76. Leipzig: Verlag des bibliographischen Instituts, 1885.

Akten zur deutschen auswärtigen Politik 1918–1945. Aus dem Archiv des auswärtigen Amts. Series B, 1925–33. Göttingen: Vandenhoeck und Ruprecht, 1966–83.

Amtlicher Bericht über die erste Versammlung deutscher Meister und Freunde der Erdkunde in Frankfurt a. M. im Heumonat 1865. Leipzig: Verlag des F. D. Hochstiftes, 1865.

Andersen, Arne. "Heimatschutz. Die bürgerliche Naturschutzbewegung." In *Besiegte Natur. Geschichte der Umwelt im 19. und 20. Jahrhundert.* Ed. Franz-Josef Brüggemeier and Th. Rommelspacher, 143–57. Munich: C. H. Beck, 1989.

Baird, Jay W. *To Die for Germany: Heroes in the Nazi Pantheon*. Bloomington: Indiana University Press, 1990.

Baird, Patrick D. *The Polar World*. London: Longman, 1964.

Balfour, Michael. *The Kaiser and His Times*. New York: W. W. Norton, 1972.

Banse, Ewald. "Über den Zusammenhang von Landschaft und Mensch." *Volk und Rasse* 7 (1932): 6–10.

Barr, William. *The Expeditions of the First International Polar Year, 1882–1883.* Calgary: Arctic Institute of North America, 1985.

————. "Wettertrupp Haudegen: The Last German Arctic Weather Station of World War II." *Polar Record* 23 (1986): 143–58, 323–33.

Bartlett, Robert A. *The Log of Bob Bartlett*. New York: Blue Ribbon Books, 1928.

Baschin, Otto. "Die Arktis-Expedition des 'Zeppelin.'" *Die Woche* 33 (1931): 972.

————. "Berichterstattung aus der Antarktis." *Zeitschrift für Geopolitik* 1 (1924): 811–17.

———. "Berichterstattung aus der Arktis." *Zeitschrift für Geopolitik* 1 (1924): 510–17.

———. "Polar Katastrophen." *Die Woche* 15 (1913): 90–91.

Bassin, Mark. "Friedrich Ratzel 1844–1904." *Geographers: Biobibliographical Studies* 11 (1987): 123–32.

Bates, H. W., ed. *The German Arctic Expedition of 1869–70 and Narrative of the Wreck of the "Hansa" in the Ice* by Captain Koldewey. London: Alston Rivers, Ltd., 1874.

Baughman, T. H. *Before the Heroes Came: Antarctica in the 1890s.* Lincoln: University of Nebraska Press, 1994.

Becker, Frido. *Unterwegs. Fehmarn, Insel zum Verlieben.* Hamburg: Christians, 1989.

Becker, Peter Emil. *Sozialdarwinismus, Rassismus, Antisemitismus und völkischer Gedanke. Wege ins Dritte Reich, Teil II.* Stuttgart: Georg Thieme Verlag, 1990.

"Bemerkungen zu K. Lampe." *Geographischer Anzeiger* 32 (1931): 147–48.

Berghahn, Volker R. *Der Tirpitz-Plan. Genesis und Verfall einer innenpolitischen Krisenstrategie unter Wilhelm II.* Düsseldorf: Droste, 1971.

"Bericht der zweiten ordentlichen Versammlung der Aeroarctic." *Arktis. Vierteljahrsschrift der Internationalen Gesellschaft zur Erforschung der Arktis mit Luftfahrzeugen* 1 (1928): 114.

Berson, A. "Alfred Wegener." *Arktis* 4 (1931): 1–2.

Bickel, Lennard. *Shackleton's Forgotten Men: The Untold Tragedy of the Endurance Epic.* New York: Thunder's Mouth Press, 2000.

Biedenkopp, Georg. *Der Nordpol als Völkerheimat.* Jena: Hermann Costenoble, 1906.

Bitterli, Urs. *Cultures in Conflict: Encounters between European and Non-European Culture, 1492–1800.* Trans. Ritchie Robertson. Stanford CA: Stanford University Press, 1989.

———. *Die 'Wilden' und die 'Zivilisierten.' Grundzüge einer Geistes- und Kulturgeschichte der europäische-überseeischen Begegnung.* Munich: Beck, 1976.

Boas, Franz. *The Central Eskimo.* Lincoln: University of Nebraska Press, 1964.

Böhme, Helmut. *Deutschlands Weg zur Grossmacht. Studien zum Verhältnis von Wirtschaft und Staat während der Reichsgründungszeit 1848–1881.* Cologne, 1966.

Börgen, Carl. "Kurze Bemerkungen über die Arbeiten der zweiten
    deutschen Nordpolar-Expedition für physicalische Geographie
    und Astronomie." In *Die zweite deutsche Nordpolarfahrt 1869–1870.
    Vorträge und Mittheilungen.* Ed. Verein für die deutsche Nordpo-
    larfahrt zu Bremen, 15–24. Berlin: Dietrich Reimer Verlag, 1871.
Botting, Douglas. *The Airships.* New York: Time-Life Books, 1980.
Boyd, Byron A. *Rudolf Virchow: The Scientist as Citizen.* New York: Garland,
    1991.
Braun, Gustav. *Die Erforschung der Pole.* Leipzig: Th. Thomas, 1912.
Brehm, Alfred. *Vom Nordpol zum Äquator.* Stuttgart: Union Deutsche, 1890.
Breitfuss, Leonid. *Arktis. Der derzeitige Stand unserer Kenntnisse über die Er-
    forschung der Nordpolargebiete.* Berlin: Ernst Siegfried Mittler und
    Sohn, 1939.
———. *Das Nordpolargebiet. Seine Natur, Bedeutung und Erforschung.* Berlin:
    Verständliche Wissenschaft, 1943.
Bremischen Comite, ed. *Die zweite deutsche Nordpolar-Expedition.* Braun-
    schweig: Georg Westermann, 1870.
Brinkmann, Jürgen. *Orden und Ehrenzeichen des 'Dritten Reiches.'* Minden:
    Auktionator Jürgen Brinkmann, n.d.
Brinnin, John Malcolm. *The Sway of the Grand Saloon: A Social History of the
    North Atlantic.* New York: Delacorte, 1971.
Bruch, Rüdiger vom. *Weltpolitik als Kulturmission. Auswärtige Kulturpoli-
    tik und Bildungsbürgertum in Deutschland am Vorabend des ersten
    Weltkrieges.* Paderborn: Ferdinand Schöningh, 1982.
Buchholz, Reinhold. *Erlebnisse der Mannschaft des Schiffes Hansa bei der
    zweiten deutschen Nordpol-Fahrt nebst Bemerkungen über das Leben der
    Thiere im hohen Norden nach brieflichen Mittheilungen.* Königsberg:
    W. Koch, 1871.
Buschick, Richard. *Die Eroberung der Erde.* Leipzig: Georg Dollheimer,
    1930.
Buttmann, Günther. *Friedrich Ratzel. Leben und Werk eines deutschen Geog-
    raphen.* Stuttgart: Wissenschaftliche Verlagsanstalt, 1977.
Cameron, Ian. *Antarctica: The Last Continent.* Boston: Little, Brown and
    Co., 1974.
Chamberlain, Houston Stewart. *Die Grundlagen des neunzehnten Jahrhunderts.*
    Munich: F. Bruckmann, 1919 (orig. pub. 1898).
Chamisso, Adelbert von. *Reise um die Welt mit der romanzoffischen Entdeck-
    ungs-Expedition in den Jahren 1815–1818 auf der Brigg Rurik, Kapitän*

Otto v. Kotzebue. Vols. 3 and 4, *Chamissos gesammelte Werke.* Ed. Max Koch. Stuttgart: J. G. Cotta, n.d.

Cook, Frederick A. *Meine Eroberung des Nordpols.* Trans. Erwin Volckmann. Hamburg: Alfred Janssen, 1911.

Cookman, Scott. *Ice Blink: The Tragic Fate of Sir John Franklin's Lost Polar Expedition.* New York: John Wiley and Sons, 2000.

Courtald, August. *From the Ends of the Earth: An Anthology of Polar Writings.* London: Oxford University Press, 1958.

Craig, Gordon. "The End of the Golden Age." *New York Review of Books,* 4 November 1999: 13.

Cranz, David. *Historie von Grönland.* Vol. 1. Hildesheim: Georg Olms Verlag, 1995 (orig. pub. 1765).

Darwin, Charles. *Voyage of the Beagle.* London: Penguin, 1989.

Delgado, James P. *Across the Top of the World: The Quest for the Northwest Passage.* New York: Checkmark, 1999.

"Die deutsche antarktischen Expedition 1939/40." *Polarforschung* 9 (1939): 1–6.

Deutsche Lufthansa, ed. *Die Geschichte der deutschen Lufthansa 1926–1984.* Dortmund: Deutsche Lufthansa, 1984.

Dickinson, Robert E. *The Makers of Modern Geography.* London: Routledge and Kegan Paul, 1969.

Döblin, Alfred. *Berge, Meere und Giganten.* Munich: Deutscher Taschenbuch Verlag, 1980 (orig. pub. 1924).

Dominick III, Raymond H. *The Environmental Movement in Germany: Prophets and Pioneers, 1871–1971.* Bloomington: Indiana University Press, 1992.

Dröber, Wolfgang. *Die Polargebiete und deren Erforschung, gemeinverständlich dargestellt.* Stuttgart: Fritz Lehmann, 1906.

Drygalski, Erich von. *Allgemeiner Bericht über den Verlauf der deutschen Südpolar-Expedition.* Berlin: Ernst Siegfried Mittler und Sohn, 1903.

———. "Allgemeiner Bericht über den Verlauf der Expedition von Kapstadt bis zu den Kerguelen." In *Die deutsche Südpolar-Expedition unter Leitung von Erich von Drygalski.* Ed. Institut für Meereskunde und geographisches Institut an der Universität Berlin, 2–40. Berlin: Ernst Siegfried Mittler und Sohn, 1903.

———. "Die Entwicklung der Geographie seit Gründung des Reiches." *Mitteilungen der geographischen Gesellschaft in Hamburg* 43 (1933): 1–11.

———. *Die Ergebnisse der Südpolarforschung und die Aufgaben der deutschen Südpolar-Expedition.* Berlin: Dietrich Reimer Verlag, 1898.

———. "Erster Bericht des Leiters der deutschen Südpolar-Expedition." *Verhandlungen der Gesellschaft für Erdkunde zu Berlin* 28 (1901): 422–28.

———. "The German Antarctic Expedition." *Geographic Journal* 18 (1901): 277–80.

———. *Die Grönland-Expedition der Gesellschaft für Erdkunde.* Berlin: Dietrich Reimer Verlag, 1898.

———. "The Oceanographical Problems of the Antarctic." In *Problems of Polar Research.* Ed. W. L. G. Joerg, 269–83. New York: American Geographical Society, 1928.

———. *The Southern Ice Continent: The German South Polar Expedition aboard the Gauss 1901–1903.* Trans. M. M. Raraty. Bluntisham, U.K.: Bluntisham Books, 1989.

———. "Die Zeppelin-Studienfahrt nach Spitzbergen und ins nördliche Eismeer im Sommer 1910." *Zeitschrift der Gesellschaft für Erdkunde zu Berlin* (1911): 1–14.

———. *Zum Kontinent des eisigen Südens. Deutsche Südpolarexpedition, Fahrten und Forschungen des 'Gauss' 1901–1903.* Berlin: Georg Reimer Verlag, 1904.

Eckener, Hugo. "The First Airship Flight around the World." *National Geographic* 57 (1930): 653–87.

———. *Im Zeppelin über Länder und Meere.* Flensburg: Verlagshaus Christian Wolff, 1949.

———. *Der Weg voran!* Leipzig: Schmidt und Günther, 1931.

Egede, Hans. *Des alten Grönland neue Perlustration, oder eine kurze Beschreibung der alten nordischen Kolonien.* Frankfurt, 1730.

———. *Die Heiden im Eis. Als Forscher und Missionär in Grönland 1721–1736.* Ed. H. Barüske. Stuttgart: Metzler, 1986.

Ehlers, Wilhelm. *In die Wunderwelt der Arktis. Schilderung einer Reise nach dem hohen Norden.* Bremen: Verlag Franz Leuwer, 1927.

Embacher, Fritz. *Die wichtigeren Forschungsreisen des neunzehnten Jahrhunderts.* Braunschweig: Vieweg, 1880.

Enzberg, Eugen von. *Heroen der Nordpolarforschung. Der reiferen deutschen Jugend und einem gebildeten Leserkreise nach den Quellen dargestellt.* Leipzig: D. R. Reisland, 1898.

Enzensperger, Josef. *Ein Bergsteigerleben. Alpine Aufsätzen und Vorträge. Reisebriefe und Kerguelen-Tagebuch.* 2nd ed. Munich: Alpenfreund-Verlag, 1924.

"Erich von Drygalski." *Jahresbericht des frankfurter Vereins für Geographie und Statistik* (1905): 151–55.

Erngaard, Erik. *Greenland, Then and Now.* Trans. Mona Giersing. Copenhagen: Lademann, 1972.

"Eskimo." In *Encyclopedia Britannica: A Dictionary of Arts, Sciences, Literature and General Information.* 11th ed., 11:769–70. New York: Encyclopedia Britannica, 1910.

"Eskimo." In *Meyers Konversation-Lexikon. Eine Enzyklopädie des allgemeinen Wissens.* 4th ed., 5: 848. Leipzig: Verlag des bibliographischen Instituts, 1885.

Farnes, Olav. *War in the Arctic.* Trans. Christopher Normann. London: Darf Publishers, 1991.

Fester, Gustav. "Polarpolitik." *Zeitschrift für Geopolitik* 7 (1930): 800–805.

Filchner, Wilhelm. *Ein Forscherleben.* 2nd ed. Wiesbaden: Eberhard Brockhaus, 1951.

———. *Sturm über Asien. Erlebnisse eines diplomatischen Geheimagenten.* Berlin: Neufeld und Henius, 1924.

———. *Zum sechsten Erdteil. Die zweite deutsche Südpolar-Expedition.* Berlin: Verlag Ullstein, 1922.

Filchner, Wilhelm, and Heinrich Seelheim. *Quer durch Spitzbergen.* Berlin: Ernst Siegfried Mittler und Sohn, 1910.

Fisher, Peter S. *Fantasy and Politics: Visions of the Future in the Weimar Republic.* Madison: University of Wisconsin Press, 1991.

Fogelson, Nancy. *Arctic Exploration and International Relations, 1900–1932.* Fairbanks: University of Alaska Press, 1992.

Frankel, Henry. "Continental Drift and Plate Tectonics." In *Sciences of the Earth: An Encyclopedia of Events, People and Phenomena.* Ed. Gregory A. Good, 118–36. New York: Garland, 1998.

Freeden, Wilhelm von. *Über die wissenschaftlichen Ergebnisse der ersten deutschen Nordfahrt von 1868.* Hamburg: Mittheilungen aus der norddeutschen Seewarte, 1869.

Freuchen, Peter, and Finn Salomonsen. *The Arctic Year.* New York: G. P. Putnam's Sons, 1958.

Friedrich, Christof. *Germany's Antarctic Claim: Secret Nazi Polar Expeditions.* Toronto: Samisdat, n.d.

Fritzsche, Peter. *A Nation of Fliers: German Aviation and the Popular Imagination.* Cambridge: Harvard University Press, 1992.

Garland, G. D. "The Contributions of Carl Friedrich Gauss to Geomagnetism." *Historia Mathematica* 6 (1979): 5–29.

Gasman, Daniel. *Haeckel's Monism and the Birth of Fascist Ideology.* New York: Peter Lang, 1998.

Gauss, C. F., and Wilhelm Weber, eds. *Resultate aus den Beobachtungen des magnetischen Vereins im Jahre 1838.* Leipzig: Weidmannsche Buchhandlung, 1839.

Gazert, Hans. *Die deutsche Südpolar-Expedition, ihre Aufgaben, Arbeiten und Erfolge.* Leipzig: Th. Thomas, 1904.

———. "Gesundheitsbericht." In *Die deutsche Südpolar-Expedition auf dem Schiff "Gauss" unter Leitung von Erich von Drygalski. Veröffentlichungen des Instituts für Meereskunde und geographischen Instituts an der Universität Berlin.* Ed. Ferdinand Freiherr von Richthofen, 46–54. Berlin: Ernst Siegfried Mittler und Sohn, 1903.

"Gemeinschaftliche Sitzung der Gesellschaft für Erdkunde zu Berlin und der Abteilung Berlin-Charlottenburg der deutschen Kolonial-Gesellschaft." *Verhandlungen der Gesellschaft für Erdkunde zu Berlin* 26 (1899): 58–87.

Georgi, Johannes. *Alfred Wegener. Polarforschung Beiheft* 2. Holzminden: Weserland-Verlag, 1960.

———. *Im Eis vergraben. Erlebnisse auf Station 'Eismitte' der letzten Grönland-Expedition Alfred Wegeners.* Munich: Paul Müller, 1933.

———. "Polarforscher Kapitän Alfred Ritscher." *Polarforschung* 32 (1962): 125–27.

Gerlach, W., and A. Sommerfeld. "Nachruf. Hermann Anschütz-Kaempfe." *Naturwissenschaft* 19 (1931): 666–69.

"German South Polar Expedition." *National Geographic* 14 (1903): 296–97.

Godwin, Joscelyn. *Arktos: The Polar Myth in Science, Symbolism and Nazi Survival.* London: Phanes Press, 1993.

Goethe, J. W. *Goethes Werke.* Berlin: Th. Knaur, n.d.

Good, Gregory A. "Geomagnetism, Theories between 1800 and 1900." In *Sciences of the Earth: An Encyclopedia of Events, People and Phenomena.* Ed. Gregory A. Good, 350–57. New York: Garland, 1998.

Gourdault, Jules, ed. *Voyage au Pole Nord des navires la Hansa et la Germania.* Paris: Librairie Hachette et Cie, 1875.

Greeley, A. W. *A Handbook of Polar Discoveries*. Boston: Little, Brown and Co., 1910.

———. *Three Years of Arctic Service*. New York: Charles Scribner's Sons, 1886.

Greene, Mott T. "Alfred Wegener." *Social Research* 51 (1984): 739–61.

Guttridge, Leonard F. *Ghosts of Cape Sabine: The Harrowing True Story of the Greely Expedition*. New York: G. P. Putnam's Sons, 2000.

Hammerstein, Notker. *Die deutsche Forschungsgemeinschaft in der Weimarer Republik und im Dritten Reich. Wissenschaftspolitik in Republik und Diktatur 1920–1945*. Munich: Beck, 1999.

Hanessian, John Jr. "National Interests in Antarctica." In *Antarctica*. Ed. Trevor Hatherton, 3–55. New York: Praeger, 1965.

Härlin, Hans. *Am Südpol. Die Entdeckungsgeschichte eines neuen Erdteils*. Stuttgart: Kosmos, 1933.

Harper, Kenn. *Give Me My Father's Body: The Life of Minik, the New York Eskimo*. New York: Steerforth Press, 2000.

Hartwig, Georg. *Der hohe Norden im Natur- und Menschenleben*. Wiesbaden: M. Bischkopff, 1871.

Hassert, Kurt. *Die Nordpolargrenze der bewohnten und bewohnbaren Erde*. Leipzig: Kommissionsverlag Gustav Fock, 1891.

———. *Die Polarforschung. Geschichte der Entdeckungsreisen zum Nord- und Südpol*. Munich: Wilhelm Goldmann Verlag, 1956.

Haushofer, Albrecht. "Alfred Wegener." *Deutsche Rundschau für Geographie und Statistik* 228 (1931): 250–53.

Hawkins, Mike. *Social Darwinism in European and American Thought, 1860–1945: Nature as Model and Nature as Threat*. London: Cambridge University Press, 1997.

Hayes, I. I. *Das offene Polar-Meer. Eine Entdeckungsreise nach dem Nordpol*. Trans. J. E. A. Martin. Jena: Hermann Costenoble, 1868.

Heinemann, Ulrich. *Die verdrängte Niederlage. Politische Öffentlichkeit und Kriegsschuldfrage in der Weimarer Republik*. Göttingen: Vandenhoeck und Ruprecht, 1983.

Heinze, Richard. *Der weisse Tod*. Zeulenroda: Bernhard Sporn, 1937.

Hempleman-Adams, David. *Walking on Thin Ice: In Pursuit of the North Pole*. London: Orion Books, 1998.

Hennig, Richard. "Geopolitische Wirkungen des beginnenden Weltluftverkehrs." *Geographische Zeitschrift* 34 (1928): 581–86.

———. *Weltluftverkehr und Weltpolitik*. Berlin: Zentral-Verlag, 1930.

Hennig, Richard, and Leo Korholz. *Einführung in die Geopolitik.* Leipzig: B. G. Teubner, 1933.

Henry, Thomas R. *The White Continent: The Story of Antarctica.* New York: William Sloane, 1950.

Hergesell, Hugo, and Kurt Wegener. "Die deutsche wissenschaftliche Station auf Spitzbergen und die Schröder-Stranz Expedition." *Petermanns geographische Mittheilungen* 59 (1913): 137–40.

Hermand, Jost. *Grüne Utopien in Deutschland. Zur Geschichte des ökologischen Bewusstseins.* Frankfurt a. M.: Fischer, 1991.

Herrmann, Ernst. *Deutsche Forscher im Südpolarmeer. Bericht von der deutschen antarktischen Expedition 1938–1939 mit Geleitwort von Reichsmarschall Hermann Göring und einer Einführung des Leiters der Expedition Kapitän Ritscher.* Berlin: Safari Verlag, 1941.

Herz, Ludwig F. *Tropisches und Arktisches. Reise-Erinnerungen.* Berlin: A. Asher, 1896.

Hildebrandt, Richard. "Fahrt der Hansa." In *Die zweite deutsche Nordpolarfahrt 1869–1870. Vorträge und Mittheilungen.* Ed. Verein für die deutsche Nordpolarfahrt zu Bremen, 24–45. Berlin: Dietrich Reimer Verlag, 1871.

Hochholzer, Hans. "Grundzüge der allgemeinen Geographie des Flugwesens." *Geographischer Anzeiger* 31 (1930): 178–85.

———. "Zur Geopolitik des Flugwesens." *Zeitschrift für Geopolitik* 7 (1930): 243–54.

Hoenerssen, A. *Neue Erkenntnisse Amundsens misglückter Flug 1925 und das Geheimnis des Nordpols.* Obermenzing-Munich: Raumkraftverlag, 1925.

Hoheisel-Huxmann, Reinhard. "Die Arktisfahrt des Luftschiffes Graf Zeppelin 1931." In *125 Jahre deutsche Polarforschung.* 2nd ed. Ed. Alfred-Wegener-Institut für Polar- und Meeresforschung, 95–108. Bremerhaven: Alfred-Wegener-Institut, 1994.

———. "Die erste deutsche Nordpolar-Expedition 1865." In *125 Jahre deutsche Polarforschung.* 2nd ed. Ed. Alfred-Wegener-Institut für Polar- und Meeresforschung, 7–13. Bremerhaven: Alfred-Wegener-Institut, 1994.

———. "Die zweite deutsche Nordpolar-Expedition 1869–1870." In *125 Jahre deutsche Polarforschung.* 2nd ed. Ed. Alfred-Wegener-Institut für Polar- und Meeresforschung, 14–33. Bremerhaven: Alfred-Wegener-Institut, 1994.

Holdermann, Karl. *Im Banne der Chemie. Carl Bosch, Leben und Werk*. Düsseldorf: Econ-Verlag, 1960.

Houben, H. H. *Der Ruf des Nordens. Abenteuer und Heldentum der Nordpolarfahrer*. Leipzig: Koehler und Amelang, 1931.

Iden-Zeller, Oscar. "Die Organisation von Polarexpeditionen." *Die Woche* 14 (1912): 2028.

Internationale Polar-Kommission. *Protokoll der Sitzungen, 1908*. Brussels: Hayez, 1908.

Irving, David. *The Rise and Fall of the Luftwaffe. The Life of Field Marshal Erhard Milch*. Boston: Little, Brown and Co., 1973.

Italiaander, Rolf. *Hugo Eckener. Ein moderner Columbus*. Konstanz: Verlag Friedrich Stadler, 1979.

Jacobshagen, Volker, et al., eds. *Alfred Wegener 1880–1930. Leben und Werk. Ausstellung anlässlich der 100. Wiederkehr seines Geburtsjahres*. Berlin: Dietrich Reimer Verlag, 1980.

Johnson, Jeffrey. "Kaiser Wilhelm/Max Planck Societies and Their Institutes." In *Modern Germany: An Encyclopedia of History, People and Culture, 1871–1990*. Ed. Dieter K. Buse and Juergen C. Doerr, 1: 542–43. New York: Garland, 1998.

Jones, T. O. "The Antarctic Treaty." In *Research in the Antarctic*. Ed. Louis O. Quam, 57–65. Washington DC: American Association for the Advancement of Science, 1971.

Kant, Immanuel. "Nachricht von der Einrichtung seiner Vorlesungen in dem Winterhalbjahre von 1765–1766." In *Kants Werke. Akademie-Textausgabe*. Ed. Preussische Akademie der Wissenschaften, 2:312–13. Berlin: Walter de Gruyter, 1968.

———. "Physische Geographie." In *Klassische Texte der physischen Geographie in Faksimile*, 2:1–7. Amsterdam: Van Gorcum, 1975.

———. "Von den verschiedenen Racen der Menschen." In *Kants Werke. Akademie-Textausgabe*. Ed. Preussische Akademie der Wissenschaften, 2:427–43. Berlin: Walter de Gruyter, 1968.

"Kassenbericht." *Arktis. Vierteljahrsschrift der internationalen Gesellschaft zur Erforschung der Arktis mit Luftfahrzeugen* 1 (1928): 115–16.

Kircheiss, Carl. *Polarkreis Süd—Polarkreis Nord. Als Walfisch- und Seelenfänger rund um den beiden Amerikas*. Leipzig: K. F. Koehler, 1933.

Kirschmer, Gottlob, ed. *Dokumentation über die Antarktisexpedition 1911–1912 von Wilhelm Filchner*. Munich: Deutsche geodätische Kommission bei der bayerischen Akademie der Wissenschaften, 1985.

"Kleine Mitteilungen aus allen Erdteilen." *Deutsche Rundschau für Geographie und Statistik* 25 (1903): 381.

Klutschak, Heinrich. *Overland to Starvation Cove: With the Inuit in Search of Franklin 1878–1889.* Trans. William Barr. Toronto: University of Toronto Press, 1987.

Knothe, H. "Moderne Polarforschung." *Geographischer Anzeiger* 32 (1931): 360–63.

Knötsch, Cathleen Carol. *Franz Boas bei den kanadischen Inuit im Jahre 1883–1884.* Bonn: Holos Verlag, 1992.

Koch, J. P. "Unsere Durchquerung Grönlands 1912–1913." *Zeitschrift der Gesellschaft für Erdkunde zu Berlin* (1914): 1–50.

Koepping, Klaus-Peter. *Adolf Bastian and the Psychic Unity of Mankind: The Foundations of Anthropology in Nineteenth Century Germany.* Saint Lucia, Queensland: University of Queensland Press, 1983.

Koestler, Arthur. *Arrow in the Blue: An Autobiography.* New York: Macmillan, 1952.

Kohl, Louis von. *Ursprung und Wandlung Deutschlands. Grundlagen zu einer deutschen Geopolitik.* Berlin: Vowinckel, 1932.

Kohl-Larsen, Ludwig. *An den Toren der Antarktis.* Stuttgart: Strecker und Schröder, 1930.

———. *Die Arktisfahrt des Graf Zeppelin.* Berlin: Union Deutsche, 1931.

Koldewey, Karl. *Die erste deutsche Nordpolar-Expedition im Jahre 1868.* Gotha: Justus Perthes Verlag, 1871.

———. "Die Fahrt der Germania." In *Die zweite deutsche Nordpolarfahrt 1869–1870. Vorträge und Mittheilungen.* Ed. Verein für die deutsche Nordpolarfahrt zu Bremen, 1–14. Berlin: Dietrich Reimer Verlag, 1871.

Koll, Johannes. *Der Kampf um die Pole.* Berlin: Deutsche Verlagsgesellschaft, 1934.

Koning, Hans. "Germania Irredenta." *Atlantic Monthly* (July 1996): 30–32.

Kosack, Hans-Peter. *Die Polarforschung. Ein Datenbuch über Natur-, Kultur-, Wirtschaftsverhältnisse und die Erforschungsgeschichte der Polarregionen.* Braunschweig: Wieweg, 1977.

Kraul, Otto. *Käpt'n Kraul erzählt. 20 Jahre Walfänger unter argentinischer, russischer und deutscher Flagge in der Arktis und Antarktis.* Berlin: Safari Verlag, 1939.

Krause, Reinhard. *Zweihundert Tage im Packeis. Die authentischen Berichte der "Hansa"-Männer der deutschen Ostgrönland-Expedition 1869 bis 1870.* Vol. 46, Schriften des deutschen Schiffahrtsmuseums. Bremerhaven: Schriften des deutschen Schiffahrtsmuseum, 1997.

Krockow, Christian Graf von. *Die Reise nach Pommern. Bericht aus einem verschwiegenen Land.* Munich: Deutscher Taschenbuch Verlag, 1988.

Krüger, Peter. *Die Aussenpolitik der Republik von Weimar.* Darmstadt: Wissenschaftliche Buchgesellschaft, 1985.

Lampe, Felix. "Erdkundliche Interessen im deutschen Publikum." *Geographischer Anzeiger* 4 (1903): 33–35.

Lampe, K. "Versuch einer politischen Geographie der Polargebiete." *Geographischer Anzeiger* 31 (1930): 105–10.

Laube, Gustav Carl. *Reise der Hansa ins nördliche Eismeer. Reisebriefe und Erinnerungsblätter.* Prague: J. G. Calve, 1871.

———. *Volkstümliche Überlieferungen aus Teplitz und Umgebung.* Prague: J. G. Calve, 1902.

Lehmann, Ernst A. *Auf Luftpatrouille und Weltfahrt. Erlebnisse eines Zeppelinführers in Krieg und Frieden.* Leipzig: Schmidt und Günther, 1936.

Levere, Trevor H. *Science and the Canadian Arctic: A Century of Exploration, 1818–1918.* New York: Cambridge University Press, 1993.

Liebersohn, Harry. "Discovering Indigenous Nobility: Tocqueville, Chamisso and Romantic Travel Writing." *American Historical Review* 99 (1994): 746–66.

Lindeman, M., and O. Finsch. *Die zweite deutsche Nordpolarfahrt in den Jahren 1869 und 1870 unter Führung des Kapitän Koldewey.* Leipzig: F. A. Brockhaus, 1875.

Lissner, Ivar. *Völker und Kontinente. Leben rund um den Erdball.* Hamburg: Hanseatische Verlagsanstalt, 1936.

Loewe, Fritz. "Alfred Wegener und die moderne Polarforschung." *Polarforschung* 42 (1972): 1–10.

Loomis, Chauncey C. "The Arctic Sublime." In *Nature and the Victorian Imagination.* Ed. U. C. Knoepflmacher and G. B. Tennyson, 95–112. Berkeley: University of California Press, 1977.

———. *Weird and Tragic Shores: The Story of Charles Francis Hall, Explorer.* New York: Alfred A. Knopf, 1971.

Löwenberg, J. *Die Entdeckungen und Forschungsreisen in den beiden Polarzonen.* Leipzig: G. Freytag und F. Tempsky, 1886.

Lüdecke, Cornelia. "Die Routenfestlegung der ersten deutschen Süd-polarexpedition durch Georg von Neumayer und ihre Auswirkung." *Polarforschung* 59 (1989): 103–11.

Luyken, Karl. "Kerguelen-Station." In *Die deutsche Südpolar-Expedition unter Leitung von Erich von Drygalski.* Ed. Institut für Meereskunde und geographisches Institut an der Universität Berlin, 41–51. Berlin: Ernst Siegfried Mittler und Sohn, 1903.

Macrakis, Christie. *Surviving the Swastika: Scientific Research in Nazi Germany.* Oxford: Oxford University Press, 1993.

Maull, Otto. "Erdumspannender Bericht." *Zeitschrift für Geopolitik* 7 (1930): 191–99.

Mawer, Granville Allen. *Ahab's Trade: The Saga of South Seas Whaling.* New York: St. Martin's, 2000.

Maxtone-Graham, John. *Safe Return Doubtful: The Heroic Age of Polar Exploration.* New York: Charles Scribner's Sons, 1988.

McCannon, John. *Red Arctic: Polar Exploration and the Myth of the North in the Soviet Union, 1932–1939.* New York: Oxford University Press, 1998.

Mecking, L. *Die Polarwelt in ihrer kulturgeographischen Entwicklung besonders der jüngsten Zeit.* Leipzig: B. G. Teubner, 1925.

Meier, Gudrun. "Aufzeichnungen über Grönland-Expeditionen des späten 19. Jahrhunderts in den Stationsdiarien der Herrnhuter Missionäre." *Polarforschung* 6 (1969): 260–63.

Meyer, Henry Cord. *Airshipmen, Businessmen and Politics 1890–1940.* Washington DC: Smithsonian Institution Press, 1991.

Meyer, Wilhelm M. *Die Rätsel der Erdpole.* Stuttgart: Franck'sche Verlagshandlung, 1913.

Meynen, Emil. "Albrecht Penck 1858–1945." *Geographers: Biobibliographical Studies* 2 (1978): 101–7.

Michalka, Wolfgang, and Gottfried Niedhart, eds. *Die ungeliebte Republik. Dokumente zur Innen- und Aussenpolitik Weimars 1918–1933.* Munich: Deutscher Taschenbuch Verlag, 1980.

Miethe, A., and H. Hergesell. *Mit Zeppelin nach Spitzbergen. Bilder von der Studienreise der deutschen Zeppelin-Expedition.* Berlin: Deutsches Verlagshaus Bong, 1911.

Mill, H. R. *The Siege of the South Pole: The Story of Antarctic Exploration*. London: Alston Rivers Ltd., 1905.

Mohr, Adrian. *Zum Pol im Zeichen des Flugzeuges*. Berlin: Otto Uhlmann, 1925.

Mosse, George. *Toward the Final Solution: A History of European Racism*. New York: Howard Fertig, 1978.

Mühlen, Patrik von zur. *Rassenideologien. Geschichte und Hintergründe*. Berlin: Dietz Verlag, 1977.

Müller, Freidrich Max. *Biographies of Words, and the Home of the Aryans*. London: Longman, Green & Co., 1888.

Müller, Johannes. *Einiges aus der Geschichte der Südpolarforschung unter besonderer Berücksichtigung der letzten deutschen antarktischen Expedition und ihrer Navigation*. Berlin: Hermann Blankes Buchdrückerei, 1914.

Murphy, David T. *The Heroic Earth: Geopolitical Thought in Weimar Germany 1918–1933*. Kent OH: Kent State University Press, 1997.

———. " 'A sum of the most wonderful things': Raum, Geopolitics and the German Tradition of Environmental Determinism, 1900–1933." *History of European Ideas* 25 (1999): 121–33.

Na'aman, Shlomo. *Der deutsche Nationalverein. Die politische Konstituiereng des deutschen Bürgertums 1859–1867*. Düsseldorf: Droste Verlag, 1987.

Nansen, Fridtjof. *Eskimoleben*. Trans. W. Langfeldt. Leipzig: G. H. Meyer, 1903.

Nansen, Fridtjof, and Leonid Breitfuss. *Die Erforschung der unbekannten Innerarktis. Karte der Höhen, Tiefen und Strömungen im Nordpolarbecken*. Gotha: Justus Perthes Verlag, 1929.

"Neger." In *Meyers Konversation-Lexikon. Eine Enzyklopädie des allgemeinen Wissens*. 4th ed., 12:39. Leipzig: Verlag des bibliographischen Instituts, 1888.

Neider, Charles, ed. *Antarctica: Authentic Accounts of Life and Exploration in the World's Highest, Driest, Windiest, Coldest and Most Remote Continent*. New York: Random House, 1972.

Neumayer, Georg. *Auf zum Südpol*. Berlin: Deutsches Verlagshaus, 1901.

———. "Zweiter Thätigkeitsbericht der deutschen Kommission für die Südpolar-Forschung." In *Verhandlungen des dreizehnten deutschen Geographentages zu Breslau am 28., 29., und 30. Mai 1901*. Berlin: Dietrich Reimer Verlag, 1901.

Neumayer, Georg, ed. *Die internationale Polarforschung. Die deutschen Expeditionen und ihre Ergebnisse*. Vol. 1. Berlin: A. Asher, 1891.

Nobile, Umberto. "Navigating the *Norge* from Rome to the North Pole and Beyond." *National Geographic* 54 (1927): 177–215.

Nordenskjöld, Otto. *Die Polarwelt und ihre Nachbarländer.* Leipzig: B. G. Teubner, 1909.

Nyhart, Lynn K. "Creating a 'Public' Nature and a 'Professional' Nature: The New Museum Idea in German Natural History." Paper presented at the Universities of Manchester and Cambridge, 24–26 February 1998.

Oberhummer, Eugen. "Die deutsche Südpolarexpedition." *Jahresbericht der geographischen Gesellschaft in München* 18 (1898–99): 94–134.

Oehlmann. "Review of Fridtjof Nansen, *Eskimoleben.*" *Geographischer Anzeiger* 4 (1903): 138.

Oswalt, Wendell H. *Eskimos and Explorers.* 2nd ed. Lincoln: University of Nebraska Press, 1999.

Paas, Willy. "Der deutsche Walfang." *Der Türmer* 41 (1939): 160–63.

Penck, Albrecht. "Antarktische Probleme." *Sitzungsberichte der königlich preussischen Akademie der Wissenschaften* (1914): 50–69.

———. "Deutschlands Seeinteressen und das Institut und Museum für Meereskunde an der Universität Berlin." *Kleinere Mitteilungen aus dem Institut für Meereskunde an der Universität Berlin* (1921): 10.

———. *Das Institut für Meereskunde.* Berlin: Ernst Siegfried Mittler und Sohn, 1907.

Peschel, Oscar. "Die deutsche Nordfahrt." *Ausland*, 8 October 1870: 983.

Petermann, August. "Die deutsche Nordfahrt, Aufruf an die deutsche Nation." *Petermanns geographischen Mittheilungen* (1866): 144–62.

———. *Die deutsche Nordpol-Expedition, 1868.* Reprint from *Petermanns geographischen Mittheilungen.* Gotha: Justus Perthes Verlag, 1868.

———. "Die Eisverhältnisse in den Polar-Meeren und die Möglichkeit des Vordringens in Schiffen bis zu den höchsten Breiten." *Petermanns geographischen Mittheilungen* (1865): 136–65.

———. "Das nördlichste Land der Erde, eine Abhandlung über die Entdeckungs-geschichte und die allgemeinen geographischen und kartographischen Resultate der Expeditionen von 1616 bis 1861 unter Bylot, Baffin, Ross, Inglefield, Kane, Hayes." *Petermanns geographischen Mittheilungen* (1867): 176–85.

———. "Nördseefischereien." *Petermanns geographischen Mittheilungen* (1866): 401–7.

———. *Spitzbergen und die arktische Central-Region.* Ergänzungsheft 16, *Petermanns geographischen Mittheilungen.* Gotha: Justus Perthes Verlag, 1865.

———. "Der Walfischfang und die Robbenjagd im europäischen Eismeer." *Petermanns geographischen Mittheilungen* (1867): 413–22.

Peters, Hermann B. *Anthropologie und Zoologie.* Vol. 6, *Wissenschaftliche Ergebnisse der deutschen-Grönlandexpedition Alfred Wegener 1929 und 1930/31.* Ed. K. Wegener. Leipzig: F. Brockhaus, 1934.

Petzina, Dietmar. *Autarkie-Politik im Dritten Reich.* Stuttgart: Deutsche Verlags Anstalt, 1968.

Philippi, H. *Ergebnisse der W. Filchnerschen Vorexpedition nach Spitzbergen 1910.* Ergänzungsheft 179, *Petermanns geographischen Mitteilungen.* Gotha: Justus Perthes Verlag, 1914.

"Plan einer deutschen antarktischen Expedition." *Zeitschrift der Gesellschaft für Erdkunde zu Berlin* (1910): 153–58.

Poliakov, Leon. *The Aryan Myth: A History of Racist and Nationalist Ideas in Europe.* New York: Basic Books, 1974.

Pratt, Mary Louise. *Imperial Eyes.* London: Routledge, 1992.

Proceedings of the Royal Geographical Society.

Quessel, Ludwig. "Kurze Chronik." *Sozialistische Monatshefte* 61 (1924): 315.

Raban, Jonathan. "The Endurance Myth." *New York Review of Books,* 10 June 1999: 14–18.

Raebel, Max. "Was ist zur Rettung der Schröder-Stranz Expedition zu tun?" *Die Woche* 15 (1913): 91–92.

Ratzel, Friedrich. *Politische Geographie.* 3rd ed. Ed. Eugen Oberhummer. Munich and Berlin: Vowinckel, 1923 (orig. pub. 1897).

———. "Die Wolken in der Landschaft." *Deutsche Rundschau für Geographie und Statistik* 112 (1902): 22–50.

Reinke-Kunze, Christine. *Aufbruch in die weisse Wildnis. Die Geschichte der deutschen Polarforschung.* Hamburg: Ernst Kabel Verlag, 1992.

Rich, Norman. *Hitler's War Aims: Ideology, the Nazi State and the Course of Expansion.* 2 vols. New York: Norton, 1973.

Richthofen, Ferdinand Freiherr von, ed. *Die deutsche Südpolar-Expedition auf dem Schiff "Gauss" unter Leitung von Erich von Drygalski. Veröffentlichungen des Instituts für Meereskunde und geographischen Instituts an der Universität Berlin.* Berlin: Ernst Siegfried Mittler und Sohn, 1903.

Riffenburgh, Beau. *The Myth of the Explorer: The Press, Sensationalism and Geographical Discovery*. London and New York: Belhaven Press, 1993.

Ritscher, Alfred. *Deutsche antarktische Expedition 1938–39 mit dem Flugzeugstützpunkt der deutschen Lufthansa A.G.M.S. "Schwabenland." Wissenschaftliche und fliegerische Ergebnisse*. Leipzig: Koehler und Amelang, 1942.

———. "Instrumente und Methoden für die Navigation von Luftfahrzeugen." In *Luftverkehr über dem Ozean. Das Meer in volkstümlichen Darstellungen*. Ed. Institut für Meereskunde, 2:102–19. Berlin: Ernst Siegfried Mittler und Sohn, 1934.

———. "Wanderungen in Spitzbergen im Winter 1912." *Zeitschrift der Gesellschaft für Erdkunde zu Berlin* (1916): 16–34.

Robinson, Douglas H. *Giants in the Sky: A History of the Rigid Airship*. Seattle: University of Washington Press, 1973.

Rüdiger, Hermann. "Geographische Nachrichten." *Geographischer Anzeiger* 40 (1939): 192–93.

Salentiny, Fernand. *Dumonts Lexikon der Seefahrer und Entdecker. Von Amundsen bis Zeppelin*. Cologne: Dumont Buchverlag, 1995.

Samoilowitsch, R. L. "Die Flüge in den Polargebieten und die Arktisfahrt des Luftschiffs 'Graf Zeppelin' 1931." In *Die Arktisfahrt des Luftschiffes 'Graf Zeppelin' im Juli 1931*. Ed. A. Berson, R. L. Samoilowitsch, and L. Weickmann, 2–30. Gotha: Justus Perthes Verlag, 1933.

———. "Die Polarfahrt des 'Graf Zeppelin.'" *Petermanns geographischen Mittheilungen* 78 (1932): 246–48.

Schiller, Hans von. "Transozeanverkehr mit dem Luftschiff 'Graf Zeppelin.'" In *Luftverkehr über dem Ozean. Das Meer in volkstümlichen Darstellungen*. Ed. Institut für Meereskunde, 2:27–41. Berlin: Ernst Siegfried Mittler und Sohn, 1934.

———. *Zeppelin. Aufbruch im 20. Jahrhundert*. Bonn: Kirschbaum Verlag, 1988.

Schlegel, Friedrich von. *Sämmtliche Werke*. Vol. 1. Vienna: Jakob Wagner, 1822.

Schley, W. S. *The Rescue of Greeley*. New York: Charles Scribner's Sons, 1885.

Schmidt-Ott, Friedrich. *Erlebtes und Erstrebtes 1860–1950*. Wiesbaden: Franz Steiner Verlag, 1952.

————. "Die Not der deutschen Wissenschaft." *Internationale Monatsschrift für Wissenschaft, Kunst und Technik* 15 (October 1920): 1–36.

Schmiedgen, G. *MacClures Nordpolarfahrt zur Aufsuchung Sir John Franklins und die Entdeckung der 'Nordwestdurchfahrt.' Dem Volke und der Jugend erzählt nach einem Tagebuche von F. A. Miertsching.* Gotha: Friedrich Andreas Perthes, 1907.

Schütte, Johann, ed. *Der Luftschiffbau Schütte-Lanz 1909–25.* Munich and Berlin: R. Oldenbourg, 1926.

"The *Schwabenland* in the Antarctic." *Geographical Journal* 95 (1940): 201–3.

Shackleton, Ernest. *South: The Endurance Expedition.* New York: Signet, 1999 (orig. pub. 1919).

Sheehan, James. *German Liberalism in the Nineteenth Century.* Chicago: University of Chicago Press, 1970.

Sieburg, Friedrich. *Die rote Arktis. 'Malygins' empfindsame Reise.* Frankfurt a. M.: Societäts-Verlag, 1932.

Simpson-Housley, Paul. *Antarctica: Exploration, Perception and Metaphor.* London: Routledge, 1992.

Smedal, Gustav. *Acquisition of Sovereignty over Polar Areas.* Oslo: I Kommisjon Hos Jacob Dybwand, 1931.

Smith, Woodruff. "Colonies and Colonial Society." In *Modern Germany: An Encyclopedia of History, People and Culture, 1871–1990.* Ed. Dieter K. Buse and Juergen C. Doerr, 193–94. New York: Garland, 1998.

————. *Politics and the Sciences of Culture in Germany, 1840–1920.* New York and Oxford: Oxford University Press, 1991.

Sokolowsky, A. "Wie der Polarmensch lebt." *Die Woche* 5 (1903): 113–15.

Spörer, J. *Nowaja Semlä in geographischer, naturhistorischer und volkswirtschaftlicher Beziehung.* Ergänzungsheft 21, *Petermanns geographischen Mittheilungen.* Gotha: Justus Perthes Verlag, 1867.

Spufford, Francis. *I May Be Some Time: Ice and the English Imagination.* New York: St. Martin's Press, 1997.

Stackelberg, Rod. *Hitler's Germany.* New York: Routledge, 1999.

————. "Racism." In *Modern Germany: An Encyclopedia of History, People, and Culture 1871–1990.* Ed. Dieter K. Buse and Juergen C. Doerr, 2:812–13. New York: Garland, 1998.

Stefansson, Vilhjalmur. *My Life with the Eskimo.* New York: Collier, 1935.

————. *Ultima Thule: Further Mysteries of the Arctic.* New York: Macmillan, 1940.

————. *Unsolved Mysteries of the Arctic*. 4th ed. New York: Macmillan, 1970.

Stehr, Albert. "Bericht über die Ballonaufstiege." In *Die deutsche Südpolar-Expedition auf dem Schiff "Gauss" unter Leitung von Erich von Drygalski. Veröffentlichungen des Instituts für Meereskunde und geographischen Instituts an der Universität Berlin*. Ed. Ferdinand Freiherr von Richthofen, 173–81. Berlin: Ernst Siegfried Mittler und Sohn, 1903.

————. "Das Südpolarschiff Gauss und seine technische Einrichtungen." In *Deutsche Südpolar-Expedition 1901–1903*. Ed. Erich von Drygalski, 1–96. Leipzig: Koehler und Amelang, 1921.

Stein, Gerhard. *Die Entdeckungsreisen in alter und neuer Zeit*. Glogau: Flemming, 1883.

Stocking, George W., Jr. *Race, Culture, and Evolution: Essays in the History of Anthropology*. Chicago: University of Chicago Press, 1982 (orig. pub. 1968).

Sütterlin, Ingmar. *Die "Russische Abteilung" des auswärtigen Amtes in der Weimarer Republik*. Berlin: Duncker and Humblot, 1994.

Swithinbank, Charles, and James H. Zumberge. "The Ice Shelves." In *Antarctica*. Ed. Trevor Hatherton, 199–220. New York: Praeger, 1965.

Swofford, Jan. *Johannes Brahms: A Biography*. New York: Knopf, 1997.

Syon, Guillaume de. "Technology as a Tool of Science and Prestige: The Zeppelins and Arctic Exploration 1907–1933." Paper presented to the National Conference of the German Studies Association, Seattle, 6 October 1996.

"Über die deutsche Südpolarexpedition." *Deutsche Rundschau für Geographie und Statistik* 26 (1904): 92–93.

Vaeth, J. Gordon. "Exploring the Arctic." In *Polar Aviation*. Ed. C. V. Glines, 78–87. New York: Franklin Watts, 1964.

————. *Graf Zeppelin: The Adventures of an Aerial Globetrotter*. New York: Harper and Collins, 1958.

Vaughan, Richard. *The Arctic: A History*. Dover NH: Alan Sutton, 1994.

Venzke, Jörg-Friedhelm. "Die deutsche Südpolar-Expedition 1901 bis 1903." In *125 Jahre deutsche Polarforschung*. 2nd ed. Ed. Alfred-Wegener-Institut für Polar- und Meeresforschung, 58–68. Bremerhaven: Alfred-Wegener-Institut, 1994.

Verein für die deutsche Nordpolarfahrt zu Bremen, ed. *Die zweite deutsche Nordpolar-fahrt in den Jahren 1869 und 1870 unter Führung des Kapitän Karl Koldewey.* Leipzig: F. Brockhaus, 1873.

———. *Die zweite deutsche Nordpolarfahrt 1869–1870. Vorträge und Mittheilungen.* Berlin: Dietrich Reimer Verlag, 1871.

Verhandlungen des deutschen Geographentages.

Verhandlungen des Reichstages. Stenographischen Berichte. Various vols. Berlin: Druck und Verlag der norddeutschen Buchdrückerei, 1899.

Vetter, O. "Alfred Ritschers Beiträge zur Verbesserung der Karten der Antarktis und des südatlantischen Ozeans." *Kartographische Nachrichten* 13 (1963): 114–16.

Victor, Paul-Emile. *Man and the Conquest of the Poles.* Trans. Scott Sullivan. New York: Simon and Schuster, 1963.

Villiers, Alan. *The Way of a Ship: Being Some Account of the Ultimate Development of the Ocean-Going Square-Rigged Sailing Vessel, and the Manner of Her Handling, Her Voyage-Making, Her Personnel, Her Economics, Her Performance and Her End.* New York: Charles Scribner's Sons, 1970.

Volckmann, Erwin, ed. *Erlebnisse eines Deutschen im hohen Norden. Aufzeichnungen und Berichte Rudolph Frankes.* Hamburg: Alfred Janssen, 1914.

Volkmann, Hans-Erich. "The National Socialist Economy in Preparation for War." In *Germany and the Second World War.* Ed. Militärgeschichtliches Forschungsamt, 1. Oxford: Clarendon Press, 1990.

Voss, Jutta. "Alfred Wegeners Weg als Polarforscher." In *125 Jahre deutsche Polarforschung.* 2nd ed. Ed. Alfred-Wegener-Institut für Polar- und Meeresforschung, 81–94. Bremerhaven: Alfred-Wegener-Institut, 1994.

Waitz, Theodor. *Introduction to Anthropology.* Trans. J. F. Collingwood. London: Longman, 1863.

Wegener, Alfred. *Die Entstehung der Kontinente und Ozeane.* Braunschweig: Vieweg, 1915.

———. *Mit Motorboot und Schlitten in Grönland.* Bielefeld: Belhagen and Klasing, 1930.

———. *The Origin of Continents and Oceans.* 4th ed. Trans. John Biram. New York: Dover, 1966.

————. "Vorläufige Bericht über die wissenschaftlichen Ergebnisse der Expedition." *Zeitschrift der Gesellschaft für Erdkunde zu Berlin* (1914): 50–54.

Wegener, Else. *Alfred Wegeners letzte Grönlandfahrt. Die Erlebnisse der deutschen Grönlandexpedition 1930–1931 geschildert von seinen Reisegefahrten und nach Tagebüchern des Forschers.* Leipzig: Brockhaus, 1932.

Wegener, Kurt. "Die deutsche Grönland-Expedition Alfred Wegener." In *Polarbuch.* Ed. Institut für Meereskunde, 22–33. Berlin: Ernst Siegfried Mittler und Sohn, 1933.

Weickmann, Ludwig. "Die Polarfahrt des 'Graf Zeppelin' im Juli 1931." In *Polarbuch.* Ed. Institut für Meereskunde, 83–110. Berlin: Ernst Siegfried Mittler und Sohn, 1933.

Weinberg, Gerhard L. *The Foreign Policy of Hitler's Germany.* 2 vols. Chicago: University of Chicago Press, 1970, 1980.

Weiser, Adelheid. *Die Völker Nordsibiriens unter sowjetischer Herrschaft von 1917 bis 1936.* Hohenschäftlarn: Klaus Renner Verlag, 1989.

Weller, Emil. *August Petermann. Ein Beitrag zur Geschichte der geographischen Entdeckungen und der Kartographie im 19. Jahrhundert.* Leipzig: Otto Wigand, 1911.

Wheeler, Harold, ed. *Marvels of the Modern World.* New York: Halcyon House, 1940.

Wichmann, Hugo. "August Petermann." In *Allgemeine deutsche Biographie,* 26:795–805. Leipzig: Duncker and Humblot, 1888.

————. "Der Stand der Südpolarforschung." *Petermanns geographischen Mittheilungen* 59 (1913): 57–59.

Wirth, Hermann. *Der Aufgang der Menschheit. Untersuchungen zur Geschichte der Religion, Symbolik und Schrift der atlantisch-nordischen Rasse.* Jena: E. Diederich, 1928.

————. "Das Geheimnis von Arktis-Atlantis." *Die Woche* 35 (1933): 1144–48.

Wodopjanow, Michael. *Die Eroberung des Nordpols.* London: Malik-Verlag, 1938.

Würzner, Karl. *Das Mysterium der Polarregionen der Erde. Eine physische-geographische und paläontologische Betrachtung im theosophischen Licht.* Bruck a. d. Mur: Hermann Schmerzeck, 1922.

Wutzke, Ulrich. *Durch die weisse Wüste. Leben und Leistungen des Grönland-forschers und Entdeckers der Kontinentaldrift Alfred Wegener.* Gotha: Justus Perthes Verlag, 1997.

———. *Der Forscher von der Friedrichsgracht. Leben und Leistung Alfred Wegen-ers.* Leipzig: Brockhaus, 1988.

———. *Kommentiertes Verzeichnis der schriftlichen Dokumente seines Lebens und Wirkens. Berichte zur Polarforschung,* 288. Bremerhaven: Alfred-Wegener-Institut, 1998.

Zeidler, P. G. *Polarfahrten. Die wichtigsten Entdeckungsreisen in den Eismeeren mit Berichten der Forscher und ihrer Gefährten.* Berlin: Deutsche Buch-Gemeinschaft, 1927.

Züchner, Ernst. *Der weisse Magnet. Polarfahrten in fünf Jahrhundert.* Berlin: Büchergilde Gutenberg, 1932.

INDEX